'I Could Write a Book...'

By Roy Reiman

It all started with a Royal typewriter
on a TV tray in the basement
of the Reiman family home.

Today one of every 10 homes in America
subscribes to at least one Reiman
Publications magazine. There are now 12
of them, none of which accept advertising.

Here's how it all happened, in the
words of the "dreamer" himself.

Foreword

WHEN Harold Ross in 1925 announced his plans to publish *The New Yorker*, he said it "would be the magazine which is not edited for the little old lady in Dubuque." He was true to his word, and the magazine found an enthusiastic, loyal audience.

Less than a half century later, a young man took his first steps toward creating what became an astonishing publishing empire that truly *was* for all those little old ladies (and little old men) in Dubuque. Yes, and all the rest of us, too.

The man was Roy Reiman, son of an Iowa tenant farmer. This book is his story, of how he built the largest "unknown publishing business" in the United States. And how he did it by defying most of the conventional wisdom in the industry.

It's quite possible that you've never seen one of his 12 magazines on a newsstand. Yet Reiman Publications has more than 16 million subscribers. One of these magazines, *Taste of Home*, goes to more than 5.3 million mailboxes and ranks *sixth* among all magazines published in the U.S.

Most amazing is that *not one* of these magazines carries advertising!

Time and again, Roy was told "You can't do that", or "It will never work" or "You'll go broke for sure." To be blunt about it, many sensible people snickered at his early publishing ventures. Yet, he steadily proved the scoffers and naysayers wrong.

His secret? First and foremost, he never lost touch with his roots…the "red states" as they were called in the 2004 presidential election. He turned out magazines for his friends and relatives in Iowa and the rest of America's heartland. And he did it with the hardheaded pragmatism of an American farmer.

Roy was born with an endless curiosity about people. He listened and learned. What did people like? What did they need? What were their interests…their unfulfilled dreams? Then he simply used his farm-boy common sense and went with what his readers would find interesting.

For example, he knew what everyone in journalism knew…that the "Letters to the Editor" section is often the best-read part of any paper or magazine. But only Roy took that to the next logical step and published a magazine *almost entirely written by its readers*. What an outrageous idea!

Within 2 years, it had topped 2 million circulation…an unprecedented growth for any new magazine. A friend told him he had created "the world's largest park bench, where people can share their memories."

Most of these magazines grew out of his observations. When Roy learned that birdseed sales were booming, he concluded more people were becoming interested in birds. Was there a place for a magazine written for backyard bird-watchers? Would they like to swap experiences? Indeed they would. The magazine, *Birds & Blooms*, also written by its readers, became an instant success with over 2 million paid subscribers.

Roy's management style was to publishing what Warren Buffet's is to the financial world. Lunch in the company cafeteria instead of at the University Club. Drive to work in a 3-year-old car instead of a chauffered limousine. Suits off the rack, not tailored in London. Trust your instincts.

Roy also had what out in the country is called "a good eye for horse-flesh". He surrounded himself with talented people and put them in an environment that encouraged ambition and creativity. It's significant that after the initial job interview, no employee ever called him "Mr. Reiman". Everyone was on a first-name basis. And not even Roy had a reserved parking spot.

To be sure, he made some mistakes. Expensive ones. But it was always his own money that was put on the line. He never complained nor blamed others. Instead, he viewed his mistake as a valuable lesson learned. After all, he was taking bold ideas into uncharted areas of publishing, so the occasional flop was inevitable.

Like many bright, high-energy people, Roy was sometimes afflicted with what Alan Greenspan famously called "irrational exuberance". Fortunately, this was offset by his total trust in the calm judgment of his wife, Bobbi. Few marriages have ever been so truly a working partnership.

If you were around Roy for even an hour or two, you were bound to hear, "I'll ask Bobbi about that tonight." He never made a major decision without her input. She was indispensable to his success.

As things worked out, Roy really never did have "subscribers". He had several million friends who were enthusiastic members of an extended family reaching from coast to coast and into Canada. They welcomed magazines that basically let them visit with each other, just as they would have over a cup of coffee with a good neighbor.

Many subscribers today take as many as five Reiman publications. In fact, more than 1,000 take all 12 of the company's magazines. Best of all, readers are fiercely loyal and renew their subscriptions at a rate most publishers only dream about.

You'll discover why as you read this remarkable story.

—Clancy Strock
Retired Chair
Advertising Department
School of Journalism
University of Nebraska

Reiman Publications Headquarters, Greendale, Wisconsin

Author: Roy Reiman
Art Director: Judy Larson
Copy Editor: Kristine Krueger
©2005 Grandhaven Group, 115 S. 84th St., Milwaukee WI 53214

International Standard Book Number: 0-9769002-0-3
Library of Congress Control Number: Applied for

For additional copies of this book, write:
Country Store, 5400 S. 60th St., Suite 7904
Greendale WI 53129. Or call toll-free 1-800/558-1013
$14.95 (plus $3.95 shipping & handling; $4.95 for two or more)

Special thanks to four people who read the manuscript for this book and provided invaluable help regarding facts, dates and rewording…even suggesting things they remembered and I'd forgotten to include.

Mike Beno, who'd served as our company Editorial Director for years and therefore had a good grasp of events as they occurred and kept me honest.

Clancy Strock, whose warm, conversational writing style is one I've always envied and admired. Clancy was the Creative Director of a large ad agency, taught journalism at the University of Nebraska before retiring and still writes a popular regular column for *Reminisce* magazine.

Samir Husni, Ph.D., Chair of the Dept. of Journalism, University of Mississippi, who is so widely known he's referred to as "Mr. Magazine" in the publishing industry—not only in the U.S., but across much of the world.

Bobbi Reiman, who was there through the years and shared the successes as well as the downright flops covered in this book.

DEDICATED to Bobbi, my wife of 43 years, who has patiently listened again and again while I've excitedly described hundreds of wild ideas—many that came to me in the middle of the night—then gave me an honest appraisal of whether or not they had merit.

Through her I've learned that—in general—women are far more intuitive and sensitive than men. They tend to make better judgments of both people and ideas. For this reason, I've never gone ahead with a new project without first listening to her insights, nor have I hired a key person without first having her join us for dinner.

Even when I sold the company, I never met with a group of potential buyers without Bobbi. She was in charge of "body language". On the way home, she'd give me "a reading" on those in the room. The buyer we eventually chose was made up of the people we both liked, and trusted, the most.

Considering we had four kids and she was pregnant with the fifth when I came home from work one day and said, "Honey, I'm going to quit my job and go on my own," I attribute a good deal of my success to her love, confidence and support. As I often tell friends, "I married up."

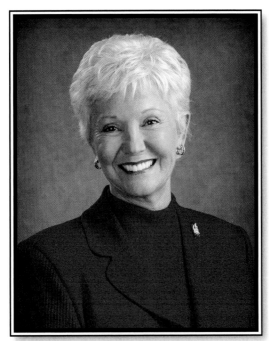

Bobbi Reiman

7

I love people with a good sense of humor,
and as I begin to write this book, I can't
help but recall one of my favorite lines
from comedian Steven Wright:
　　"I have the perfect retirement plan.
I'm going to write my own unauthorized
autobiography...then I'm going to sue myself."
　　　　　　　—Roy Reiman

Pssst! We were the first to *hide* something in our magazines. Now I'm going to be the first to hide something in a book.

Yes, just as we've regularly hidden things such as a "needle in a haystack" in our magazines, there's now a needle *hiding* within the pages of this book. *That's not it above.* That's just a *sample* to show you what it looks like. It could be smaller, but it's hiding some-where—it could be in a margin, in a photo, in a headline...

Find it and you may win a prize. You won't be clueless after you read Chapter...well, wait, you'll just have to search for that, too.

Here's What's Ahead...

It Wasn't My Idea...

THIS BOOK wasn't my own doing. Executives who studied the prospectus I wrote when we prepared Reiman Publications for sale—plus others who simply heard about our rags-to-riches growth—have urged me repeatedly to turn this incredible story into a full-length book.

So, I'm finally doing it...with some reluctance. As an ex-Iowa farm boy, I'm aware there are two things that upset any Iowan: Being called "lazy"; or even worse, "a bragger".

To me, putting all these personal accomplishments on paper leans a little toward the latter. On the other hand, if sharing these successes (along with some really dismal failures) allows others to dream dreams and pursue them, doing so should be worth the risk.

I hope it will help other firms prosper and add more *fun* to the daily lives of their employees as well. We've tried to provide an upbeat atmosphere where people look forward to coming to work every day. Happy employees equal happy customers.

Truly, this story traces *my* dream, from losing everything I had on my first venture (and learning so much from it, I've long regarded that failure as my "Master's Degree") to eventually having the kind of success even I find hard to believe.

I've always wanted to fly. And I have, but not in the way I'd planned. I wanted to take flying lessons so I could pilot my own Cessna, but I could never find time for the training.

Instead, I ended up "flying" this company. From the start, it responded and grew so fast it simply *soared*, unbelievably higher every year.

What's made it enjoyable is that it's flown in such an unconventional way. Who ever heard of a national magazine not only surviving, but *thriving*, without advertising? Much less an even dozen national magazines, all supported solely and wholly by subscriptions.

While we're best known for our unusual no-ads approach, doing a lot of things differently was also the mantra for the way we operated. While these differences should prove interesting, some of them may arch your eyebrows and have you shaking your head.

For example, we never had a "business plan". We never had a company organization chart, either. Such charts tend to put parameters on people—"That's not my job."

Nor did we bother much with giving people titles; we just worked as a *team*. We maximized everyone's involvement and encouraged their input—it made them all feel important.

We managed the business, not the earnings. I'm no fan of bureaucracy, so we resisted "paper wars"—memos back and forth rehashing plans, problems and opportunities. We kept the unnecessary work out of the system.

For the same reason, we never had strict annual budgets or year-end goals. The biggest chill to creativity is calculated planning.

Finally, we rarely held meetings. We met only when there was a reason to meet, then kept it brief because we wanted to get back to "work".

I put "work" in quotes because none of us regarded it in that fashion. We were collectively involved in a mission to prove that magazines *could* make it without advertising. Together we became a family that enjoyed the challenge and looked forward to each day.

Essentially, we just kept at it and the company simply evolved...to the point where every 10th home in America now receives at least one of our company's magazines. (All circulation figures are current as this is written.)

What an experience! My career has given me fascinating insights into thousands of people's lives and businesses. Being a journalist is like taking a different graduate course month after month. And instead of paying for it, you get paid for it.

What a job. What a life. What a joy.

I won't need any references to write this story. Nor will I need to interview anyone or phone people for details. Because this is my story...the story that begins on my parents' rented farm in Iowa and describes the beginning, the present and the potential of Reiman Publications.

In varying degrees, this will be the *easiest*, the most *difficult*, the most *personal* story I've ever written.

Easiest...because I've lived and enjoyed it. Difficult...because all the other stories I've written over the years have been about other people and other companies. Personal...because this company became a part of me, almost as much as one of my limbs.

To look in the rearview mirror and trace this company's here-to-there history is an emotional experience. And to finally sell it was as difficult as if I'd put up one of my kids for adoption.

This, then, is that story...from the basement to the boardroom...along with all the *fun* I had during the trip.

Roy Reiman

*Happy are those who
dream dreams and are
ready to pay the price
to make them come true.*
—*Jerry Litton*

CHAPTER 1

'No Ads?' 'NO WAY!' 'Oh, Yeah?'

WELL…how do you like this book so far?

Okay, it's a little early for that question, but I ask it for two reasons:

1. I want you to know this isn't going to be a stuffy, these-are-the-facts kind of book about my technical experience in the publishing industry. I think you're going to find some chuckles in the pages ahead. I've always encouraged levity at work, so I'd like those who read this book to experience the same kind of lightheartedness here.

2. The other reason I ask that question—or at least would like to ask it about 20 pages from now—is because it's been my experience that a lot of people think "they have a book in them". They feel they've lived an incredibly exciting life, have learned so many lessons and have had so many fascinating experiences that they're almost *obligated* to share them.

Yet, while their life and their proposed book may seem exciting to *them*, they don't stop to ask themselves, "Will it be that exciting to *others*?"

Bottom line is, sure, a lot of people can *write* a book. Question is, when they get done, how many people will want to *read* it?

This sobering concern crossed my mind as I began this project. Sure, I think I've lived an exciting life…I've traveled broadly…met fascinating people…chased a lot of dreams…caught a few…and experienced a few crash-and-burn failures that were right up there with the guy who designed the Edsel. But will *others* find it interesting?

I have no doubt this book will have broad appeal to the publishing audience, since many industry people have told me repeatedly they can't *wait* for me to bare my soul and explain how on earth we keep launching successful national magazines *without advertising*.

Many of them have been among the "experts" who have said, "No ads? *No way!*" To which we've responded, "Oh, *yeah?*" Those people will probably buy this book just to read the chapters disclosing that unique approach.

Actually, this will be the first time I've ever detailed this no-ads concept.

For years I've been asked to speak at publishing gatherings to "share the secret" of our unique approach. But until I sold the company and my 5-year non-compete agreement expired, I saw no legitimate reason to teach our peers how to compete with us.

If you're not in publishing, hang in there. Just smelling ink on paper is enough to get most journalists excited. But if fresh ink doesn't turn you on, I want you to know this book is about much more than publishing.

From my biased point of view, what's in the pages ahead should interest people who have nothing to do with the print industry. Why? Because we've bent or broken most rules of management, promotion, sales and "standard procedure" over the years.

Sharing these things should prove beneficial to anyone in business. In fact, if Bill Veeck was still around, even he might have admired a few of the off-the-wall ideas and "You gotta be kidding!" promotions we've tried.

As I started on this book and pondered over which of all these experiences I should include, I decided the best approach would be to list and rank them. So, I began assembling a file of them...jotting down a word or two about this event and that as each one resurfaced in my mind.

> *"From allowing readers to 'rent a cow' to adding scratch 'n' sniff to our pages, we tried some wild things..."*

Sometimes these were part of my "shower notes". Nearly every day, as I finish my morning shower, I hurriedly jot down ideas before I forget them. I've done this for decades and always wondered why this was such a creative time for me. Then I read somewhere recently that "Water running over one's body spurs creativity." Hmmm...

To my wife's chagrin, I also scribbled these memories on a bedside notepad in the middle of the night. Some years back, after she tired of my turning on the nightstand light to jot down ideas at all hours, she found a little notepad set; a pen snaps in at the top, and when you lift the pen, a tiny light illuminates the page. I wear out the batteries in that thing at least twice a year. It's one of the best gifts she's ever given me, and I'm sure she'd readily agree!

And—okay, I'll admit it—I also scribbled some of these notes on the small pad on my dash while I was driving. But I have a rule for that—I *never* write a note or look at a map when there's an oncoming car within sight. I wish drivers I meet would have the same rule for using cell phones.

So, I kept carrying batches of these little notes to the office and tossing them into a file folder labeled "The Book". Recently, as I *finally* got ready to begin this project, I opened that folder...and the task ahead almost overwhelmed me!

There were well *over 200 no*tes in there; *238* to be exact, some with three or four recollections jotted on a single slip. Each was a small note, but some of those reminders could take a good deal of explaining.

We did all that??? As I pored through all my scribbled notes in the

Ideas are funny little things—they won't work unless you do.

14

folder, even I was taken aback by the dozens of sometimes crazy ideas we've tried over the years, not only in formatting our magazines but in management and promotion. We'd been over some exciting, risky, bumpy roads.

It didn't take long to realize I'd definitely have to limit my selections. Otherwise this book will make *War and Peace* look like a pamphlet.

These wild ideas ranged from hiding a "needle in a haystack" in each of our issues…to allowing readers to "Rent a cow" as a unique Christmas gift…from adding a scratch 'n' sniff scent to our pages to give subscribers their first whiff of spring…to buying 1 acre of land in all 50 states so we could deed a square inch in each state to each of our subscribers…from having our readers write most of the copy for our magazines…to hiring a handwriting analyst to see whether men or women were signing subscription checks.

I'm tempted to list here more of the innovative things we tried—from sneaking $100 bills between pages as pot-of-gold treasures in our "rainbow issue"…to driving a company-owned six-horse hitch from Maine to California. Including a larger sampling of these promotional efforts would provide you with sort of an overture before my opera—so you could scan them and get a pretty good idea of whether this book is for you.

But I'm going to put off that list for a few chapters, because when people ask about our company—and how something got this big after starting so small in the basement of our home—they always seem to inquire first about my roots.

They want to know how my growing up on a rented farm in Iowa could possibly spark all these whimsical ideas. As if I knew.

So I'll deal with my pedigree first, then get to the good stuff later…about how we managed to launch a dozen national magazines without advertising…*after* struggling through the effects of my original outright "bomb".

A man can succeed at almost anything for which he has unlimited enthusiasm.

You can't plow a field by turning it over in your mind or build a home by hammering it around in your head. You have to just <u>do</u> it.

Life's not measured by the number of breaths you take, but by the moments that take your breath away.

CHAPTER 2

The 'It's All About Me' Chapter

I OWE a lot to Iowa. That may sound like a lyric by Meredith Wilson, but it's simply true. While most people are partial to their home state, I doubt many are more loyal to their roots than I am. Even now when I read the "Across the Country" section in *USA Today*, I always check out the snippet about Iowa first.

I've traveled in all 50 states; many of them offer much grander scenery. Iowa doesn't have mountains, ocean views, verdant valleys, sandy beaches, redwood forests or the Grand Canyon. Nor does it have man-made features such as the Statue of Liberty, the Superdome, the Golden Gate Bridge, the Space Needle, Mount Rushmore, the Arch or the Sears Tower.

Iowa isn't exactly a sports mecca, either. Few people are aware that it's one of the few states with no professional sports team of any type. High school and college games are as good as it gets.

So what does Iowa have? The answer's easy: It has incredible *people*.

Honest, hardworking, unpretentious, churchgoing, no-hands-out folks who take a great deal of satisfaction in earning their own way in life. They have an uncomplicated perspective: They feel God didn't put them here to be lazy. They look forward to each season. They know where milk comes from and which way is north. They define neighborliness.

As a whole, they just enjoy doing the right thing. I recall a small but vivid example: Years ago when Bobbi and I still had wee ones, we left Wisconsin in our Ford station wagon for a trip back to Iowa. We had just crossed the Iowa state line when my wife said she needed milk for the baby.

Naturally, like every other male who drives anywhere, I looked for a place where we could get gas, food and rest rooms *all in one stop*, right?

Well, as we pulled in, Bobbi said, "Gee, I always hate to ask to have milk warmed for the baby. Some waitresses aren't too happy about doing that."

I mentioned having my own problem—the rack on top of the station wagon was rattling and I needed to borrow a screwdriver to fix it.

So, as she went into the restaurant, I walked over to the guy near the

"THE REIMAN BOYS", we were called. I'm little squirt on left of my four brothers.

grease rack. I told him I needed to borrow a screwdriver and a pliers for a few minutes, then handed him my wristwatch.

"Why are you giving me your watch?" he asked.

"So you know I'll bring your tools back," I answered.

He looked at me like I must be some weird big-city guy and said, "Why don't you just let me take care of that for you?" And he did.

Minutes later, before I could tell Bobbi my experience, she said, "Guess what—when I asked the waitress to warm some milk, she not only smiled, she said 'I'll be happy to!'"

My response: "Well, we're back in Iowa, honey!"

The smile part didn't surprise me. People smile easily in Iowa. In general they're a happy bunch who seem pleased with their lot in life.

I sometimes think it isn't a coincidence that the outline of Iowa is shaped like an old security blanket with a few ragged edges. For natives like me, returning home now and then and grabbing hold of those fuzzy edges has a calming effect when our world is reeling.

But the part of Iowa that's paid off most for me is its work ethic. Iowans don't just dislike laziness, they *loathe* it. On the contrary, they take a good deal of satisfaction in hard work. Physical work. "Real work", some Hawkeyes would call it.

I grew up in that environment, and it's served me well. On a farm, you learn to be a contributor, not just a taker. And you stop working when the job is finished, not when the clock points to a certain number.

As a result, I was never a clock-watcher; when I got involved in a project, it was sometimes after 1 p.m. before I realized I'd missed the lunch hour. And I often stayed right into the evening to get a job *finished* rather

18

IN photo booth at 13.

than re-gearing and starting over in the morning.

You don't *whine* when you're from Iowa, either, and you avoid confrontations if at all possible. If something you'd like isn't on the menu, you just order something else. And if it isn't prepared quite the way you wanted, you don't send it back—you just say to yourself, "Well, it's not quite like Mom's", and eat it anyway.

You don't make a fuss about things. You just try to "get along". For all these reasons, Iowa was a great place for me to grow up.

I was the youngest of a family of five boys. Well, I guess I still am. But that served me well, too—trying to keep up with four older brothers, whether we were making hay, feeding cattle or hauling manure.

Like a lot of people, we kids grew up poor but didn't know it. Our mother was a good cook, we always had plenty to eat, there was plenty to keep us busy and we had clothes to keep us warm. Being the youngest, I wore hand-me-downs. Didn't bother me; I just assumed everyone did.

That background helped shape my outlook on life—I know what it's like to not have things. Wealth was never one of my goals. Working hard, having a nice family and "making an honest living" pretty much encompassed all I ever hoped for.

Rising early became a habit, too. Dad got us boys up at 5:30 every morning. Even in winter. He never wanted to "waste daylight". If there wasn't any work, I think we just looked for it.

I've been an early riser ever since and usually have been one of the first to show up at work. That proved beneficial, too: No matter how big your company gets, the leader sets the pace.

Dad never owned any land, but I don't recall him ever complaining about it. I don't remember him ever being depressed, either—he always seemed to have an "It'll rain tomorrow" attitude.

We were tenant farmers. In all, I grew up on four different farms, and our family cleaned up every one of them.

By that I mean Dad was a fixer-upper farmer and the "neat-nik" of all neat-niks. It was important to him that our place always "looked good". So we painted the barns, repaired the fences, wiped out weeds and picked up litter—we even cut the grass with a lawn mower right out to the road.

Dad was such a stickler for appearances that one day when I was with him in our pickup truck, he pulled onto the shoulder, climbed the fence into our oat field and walked about 50 yards out to pull one lone weed. I concluded he felt that weed might project a negative image to all who passed as to the kind of farmer he was.

That weed and that act made a statement to me: It's important to take pride in everything you do, and make any project you're involved in appear as good as possible.

Dad's corn rows were so straight, you could "aim" from one end of the field to another. And while we couldn't afford carpeting in our home,

There's no incentive to be punctual if there's no one there to appreciate it.

Mom kept the linoleum floor shining like the Johnson Wax headquarters.

I got my sense of neatness and structure from them. To this day, I guarantee that if I visited your home and you stepped out of a room, I'd straighten any crooked picture on your wall.

I think that's why I've insisted on "squared captions" (I'll explain that later), framed pages, white margins and other touches of "orderliness" in our magazines. I'm sure many of our readers don't notice all of these little extras, but they often comment on how clean and neat our pages are. In other words, our magazines—like Dad's farms—just "look good".

I learned a lot of other things by working alongside Dad that I've carried into my own life. For example, I noticed when I was young that Dad always took the worst or hardest job. That way none of us boys could complain about ours.

I did the same when running my own company. I always tried to make people think they worked *with* me, not *for* me. I wanted them to feel we were a *team* and I didn't outrank them.

When we drove somewhere, I jumped into the backseat instead of the front. When mailings needed stapling late in the day, I grabbed the stapler and pitched in. If three of us were on the road and the hotel had only two rooms and one suite, we quickly played a hand of "Showdown" to see who got the suite.

One time when we moved to other offices, I became aware some of our staffers would have to get by with less space than they'd had before. I quickly took the smallest office so no one could complain. Thanks, Dad.

Growing up among five boys, I loved sports. Being the youngest, I was always available when one of my brothers wanted to play catch or shoot buckets at the hoop we'd mounted above our concrete hog lot.

AUBURN TIGERS team apparently let me hold the ball during 1952 squad photo.

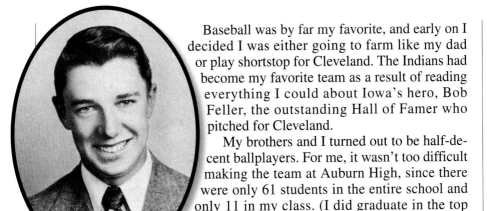

HIGH SCHOOL graduation picture in 1952.

Baseball was by far my favorite, and early on I decided I was either going to farm like my dad or play shortstop for Cleveland. The Indians had become my favorite team as a result of reading everything I could about Iowa's hero, Bob Feller, the outstanding Hall of Famer who pitched for Cleveland.

My brothers and I turned out to be half-decent ballplayers. For me, it wasn't too difficult making the team at Auburn High, since there were only 61 students in the entire school and only 11 in my class. (I did graduate in the top 10, by the way.)

Despite that meager enrollment, we had some good athletes—our team won Iowa's state high school fall baseball tournament! That was a pretty big deal for our 300 residents—if a fire had started, the whole town could have burned down during that tournament; *everyone* from Auburn attended the games.

Unfortunately, nobody from Cleveland called me when my senior season was over. Fortunately, I had another option:

I had a high school English teacher, Mrs. Kluever, who recognized early on that I had some ability to write. She knew my main interest—if not the only one—was sports, so she made me the Sports Editor of the high school newspaper.

When she saw the quality of the write-ups after each game, she convinced the publisher of the *Auburn Enterprise* to print those reports in our weekly hometown newspaper—with my *byline*, no less. That made me work even harder—people began stopping me on the street to comment on the articles.

None of Mrs. Kluever's English students had ever gone on to college to major in journalism, and that may have been what drove her. She stayed on my case all 4 years. When she began suspecting I was still just going to end up farming if Cleveland didn't call, she took me to the next level—she assigned me the task of interviewing "celebrities" who came to town.

See, in those late-1950 days in rural Iowa, it was common for a small community like ours to hold Adult Education Classes at the high school every Wednesday evening during the winter months. I really don't know how much any of our parents learned at those classes. More than anything, it was a good excuse for a gathering, and such bonding is important to small communities where people depend on each other.

But one thing's sure when folks gather in Iowa: You never send them home without feeding them something.

So, at the end of the evening, cake and cookies were served—all potlucked in by local women. And while these treats were being enjoyed, there was a little entertainment by singing groups or informative speakers.

An entrepreneur is someone willing to go out on a limb, have the limb cut off behind them and discover they had wings all along.

STATE WINNER of Iowa writing award. Who knows—I may have been only entrant!

Well, Mrs. Kluever decided that I should interview these celebrities and "review" them for both the school and town paper. I found that pretty interesting; travel in our family had ranged from nil to none, and these people had exciting lives to describe.

That's how I met Andy Williams. Yes, one of the singing groups that performed was "The Williams Brothers", four brothers from nearby Wall Lake, Iowa. They were far from famous at the time (or they wouldn't have been singing in the gym at our little high school).

Their claim to fame then was that they'd recorded a Shinola shoe-shine commercial that played on Des Moines radio stations. Lawrence Welk and Ed Sullivan hadn't heard of them yet. The youngest of the brothers was Andy, then in his mid-20s, and he was so un-famous, I didn't even single him out in my review. Ironically, I've often been told I look like Andy Williams by people who are unaware of this early experience.

Anyway, once the winter season was over, I pretty much forgot about my celebrity interviewing experiences. Until high school graduation, that is. That Sunday afternoon, at the cap-and-gown occasion, shortly after *all 11 of us* paraded up the center aisle to our seats, Mrs. Kluever called me up on the stage. The thought flashed across my mind maybe I'd flunked after all.

But that wasn't the case. She beamed ear to ear as she presented me with a framed certificate. She read aloud its engraving—the Quill and Scroll

Honor Society had named me the state winner of Iowa in interview writing!

My mouth must have hung open for a full minute. I didn't even know there *was* such an organization as Quill and Scroll. Mrs. Kluever had never mentioned it, but without my knowledge, she'd put together a collection of all my celebrity interviews and sent them off to this society.

For all I know, I might have been the only entrant in the state! But that certificate was pretty impressive. It was the first time in my life I was recognized for my brain rather than my bat or hook shot.

With that, Mrs. Kluever really turned up the heat: She contended I just *had* to go to college and study journalism.

I still wasn't sure. Not many kids from our small community went to college in those days. Plus, I wasn't exactly an "A" student; it seemed safer not to go than to suffer the humiliation of flunking out.

Sensing again I was leaning toward taking the easy way out, she called me into her office one day and said: "Roy, I'm only going to tell you this once. God doesn't spread talent like yours around too loosely, and when He does, you shouldn't waste it. Now you go home and think about that!"

How's that for a guilt trip? I mulled over the decision a lot that summer, changing my mind about as often as Iowa's weather. My second oldest brother, Ray, was a big influence.

Ten years my elder, he had begun a business career shortly after high school, but repeatedly found his chances of promotion limited without a college degree. So, by the time I graduated from high school, he was taking courses at Iowa State College (now Iowa State University) in Ames while continuing to stay employed.

When I discussed my go/no-go decision with him, and admitted my fear of failing, he said simply, "Fear is a great motivator. You won't fail if you try your best. It's people who don't study and don't try who flunk out. In college, it's all up to the individual." I've always been grateful for his nudge, because he proved to be right.

"Reiman, you're too damned dumb to go to college!"

I finally made the decision to enroll. But I then faced another problem—I lacked the funds to sign up for the fall term. Dad was in no position to help even if I'd asked him, and it never crossed my mind. The only choice was to find a good-paying job, which would allow me to start at the beginning of the winter session in January.

I found employment at a creamery in Carroll, about 10 miles from our farm. The job paid well because it was hard work and required long hours. Six days a week I reported to work at 4 a.m. That early start was necessary to get my assigned truck ready for my morning rounds in a 30-mile radius of the plant, picking up milk in large cans from dozens of farmers.

Those farmers got up before the sun, had their cows milked (so they could get started on the "real" work of the day), and they wanted that milk

Opportunities are never lost. Someone else will take over the ones you miss.

picked up before it got warm.

Getting up that early was sometimes a challenge, since I was still playing on a baseball team—with practices in between—plus enjoying a little social life. When I went to the Tuesday night dances at the Arcadia ballroom, I'd get home after 1 o'clock in the morning. So I'd just change clothes, drive to the creamery and take a nap in the truck until 4 a.m. Ah, the endurance and energy of an 18-year-old.

As I thought ahead, the challenge I'd face in getting passing grades at college still concerned me during those fall months, but never more than on the day I made a mistake in stacking crates of small milk bottles—24 to a case, eight cases high, a dozen cases across—on a large, flat cart.

Suddenly, the whole load started tipping over! Before I could stop it, several *hundred* bottles *crashed* to the floor, splintering into thousands of pieces! The horrible noise of all those bottles hitting the concrete floor in that hollow building must have been heard a full block away.

For me, the only sound that was worse was what followed it: The booming voice of the creamery manager, Bob Ware. A gruff guy to begin with, he bolted out of his office, looked at the huge pile of shattered glass, threw up his hands and yelled, "Reiman, you're too damned *dumb* to go to college!"

Just the confidence booster I needed.

Nevertheless, I registered for the winter session beginning in January, and headed to Ames. It was easier than facing Mrs. Kluever's wrath.

To me, the greatest pleasure of writing
is not what it's about,
but the music of the words.
—Truman Capote

CHAPTER 3

Man, I *Loved* College!

THAT CREAMERY JOB was the first of all sorts of jobs that financed my college expenses. I worked long hours during the summer and as many as 30 hours a week during the school year. Even so, I was in and out of the college loan office so often they started greeting me by first name.

Looking back, all those were good experiences—I learned almost as much from those jobs as I did from classes and books. For beginners, I learned that if you *present yourself* and show a real *willingness to work*, you can get just about any job you want.

An example is the first summer I returned home after my freshman year. I headed directly to Carroll again to apply for a summer job; I'd heard they were hiring at three construction sites in town.

That's when I learned students at the University of Iowa got out of spring classes more than a week before we did at Iowa State—and those Hawkeye students already had all the available jobs buttoned up.

The foreman at the first site, a school renovation project, said, "Sorry, got all the college kids I need." The foreman at the second site said the same thing. So did the foreman at the third and last site. I was *frustrated*; to my knowledge, there were no other jobs available in town.

After thinking about it a minute, I walked back to that third foreman and said, "Look, I don't just *want* this job, I *need* this job in order to go back to college next fall. I'm a farm kid and a good worker.

"So, tell you what I'll do—I'll work today for nothing just to show you what I got. By the end of the day, you're either going to add me on or re-place one of those other guys."

The big foreman—a Marine-type guy who turned out to be tough but fair—narrowed his eyes at me, paused a bit, looked me up and down, then said, "Okay, kid, grab a shovel."

At the end of summer, out of the dozen college kids on the crew, there were only three of us left. I shoveled gravel, muscled heavy wheelbarrows and lugged mortar up long ladders. It was hard work, but well worth it, because it covered my tuition the following fall.

I absolutely *loved* college! Till then I had never traveled—honestly, I'd only been outside the state once, to North Dakota. Yet here on this campus I was tossed amid a world I didn't know existed.

Classes and textbooks were challenging and enlightening, but I also learned a great deal from ancillary experiences—mixing with people from all over the globe…listening to widely differing opinions…delivering a speech in front of a large class…joining a fraternity…trying out for the college baseball team…handling publicity for homecoming festivities…writing and performing in college variety skits…and much more.

My campus jobs offered lessons, too. I worked at the college print shop, where I learned things about the printing industry that greatly benefited me later. I wrote releases for the college extension service, which taught me what a land-grant college was all about. I waited tables at a sorority house, which taught me "sophisticated" table manners.

I reported agricultural market news on WOI radio that reached farmers across the state. I worked as a spotter for the play-by-play announcer at Iowa State's home football games. I also sold advertising for an Ames printer, and yes, I even sold cookware for a while.

Selling ads for the printer turned out to be my first venture into the world of entrepreneurs. (I had so much "farm" in me, the first time I heard that word I wondered whether they'd said "in the manure". I eventually decided the two versions may have a little in common.)

The printer hired me to sell ads on bowling score sheets. There was no salary, but the commission was good if you were successful. Now, let me explain the premise here, as he did to me:

In the days before automated scoring, bowling centers used *lots* of score sheets. Those large sheets were expensive to print and bind into pads with perforated edges. So, when I'd walk up to a bowling proprietor and tell him he can have a year's supply of those sheets *free*, I'd get his attention real quickly.

> *"That was the key to making people not only read but study each ad…"*

Then who pays for them? The local *advertisers*, and it was my job to sell blocks of ads around the outside margins of these sheets. "Not only will those local businesses cover the cost of the sheets with these ads," I'd tell the owner, "but they'll become interested in your business because they'll be 'partnering' with you."

Well, with nothing to lose, the bowling proprietor wasn't hard to convince. He likely didn't think I'd be able to sell that many of those ads, anyway, since I had to sell *all* the blocks of ads around the perimeter of those sheets—about 16 ads, depending on the size of each ad—in order to make the thing work.

When I began, these ads did indeed prove hard to sell…until I came up with a gimmick. I quickly learned that almost any ad buyer's first and toughest question is, "Yeah, but who's going to *read* these ads?"

I knew I had to come up with a good answer to that to sell these small blocks of ads. So I watched people bowl for an evening, and watched how they kept score (a lot of this was new to me; I didn't do a lot of bowling while growing up on our farm, either).

I noted what bowlers got most excited about—things such as three strikes in a row, picking up a tough spare, scoring a 250 game were biggies. Suddenly it was clear to me that right there was the key to making people not only read these ads but *study* each one of them!

I convinced each advertiser to give a *prize* for any of these exciting feats—five strikes in a row would get 2 free gallons of gas from Geiers Standard Station…picking up a 7-10 split won you the dessert of your choice at Betty's Cafe…a 300 game won you a $25 deposit in your account at First Savings Bank (if you didn't have an account there, this just might induce you to open one).

I strategically put together a list of every conceivable kind of bowling achievement I could think of, then started making sales calls. The local business owners immediately understood *why* bowlers would not only read these ads but get excited about them.

The approach proved golden. In no time these owners got *involved* in these ads, talking it over with their employees, deciding which of these feats they should choose—should it be three strikes in a row or four?—and what the prize should be.

Once I got this gimmick perfected, I could drive into a town on a Saturday morning, find the bowling alley and have the whole border of ads sold by early afternoon. I once tried to sell the program in two towns in one day just to see if I could do it, but only came close.

Still, my commission on those sheets was $150.00 per bowling center, and that was *good money* back then.

The "Co-ed Catalog" was even more profitable. I didn't come up with this idea; I just perfected it. During my junior year, a friend of mine, Jere Wise, and two others came up with the idea of publishing a "dating booklet".

There were a lot of mixers and blind dates back then, and you often got paired up with someone you didn't know. What's more, there were *four male students* to *one female student* at Iowa State at that time, so there was a lot of interest in and pursuit of the available girls.

Blind dates were more common then. So, if a guy found he'd been paired up on a blind date with "Jane Smith", he quickly got out last year's college yearbook and looked up her picture, hometown, etc.

But…what if Jane Smith was a freshman??? Freshmen don't appear in the yearbook until after their first year. And *there* was where Jere and his buddies saw an opportunity—a booklet that would include pictures of all the freshmen girls on campus!

With four guys to each gal, a dating booklet like that would sell like hotcakes, right? Well, I'm sure it would have, but they got a late start on it,

Kites rise highest against the wind, not with it.

ran a little short on cash and the project sort of sputtered.

Still, I was *fascinated* by the concept and felt their idea had incredible potential if done right. My chance was coming—Jere and his entrepreneurial pals graduated the following spring, while I had another year to go. So I'd have the whole summer to think about doing it *right*.

Turned out I had a *lot* of time to think—that summer I operated a bulldozer on a road construction crew. Six days a week I reported at 6 a.m. and worked till 5:30 p.m. with a half-hour break for lunch. The best thing about those 11-hour days was that by noon on Thursday, we were already on overtime. So by 5:30 on Saturday we had 26 hours of overtime per week.

Well, over the roar of my Caterpillar's diesel engine, I gave a good deal of thought to this "dating brochure". The solution to the cash shortage Jere and his pioneer friends had run into, I decided, was to sell enough *ads* to support the printing costs *before* it was even printed. Otherwise, without those funds in hand, no printer would take a chance on a college kid being able to pay the bill.

Thinking back on my bowling sheet sales, I knew I first had to come up with the answer to, "Yeah, but who's going to *read* these ads?" One day as I pulled back the throttle on the dozer, I came up with the answer:

I'd hide the phone number of a different co-ed in each ad! The first guy who got a date with that girl would then bring her into the establishment, prove by the picture, phone number and driver's license she was that girl, and he would win a prize!

It would add *fun* to the whole thing. *Perfect!* Can't miss!

With this foolproof scheme in mind, I headed to campus a week before fall classes started and eagerly began my ad sales campaign. As I'd guessed, the merchants loved it.

Just like the bowling sheets, they knew these ads would be *read* (and probably *discussed* by dozens of guys saying, "Hey, Larry, look what you can win if you date this gal…").

These merchants, too, enjoyed picking the prizes—a free shirt from Joe's Men's Shop…five large pizzas from Connie's Pizza…$25 deposited in your account at College Savings Bank (some of the bowling gimmicks were easy repeats), etc.

Since I had hit the campus well before other students started selling ads for the college newspaper, various brochures or whatever, the fall budget of these merchants was ripe for pickin'. In just 3 days, I'd sold enough ads to cover the complete cost of printing 3,000 of these catalogs. So…the 50¢ each I'd charge for each catalog would be pure profit!

Taking the photos for the catalog proved easier than I thought, too. I lined up a good student photographer, Ted Doty, then contacted each sorority, asking if they'd like to have their freshman pledges included in the catalog.

No problem. They saw it as a lighthearted dating service, too, and readily agreed to it (trust me, things were different back then). Girls who were interested in the annual sorority rush week came to campus early to make

If something was worth doing, you've already been paid.

28

their rounds, which would give us an early start on the photos.

Timing was important; I wanted this booklet printed and ready to sell when the majority of the students—again, mostly males—came back to campus. That's when they'd be standing in those long lines to register, sign up for activities, change classes, assign dormitories, etc.

There were no computers to handle those things then; you just put in your time in those long lines and waited your turn. I was confident that selling this *Co-ed Catalog*, as I'd named it, along these lines would be like selling ice water in the Mohave Desert!

For the photo shoots, Ted and I put together a small set of bleachers in the middle of sorority circle. We shot all of the pictures in 2 days, scheduling the pledges to come for their group photo at a preset time.

"Why would the dean want to talk to me?"

As we prepared to take the picture, we passed a clipboard down each of the three rows on the bleachers, asking each girl to print her name, her residence, her phone number and her *height* (I thought of this detail on the dozer, too, as a benefit to both parties).

When we finished, Ted started processing the photos and I headed to the journalism building to lay out the booklet, design a cover, type the hundreds of names, etc. We both worked right through the night and delivered all the pages and photos to the printer by the middle of the next day.

While the press was chuggin' away, I met with members of a campus journalism group that was looking to raise funds. I hired them as "salesmen", offering them 10¢ commission on each 50¢ copy they sold. They saw its easy sales potential and jumped at the opportunity.

The following day, our "sales force" hit the lines, carrying heavy boxes of catalogs. My estimate of the expected response turned out to be conservative—the thirst was so great it was like selling iced *beer* in the Mohave!

By the second day we were running out of catalogs, and I raced to the printer to get another thousand copies run off. That turned out to be my undoing...because before I could get that next batch of *Co-ed Catalogs* back to the campus, I learned I'd received a call from a "Dean Helser".

Yep, that was what the note said back in my fraternity room, "Call Dean Helser". I recognized the name—he was Dean of Men and well known on campus—but I'd never met him. Why would the *dean* want to talk to *me*?

I called the number on the slip with more than a little trepidation; I'd never been in any kind of trouble on campus and my grades were good. My brother's "fear factor" advice had served me well. Why would any kind of dean want to see me???

When I called, the secretary said the dean would like me to come to his office that same day for a "brief meeting". This was getting even more mysterious. And it was cramping my schedule, too—I needed to check on those extra copies of the catalog and get them to my campus crews while the feeding frenzy was still at its height.

But, with anxiety growing by the minute, I put on some good clothes, added some butch wax to my crew cut and headed over to Beardshear Hall, not even certain where in that building the dean's office was. After finding it on the directory, I checked in with his secretary and was escorted into his *huge* office. Dean Helser stood up at his desk, smiled, introduced himself with a handshake and asked me to have a seat.

That's when I saw a copy of the *Co-ed Catalog* laying on his desk. Yet, with my farm-boy naivete, I still didn't get what the meeting was about. But that only took a minute.

"Did you publish this, Roy?" he asked, picking it up. Well, with bold type on the front cover stating, "Roy Reiman, Publisher", this was hardly the time for denial.

> ### *"Gee, Dean, I never thought of that!"*

After my hesitating answer of, "Um…yes," he said, "Well, I need to inform you, Roy, that Dean LaBaron, the Dean of Women, brought this to my attention, and she isn't too happy about it."

My naivete becoming even more obvious, I asked, "Why?"

"Well, she doesn't think it's proper that you're—as she put it—'selling her girls'."

He smiled as he said it, though, and I got the impression he personally thought she was overreacting.

I explained that I had "cleared" it with each of the sororities and dorms that were involved, and that they had all not only okayed it, but were supportive because they thought it was sort of a dating service.

"Well, Roy, be that as it may, I have to ask you to stop selling these booklets. After all, we have a rule here that no private enterprise can operate on campus without first going though proper clearance channels and receiving approval."

When I said I had no knowledge of that, he responded, "Oh, yes. If we didn't have a rule like that, somebody might set up a pop stand right here outside Beardshear."

Seeing a twinkle in his eye and deciding to try a little humor, I said, "Gee, Dean, I never *thought* of that!"

He threw back his head and roared, and we had a nice conversation after that. He told me he admired my entrepreneurship, said he'd checked on my grades and conduct, and asked me what my career goals were. Then, once again clarifying I could sell no more copies of my catalog on campus, he patted me on the back and sent me on my way.

But he didn't forget me. Whenever our paths crossed on campus from that day on, he'd single me out in the crowd and ask, "Hey Roy, how's the pop stand doing?" (In Iowa "pop" is what they call soda or Coke, and that response of mine had apparently really tickled him.)

Tickled or not, the meeting cost me dearly. I'd made a really good profit from the first 3,000 *Co-ed Catalogs*—enough to cover about half of that year's tuition plus room and board—but I had to pretty much "eat" the extra thousand copies I'd printed.

Trying to sell the leftovers wasn't worth getting in trouble with this Dean LaBaron, who had obviously sensed the "women's movement" long before others—especially me—had any idea it was on the horizon.

I nearly became a veterinarian. I was wrestling with a lot that summer between my sophomore and junior years when I bounced around on that bulldozer. I enjoyed the creative challenge of coming up with ideas for promotional ventures, but one thing kept bothering me:

If I continued in journalism, it was likely I would end up in some big city, because that's where the good-paying jobs were. That didn't appeal to me; I was still a country boy at heart and had no desire to locate in some large, urban area.

The more I thought about it, the more I concluded I was on the wrong path in pursuing a journalism degree. And that's when I started thinking about switching to veterinary medicine. I'd always liked working with livestock, I had good grades, and Iowa State was one of the pre-eminent vet schools in the nation.

So shortly after the fall session started, I met with my counselor, Harry Heath, a journalism professor, and told him my plan to switch to pre-vet. He threw a small fit! I had another Mrs. Kluever on my hands! He wouldn't hear of it; he contended I had writing talent and great potential if I stuck with journalism.

> *"I'd sold my first article—*
> *I was ecstatic!"*

Then he did something that had long-lasting effects: He set up a series of courses that were required in *both* journalism and pre-vet, so I would have the fall semester to think about my decision without losing any credits.

But, knowing how financially challenged I'd been up to then (he apparently hadn't heard about the "catalog"), he suggested I take one senior course in "Magazine Freelance Writing". He explained how this would provide me with extra income if I succeeded in selling any articles, as well as give me a better idea if I "had what it takes" to write at that level.

I went along with his recommendations. The first day in this senior course I learned that our grade was based primarily on whether we were able to *sell* articles to off-campus publications. If we succeeded in selling three articles during the course, we received three hours of "A"; if we sold five articles, we got five hours of "A", which was as good as it could get.

Three weeks into the course, I sold my first article to *Hoard's Dairyman*, a magazine in Fort Atkinson, Wisconsin. They paid me *$60.00* for that article (detailing how to rid pastureland of pocket gophers, which was becoming a real problem for dairy farmers). *I was ecstatic!* For a number

Many would like to move mountains, but few are willing to practice on small hills.

of reasons: For one, it was the first time I was *paid* for something I'd done with my brain instead of my back. I had done nothing more than just sit down for an hour or two to write this article, and they paid me *big bucks*—$60.00—for it!

Secondly, they'd paid me for something that wasn't "work"; it was something I had actually *enjoyed doing*.

In a way, that somehow didn't seem ethical to me. Till then, I'd only been paid for things that were physically difficult. It didn't seem right to get paid for something that was enjoyable. But...I got over that guilt aspect pretty quickly.

With that encouraging start, I really dug into this freelance writing course. And the success kept coming.

Since I was working as a part-time writer at the college Information Service—interviewing various college crop and livestock authorities for articles provided free to media across the state (which is an obligation of land-grant colleges)—this provided me with numerous leads for longer, in-depth articles that farm magazines were interested in.

By the end of that course, I had sold *27 articles* to various publications, picked up five hours of "A" and never gave another thought to veterinary medicine. I figured maybe I could avoid the big cities—maybe I could just write and sell articles from the boondocks the rest of my life.

I continued freelancing after that, and by spring of my senior year—between the freelance income and what I made off the *Co-ed Catalog*—I actually had to pay income tax, which was another learning experience.

One Cadillac, 14,000 buyers. While my first meeting with Dean Helser was somewhat confrontational, I eventually became one of his biggest fans.

I never had the opportunity to have long conversations with him, yet whenever he saw me, he not only joked about the pop stand, but he took the time to ask how I was doing. It was obvious he took an interest in me. He was an extremely handsome man, he looked the part of a dean and he had a demeanor I greatly admired.

Apparently I wasn't alone in my high regard for him, as evidenced by a later opportunity I was given to become part of a group effort to honor this man in a very unusual way.

Some students were sitting at a table in the Memorial Union one day when one of them said, "I heard that Coach Evasheski is retiring at Iowa U., and the students are collecting money to give him a Ford station wagon."

Now, you have to understand that the rivalry between the University of Iowa and Iowa State University was and still is...well, *ripe*. Back then, they called us the "Cow College" and we called them "Moo U". The rivalry was so intense, the two schools didn't even compete in sports for nearly 25 years; the administrations feared the campuses might be torn apart.

So, here was the situation: Forrest Evasheski had been Iowa's football coach for eons, had been highly successful and now those Hawkeye stu-

It takes more backbone than wishbone to make success.

"OPERATION CADILLAC" was kept a secret by 14,000 students. Several hundred of them showed up at the dealership to help select color and interior accessories.

It's not how many hours you put in—it's what you put in the hours.

dents were going to buy him a Ford station wagon.

"Shoot, they're going to get all kinds of publicity out of that," one of the students said. "You know what, since they're the 'jock college' and we're the 'academics college', we oughta give Dean Helser a *Cadillac* when he retires this spring."

In an instant, he and his listeners realized what he'd just said, and what an incredible idea that was!

I wasn't in on that original conversation, but I was soon contacted by the organizers to help formulate and publicize the plan. We decided this would be all the more fun if we could keep the whole thing *secret* from Dean Helser.

This presented a challenge, because while we wanted the entire student body to know about this exciting project, we couldn't publicize it in the student newspaper, *The Iowa State Daily*.

So I turned out a flyer that was inserted in the message boxes at the Union; there was one box there assigned to each fraternity, sorority, dorm and group house on campus for the purpose of distributing campus-wide announcements. That flyer privately touted the "secret" to the heart of the campus, and we mailed it to the 1,500 students living off campus.

My headline in small italics at the top of the flyer stated: *"Sh-h-h-h! Can you keep a SECRET?"* Then it went on to explain exactly what we had in mind—we were going to "top" that Ford for Iowa's coach by giving a *Cadillac* to one of Iowa State's most popular deans!

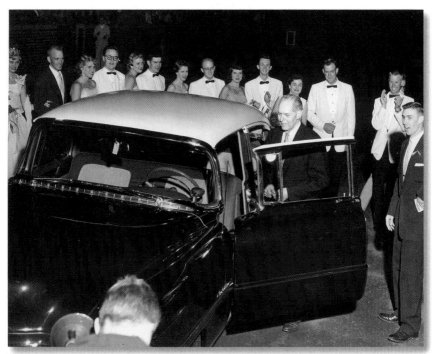

THE DEAN was still in bit of shock when the students presented him with the car.

34

"Dean Helser doesn't have any idea we're doing this, *so let's see if 14,000 students can keep a collective secret,* okay?" the copy read.

"Now, all we want is for every student to give *just 50¢* toward the purchase of this car. That way every student can get involved, and every time the dean drives this Cadillac on campus, you'll be able to say with pride, "*I* helped buy that car!'"

The flyer went on to explain that members of our group would be spreading out over campus to all the houses at specified evening hours during the following week, to detail this exciting project, answer any questions and collect the funds.

Well, while we'd only asked for 50¢ each (a new Cadillac in 1957 only cost around $6,000), students found this whole "secret gift" idea so exciting that many of them threw in a dollar or even more. When our group got together to count the take on Thursday night, we had nearly *$7,500*!

We decided to use the leftovers to start a "Dean Helser Scholarship Fund", and we were on our way. But since Cadillacs came in such a variety of models and colors, we weren't sure what to choose.

That's when we decided to let Mrs. Helser in on the secret. We asked her to join us at the local Cadillac dealership after classes the following Monday afternoon to help with the decision.

While word of "Operation Cadillac" never once reached the dean, it seemed everyone on campus was whispering about it all day Monday. I got the impression a *lot* of students were going to show up at the dealer-

THE HELSERS BEAM as the dean holds keys and salutes the throng of students.

In the midst of difficulty lies incredible opportunity. —Albert Einstein

ship to experience the excitement of Mrs. Helser picking out their car.

It also occurred to me that a story was building here. So I grabbed the best camera I could borrow from the journalism department and headed to the dealership myself.

A few dozen students were there as I started shooting, but it soon became a *mob scene*. Several hundred pumped-up students eventually surrounded the cars and crowded a small balcony. Those who couldn't get inside the building were looking through the windows.

I shot several rolls, including some overall views from the balcony and some great close-up shots of Mrs. Helser with beaming students leaning in around her. When she finally chose a two-tone model with a navy blue bottom and cream-colored top, the students applauded!

The next day, I airmailed (no FedEx then) some of those pictures to *LIFE* magazine in New York, with a bit of the details. Sure enough, I got a call from one of their editors later in the week, asking when the car was going to be presented to the dean.

"Next weekend at VEISHEA," I responded, then explained the acronym was formed by the first letter of the college's majors—(V)eterinary Medicine, (E)ngineering, (I)ndustrial (S)cience, (H)ome (E)conomics and (A)griculture. "It's a spring celebration event, and he'll be given the keys during a surprise presentation on Saturday night after a student variety show on the football field."

The *LIFE* editor told me they were definitely interested in some pictures showing the dean's reaction, along with some brief copy. But, he emphasized, they had a Monday morning deadline, and I would have to somehow get those pictures to New York by no later than Sunday afternoon. I told him I'd do my best.

"If I'm dreaming, please don't wake me!"

Man, think of it, a college kid having a chance to get something published in *LIFE* magazine! It was a weekly national publication then, easily one of the country's biggest and most popular. It seemed everyone read *LIFE* at the time.

The Saturday night presentation came off like a movie script. At the end of the evening's skits, songs and dances on the huge stage set up on the 50-yard line, the student body president called Dean Helser from the audience and asked him to come up on stage.

When the dean got there and faced the crowd, *the Cadillac* slowly appeared on the other side of the field behind him, with spotlights thrown on it. The students started yelling and screaming, and Dean Helser didn't have a clue what was causing the ruckus—the backdrop of the stage totally blocked the car from his view.

The student president kept talking to the dean, holding his attention, as the car slowly moved down the track in the background, made the turn behind the goalposts, then headed toward the front of the stage, with the din growing louder by the minute.

THIS IS PHOTO in *LIFE* magazine showing Dean driving off with grandchildren.

The gleaming car finally stopped and the roar reached a new crescendo. Then it got suddenly silent—everyone wanted to hear the dean's response as the student president explained that this car was a retirement gift from *all* the students of Iowa State, and handed him the keys.

I was standing nearby, shooting film like crazy, but also listening for the dean's response in hopes of getting a good quote. I couldn't have written one better: Dean Helser was shocked. He just kept shaking his head in disbelief, then finally said one sentence: "If I'm dreaming, please don't wake me!"

I really don't know what happened after that, because I raced off to get the pictures processed. I was in such a rush, I actually printed several off wet negatives. It was close to midnight when I jumped in my old Chevy coupe and headed for the Des Moines airport, about 40 miles away. I put the package on the next flight to New York and hoped for the best.

I couldn't *wait* till next week's issue of *LIFE* came out. When it did, I was more than pleased. There, on a left-hand page in a summary of "What Happened Last Week", was my picture of Dean Helser in his Cadillac, with

Enthusiasm is the yeast that raises a lot of dough.

a caption that led off with, "If I'm dreaming, please don't wake me!"

I was no longer taking that freelance course, but what I'd learned in that class helped me accomplish this. There was no photo acknowledgement with the *LIFE* item, but I knew how that picture got there, and the satisfaction of achieving this was enough credit in itself.

Graduate one minute, in the Army the next. I was also enrolled in ROTC (the Reserve Officers' Training Corps) while in college, which provided additional income on one hand, but on the other meant I had to go directly into service upon graduation.

Directly it was. On graduation day, all of us in the ROTC program were required to wear our military uniforms under our gowns. After we received our degrees, we didn't return to our seats like the other graduates—we circled behind the stage, where we removed our caps and gowns, then put on our service hats and waited.

The minute the graduation services were complete, we were marched back out in front and sworn into the Army. Within a week, I was on active duty at Fort Sill, Oklahoma, beginning a 17-week officers' training course, which proved even tougher than any college course because of the physical as well as mental stress, combined with the pomp and polish requirements.

I followed that with duty at Fort Leonard Wood, Missouri and later at Fort Carson, Colorado, eventually reaching the rank of Captain before I hung up my spit-shined boots.

There were parts of my term I didn't care for, much like everyone else, but overall I enjoyed my stretch in service, particularly the travel and meeting guys with even more diverse backgrounds than I'd known in college. My journalism degree helped me pull some good duty, too, including editing the camp newspaper at two different sites.

Still, I was eager to finish my obligation and get out into the "real world" of publishing. When I did, I was pleasantly surprised to learn that—through those freelance articles I'd sold them during college—several magazine editors were eager to talk to me.

Stand at attention, one last salute, click of the heels, I'm out of the Army. And I'm *ready!*

Don't clutch the past so tightly that it leaves your arms too full to embrace the present.

*Find something you like to do
so much you'd do it for free...
then do it so well that people will pay you for it.*

CHAPTER 4

First Job—All I'd Hoped for, and More

AFTER a series of interviews, I chose to work for Capper Publications in Topeka, Kansas, a company that published several magazines as well as the local newspaper, and also owned the city's major TV and radio stations. It turned out to be an excellent choice.

At many points of my career, I've been fortunate to be at the right place at the right time. Still, for me—as for anyone—it's important to make the most of opportunities when they're presented. Capper's was a case in point.

The magazine I would work for was *Capper's Farmer*, which then was one of the three largest national farm magazines in the country. I was told in the interview that they had the position of Managing Editor open for that magazine...but not immediately.

They had a pretty seasoned staff. "We feel it's time for some young blood," the salty-tongued publisher said, explaining that rather than promote someone internally, they were looking for a young editor they could groom for this Managing Editor position over the next 3 to 5 years.

I was a young man in a hurry, and I made it in 9 months. I was rightfully proud to be named Managing Editor of a magazine with 1.3 million subscribers at the age of 23.

They groomed me by moving me from department to department, working with this editor and that. The first of these assignments involved working with the Livestock Editor.

Problem for me was, after my stretch in service, I was pretty out of touch with the livestock industry. I decided a good thing for me to do would be to *get involved* by owning a few cattle of my own.

I found a good cattle feeder near Topeka and asked if he'd be interested in selling me a couple of his steers so I could "get back in action". I explained I didn't want specific steers, but simply a small *percentage* of his feedlot of 80 steers so I could be on the same page as him and think like him.

He was enticed by my offer and said he'd be fine with it. (I'm sure it

If you want to feel rich, count all the things money can't buy.

39

crossed his mind that he'd be getting direct access to our magazine's Economics Editor's take on what the market was going to do.) He asked how many I'd like to buy, and I said four of them would be about right, but I'd have to borrow the money to cover them.

That presented a brief problem, too. I'd just gotten in town and had no credit rating; likely no bank would loan me close to a thousand dollars to "go out and buy a few steers". So, I went to four separate men's stores in town and bought at least one item at each of them (I was pretty short of business clothes anyway, just coming out of the Army).

Then I charged each item and said I would pay them next week when I got my first paycheck. Getting them to go along with that didn't prove difficult, since I was able to show I was employed by Capper Publications, which was well known in town.

True to my word, the day I got paid, I went back to those stores and paid each bill in cash. Then after a few days, I went to the bank to borrow the money for the steers. No problem—I now had an "excellent" credit rating.

My weekend drives out to see "my steers" not only directly entrenched me in the livestock industry, but got me involved in a good farm family as well, which helped me relate to this audience as I edited copy for the magazine.

Being sent from one department to another had a huge benefit—I began to learn what was going on in every aspect of farming, even in farm kitchens when I worked with the food editors. It was like getting a quick catch-up course in agriculture and rural living.

Meanwhile, the job also taught me *tact*. When you're 23 years old and you walk up to the desk of an editor in his 50s—who's been doing his job a *long* time—and tell him you think he needs to rewrite some of his copy, that takes *TACT*.

Handling that task was sometimes so difficult that I would first sit at my desk and *write out* what I planned to say (I've always typed better than I talked). Then I'd pretty much memorize it before I approached the editor involved.

Fortunately, I had the backing of the Editor in Chief. During the first few weeks, I would first go to him to see whether he agreed with the changes I was about to suggest.

He nearly always agreed with me, and once he'd made that known to the staff, things went better than I first expected. I gradually won their respect, they began inviting me to coffee with them and we developed a good relationship. They were a great bunch.

The thing that turned the tide for me and led to my early promotion was a special project one of the editors was working on. The project was a 16-page insert—"What City People Should Know About Farmers"—that was to be bound in the center of an upcoming issue.

The editor to whom this project was assigned had worked most of a month on it, and when he finally finished it, he put it on my desk in a spe-

40

cial folder for my review. He'd worked hard on it, and I could tell he was really proud of the effort.

A half hour later, I wondered why he felt that way. I'd closed the door to read this long piece of prose…and I was really disappointed. It had lots of facts, but it had no "zing". It wasn't written in an interesting style…it wasn't compelling. It lacked any excitement—reading it was like having a back rub after a big meal.

Here he'd done all that work, our staff had been anticipating this challenging venture and now we had a big yawn on our hands. I didn't think our subscribers were going to read through the whole thing…much less pass it on to their urban friends, as we'd hoped.

> ## *"Man, this pretty girl could dance!'*

I went to the Editor in Chief (who I'd started referring to privately as the "Big Guy") and told him my concerns. He simply said, "If you think you can do better, rewrite it."

So I did. I was single at the time, had no one to get home to, so I pulled up to my typewriter with a ream of paper alongside and had at it. Once I got rolling, I couldn't stop. I went right through the night and finished it in time to put it on the Big Guy's desk before heading home to shave, shower, change clothes and get something to eat.

When I got to the office, he called me in. He told me he was so pleased with the result of this effort and my other work, he was promoting me immediately.

He put out a memo later that day naming me Managing Editor, after just 9 months. That was one of my proudest days, and despite having only a few hours of sleep, I left the office feeling frisky as a colt.

That wasn't the best thing that happened to me in that job. Bobbi was.

After I'd been on the staff for about a year, Capper Publications' management decided to shut down one of its other magazines named *Household*. Its offices were located in another part of town, and when the closure was final, Big Guy decided to interview three of the top secretaries from that staff to add one to ours.

When I saw this really pretty auburn-haired girl walk in, I thought, *I hope he hires her.* And he did. Apparently he was as impressed with her brains as her beauty, because he selected this girl named Bobbi as his Executive Secretary.

Well, I put in a lot of hours at that magazine, but I didn't work *all* the time. By then I'd made local friends and went out evenings to the various bars and dance halls around town. One hot Kansas summer night we went to a place called "The Moon", and there I spotted this "Bobbi" dancing up a storm. Man, this pretty girl could *dance.*

Since I've always liked to dance, and have always liked pretty girls as well, I soon had my arm around the waist of that cute secretary and was

The trouble with reaching a crossroads in life is the lack of signposts.

making moves with more than my feet. And that was the start of a long-time relationship.

I hadn't gotten to know her that well at work, but beginning with that night, I got to know her better and better after work. She was from a rural town, too, where her parents ran a small cafe. She had my kind of energy, big brown eyes and a ready smile. I was "smitten".

But there was a problem. The company had a strict policy against "interdating". I think a lot of companies had policies like that back then. So she and I knew it was highly important to keep our growing relationship on the Q.T.

I thought we did that pretty well. That is, I thought so until one morning Big Guy asked me to go out to coffee at a nearby restaurant with him. Here comes my farm-boy naivete again—I thought maybe he was going to talk to me about a raise or another promotion!

Was I wrong! He'd found out Bobbi and I were seriously dating, and I was in deep do-do. He lectured me good for a full 5 minutes. He was good with words and he used a lot of them.

I quickly concluded my whole career there was over and I was a goner because he kept saying everything in past tense—as in "You knew what the policy was…", "If you thought you had a future in this company…" and "You should have known better…".

Worse, I did a terrible job of defending myself, because frankly, I was guilty as sin. I just kept nodding and mumbling "I know" a lot.

Finally he stopped and just sat there for a bit. I thought, *Oh boy, here it comes. I'm gone!*

But he surprised me. He took a deep breath, looked me right in the eye, then said rather softly, "Having said all that…I think you're good for each other."

I was pleasantly shocked. It was as though he'd done his job, said what needed to be said and now it was up to me. He told me to be even more discreet, that Bobbi and I needed to keep our relationship at the office on a very professional basis, and we were never to discuss business issues that needed to be confidential between him and her.

With that, he walked out of the restaurant. It took quite a while before I could follow him.

I was *very appreciative* of that gesture on his part because, as I thought about it later, I knew that if I'd been forced to decide between the job and Bobbi, there was no doubt which I would have chosen.

I think he knew that, too. For me, as good as the job was, it was a temporary thing. My relationship with Bobbi was going to be a permanent thing.

So, I've always contended that the best thing I got out of Topeka was Bobbi. After 43 years, I still say that.

Indulge in things you love…even when it seems hopeless.

42

*The only place success comes before work
is in the dictionary. —Vince Lombardi*

CHAPTER 5

Milwaukee's Famous for More Than Beer

WHILE beer is the first thing that pops into most people's minds when you say you're from Milwaukee, Wisconsin, what isn't well known is that the city is one of the country's largest printing centers.

Numerous magazines such as *TIME*, *Newsweek*, *Playboy*, *U.S. News & World Report* and other national publications are printed there. Our company's magazines add 16 million copies to the total every other month.

How did Milwaukee become such a printing mecca? Well, for one, Wisconsin has *lots* of trees, offering a vast source of paper. And Milwaukee's early settlers included large numbers of German immigrants, who were particularly adept at manufacturing and operating printing presses and linotypes.

While I wasn't smart enough to plan it that way, Milwaukee turned out to be the perfect place to launch a publishing company of my own. But that was far from my mind when I moved there in 1960.

Earlier that year back in Topeka, Capper Publications was acquired by Stouffer Communications. Those of us on the editorial staff of *Capper's Farmer* didn't know it at the time, but the Stouffer family was far more interested in the city's main newspaper and its TV and radio stations than they were in our farm magazine, which was something they had to take along with the deal.

The new management didn't give us a lot of support to begin with, but when we started losing money, they decided to pull the plug real fast. How *Capper's Farmer* began losing money is a story in itself.

Today, almost all magazines are audited by outside firms. Publishers have to validate their circulation list annually now, to openly show advertisers exactly the kind of people they reach. If a publisher says the magazine goes to 200,000 CEOs, for example, the independent audit will provide proof or lack thereof.

But there was no "Standard Bureau of Auditing" in the late 1950s. Back then most people just took another person's word for things, and if

People who are busy rowing seldom rock the boat.

you said your magazine went to a million farmers, well, then that must be true.

It gradually became less true at *Capper's Farmer*, and that was what led to its demise. Old Senator Capper, the founder and father figure of the magazine, employed a large field sales force to sell subscriptions.

The salesmen were paid mostly through commissions, and when Senator Capper decided to have them offer *insurance* in addition to subscriptions, those sales reps started making more off the insurance premiums than the subscriptions.

But there was one catch to selling the insurance: It could *only* be sold to people who subscribed to *Capper's Farmer* magazine.

The good Senator likely felt he'd come up with a clever way of boosting subscription sales, but that move proved to be loaded with arsenic. The sales force, now eager to sell a subscription first so they could then sell the more lucrative insurance, found it was easier to sell subscriptions door-to-door *in towns and cities* rather than to go farm-to-farm and run down Clem Corngrower on his back forty.

They had been given no provisions that the subscribers to *Capper's Farmer* had to be farmers. And likely the Senator didn't mind too much in the beginning, either, because the magazine's circulation was going up, and he, too, was making more off the insurance than the subscriptions.

But then one day the wall came tumbling down. Someone in the advertising department at John Deere in Moline, Illinois became suspicious and did some checking, and to his surprise (and to many of us editors) he found that nearly 50% of *Capper's* subscribers lived in urban areas.

With that, John Deere—one of our two biggest advertisers—quickly pulled its entire ad schedule from the magazine. Next issue, International Harvester—our second largest advertiser—followed suit.

Our ad staff asked the IH people why, since IH hadn't done any similar study. They simply replied, "Well, John Deere dropped out, and they must have had a good reason. So we're following suit." With each following issue, more advertisers did the same.

I never forgot that lesson of how one major advertiser can start a parade of naysayers that can quickly have a well-known magazine swirling down the toilet. *Capper's Farmer* had over a million subscribers, was one of the "big three" in farm magazines, had been published for over 80 years, and we were shut down within 6 months after some "Green Detective" at John Deere admirably did his homework.

"I saw editors crying at their desks...not just the women."

That final day—when it was officially announced that we were going to cease publishing—was one I'll long remember, too. I saw editors crying openly at their desks. Not just the women, but the Crops Editor and the Machinery Editor as well.

They took it very personally. Editors become involved in a magazine. It's not just a bunch of pages bound together each month, it's part of *them*.

What made matters worse is that most of these editors were in their 50s, some beyond. I was young, and there would be lots of jobs open to me; for them, there were few if any jobs waiting for them. The other two major farm mags were fully staffed. It was a very sad day.

For me, the phone began ringing almost immediately. I'd gotten good exposure through the magazine over the past 3 years, and I'd met management people from other publications at conventions and industry open houses. Within a week, I was contacted by nine publishing companies and ad agencies.

Of all these, the one that enticed me most was a firm in Milwaukee called Agricultural Publishers. They produced sponsored magazines—contract publishing, as it's now called—which sounded new and challenging.

For example, they published a magazine for Massey-Ferguson, a national farm equipment company. The publication was called *Farm Profit*, and it was sent free to all farmers who owned M-F equipment. They also produced *Ford Farming* and *The Ford Almanac*, again sent to customers and prospects of Ford farm equipment.

They felt they had the opportunity to substantially increase the Ford business by putting someone full-time on the account, and were offering me a salary that was a third more than I'd been making.

What I liked best about this company is that the head honcho kept saying, "At this company, you set your own salary—you can make as much as you're worth."

He explained that the staff was small, and there was no "seniority" or organizational structure that limited compensation: "If you produce more than the other guys, you'll get paid accordingly; your salary won't be based on what anybody else is making. Here, it's up to you what you make."

Having the opportunity to get paid on that basis sounded awfully good to me. So did what he described as the "Million Dollar Idea Meeting" that the company held every quarter.

I don't think the term "brainstorming" had surfaced as yet, but that's basically what this was. Each editor was to come to these quarterly meetings with an idea that would make the company a million dollars. That figure was used to add a little levity—anything less would do.

This all seemed exciting and challenging, but I kept hesitating, putting off a decision. When the owner asked why, I explained that I was engaged to this young woman in Topeka, and that the distance between Wisconsin and Kansas was a concern, especially since I had another offer in Kansas City, a short drive away.

He thought a bit, then said, "Okay, here's what I'll do. I'll add $500 to what I've already offered you in the form of an expense account. That will allow you to fly back and forth (airfares were much cheaper then), with the provision that you pick up an article and photos there in Kansas each trip so it's a legitimate expense."

That thinking impressed me, too; no wonder this guy was so success-

Living on Earth is expensive, but it does include a free trip around the sun every year.

ful. That closed the deal, and *that's* how I ended up in Milwaukee and have been there ever since.

As I dug into this new job, I found it paid well, but the expectations were high, too. Still single, I put in long hours, working many evenings and weekends, plus I traveled a great deal, especially to Detroit and back.

I ended up handling a number of different publications for Ford Motor Company, not just for their ag division, but for their car division as well. Spending a good deal of time at what was called "The House of Glass", Ford's main office in Dearborn, also provided me with an insight into the regimentation and an almost aristocratic "pecking order" that existed in large companies like this then.

I learned little things meant a lot to executives at Ford. As a result of my frequent visits to the company's headquarters, I could nail a person's "rank" and salary level within minutes of being in his office, based on status symbols such as:

What floor was the office on? (Salaries went up with altitude at Ford.) How large was the office? Was it near the center of the building or near the end? If it was a *corner* office, you were dealing with an exec who was in tall grass!

That was just the beginning. How big was his desk? Was it straight or L-shaped? Did he have a credenza or not? Did he have a private secretary outside his door or share one from the pool?

It didn't stop there. In his office, did he have a metal in-and-out basket...or a walnut-colored one? Did he have real art on his wall...or just prints? How expensive was his suit?

And here was a biggie—did he have a *water pitcher* and matching drinking glasses??? That status item, I learned, could make a salary difference of $20,000 a year more compared to the guy without one.

I even noticed the secretaries for the water-pitcher guys made a big deal out of freshening up that water regularly; it appeared they didn't have a lot of other things to do. Most of these girls, too, looked like they weren't selected solely for their ability to type. The executive levels at Ford took on the aura of a pageant.

> *"This was an introduction to a world I didn't know existed..."*

Another important thing to notice: What dining room was one privy to? The Ford headquarters had three types—the general cafeteria, where all the low-echelon types ate; a mid-level restaurant, where mid-level execs could order off a menu; and then, ahem...the "Executive Dining Room"!

I was only invited to lunch a few times in this palatial room on the top floor of Ford's huge, glass-encased headquarters, and it was an experience. Here, things were taken to a whole new level of decorum. Each waitress was assigned to only three or four specific execs.

Many people drank at lunch then, and "his" waitress knew exactly

46

what he wanted to drink. She also knew when he was coming and had his drink ready; as soon as he sat down, she put his martini with three olives in front of him, made with his choice of gin.

There were gourmet choices, fine china and crystal in this opulent room, and everything was served with elegance. For example, it was the first time I'd seen those little "swirlies" of melted chocolate around the edge of the dessert plate. (Mom *never* did that back on the farm.)

These subtle "power symbols" were never mentioned at Ford, but there was no doubt everyone noticed and *recognized* every one of these status emblems. These outward symbols were like stripes or bars on a serviceman's uniform, and executives who earned them were lavished with accorded respect.

Likewise, if you wanted to do business there as an "outside vendor"— that's what I and others were called—you'd better pick up on these things in a hurry. I learned who I could greet by first name, and who I'd better address as "Mr." When I got to one of those corner offices, I even used "Sir" a lot.

For a young guy like me—still not that many years off an Iowa farm— this was an introduction to a world I didn't know existed. But I kept alert and learned, minded my p's and q's, and our company's business with Ford continued to grow.

Spending that much time in Detroit over the next 3 years did present one problem, though. Traffic in the "Motor City" moved about 20 to 30% faster on the same roads compared to Milwaukee. As a result, I kept getting stopped in Milwaukee for driving over the speed limit.

I got two tickets on the same four-lane boulevard in a single month—one for going 27 mph and the other 29 mph! When I complained to the policeman that there was no speed limit posted on that boulevard, he simply said, "If it's not marked, it's 20 miles per hour."

Traffic in Detroit moved 30 to 40 mph on that kind of boulevard. But here I was, with a speeding fine and 6 points. Worse, a few weeks later, I got a *third* speeding ticket within the Milwaukee city limits for driving over 30 in another one of those 20-mph zones.

This was *serious*! I now had 9 points, and one more ticket—12 points— I'd lose my license! I wouldn't have been able to drive to work and back or anywhere. By then Bobbi and I were married and had a baby, and it would have been *extremely difficult* for her to drive me to work in downtown Milwaukee each day, take me to the airport and to my weekly meetings in the Army Reserves. (I spent 8 years in the Reserves, requiring 2 weeks at camp each summer—which meant Bobbi and I had no summer vacation those first 8 years.)

I could *not* get another speeding ticket. So I stuck a *"You're in Milwaukee!"* note on my dash and drove like a little old retiree for as long as it took to melt some of those points away. It worked, but I hated it; I'm always in a hurry when I'm going somewhere.

The job at Agricultural Publishers continued to be challenging and interesting, but eventually it became obvious the company wasn't keeping its "We'll pay you what you're worth" promise. While I kept grinding out copy and coming up with more ideas that brought in new business, my salary and bonuses sort of leveled off and stayed there.

True, I was being paid well, but I got the impression they felt what I was receiving was adequate and they'd put a lid on it. Yet, being from Iowa, I have an acute sense of what's fair. Gradually I became less content...and started considering other options.

In retrospect, it's interesting that—just as Senator Capper's clever insurance program led to his magazine's demise—it was my boss' clever "Million Dollar Idea Meetings" program at this company that eventually led to my leaving. You'll learn why in the chapter ahead.

Don't be afraid to try something new.
Remember that a lone amateur built the ark,
while a team of professionals built the Titanic.
—Dave Barry

CHAPTER 6

First the Idea, Then Itch to Try It

WHAT I'D LOVED about that Milwaukee publishing company was its entrepreneurial spirit. I'd never been challenged like that before in my career. Here I was constantly urged to come up with new ideas, new projects and new ways to boost this small firm's profits.

At the heart of this were those quarterly "Million Dollar" brainstorming meetings. I really geared up for those, because that's when the "big boss" (the majority owner who lived in Illinois) would show up for what usually proved to be a full-day session.

You were encouraged to have your ideas in writing and make a verbal presentation of your thoughts and why you felt this new publication or potential project would succeed. It was that "come-up-with-something-that-sells" challenge that I enjoyed most.

Quarter after quarter I came up with new ventures or ways to expand our business with current clients. Eventually I was handling seven different pieces of business for Ford Motor Company alone, several that had been conceived through these meetings.

Another account I worked on was the A.O. Smith Harvestore company in Kankakee, Illinois—the company that made all those blue metal silos you see on farms around the country. We began publishing the *Harvestore Farmer* for them, a newsletter that was mailed to their customers.

As I interviewed Harvestore owners for that publication, they continually had a variety of questions on the structure's use—how fine should they chop their silage…how should they adjust the unloader…how should they deal with breakdowns…what were the best ways to mix the feed…where could they go for parts and repairs, etc.

So, for the next quarterly meeting, I proposed a "Here's How…" book for all these Harvestore owners. It would answer all these questions and more. I suggested a three-ring notebook format, so when new ideas, new suggestions and new products surfaced, we could produce extra pages and send them to each farmer to be inserted as directed.

The book would be a steady profit item for our company, too, I emphasized, because it would be sort of a continuous process; we would keep updating it in the years ahead.

Our brass liked it, so we went down to "K-3" (which is what locals still call Kankakee) and I presented the idea at Harvestore's headquarters. Their management loved the concept (eventually so did their customers).

When I finished the presentation, the discussion soon got around to what our company would charge for this project. That's when I was asked to leave the room to "get a cup of coffee".

That was the usual procedure, and back then I wasn't really bothered by it. I wasn't involved in the company's ownership nor privy to the profit structure, so it seemed reasonable that when they talked prices I wasn't included.

After Harvestore okayed the project, I put in a lot of hours pulling this extensive "Here's How..." book together. When it finally went off to the printer, I received a bonus for my efforts. That was expected and appreciated, but this time the amount puzzled me. The check was for $220.

My annual salary was $11,500 at the time (hey, this is in the early 1960s, and that was good money for someone my age then). So a bonus of a couple hundred dollars was adequate. But why *$220???*

It just seemed like an odd figure. If it had been $200, or $250 or $300, I wouldn't have questioned it. But that $220 figure just stuck in my mind.

Then one day the bookkeeper walked up to my desk, told me the office manager was out of town, and said she had a question on the "Here's How..." book that I might be able to answer.

She flopped open the big budget book on my desk and pointed to some figures on the upper left-hand page. But my eye fell on the figure on the lower right page, which was right in front of me. And there, as plain as the nose on my face, I saw: *Net profit—$22,000.*

So *that's* where that $220 figure had come from! My bonus had been 1% of the net profit.

That single revealing moment had a direct effect on my life. A seed had just been planted. I really hadn't given any thought to going on my own until just after I saw that figure.

I sat there for a few minutes, recalling the whole process: I'd come up with the idea, made the presentation, successfully sold the concept to Harvestore, gathered all the material, took the photos needed for illustration, wrote the copy and directed the layout—I'd produced this project pretty much single-handedly from the start through printing and delivery.

It occurred to me that I could have done this all by myself, without the aid of the company. And the net profit of $22,000 was *nearly double* my annual salary!

What's more, this was just *one* of the projects I'd come up with that year. As I reflected on other projects I'd originated during the past couple of years, I was sure some of them were likely more profitable than this one.

Ironically, those "Million Dollar Idea Meetings" that had proven so successful for the company had provided me with a great deal of experience and confidence—the very kind I'd need to succeed in this type of business on my own.

Still, making a move like that was risky. By then I'd been with the company for a number of years, and we now had four kids, which made the security of a good-paying job more important.

Once I had the idea in my craw, though, it gradually got to the point where I had to spit it out or swallow it. The challenge and the excitement of trying something of this magnitude just gnawed at me.

Great golfers must experience similar feelings when they wonder whether they can make it on the tour, and are torn whether to give up a good club pro job to take the chance. I tend to put lots of things in the working world on a sports basis, because in many ways business is a game; it allows you to compete with "pros" on any level. In business, you can be in Podunk Center, Nebraska and compete head-on with somebody in the heart of Manhattan. That's exciting!

"I longed to write upbeat stories about how to lead a life rather than how to make a living..."

Three things made me lean toward trying it. One was my farm background. Even if I didn't succeed, I knew—and Bobbi knew—I'd feed those kids.

When you grow up on a farm, there's no job below you. You've already done most of the worst ones. So if I struck out on my own and failed, I knew we wouldn't starve. There's work to be found for those willing to earn their pay.

I've always been of the opinion that most people who can't find a job just can't find the job they're willing to do. Some keep looking for that "perfect job" and are unwilling to do other work until they find it. Much better, I think, to *take the job that's available* and work hard at that until a better job opens up.

So I was confident that if I failed I'd support our family some way. If, to put food on the table, I'd have to work at a gas station, a tannery, a chicken processing plant...you name it, I'd do it. We might not live as well as before, but we'd get by.

Secondly, I was eager to try something *different*. I'd been writing primarily how-to pieces for various types of agricultural publications—telling farmers how to grow bigger crops, put more pounds on their livestock and basically how to make more money.

I longed to write more upbeat, lighthearted stories about how to lead a life rather than how to make a living. I was eager to write more about sports, too, which had continued as a major interest (I was still playing on a local softball team in summer and a weekly basketball league in winter).

The third and clinching reason to try it on my own came about when I happened upon a high school sports clinic at the Milwaukee Bucks arena in

Some people treat religion like a spare tire—they never use it except in an emergency.

downtown Milwaukee one Saturday morning. Hundreds of young athletes were there—90% of them girls—all brimming with enthusiasm.

There were cheerleaders, pom squads, marching bands, pep squads, booster clubs, dance teams and gymnasts, all accompanied by each group's school adviser. Basically this clinic was aimed at boosting "spirit" at their respective schools.

I didn't know there were clinics such as this. It was, from what I was able to learn, the first of its kind in the Milwaukee area. The guy in charge was an ex-college cheerleader, and he was supported by a number of college students with some expertise in each of these areas.

It was a wild scene as these clone-like kids bounced around like they'd all had too much sugar for breakfast. When I learned they'd each paid $15 to attend, I concluded this had to be a highly profitable affair for that middle-aged cheerleader who'd organized it.

Yet, the kids obviously loved it. As I observed groups of cheerleaders from various schools exchanging the words for different yells, saw pom squads sharing the choreography of different dance routines and watched each of the other segmented groups doing the same thing, a thought suddenly occurred to me:

There should be a *magazine* for kids like this all across the country, filled cover to cover with the same type of advice and suggestions and the kind of networking they were experiencing at this clinic!

Hey, if they were willing to pay $15 for just a few hours at this event, surely they'd be willing to pay $5 (the going sub price for mags then) to get regular issues of such a publication for an entire year, right?

What a *great* idea!

The following week, I did some checking and got even more excited about its potential. I found that (1) there was no magazine like this in the country; (2) there were *32,000* high schools across America; and (3) an average of more than *100 kids* in each school was involved in some aspect of this "sports spirit" activity.

"I did the math—the potential was incredible..."

I did the math, and with paper and postage costs being what they were then, I could turn a profit with as few as 20,000 subscribers.

That seemed an easy mark what with—let's see, 32,000 times 100 students each—over *3 million potential subscribers* out there.

If only *one* adviser at each of these 32,000 schools signed up, I'd already be on my way. And if just a half dozen of the 100 students at each school wanted *their own* copy mailed to their home, that would be nearly *200,000 subscribers*! Five dollars times 200,000...wow, that was a *million dollars*!

The more I worked the math, the better it looked. Especially after I quickly came up with other avenues of income—I could create national "clubs" or associations with fees for each group—such as The National Cheerleaders Assn. and The National Marching Band Assn. Kids like to *belong*, and they'd each get not only an official card to carry with them, but a "Certificate of Membership" to frame and hang in their room.

And think of the potential garment sales—we'd sell shirts with the association insignia, plus hats, caps, scarves, membership pins, socks, warm-up outfits, shorts—we might even offer our own "exclusive" shoelaces!

Naturally, these items could *only* be purchased if you were a *subscriber* to the magazine…which would boost subscriptions even more when kids saw these colorful items and learned there was only one way to get them.

The potential was *endless*. By now, my mind was racing toward even bigger things. The magazine could sponsor and promote much larger and better "clinics" in every state. There would be a separate one for each segment of these sports booster groups, each one far better managed and more professional than the one I'd seen, which was obviously locally produced.

Besides the admission that we'd charge at each of these clinics, just think of the garments and paraphernalia we'd sell at those events! We'd offer not only our regular attire with our national insignias, but we'd sell the usual "I Attended the So-and-So Clinic" shirts that teenagers love to wear to show where they've been.

> ***"I finally had to decide —stay, or go?"***

In addition to instructions at each of these clinics, we would hold statewide competitions among cheerleaders, bands and pom squads (think ribbons, plaques and trophies). The state winners would then qualify for a *national* competition each year (yes, exactly like the one that is now being hosted annually in Florida by ESPN).

And at this national event—maybe at the statewide venues as well—we would rent exhibit booths to all types of companies who sell teenage gear, from garments to tennis shoes to cosmetics. This could be *huge*.

I had still more ideas—too many to detail here. Suffice it to say that all this was becoming a distraction to my work, and that began to bother my conscience. This time that sense of fairness was beginning to work the other way—I felt I either had to devote 100% of my time and energy to the company that was paying me…or quit and go with this idea on my own.

An option could have been to present this idea at the company's next quarterly brainstorming session—but this was an agricultural publishing firm, and this project just didn't fit with anything we were doing. Besides, I thought the "head honcho" would start looking at me a little sideways when I started describing this magazine for, what, "high school *booster* groups"?

Nor did I think the company's leaders would *understand* this whole new endeavor. The management group was older and likely wouldn't relate to this youthful audience. Even if they did, they would certainly have put some limits on what I could do.

And that very "lack of limits" was what I found so exciting about doing this on my own. It was the "abandon" with which I could approach this project as the ideas kept coming. I wouldn't have to sell or convince any-

Nostalgia is the sandpaper that removes the rough edges from the good old days.

one else of their potential or validity before I sped off and tried them.

I finally had to decide. So I drove to a rural area one Saturday, sat on a stump near a pond…and pondered. A long time.

Gradually, I again centered on the three things I described earlier as reasons to go for it: (1) If I failed, I'd somehow still feed the kids; (2) I was itching to try something "different"; and (3) more than anything, I wanted to know whether I had what it took to make it on my own.

I'd made my decision.

If you have a good idea,
you need to act on it quickly.
Otherwise it's like selling
Christmas trees at New Year's.
—Will Rogers

CHAPTER 7

'Honey, I'm Going to Quit My Job!'

EVEN THOUGH I'd fully committed to take the big step to go on my own, I hesitated to tell Bobbi. After all, by now we not only had four kids, she was pregnant with the fifth.

She knew I was thinking about this—I'd always used her as a sounding board for my wild ideas. But I hadn't filled her in recently on how far I'd gotten with it, nor shared how enthused I was about the additional ideas I'd piled on top of the original ones.

I'm sure she shared my confidence that somehow we'd get by if striking out on our own didn't work. Even so, that could mean some big sacrifices right at a critical time when security and comfort were understandably very important to her.

I suppose I could have put off making this critical move until after the baby arrived and things had calmed down a bit. But again, that didn't seem fair to my employer. My heart was no longer in my job now that I'd privately made the decision to move on. Plus, I was eager to *get on* with this exciting venture.

I waited until one Wednesday evening, right after dinner, when the kids had headed off to do homework and other things. The time seemed right, so I looked at her and said, "Honey, I've made the decision…I'm going to quit my job and go on my own."

Her brown eyes opened wide. She looked at me with a smile that had a little worry in it, then simply said, "Well, let's talk it over after the kids get to bed." *That's my Bobbi*, I thought.

We discussed it till 2 o'clock in the morning. The longer I talked, the more wound-up I got. I explained how this could be so much more than just a magazine—I described the clinics we'd hold across the country, the garment sales, the association membership fees, the statewide and national competitions that would give us great exposure.

Finally I had to get to the tough part—finances. We had $6,800 in our savings account, and it had taken us a long time to get it there. We were

The quickest way to double your money is to fold it and put it back in your pocket. —Will Rogers

going to need every penny of that to get a sample issue in the mail to the 32,000 high schools.

Yep, this would wipe us out, savings-wise. "But honey, we should get that money back in spades within a month or so when the subscriptions start pouring in, what with the advisers and hopefully a half dozen kids at each of 32,000 schools signing on…" In fact, the payback could be *huge*.

By 2 a.m., I had either been a great salesman or she got tired. She finally said, "Okay, I'm with you—let's go for it!" Now we'd both made the decision. As it's said, "Doing is better than stewing."

I didn't waste any time. I told my boss the next day. It caught him completely by surprise. When he got over the shock, he started offering me more money to stay. First he offered a salary increase of $1,000, then $2,000, then $3,000.

That's when I *really* knew I was going to quit. As a result of that experience, I've never once offered an employee a "shotgun raise" to encourage him or her to stay. They'd likely conclude, as I did, that they should have been paid that amount all along; that their value didn't suddenly increase just a few minutes after they decided to quit.

When he could see my mind was made up, he asked whether I would stay a month to phase out of some of the things I was involved in, and I agreed. They'd treated me pretty fairly, and it seemed only right to do the same for them.

We called it a basement "office". But that description was really stretching it a bit.

As Bobbi and I began this venture, we couldn't afford to rent any office space outside the home, and our small three-bedroom home was fully in use. So a corner of our basement would have to do as the "office".

I went to a secondhand furniture store and bought an old wooden desk that looked like it had been lifted from some Army sergeant, a secretarial-type chair and a couple of metal cabinets. None of it matched—I later referred to this decor as "Early Army". Then I went to an office supply store and bought a stapler, dictionary, carbon paper, file folders and the most important item of all—a secondhand Royal typewriter.

> *"The old Royal swayed on the TV tray…"*

I arranged all this in one corner of what was a totally open, unfinished basement. There was no partition separating me from the rest of this dim room, with only a few small window wells for outside light. It had the standard concrete block walls, open pipes and ducts, and a concrete floor that sloped toward the sump-pump drain.

Calling this a "business office" was akin to calling the small hill behind our house "Mount Everest". But while spartan, it sufficed. The directors of any of today's TV extreme makeover shows would have salivated if they saw it.

To further conserve our funds, I didn't buy a typing stand. Instead, I

Eventually you will reach a point where you stop lying about your age and start bragging about it.

simply set the old Royal on a TV tray, and later when I pecked away, I locked my knees against legs of the tray to keep it from swaying. In winter, I doubled up a rug below it to keep my feet off that cold concrete. (That Royal typewriter and TV tray—at left—are now on display at the company Visitor Center in downtown Greendale.)

Bobbi did as much typing on that machine as I did, at least in the beginning. Wait'll you hear why.

I found a book in the Milwaukee library with the addresses of those 32,000 high schools across the country. I don't recall whether anyone rented mailing lists then, but if they did, we couldn't have afforded it anyway.

So we—make that mostly Bobbi—*typed those 32,000 addresses from that book!* Fortunately, Bobbi was an incredibly fast typist. (They used to have secretarial speed tests, and she once averaged over 100 words a minute for 10 minutes on a standard typewriter—as in "non-electric"—after deducting five words per error.)

Even so, typing 32,000 addresses took a *long* time. That typewriter got a lot of use as we traded off—I used it to type numerous letters and articles, and she used it for the addresses when I was out taking photos and gathering material for the first issue.

Buying the camera I needed to take those photos brings back another short memory. There was a camera shop in Milwaukee that applied a unique sales tactic: The owner would display a used camera in the front window, and each day he would lower the camera's price by $10 until somebody bought it.

When I was still working downtown, I particularly had my eye on one Rolleiflex he displayed. I walked by the store each noon, watching that price go down by the tens. I decided that when it reached $150, I'd buy it. It got down to $160, and the next day when I hurried back there, it was gone!

Somebody else's buy-mark had obviously been $10 higher than mine. Still, I admired the owner's tantalizing approach and decided if I ever went into any type of retail business, I'd try something like that. As evidence

The older we get, the fewer things seem worth waiting in line for.

of its effectiveness, when he put out the next used Rollei, I made my move sooner and bought it for $175.

The Premiere Issue went together well. The material I gathered was even better than I'd anticipated. Great photos, good advice, tips, ideas and suggestions poured in. Schools, advisers and students were extremely cooperative. They were excited to hear there was going to be this kind of magazine and eager to "be published" in any way they could help.

I collected most of the features for that first issue by mail. I simply wrote to high schools in each state, asking cheerleading captains for the words to their best "yells"…pep squads for their methods of motivating fans …pom teams for their choreography to various routines (many sent sequential photos, while some sent original sketches with "stick people" illustrating their moves)…and advisers for their best fund-raising ideas.

Within weeks I had enough to fill a *book* rather than just a 48-page Premiere Issue. This was going to be a fact-filled, *helpful* opening edition.

Finally it was time to pick a name for this publication. After considering a lot of them, we settled on *The Pepperette*. That may sound a little corny now, but back then—with its largely female audience and school spirit as its main theme—that title seemed to fit.

In the end, one thing about the contents wasn't female-oriented. As I was putting that first issue together, it occurred to me that we should have something in its pages for high school *boys* as well to expand its audience even further. A few pictures of boys shouldn't hurt our appeal among teenage girls, either.

So I decided to pick a national high school "Athlete of the Month" in each issue, along with photos and copy on several runners-up as well. To kick off the series, I thought I needed to draw attention to it by featuring some well-known athlete.

I was a devout Green Bay Packers fan (still am), so I wrote a letter to Bart Starr. I knew he and the team were flying to Los Angeles to play the Rams the next weekend, so I told him what my intentions were and asked if he'd answer my questions during the flight. I suggested he just write his answers in the space below each question, then mail it in the postage-paid envelope when he got to L.A.

> *"Bart Starr handwrote the answers—<u>free</u>. Can you imagine a professional athlete doing that today?"*

That's *exactly* what he did! I received the three-page response the next Tuesday. Can you imagine a professional athlete doing that today??? That quickly and willingly, *free*?

But back then, I wasn't hesitant to ask that of him. And I wasn't even surprised that he cooperated to that degree. I did, however, have such a high regard for what he did that I saved that letter and still have it displayed on my office wall today along with a personal letter from Norman Rockwell and other memorabilia.

Bart answered my questions in so much detail that in some cases he continued writing on the back of the sheet. And his comments were just the kind of thing I was looking for—the benefits of being part of a team, the importance of playing fairly, what you can learn from athletics that will help you later in life and so on.

I titled the article, *"So You Want to Be a Starr!"* and ran it along with a picture of Bart I acquired by mail from the Packers headquarters. Free, of course.

I worked with a freelance artist on the format and the layouts for the Premiere Issue, then got all the copy typeset, proofed and re-proofed it, and it was finally ready for the printer. I actually went there to watch—it was highly exciting to see that first issue rolling off the press.

Next came affixing all those 32,000 addresses. We'd typed them on sheets of small labels with glue on the back, each of which had to be moistened to attach to the issues. Bobbi and I did all that ourselves, too, then hauled the magazines to the post office by making multiple trips with our car.

We paid the postage with borrowed money. Actually, that wasn't all we borrowed—the bills had mounted considerably above my original estimate, and our $6,800 of savings wasn't enough to cover them. We had to take out a loan and use our house as collateral to cover the extras needed. Our total cost of getting that first issue in the mail was right at $10,000.

But it was now done, and the issue looked good.

It's in the mail. Now the waiting. With the slow delivery of bulk mail, I allowed a week for the magazine to get to the schools. I estimated it would then take a week or so for the advisers and students to respond, so by the third week, I figured the subscriptions should start coming.

My calculation of the timing was pretty accurate. I wish I could say the same for the response. The first few subscriptions arrived near the end of the second week, and a few hundred came the third week. A hundred or so more came the fourth week.

But so far they were only in hundreds. Where were the *thousands* I'd anticipated?

They kept coming, but in a drizzle, not a downpour, and after nearly a month, we had about 1,500 subscriptions. I began to worry. I decided to go to a few schools in the Milwaukee area to personally see whether the Premiere Issue had reached them.

In each case, they'd received it, they "loved the magazine" but hadn't subscribed. Why? There seemed to be multiple reasons:

For one, I learned that schools received a lot of publications free. These publications were sponsored by advertisers or companies who had good reasons to get them into high school libraries. Some of the students actually seemed a little surprised that someone was going to have to *pay* for this magazine to keep it coming. Obviously I hadn't emphasized that clearly enough—they assumed it would just keep coming free.

Secondly, when I talked to a few of the advisers, they said if the magazine wasn't free (they'd made the same assumption), they would have to get a subscription acquisition cleared, and that could take some paperwork and time to accomplish.

Thirdly, as far as my expectation that these teenagers would subscribe so they could receive their own copy at home, that didn't seem to be an option—at least if they were going to have to pay for it *themselves*. I soon concluded that teenagers will spend money on movies and malts, but not magazines. "If *Mom* will pay for it, I'll get it," one said. So make that movies, malts or Mom.

I made a few long-distance phone calls to other areas—couldn't afford many—and got pretty much the same response in every case. Again, the teenagers wouldn't spend their own money on the magazine, and the advisers didn't seem eager to go through the process of getting a subscription approved. So it became more and more obvious—if it wasn't Mom's money or the school's money, it probably wasn't going to happen.

Things didn't look good. By the middle of the second month, the ship was listing. I was devastated. All my hopes, all my exciting ideas, all my optimistic forecasts to Bobbi… (Footnote: She never once complained or suggested "We shouldn't have…" all through this.)

I now had just over 3,000 subscriptions, but instead of the pace picking up, it was dropping off. I was facing another decision: I could use the money from those 3,000 subscriptions to cover the cost of the second issue…but would I just be pouring more good money on top of bad?

I kept waiting and watching as long as I could. Predictably, I soon began hearing from subscribers asking why they hadn't received the next issue.

Discouraging and depressing as it was, it was time to face the fact. My dream had failed, and I would have to fold the tent.

But how was I going to square things with those 3,000-plus subscribers who'd sent in their $5? Was I going to send each of them a refund check and deduct one issue? Likely, most of them would expect a full refund. Worse, buying envelopes and paying first-class postage to mail those checks would put me in even deeper debt.

I finally came up with a solution: I had a lot of good material available for what was planned for the upcoming issues. So I gathered the best of it and compiled it into a small book, put a $5.00 price tag on the cover and sent a copy of it to each of those subscribers.

With it I put a letter that basically said, "I wish there were more people like you! If there were, you would be receiving your second issue now. But because the response has been less than we expected, we have to suspend publication for now. In the meantime, please accept this $5.00 book, which contains the *best* of what was planned for future issues. We hope this is satisfactory to fill our obligation to you. If not, please write and we will send you a refund."

It worked. Producing and mailing this book cost us far less than sending the full refund. We received fewer than 20 requests to return their money, which we did. Gratifyingly we received more than twice as many letters expressing their regret, and even thanking us for the quality book.

While greatly disappointing, I've often looked back at this first experience as my Master's Degree in publishing. While it sucked up all our savings and more, where can you get a Master's Degree for $10,000 and cover the entire course in less than 6 months?

What's more, it's a fact that you learn more from mistakes than you do successes. And when you're personally involved like this, with your own money on the line, you learn fast and remember well.

I was so naive when I started this first magazine! I'll elaborate on that naivete in upcoming chapters, but basically, (1) I hadn't done my homework regarding how magazines are purchased at schools; (2) I didn't know my audience's buying habits; and (3) I knew nothing about testing a mailing list.

As for the latter, instead of typing and sending a sample copy to all 32,000 high schools, I should have simply *sampled* the list first by sending a copy to, say, *every 10th name* on the list. By testing with just 3,200 copies, I could have cut my costs by 90% and learned nearly as much as I did by foolishly mailing a copy to all 32,000.

> *"It was time to face the fact —my dream had failed..."*

As they say, "Experience is expensive." Or, as Abigail Van Buren once put it, "If we could sell our experiences for what they cost us, we'd all be millionaires."

At another time, with more funds to spend, maybe I could have hung in there and made a success of this first magazine and its ancillary products. (In fact, there is now a magazine called *American Cheerleader* that is very successful. There is also the National Cheerleaders Association, which has *thousands* of members. I was just way ahead of my time.)

However, at this particular phase of my life, carrying on with the magazine wasn't a choice. I was now broke financially, but not mentally. I'd just been bucked off a horse, yet with what I'd learned, I vowed I'd climb back on another one soon.

That "horse" walked up to me within a year, and this time I rode it. Next chapter I'll describe that exhilarating ride.

Cheerfulness is the window cleaner of the mind.

Success is never permanent,
and failure is never final.
—Mike Ditka

CHAPTER 8

Life Is Not Always Like a Movie

MY EXPERIENCE with this first dismal failure proved to be more like a documentary than a movie, one with a very sad ending at that. I was just one of those blinded-by-my-dream publishers I still see today who feel the world is waiting for their idea, so I had jumped in with both feet and launched it.

I'd heard the old expression "It's not whether you win or lose, but how you place the blame." I'd lost big time with this first launch and it was tough to swallow, because I had no one to blame but myself.

Yet, there was no time or benefit in being dispirited. Life includes hard knocks and doses of reality. So I needed to file this under "lessons learned" and move on.

We were down to our last dollars and I had to start earning something fast. Bobbi had already come up with several dozen macaroni and cheese recipes as well as a dozen new ways to make SPAM interesting!

I could have looked for a job with another publishing company, but that would have meant relocating at a difficult time—remember, Bobbi was still expecting our fifth child. Beyond that, I was now more determined than ever to start another magazine of some type.

I well knew what I'd done wrong in this first attempt, and I was sure that if I applied those lessons next time around, I could make it work. It's hard to convince a stubborn German ex-Iowa farm boy that he can't succeed at something!

I had a lot of friends and contacts among the staffs of farm magazines around the country, so I decided to freelance until that next big idea came along. I had pretty quick success, it was something I could do from home, and payments for articles and photos began coming in.

One of the hardest parts of freelancing, though, was the amount of travel it required. It got to be a routine—I'd help Bobbi put the kids to bed on Sunday night, then leave about 8 o'clock in my Volkswagen Beetle. I'd drive south through Chicago to a little ma-and-pa motel at the edge of Gary,

If at first you don't succeed, you're running above average.

FREELANCE DAYS involved lots of travel for farm interviews and photos.

Indiana. The place was low-cost and clean, and these nice people gave guests free coffee and a cinnamon roll to start you out in the morning.

I chose Gary because it was a good jumping-off point for Monday mornings. I was still pursuing primarily agricultural stories, and about all I could muster in Wisconsin were dairy stories. But from Gary I could cover northern Indiana and get over to Michigan and Ohio as well.

The nights were lonely out there on the road, and so were the meals. That mostly involved evening meals, because I never stopped for lunch when I was out there. Lunchtime was the best time to catch farmers. They came home to eat, and I could interview them just before or after instead of trying to find them somewhere out on their back forty.

I'd gotten pretty handy with a camera by then, and I used it to illustrate the features I wrote. In fact, I managed to sell seven front cover photos to major farm magazines that year.

One "almost cover" was particularly memorable, when I did something really stupid on a farm in Indiana. On a beautiful autumn day, I spotted a herd of cattle in a green pasture with multicolored trees in the background. With a blue sky and cotton clouds above, it had "cover photo" written all over it. (Most farm mags paid $250 to $350 for a cover then, so they were well worth pursuing.)

I pulled my Volkswagen Beetle off the rural road, grabbed my loyal Rollei camera and climbed the fence. I'd grown up with cattle—we raised registered Herefords on our Iowa farm—so I had no fear of the large herd as I walked across the pasture toward them.

When I felt I was close enough, I looked down into the lens to see what I had. As I adjusted the focus on one particular animal, it began moving, so I switched to another one. But then I remembered that first animal had been moving toward me, so I aimed the camera back to it.

That's when I noticed it was a bull...and it had a *ring in its nose*! Now, I had enough farm in me to immediately be concerned—cattlemen only put a ring in the nose of bulls that are *mean*. That ring is something to grab to control him if he ever attacks you!

> ## "I could hear that bull gaining on me as I ran..."

I looked back at the fence, and it was like 50 yards away. I snapped a quick photo of him, then started retreating *slowly*. Another thing you learn when growing up on a farm is never to run from a bull; that will only encourage him to chase you.

But this large bull wasn't cooperating. He was walking toward me faster than I was retreating. So I picked up the pace. So did he. When he began trotting, I trotted, too...and soon I began *running* for all I was worth. The Rollei was suspended from a strap around my neck, and the heavy camera banged hard against my chest.

What probably saved my life is something that Dad always discouraged my brothers and me from doing when we grew up on our Iowa farm. We would run at a fence, grab the top of a wood fence post and "pole-vault" over it. Saved a lot of time compared to climbing over. Dad warned us again and again that, just once, we weren't going to make it over and we wouldn't be fathering any children, or something like that.

Now as I ran, I looked for a wood post along that fence—you can't grab hold and pole-vault from a skinny steel post. I could *hear* that bull gaining, and I picked up my pace even more. Fear is a great motivator.

I picked out a wood post, sped toward it, grabbed the top and swung over the fence just like I'd done hundreds of times about 20 years earlier. My body made it over, but the camera strap looped over the post and suspended me, holding the back of my neck and swinging my face right against the fence.

That bull slid right up against the wire—his face was so close, I could hear and smell his breath! Inches away, he glared at me with big dark eyes, pawed the ground for a bit and waggled his head to make his point, then sauntered back toward the harem he was "protecting".

I was so frightened, I just stayed there on the ground awhile. I couldn't tell whether my chest was hurting because the camera had pounded me so hard or my heart was pounding that hard. When I finally got up and un-looped the strap, I found I had cockleburs stuck all over my pants. I normally hated those things, but as I picked them off, I thought even those prickly things felt good compared to what I might have experienced.

I got more evidence of how scared I'd been when I got back in my Bug. It had a stick shift, and for the first 5 miles or so, every time I pushed in the clutch, my knee would jerk like crazy! I couldn't even hold the gas pedal steady. Truthfully, if I hadn't made it over that fence, that bull might have killed me. This happened along a remote rural road with little traffic, and there was no one in sight who could have helped me.

Scary as it was, there was an upside to this tale. Remember, I'd snapped that one picture of the bull as he started toward me. When I developed the film, the photo was so clear, you could see that ring in his nose.

So I wrote up this whole experience with a headline something like: "Farm Photo Develops into Fearful Finish", then sold the story to *National Livestock Producer* magazine for $225. Proves again there's something good in everything.

"The Idea" suddenly surfaces. I'd usually return home Thursday afternoon, immediately take the film to a processor and begin writing the articles. I'd often write well into the night. I recall one of the hardest parts was to have dinner with the family, help Bobbi put the kids to bed, then I'd head back down to the basement around 8 o'clock.

What made this difficult is that was prime time, when all the better shows came on TV, and since our TV was right above my office area, I could hear the laughter—both that on TV and Bobbi's—as I wrote. I've always loved any type of entertainment, so I envied what I was missing as I kept pounding away on the Royal.

By Saturday I had the pictures back from the processor, so I could write captions for them and finalize the pieces. Sunday was sort of a day of rest with the family—till 8 p.m., that is, when I took off for Gary and did it all over again.

Bobbi played a big role in this freelancing effort. She was a much better typist than I was, and while I was gone, she retyped all the articles and accompanying letters to the editors and put them in the mail. During my calls from the road, she would regularly give me a report of which articles had sold and for how much. Even at freelancing we were a team.

> *"In the ledger, Bobbi had written, 'What net profit???'"*

She also kept our financial records in a leather-covered budget book. I found while scanning it one day that at the end of one month, on the line titled Net Profit, she'd written, "*What* net profit???" I learned recently that our son, Scott, still has that ledger book and cherishes it.

In addition to freelancing for magazines, I began writing collateral materials for various ag firms. These amounted to promotional brochures and

THIS was one of seven cover photos I sold during my freelance days. It won first place in the single editorial photo category of the annual Agricultural Editors' Association contest in 1977. Only a dairyman would enjoy a cow sniffing his ear!

catalogs for Allis-Chalmers, Reynolds Aluminum, Republic Steel, Cuckler Buildings, the Iron & Steel Institute and others.

For some reason I started gaining more clients who were selling supplies for the construction of farm buildings, and that's where "The Idea" for my first successful magazine suddenly surfaced.

I'd just finished producing a full-color brochure for Russ Lehe, who was the Marketing Manager for Reynolds Aluminum's farm roofing and siding division in Arlington Heights, Illinois.

Late that evening, we chatted at length in a bar-restaurant. He was drinking martinis and getting honest; I was sipping beer and listening closely. He suddenly volunteered, "If you could get that brochure in the hands of farm building contractors across the country, I'd pay you twice the price for it!"

Even with my rural background, I hadn't heard that term before. "What's a 'farm building contractor'?" I asked.

"Young man," he answered, "let me give you an education." And he most certainly did.

Swallowing angry words is much better than having to eat them.

67

He explained that "farm building bees" were now a thing of the past. During the days of those "bees", when a farmer needed a new barn, his neighbors gathered to help him construct it…just as he'd do in return when they needed one.

"Today's farmers are getting far more independent," Lehe explained. "They're now operating so many acres, they don't have time to exchange help and assist each other with barn raising tasks."

What's more, he pointed out, new farm buildings were getting so sophisticated that farmers likely couldn't erect them even if they wanted to. "Today you need a lift or a crane to put up these large structures," he explained, "and you need to know electrification, mechanization, insulation, ventilation and more.

"When you have several hundred head of cattle or hogs housed inside a confined building, you'd better know something about air movement and moisture control. You don't even call these buildings a barn anymore. They're now called 'structures', 'units' or 'systems'."

As a result, he said, a new breed of carpenter was coming into his own across rural America. "These specialists are called 'farm building contractors', and it's getting to a point that they absolutely *dictate* every product that goes into the structures they erect.

I SPOTTED the name on this mammoth tractor and couldn't resist posing with it.

"Sometimes a farmer today doesn't even know whether he's getting a steel roof or an aluminum one, much less whether it's Reynolds or Alcoa," he related.

"The farmer's only told it's a 'metal' roof. It's like when you buy a car—most buyers don't even notice or care whether it has Goodrich or Firestone tires. They come as part of the package.

"So the brochure you just finished isn't going to do me or Reynolds much good if we put it in the hands of one farmer who *might* put up one building this year—we need to get it in the hands of these farm builders, many of whom now put up *several dozen* farm buildings a year.

"I need to somehow connect with these farm building contractors to get them to recommend and use my product in these buildings. Each one I convince could mean selling enough roofing and siding for 20 or more buildings. But I just can't find a way to reach them."

"You mean there's no mailing list for these rural contractors?" I asked.

Nope.

"So there's no *magazine* for these contractors?"

Nope.

BINGO!!!

In rapid fire, I started asking more questions. I learned there were all sorts of companies trying to reach this new, growing rural industry. Companies that sold lumber, nails, trusses, screws, ventilation ducts, doors, lighting, flooring, lightning rods, fire alarm systems, cooling units and, of course, lots of roofing and siding.

Lehe lamented he was sure all his competitors and other suppliers selling to this growing industry had the same problem as his. "There's just no way to reach these guys."

It was past midnight as I headed up I-94 to Milwaukee, but I was suddenly more awake and alert than I'd been all day. *This* could be the idea I was looking for!

The next morning, instead of heading downstairs to the basement, I drove downtown to the public library. This time I was doing my homework. The Reynolds exec was right—there was no publication for farm building contractors or the rural construction market in general.

The opening was there.

But how do I fund it? Those days of driving that Volkswagen Beetle along hundreds of miles of rural America each week were mighty lonely. But there was one benefit—when you don't have anyone to talk to and you eat most of your meals alone, there's plenty of time to *think*.

I now had the idea for this farm building magazine, but no funds to launch it. Still, this publication had such incredible potential that I just would not give it up. I needed to come up with some way of financing the start-up.

It took most of a week, but while bumping over those gravel roads, I finally formulated an approach I felt just might work.

When I got home, I put together an extensive business plan, banking on what I'd learned from those Million Dollar Idea Meetings. The plan detailed this growing construction market and described the void facing suppliers trying to reach it.

Then I made an appointment with the president of a small printing company whom I'd gotten to know well. I'd learned how to make sales presentations, too, and leaned on that experience to make a lengthy pitch to him, supported by my 12-page plan and financial figures.

I then described the magazine I had in mind and why I felt it would be a huge success. When I finally finished, he agreed it had great potential. That's when I told him my problem—I had everything but money.

"Here's the deal," I said. "If you'll wait to get paid for the first 6 months, I'll guarantee in writing that I'll leave the printing account with you for at least 2 years. What's more, you have my word that I'll stick with you be-

When you hold a conversation, don't forget to let go once in a while.

yond that period if your price and services are right."

He thought about it overnight, then called me the next day to say he'd take the deal. *Yes!* To me, that was a great affirmation; it was no longer just me who believed in this magazine's potential—I now had a respected businessman who believed in it as well.

I then repeated the process and struck the same deal ("Wait 6 months to be paid in return for a 2-year commitment") with every type of supplier I needed to get out the first issue—a typesetter, an engraver, a photo processor, a mailer and so on.

Several turned me down, but eventually I got enough suppliers who agreed to it, which further bolstered my hopes. I now had seven separate businesses that were convinced of this publication's chances as well.

The only supplier I didn't even try to convince was the Post Office. They don't make deals, they don't take promises, they just take cash. So, to cover the postage, I took out a second mortgage on the house.

The key to launching this publication was getting "the list" together. Lehe was right—there was no existing list of farm building contractors.

So how would I compile this list? Again, all that thinking time on the road had led me to the solution. I asked Lehe for the name of a good farm builder that he knew. He suggested Ed Bahler of Remington, Indiana.

I called Ed, then drove down to Indiana and rode with him in his pickup truck for a day. This was key to my plan: I wanted to learn *where he and other farm builders bought the bulk of their supplies.*

> *"The only supplier I didn't try to convince was the Post Office..."*

Ed and I enjoyed each other's company and ended up good friends. But I learned what I was looking for quickly. Ed bought more lumber than any other product, so his No. 1 supplier was his local lumber dealer. He said that was likely true for most other rural builders.

With that knowledge, when I got back, I returned to the Milwaukee library again. Sure enough, there *was* a source of names and addresses of lumber dealers all across America. And *that* would provide the link to the rural builders!

I then put together a full-color brochure that—when mailed to these thousands of lumber dealers—basically introduced *Farm Building News*. It gave them an idea of the kind of publication it would be; it included sample articles and some great photos of farm structures being erected.

The letter with this brochure was key: It told the lumber dealer that *if he would supply the names and addresses of all the farm building contractors in his area*, we would send this new publication to each of those contractors...and *give him full credit for it—FREE.* (As in, "Sent to you by JENSEN LUMBER COMPANY in appreciation for your business.")

This time I tested the idea. While I had the addresses of thousands of lumber dealers, I printed only enough copies of the brochure to go to

The one thing you can give and still keep is your word.

70

every *10th name* on that list. I don't learn fast, but I remember well; this time I would "test" the response before rolling out a mailing to the entire list.

It was terrific! The names and addresses poured in, and as quickly as I could I sent the brochure to the other 90% of the lumber dealers. Within a month, I had the addresses of nearly *20,000* farm building contractors coast to coast. What's more, it was the *only list of its kind.*

I learned something from this experience: If a mailing list is hard to come by, and you find a way to assemble one, you'll have little or no competition. Conversely, if a mailing list is easy to come by, anyone can compete with you by obtaining the same list.

If I'd known then what I know now, I would have recognized that this list I'd just compiled was so valuable that I could have simply *rented* the list to all those eager suppliers and made some pretty good money with it. But I probably wouldn't have done that anyway; I was bent on launching a *magazine*, and this time I wasn't going to get bucked off.

Before I got ready to put the first issue together, I did something else that proved very beneficial. I sent that same introductory brochure to the marketing manager of every building trade supply firm I could find. I reasoned each of them—just like Russ Lehe—would be eager to know there was now a way to reach these farm building contractors.

COVER of the Premiere Issue of my first success!

The accompanying letter told each of these sales managers about our planned launch of this magazine for farm builders and to "Call for ad rates" if they were interested. I did so partially because I had no idea how high to set the rates; a good deal of it would depend on the demand.

It didn't take long to get an indication of how eager these firms were to reach this market: The president of Deniston Nail Company in Chicago called me at our home the following *Saturday morning.*

"I want the entire back page of the first issue," he said, even before asking about the rates. "And I want to reserve it for the following issues as well. I've been trying to reach this booming farm building market for years!"

A speech is like a wheel—the longer the spoke, the greater the tire.

Calls soon followed from other advertisers, all willing to pay what I'd soon set as a premium rate—$1,500 a page—for a circulation of 20,000 rural builders. So many ads came in that we came close to *breaking even* on that first issue! That was as unheard-of then as it is today.

I quickly rented a small office downtown so I'd have a Milwaukee address and would thereby appear more official, but some advertisers still called me at home in the evening to get their ads in the second issue. It was as though I'd opened up the only candy store in town, and they wanted to get in before the door was closed.

I turned a good profit on the second edition, even more on the third, and we were off and running. Of course, my printing suppliers were almost as delighted as I was. They'd agreed to wait 6 months for their money, but I paid each of them in 2 months and had money left over. (So long, SPAM… hello, T-bones!)

Still, I stuck with every one of those people not only for 2 years as originally promised—in appreciation for their confidence and support—but much longer. In fact, we still work with many of those same suppliers today, and they've grown right along with us.

When you have the good fortune to have success in life,
that's precisely the time to reinvent yourself.
—Robert Redford

CHAPTER 9

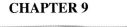

Success Is a Wonderful Tonic

THOUGH our first attempted launch from the basement was a bomb, this second launch of *Farm Building News* was an immediate and incredible success.

But that success didn't come without a lot of long hours and hard work. With the experience I'd gained writing for these farm building supply firms, I already knew a rafter from a purlin, but I was far from an expert when it came to the intricacies of construction.

I didn't feel I was adequately prepared—I didn't know enough about their industry, how they went about their work and what their everyday lives were like. I needed an in-depth knowledge of that in order to edit a magazine for them and "talk their language". After giving it some thought, I settled on the perfect solution:

I ran a picture of myself in the first issue—holding a hammer and wearing a hard hat. Below it was this headline: *"Editor For Hire...Cheap!"*

I offered to work for a full day on the building site of the highest bidder before each issue. I told readers I would then write a "diary" of my experience for the next issue, and that my day's "salary" would be given to the charity of their choice.

That series was such a hit with readers, I continued it for several years. Many of those days working at building sites across the country were *long, hard days.*

I drove or flew in the night before, and if the crew started their workday at 6 a.m., I was there on time, dressed just like them. I pushed wheelbarrows of concrete, nailed down siding, carried heavy lumber, fastened roofing during hot days in summer and frigid days in winter.

Sometimes by late afternoon I thought this was the absolute *worst* idea I'd ever come up with! I came back with blisters, splinters and sometimes a swollen left thumb. But I also learned that the harder the work, the better the diary, and the more the readers enjoyed it.

The one diary these builders always brought up to me later at conven-

How long a minute is depends on which side of the bathroom door you're on.

There are no shortcuts to any place worth going.

WORKING alongside rural builders was often hard, hot and…"odorous", but a great experience.

tions was when I described my day helping erect a new manure pit in 95-degree heat on a large hog farm. *Phew!*

I contended in that diary that, during the plane flight home that night, the stewardess wouldn't even get close enough to offer me peanuts! That was a bit of an embellishment, but any guy who had worked on a hog farm on a hot day *related* to that experience.

As a result of those diaries, I learned an incredible amount about the day-to-day lives of my readers. Even better, those diaries were so personal that they began to know *me* and regarded me as a friend.

More than just a magazine. While that first publication for teenagers was a financial flop, there were some ideas and concepts that I thought had merit this second time around. After all, I'd paid dearly for that expe-

I HELPED POUR CONCRETE, nail down siding, whatever, then wrote "diary" about day in next issue.

rience so I might as well use it!

For example, as *Farm Building News* soon became *the* magazine for the rural construction industry, we quickly launched a "National Farm Builder Show". That show *quadrupled* our profits the second year and beyond due to a unique advertising tie-in:

We sold no space at the show. Instead, we gave it away.

That is, we gave away *free* exhibit space, but only to our *advertisers*. It was a gesture on our part—we showed our appreciation for their support of our magazine by allowing them to "talk nose-to-nose to the builders you've been reaching with your ads."

The arrangement was pretty simple—one full-page ad qualified a company for one 10- x 10-foot booth, two pages got them a 10- x 20-foot space, etc. Advertisers who booked a full page in all six bimonthly issues got six free booths if they wanted them, cost free.

Admittedly, we initiated this arrangement because we knew it would motivate firms who hadn't as yet committed to advertising. And it worked like a charm. More and more suppliers gradually became aware of this annual convention and were eager to exhibit their product or service to the more than 2,500 contractors who regularly attended.

But only if they became one of our advertisers would we allow any firm to exhibit at this show. No ads, no booth.

So, instead of their paying us $1,000 for a sizable exhibit, some of these companies were soon spending $5,000 to $10,000 and more for advertising in *Farm Building News* to qualify for the amount of space they needed at the show.

OUR STAFF WARMING UP for annual "Farm Building All-Industry Band" event.

ATTENDANCE neared 3,000; even the Chicago Bears cheerleaders performed.

Chevrolet, for example, wanted to exhibit two of its trucks at the show (after we informed them and Ford that the average farm builder owned a half dozen trucks). To fit those two trucks on the exhibit floor, Chevrolet took *four pages* of full-color ads in the pre-show issue.

Our pre-Builder Show issues in later years had as many pages as *Architectural Digest*. Some were so thick—well over 200 pages—that we had difficulty binding them.

This National Farm Builder Show became a huge success in itself. We held it in February, when builders in the northern part of the country had some downtime, and we booked it in appealing places, including Phoenix, Memphis, New Orleans, Tampa and Chicago.

PRE-SHOW issues often topped 200 pages.

Attendance consistently topped 2,500 to 3,000. We had speakers and presentations on every aspect of the farm construction business, plus separate programs to interest their wives.

We made sure people had *fun* at the event, too. Each opening night we hosted "The Frost Breaker Hospitality Suite" and mixed in some surprises to make it entertaining.

In fact, the year we held the show in Chicago, when we opened the doors to the exhibit hall, we had a marching band and the Chicago Bears cheerleaders lead the attendees in a "snake dance" that wound through the entire exhibit hall. We were pleasantly surprised to see that all the builders and their spouses stayed right in line, marching and zigzagging among the booths and having a great time.

We also became aware that a number of the builders played a musical instrument, so in future years we encouraged them to bring their trumpet or whatever and join the "Farm Building All-Industry Band". Dozens of them did, and this opening march through the exhibit hall became a great annual event they all enjoyed.

Simple idea that worked. We soon learned that all the exhibitors wanted a booth as *close to the entrance* as possible. That's where the traffic would be. When that area filled up, it became harder to get people to accept space farther back in the hall. Until we came up with this idea:

We put a large "treasure chest" at the extreme rear of the facility. As each

Doing what you like is freedom. Liking what you do is happiness.

RURAL BUILDERS learned during seminars at the shows, but had some fun, too.

person came into the hall, he or she was given a key to try in the lock of that chest. Only one key in several hundred worked, but when it did, there was a crisp $100 bill, or a portable radio or some other prize in that chest. This gimmick drew so much traffic that we eventually had exhibitors request "a booth near that treasure chest".

Overall, editing *Farm Building News* and running this annual convention was a challenging, educational experience. I became close friends with many good people in the industry. And I'd like to make this point before I move on to describe the launch of our first ad-free magazine:

> *"We sold no exhibit space at the show; we gave it away..."*

Some people look at our 12 publications today—all which depend on subscriptions alone and accept no advertising—and come to the conclusion that everyone at our company must be "anti-advertising".

As you can tell from the story I just related about our first successful magazine, *Farm Building News*, nothing could be further from the truth. In the right places, advertising makes the world go 'round. It's just that we've since proven there are places for ad-free magazines as well as places for ad-supported magazines.

Truthfully, I find much more enjoyment and satisfaction in producing the

78

ad-free ones. When you go this route, you don't have the pressure sometimes exerted by advertisers, you don't have to travel extensively to meet, wine and dine them, and you simply have more freedom to do it your way.

That's why I eventually sold *Farm Building News* to another publisher so I could concentrate on the ad-free route. That publication, which was launched from our basement in 1967 with zero seed money, a typewriter and a handshake agreement with seven appreciated suppliers, was sold in 1981 for $3.2 million.

Success stories like that are a lot more fun to tell than those describing failures. But in this case, like many, what I learned from my original failure provided the very experience needed to turn this second attempt—with *Farm Building News*—into a solid success. You often learn a great deal more from mistakes than successes.

Dreams come in a size too big so that we can grow into them.

THE DENISTON NAIL COMPANY was *Farm Building News'* very first advertiser —the owner called me *at home* on a Saturday morning to reserve the back page of the first issue. The company never missed an issue after that. Here, Ad Manager Dick Bowman (left) and I present a plaque to Doug Deniston, the owner's son.

Good things take time.
Great things happen all at once.

CHAPTER 10

Second Idea Suddenly Surfaces

THAT first successful magazine, *Farm Building News*, had its upside and its downside.

The upside was the satisfaction of succeeding after that first, dismal failure. I also got to meet many of these farm building contractors personally, who were honest, hardworking, enjoyable people. And I found it gratifying to produce the kind of articles and issues that were genuinely helpful to them, as well as producing and emceeing the annual National Farm Builder Show. They even laughed at my jokes.

The downside was constantly dealing with advertisers. To be fair, many of these were wonderful people, too…but then there were the demands and quirkiness of others.

We constantly dealt with the things that most other ad-supported magazines deal with regularly: "Why wasn't our ad closer to the front of the issue?" "We asked that our ad be put on the *right-hand* page; you put it on the *left*!" "The color of our ad was way off—you owe us a 'make good'!" (A "make good" is a demand to run the ad again with no payment.)

And there was the excessive travel. I had more than a dozen staffers by now, as the magazine and annual convention continued to grow. Two of these were ad salesmen, and they were the ones who kept asking for more of my time, travel-wise.

It was, "You just have to go to Cleveland with me to talk to the guy at Republic Steel," and "I need you to come to Pittsburgh with me to close the deal with the Alcoa people." Some advertisers not only like to be wined and dined, they insist on talking to the "top dog". In this case, that dog was me, the publisher.

These constant requests to travel with our ad reps really cut into my productive time, since I was never willing to give up the writing end of the business. (And I never have since. I've seldom had a day that I came to the office and didn't write something. Writing is what I enjoy doing, and to promote myself to a non-writing role would be akin to a company promoting its best salesman to sales manager, and then have him do none of the selling.) I turned out more copy for each issue of *Farm Building News* than anyone on my staff. Fitting in the necessary travel made my days not only longer, but required spending most Saturday mornings at the office as well.

It was this hectic schedule—especially from the ad side—that likely perked up my ears when I saw an opportunity to take the ad-free route. Here's how that came about.

New way of thinking. Once this *FBN* publication jumped into the black, and our kids jumped into a Ford station wagon instead of cramming into a VW Beetle, there was no stopping me.

From that point on, I regarded Uncle Sam as my partner: Since we were now in the 50% tax bracket, I figured Ol' Sam took half the risk on any new publication we launched. Since he received 50% of the *profit* when a new magazine succeeded, it only seemed fair that he was handed 50% of the *loss* when a new one failed.

So I began thinking about other magazines and keeping my ears tuned to potential ideas. Being consciously open to opportunities is the key to recognizing them when they occur. And it worked.

The idea for our second publication sifted into my open ears late in 1970 while I was having lunch in Chicago at the annual Agricultural Editors Association meeting. (From the way this is beginning to sound—with my picking up the idea for the first magazine while having a drink in Chicago and this second one while eating in Chicago—I should have spent more of my time dining and drinking in Chicago instead of typing in Wisconsin!)

> *"From that point on, I regarded Uncle Sam as my partner..."*

Ralph Yohe, the editor of Wisconsin's state farm magazine, was at my table and, to my surprise, he said he'd just learned the two largest farm magazines, *Farm Journal* and *Successful Farming*, were both dropping their Women's Sections!

I was shocked. The women's pages had always been an important part of every farm magazine. I quickly visualized how that news was going to hit my mother.

Mom had always read and appreciated farm magazines even more than Dad did. He usually fell asleep in the chair with them around 9 o'clock in the evening, but she read those Women's Sections thoroughly.

I thought of all the other farm wives across the country just like Mom who were going to feel "jilted". I just knew they were going to be downright upset to learn that these two major farm mags would no longer include the recipes, decorating ideas, homemaking tips, family fun and human interest stories they'd always looked forward to.

I sought out Dick Cech, a friend of mine on the *Farm Journal* ad staff, and asked if it was true they were dropping their Women's Section, and if so, *why*. He confirmed the decision and pointed out two reasons:

Facts do not cease to exist because they are ignored.

First, ads in that section were becoming harder to sell since television was becoming a bigger competitor for ad dollars, and farm numbers were starting to decline. What's more, several new women's magazines, including *Woman's Day* and *Family Circle*, were becoming formidable competitors.

Second, he noted that the makeup of farm magazines was making it increasingly difficult to incorporate agriculturally oriented ads within the Women's Section.

"Here's what I mean," he explained. "Our magazine is saddle-stitched—the spreads come down the press folded over in the middle like a saddle. So, when we assemble our issues, we put all the two-color pages on first, then put all the four-color pages on top, which means the outside pages in front and back of the issue are where the color is.

"Well," he continued, "the Women's Section is traditionally in the back pages. After we've used up all the available four-color ad spots in the front, we move the rest of the color ads to the back, and this sometimes places an ad for rat poison or a manure spreader smack in the middle of the food section!"

He said this had been a growing problem for a long time, especially with the women's advertising dropping off dramatically in the past year.

"We finally just decided to drop the Women's Section entirely and make ours a pure farm production magazine. That way we can run any ad anywhere," he related. "I guess you could say we're taking the fun out and putting the profit in."

That closing comment bothered me a lot. I'd felt for several years that one of the reasons so many young folks were leaving the farm is that it was getting to be all work and no play. I *enjoyed* growing up on an Iowa farm. We worked long hours, but we had fun, too. And here the largest farm magazine in America was espousing a new theme to its readers—"You're in farming primarily for money, not enjoyment."

What's more, I felt they were *wrong*. I knew a lot of farmers and ranchers who didn't feel that way. Sure, they wanted to turn a profit, but that was far from their *only* goal.

Even today, many farmers and ranchers stick with it through thick and thin because *it's a way of life*. A good life, to be sure. They believe farming offers a challenging, independent, enjoyable livelihood, along with being a good place to raise a family and teach responsibility.

A farm or ranch is definitely a great place to raise kids. It allows you to *work* alongside them. City life offers opportunities to play with children, but not many chances to work with them. Shooting baskets or tossing the football around with kids in the city doesn't build the same relationship as sharing work on a farm, whether it's milking cows, planting corn or weeding the beans.

You also get a better read on a farm kid's attitude and willingness to be part of the team. When you say, "Help me move this feed bunk from here to there," you can note how quickly his end of the bunk comes off the ground, and whether he did it willingly or begrudgingly.

Plus, farm kids sense *achievement*. There's not much satisfaction for city youths in cutting the lawn or cleaning a room. By comparison, a farm kid can see results—he sees a calf fatten, a crop grow and how his efforts affect the family income.

Most rural parents recognize those things as tangible benefits to their choice of livelihoods. Yet, here were the country's two largest agricultural magazines turning their backs on these important aspects of rural family life by concentrating solely on profits.

As far as most farm women were concerned, these magazines were removing the mainstay of their issues—that is, the down-home and hearty recipes for main dishes and desserts that added variety to the meals of hungry farm families. (Even breakfast is a big meal after doing an hour of morning chores.) It's oft said that "good eating is part of good farming".

Worse, these two magazines weren't stopping there—they were also removing all the other things that farm women looked forward to in each issue: Cooking shortcuts, home improvement ideas, decorating and fix-it tips, parental advice, family fun suggestions, lighthearted human interest stories and even a few humorous items.

These topics had always been part of the mix. They weren't just farming magazines, they were *family* magazines.

That evening, as I headed north to Milwaukee in the Beetle, I mused on how the elimination of these Women's Sections was going to jolt more than a million farm and ranch wives across the country. (*Farm Journal* had a circulation of more than 1.3 million at that time.)

I anticipated their editors were going to be hit with a backlash like they'd never anticipated. (I was right; a *Farm Journal* staffer told me a year later, "We responded with a form letter to each angry reader, and after mailing out 5,000 of them, we just gave up and went on with our business.")

Suddenly the idea hit me! I was cruising up I-94 past Kenosha when I thought, *Wait a minute! What if I produced the first-ever magazine exclusively for farm women?*

It would be filled cover-to-cover with *all* the things these other magazines were *eliminating*. For beginners, it would have far more recipes than they'd ever found in a farm magazine before, and we'd encourage these women to "exchange" household hints, decorating ideas, family advice and much more. It would allow them to "network".

We'd let these women *talk* to each other through our pages! We'd call it *Farm Wife News* so they'd know *exactly* who we were addressing and what the publication contained. And we'd make it fun to read, even allowing farm women to 'fess up to "The biggest mistake I ever made in the kitchen", "My most embarrassing moment when we started farming" and similar confessions.

We wouldn't deal with any farm management issues; we'd leave that to the other farm magazines that were pushing profits. The copy on our masthead would say, "We don't tell you how to make a living...we tell you how to lead a life."

I got so excited, I found I was now driving well over the speed limit. Then, as I drove past Racine, a sobering thought hit me that slowed both the car and my optimism. It was this:

"If *Farm Journal* and *Successful Farming* can't sell enough advertising to support a *section* of their magazines, how in the world can I possibly sell enough advertising to support a *whole* magazine?"

That dose of reality tempered my enthusiasm, but not for long. When I got home, I sat in the car awhile, mulling it over. The answer became obvious: I'd have to make it on subscriptions alone, without advertising.

Could that be done? Well, I recalled that *Reader's Digest* had survived nicely for its first 50 years or so without advertising. So did another magazine I was familiar with, *Changing Times*. The *Digest* eventually accepted advertising to boost its profits, but it got along fine without it for a long time.

Then another thought occurred to me as I sat in the dark garage: When you buy a book, there is no advertising to offset part of the cost. You either want the book badly enough to pay the whole price, or you don't get it.

That being the case, I reasoned, why can't the same be true with a magazine? If I turn out a magazine with material that can't be found anywhere else, wouldn't people be willing to pay a little more for a subscription?

In this case, wouldn't farm women pay more for a magazine published *just for them*, filled with all the things that were now *missing* from their favorite farm magazines?

Plus, there was a huge universe out there—1.3 million *Farm Journal* readers alone who would be "ripe" for this magazine when they learned their Women's Section was being scratched.

I was just as excited and optimistic the next morning when I talked it over with Bobbi, my sounding board. She liked the idea as much as I did, and it wasn't long before we decided to launch this new magazine solely for farm women!

I felt one of the keys was to get this first issue out *fast*. *Farm Journal* and *Successful*

BUSINESS must have been good at this point.

Farming were going to announce their "Sorry!" change in their next issues, just a month away, so I wanted my Premiere Issue to arrive as soon after as possible, to catch their readers on the rebound right after they'd been jilted.

I pushed everything aside as best I could and dug into the exciting task at hand, gathering copy and photos for that initial issue. A couple of staffers pitched in to help. We sent a lengthy letter to several hundred farm wives, telling exactly what we had in mind and what we needed—recipes, household tips, photos, decorating ideas and family fun suggestions. We emphasized it was their chance to "be published" in the Premiere Issue of a totally new type of magazine.

> *"Farm women told us how upset they were…"*

The response from these selected rural women *poured* in quickly, letter after lengthy letter. Within little more than a week, we literally had enough material to produce several issues, which allowed us to pick the *best* material for that first issue.

Again and again, these farm women told us how upset and even downright *angry* they were to learn these two farm magazines were excluding them from their pages. We decided to include a few of those comments in the Premiere Edition to add a little coal to the fire.

Best of all, these farm women kept telling us how *excited* they were to hear there was finally going to be a magazine "just for them". This gave a big boost to our optimism as we hurriedly put that first issue together.

The softest pillow is a clear conscience.

I've never seen a monument erected to a pessimist.
—Paul Harvey

CHAPTER 11

Here We Go—with No Ads

AGAIN, I thought getting this first issue out fast—while more than a million rural women were still riled up about the news of "no news" for them in two of the nation's largest farm magazines—would have a direct effect on our response. Being a hero is sometimes all in the timing.

So we worked furiously. We cranked out that first sample issue and had it ready for the press in just 3 weeks.

Rather than using a magazine format, we produced this new publication in a tabloid-size newspaper format. But it was *four-color* throughout its 24 pages and printed on slick "magazine stock". That was a key to making it "different".

Back then, there was no *USA Today*, and there was seldom any color in any of the nation's newspapers. This fact set ours apart and caught any reader's attention. People expected to see color photos and colored headlines in a *magazine*. But when they saw color like ours in a *newspaper*, it pleasantly surprised them.

Another benefit: People tend to regard a 24-page magazine as a "skinny little magazine". But they regard a 24-page newspaper as a "thick little newspaper". Their perspective changes.

We couldn't afford more than 24 pages, so using this newspaper format worked in our favor—it *looked* more expensive. Yet, the difference between the cost of applying four separate colors to a 24-page magazine and a 24-page newspaper is pretty much the same; you're just using a larger sheet.

Still, without ads, these 24 pages carried a *lot* of copy—likely a full hour or more of reading—and some vibrant color photos. Basically, farm and ranch women wrote that first issue. After all, we'd gathered all of the material from them.

For the first time, we'd given rural women a "voice". We'd asked for their opinions and input on a variety of things, and they'd responded big time, mostly in handwritten letters.

We included some of their salty comments, too, such as this one from

Before you can score, you must have a goal.

Ellen Thompson of Shelby County, Illinois:

"I cancelled my subscription to one of the big farm magazines as soon as they stopped printing their Women's Section. They ought to know it's the farm wife, not the farm husband, who signs most of those subscription checks!"

Another response we ran was from Susan Talworth of Salina, Kansas. "That's *wonderful* news!" she said about the launch of *Farm Wife News*. "We've been needing a publication of our own for years. *McCall's* and *Ladies' Home Journal* and those other women's magazines just don't fill the bill for us—we farm wives have problems and interests that just aren't common to city women."

That first issue was a dynamite edition. It was filled with just about everything a farm woman would find interesting. Such as:

A "Rural Recipe Roundup" feature, which announced a national recipe contest planned for each issue (the winner received "Free dinner for four at the restaurant of your choice within 100 miles, and we pay the mileage!")...a Craft Corner...a Farm Wife of the Month contest...Decorating Ideas *from* farm women *for* farm women...Farm Wife Savers (Heloise type tips)...A Day in the Life of an Amish Farm Wife (a dawn-to-dusk diary).

There was also "Ask *Farm Wife News*", a column designed to help rural families deal with mail-order houses and other businesses, as well as "Dear Aggie", a takeoff on Dear Abby, with a professional counselor answering questions on social and personal problems of farm people.

> *"We'd finally given farm women a 'voice'…"*

There was a Farm Photo of the Month...Rural Rhymes..."I Remember When" (nostalgia series)...Mailbox of the Month...and "Farm Women on the Go". We also featured a product comparison in each issue—the Premiere Issue led off with a panel of farm women rating the latest dishwashers (without advertising, we let these women get downright honest about the negatives and positives).

We covered some meaningful topics, too. One article dealt with "What Dangers Do Farm Chemicals Pose for Your Husband?" We started a "Legally Speaking" feature, which gave readers an opportunity to ask a respected attorney for pertinent legal advice regarding estate planning, wills, record keeping and purchase agreements.

But we remembered to keep some *fun* in it, too, with "My Most Embarrassing Moment"...and "Little Humor", a column that encouraged readers to send in cute quips of farm kids. We included a hilarious piece by an Iowa farm wife entitled, "Sorting Hogs Is Hard on Husbands (especially when wives help)".

The latter piece was long but so funny, I considered having it continued in the second issue...so people would have to subscribe in order to finish it! Fortunately, I decided against that and ran the whole yarn.

Looking back, we didn't miss too many bets with this Premiere Issue.

Don't worry about making mistakes…but don't make the same one too often. —Sam Johnson

We encouraged readers to give gift subscriptions of *Farm Wife News* to friends during the approaching holiday season, even including a sample of the gift note we'd send the recipient that began, "Here's a happy holiday note. A thoughtful friend of yours requested and paid for a year's subscription to *Farm Wife News* on your behalf…"

All and all, it was a pretty powerful package of food, fun, facts and photos. We couldn't *wait* to test it, and we did it with a mailing list that we'd garnered in an unusual way.

At that very time we were producing a publication for Allis-Chalmers that was being sent to a list of 400,000 farmers and ranchers throughout the United States and Canada.

PREMIERE ISSUE of *Farm Wife News* was in full-color newspaper format, not common then.

I'd learned the A-C executive in charge of that publication was short on funds, so I struck a deal with him: We would do the editorial package for one issue of his publication *free* in exchange for a single use of that mailing list.

He hesitated, studied his budget pinch, then took the offer. With that list of 400,000 farm families in hand, we were ready to send out a sample of *Farm Wife News* in September of 1970.

Once again, we "10thd" the list, deciding to send the trial issue to 40,000 people—every *10th* name on that list of 400,000. To urge a quick response, we told the readers the 1-year price was just $5 if they subscribed *before October 20.* "The price will go up to $7 after that."

Being the eternal optimist, I immediately told the printer to have the extra paper on hand and be ready to roll out copies for the other 360,000 people as soon as we got a positive read on the first 40,000.

Then, once again, the waiting began.

But we didn't have to wait long. We didn't list a phone number in that first issue, but a few women still began calling us long distance, at their expense, to tell us how delighted they were with *their* magazine.

Then the mail started coming in. The first day, the postman smiled as he carried a bag filled with subscriptions up the stairs to our second-floor

People who say they "sleep like a baby" never had one.

office. By the third day, he was no longer smiling—he asked us to come down and help him carry up the bags!

Most publishers who launch a direct-mail campaign hope and pray for a 2% response. I'd set our goal at more than double that—a 5% response —because we'd have to make it on subscriptions alone. I decided in advance that the day we hit 5%—that is, 2,000 paid subscriptions—I would pick up the phone and say something like, "Roll 'em, Lester!" to the printer.

We topped the 2,000 mark on just the *fourth day* after the first subscription came in! Actually we topped it by more than 500 on that day.

I called the printer and urged him to get those 360,000 copies off the press as fast as he could. (I'll detail later why following a "test" mailing with the "rollout" is highly important.)

> *"Those figures were true! You actually did get that kind of response..."*

Even hurrying, it took more than a week to get those extra copies in the mail. By then we had well over 4,000 subscriptions, a more than *10% response*, and the pace was picking up rather than tailing off.

That was nothing compared to what we were about to experience when those 360,000 copies reached farm and ranch women across America. It wasn't long before we could no longer handle the mail in our compact offices (our entire "staff" at the time was just a dozen people, and two were part-timers).

Finally, out of desperation, we rented the second floor of an empty Schlitz Brewing Company warehouse, just for the month of December. We hired college and high school kids during after-school hours and during their holiday break.

There was no furniture in this large warehouse. We just dumped the mail in a big pile in the center of the room with the kids sitting on the floor around it. (Thinking back on that sight now, it's a career highlight.)

We brought our spouses downtown to help supervise the process, because back then it was common to put cash in the mail. Many of these subscribers just put a $5 bill in the envelope with the form, and we needed to keep an eye on all that money.

Both frustrating and flattering was the fact that most women didn't just cut out the coupon and mail it with their payment—the majority of them wrote *long*, heartfelt letters along with their subscriptions, complimenting us for being the first magazine to recognize the role farm women played as "partners" in American agriculture, and telling us how much they looked forward to future issues.

At first we thought we could put these letters aside to read later, when we'd have more time to screen them for material to use in future issues. But we soon learned we were wrong—each of these letters had to be scanned closely because

AT RIGHT is a montage of just a few of the timely topics covered in first issue of *Farm Wife News*, from food, facts to fun.

"I Remember When..." (first of a series)

Cooking for Threshers Was Social Affair

By Kathryn McGaughey
Wheatridge, Colorado

MODERN MACHINERY has changed a lot of things about ...

tapered weather-shunning mound, and hauling the grain and shoveling it into the granary. Usually the men worked right through the noon hour, and trudged toward the house in "shifts" so the other ...

chaff-itchy fellow behind him.

When they tromped into the house they were hungry, and the women were ready. The middle of the large table was so filled with food it seemed it might need ...

Rural Recipe Journal

Farm women have envied reputations as the country's best cooks . . . and Farm Wife News will gather the best of the best.

AS EXP...

All Coo...
page wil...
recipes

...ED in the "Calling family," and they, too, disap- ...

dren from Milwaukee who come to the farm each spring and fall.

DECORATING IDEAS
from farm women *for* farm women

...ed by Helen Toman, Decorating Editor

...VE SOMETHING interesting to your farm home recently? We'd like ...ear about it, and will pay $5 for each decorating item we publish ...

Framing a Tapestry Ca...
Be Fun and Fulfilling

Farm Wife of the Month... first of a series

Idaho Wife Is a Working Partner

First winner of "Farm Wife of the Month" title (see back page) is as capable in the field and in her community as she is in the kitchen.

By Anne P. Wallace
Latah county, Idaho

LILA KITT mak...
sun sh   Farm Wife News
care of

heat it up, cook potatoes, make gravy and fix a sal...

couple ...

...started
...way—I

BY ...orking
social
indivi
psych every
Et...
and ...
serves
indus
subm
unde...
W...
socia...
will
quest
"I...

Dear Aggie,

Answers by a professional consultant to the social and personal problems of farm people.

TAKE JOB IN TOWN?

Dear Aggie: Farm wives all around us are taking jobs in town. I am a registered nurse and the local hospital is pressing me to return to duty. My husband says it is up to me, but I can't make up my mind

exactly when and how everything should be done around the farm.

His ways are not the modern ones, and we want to have an up-to-date farm. How can we kindly but tactfully handle this situation? FOURTH GENERATION

Dear Fourth Generation: By firm-

work.

He is conscientious and wants to do a good job, but is hampered by the attention and the interruptions. We don't want to keep him from getting acquainted, and don't want our neighbors and the young people in the community

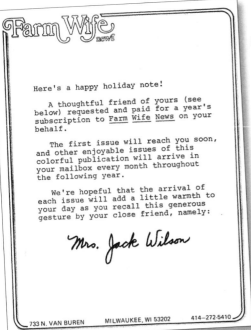

Here's a happy holiday note!

A thoughtful friend of yours (see below) requested and paid for a year's subscription to <u>Farm Wife News</u> on your behalf.

The first issue will reach you soon, and other enjoyable issues of this colorful publication will arrive in your mailbox every month throughout the following year.

We're hopeful that the arrival of each issue will add a little warmth to your day as you recall this generous gesture by your close friend, namely:

Mrs. Jack Wilson

733 N. VAN BUREN   MILWAUKEE, WI 53202   414-272-5410

THIS GIFT NOTE succeeded in bringing in thousands of Christmas subscriptions.

sometimes on page 3 they'd write, "By the way, add my Aunt Helen and sister Judy to your subscription list and bill me…"

That's what took up so much time. Plus, the kids kept saying, "Oh, this letter is so sweet…you just *have* to take time to read this one!"

As a result, we got so buried and behind in the mail that some of the people who subscribed in November never received the second issue because we were unable to get them on our mailing list until early the next year!

There weren't outside "list services" to handle things like this then. But that didn't matter—even if there was, we couldn't have afforded them anyway.

I'd done my math and determined we needed 38,000 subscriptions at our sub rate to break even during the first year. By December 31, even though we still hadn't made another mailing to additional lists, we'd topped *84,000 subscriptions!*

It wasn't until later that we learned part of the reason: The women who received those first 400,000 copies had become great "sales reps". Through word of mouth and by sharing that Premiere Issue with friends and neighbors, many of those charter subs were referrals.

If those figures sound unbelievable to you, you're not alone. Late the second year we brought in a direct-mail specialist from New York to advise us on some procedures. After studying our books at length, he suddenly said, "Those figures were true! You actually *did* get that kind of response."

When I asked what that meant, he said, "Well, some industry people in New York heard those figures…but nobody really believed them." Once again the "twains" had met—New Yorkers and Midwesterners often have difficulty finding each other credible.

He and his cohorts likely had even more trouble believing the success that followed. By the end of its second year, *Farm Wife News* topped *340,000 paid subscriptions*, thanks in part to thousands of gift subs readers gave to their friends.

More amazingly, the profit we were making from an *ad-free* magazine was unbelievable—even to us "dreamers".

Problems are opportunities in work clothes.

CHAPTER 12

'Problem' Creates Ancillary Business

I'M A BIG BELIEVER in the philosophy that, "Every problem offers an opportunity if you come up with the right solution."

Problems force you to think creatively. Some of our company's most profitable projects and even some complete divisions of our company were launched because we literally stumbled onto them while trying to solve a problem elsewhere.

Our Country Store catalog division is a prime example. That division might never have become a reality if we hadn't been confronted with a problem related to *Farm Wife News*. Here's what I mean:

The mailing list business wasn't nearly as sophisticated in the 1970s as it is now. If it was, we were too unsophisticated to know it. So when we'd used up that first list of over 400,000 farmers, we contacted several farm magazines—including *Farm Journal* and *Successful Farming*—asking whether they'd rent us their mailing lists. We were turned down cold!

We got the same reaction from other farm magazines we contacted. *Not one* of these publications would rent us their lists. It was like a boycott. We soon learned why.

It became apparent that we'd proven to be an embarrassment to these publishers. They were still getting letters and even cancellations from irate farm women who were bitter about the reduction or total elimination of the Women's Sections from those magazines.

It was true we'd called that cutback to the attention of our readers and sort of blew the whistle on them. In retaliation, they refused to rent us their mailing lists.

We were stymied. We desperately needed more farm addresses, because when farm women saw a copy of our magazine or learned this just-for-them publication existed, a high percentage subscribed. Without these lists, we were forced to look for other ways to inform the more than 1 million existing farm families that there was such a thing as *Farm Wife News*.

We tried the obvious. We sent a news release and a sample copy to ru-

Setting a good example for children takes all the fun out of middle age.

OUR STAFF AND KIDS posed for many of our early product catalogs. The modeling fee? Everybody got to keep the garment…and point to, "Look, that's me!" later.

94

THIS SHIRT started our catalog division, leading to variety of products as shown at left.

ral newspapers across the country. That resulted in minimal success. For the same reasons, rural newspapers had begun cutting back on their women's pages; therefore they weren't about to give a boost to a publication that was exposing and exploiting this fact.

Secondly, newspaper editors didn't take us seriously. They likely agreed with the opinion of one editor who wrote back, "Look, you're not going to make it without advertising, so we're not going to urge our local folks to subscribe to something that's bound to fold!"

About the only other route available to us would be to purchase advertising in rural newspapers and on rural radio. But that would be far too expensive.

Part of the solution came to me one night when I was mowing the lawn. Frustrated by this lack of exposure, I wondered what would happen if we turned out a woman's sweatshirt with bold artwork that stated, *"I'm Proud to Be a Farm Wife."*

Hey, not a bad idea. If we included a large *FWN* logo in the shirt's design, it would be a breathing billboard. When people noticed and asked, "Where'd you get that shirt?", the wearer would answer, "From *Farm Wife News*." And when she explained the background, we'd have ourselves another subscription prospect.

It seemed worth trying. So, we came up with an attractive shirt design, then priced the shirt at exactly what it cost us. (We wanted it to be a bargain so we'd sell as many as possible to spread the word, and secondly, it just didn't seem proper to make money on our promotion piece—we'd be satisfied with breaking even.)

The response was amazing! We sold over 4,000 shirts in the first month after offering it in the magazine. Our five oldest kids—those macaroni and SPAM eaters from 7 years earlier—now had a summer job. They sat around our conference table and became our "merchandise fulfillment department".

There was nothing sophisticated about this operation. They just hand-addressed each envelope, stuffed a shirt inside—with no slip or form recognizing the order or whatever—and tossed it in the mailbag. It worked incredibly well for a crew that was getting a dollar an hour supplemented by cheeseburgers and malts at noon.

Then one day a staffer handling the purchase of these shirts walked into my office and said, "Guess what—we're now making 50¢ a shirt! We're ordering so many, the supplier reduced the price due to volume."

Geez, I was already feeling a little guilty about selling our promotion and

Gray hair and wrinkles never conceal dimples.

COUNTRY STORE

Retirement is when the alarm clock is no longer alarming.

breaking even! Now I was even more chagrined to learn we were making a *profit* on our promotion.

Once again, I got over the guilt pretty quickly. So much so that I suggested we run the picture of the shirt in *full color* in the next issue. It doubled the sales.

Orders for the sweatshirt continued coming in at a good pace for some time. We'd sold well over 5,000 of them, and that would have probably been the extent of the "shirt business"… if it hadn't been for a single letter and exquisite timing that led to the birth of what is now our catalog division.

The timing was the result of my having walked to the coffee machine at the precise moment that several of our secretarial staff were laughing about a "funny letter" one of them had received. When I asked what was funny, they told me a farm woman had written: "My teenage daughter loves my new sweatshirt, but she can't wear it because it says, 'I'm Proud to Be a Farm Wife' on it. Why don't you folks turn out a T-shirt that says, 'I'm Proud to Be a Farmer's Daughter'?"

"Wow!" I said. "Where's that letter? I don't think that's funny. I think that's a *fantastic* idea. We'll sell 10,000 of those shirts!"

I was wrong. Those Farmer's Daughter shirts started moving so well that we could hardly meet the demand. We quickly offered them in every size, from toddler to kids to teens. And we ended up selling *143,000* of those Farmer's Daughters shirts in the first 12 months!

With that experience, we began watching the mail for other ideas, and it wasn't long before another farm woman wrote to tell us, "I have three daughters and two sons. I can't order something for the girls and not for the boys. Why don't you offer a T-shirt that says, 'I'm Proud to Be a Country Boy'?"

We had that version ready in 3 weeks and sold over 50,000 of those boy's shirts in the first year as well. *Country Store was born.*

We now found ourselves in the garment business big time, so we started giving

SHIPPING CREW. Our six kids hand-addressed packages and shipped out all the shirts in early months as our mail-order division got off ground.

He who watches the clock often remains one of the hands.

97

this merchandise area more creative thought. We soon became the only national firm turning out farm-sloganed T-shirts for nearly every aspect of agriculture. They ranged from "Ag Is My Bag" and "I Dig Pigs" to "We're Poultry Producers...We're a Real Chicken Outfit" and "Bulls Live Happily for Heifer and Heifer".

The slogans got even worse and the orders got even better: "Get High on Milk...Our Cows Are on Grass"; "I'm a Beef Producer...Pleased to Meat You"; "Milk Is Udderly Fantastic"; "I'm Rooting for Hog Prices"; "Never Give a Heifer a Bum Steer" and many more.

We didn't sell those corny slogans just on shirts—we sold them on caps, sweaters, jackets, aprons, bibs, head scarves, mittens, tote bags, belts, buckles, cups, plates and even country-oriented costume jewelry. We sold mud flaps, too (with "Crime Doesn't Pay" on the left and "Farming Doesn't, Either!" on the right).

Looking back, those were some pretty sorry slogans, but the market and what was politically correct was different then, and the shirts sold as fast as we could print them. We even bought our own imprinting equipment and started a silk-screening department in our warehouse.

"We ended up selling over 143,000 of those shirts in the first 12 months!"

The rest is history. Our Country Store mail-order division now sends out millions of full-color catalogs a year, plus millions more small flyers that are mailed with our magazines. This division sells everything from country-oriented garments and household items to gardening and grilling equipment, along with several gadgets we invented ourselves...including a "Tomato Booster" kit that's now sold over 3 million units. More on those items later in this book.

And, in recent years, this department has turned up the burners on its most profitable items—proprietary books. Especially cookbooks. As a result, we've become the country's largest publisher of cookbooks, selling more than 4 million cookbooks a year. In fact, in the past year (2004), we sold over 2.3 million copies of a single cookbook.

Again, it's likely none of this would have happened if farm magazines hadn't been reluctant to rent us their mailing lists after we launched *Farm Wife News*. Had they readily come forward, we wouldn't have had to think of other ways to bring attention to our magazine. Fortunately, coming up with a solution led to a whole new segment of business we'd never have known existed.

It's proof again that in business you shouldn't look at problems negatively. Solving them forces you to think creatively, which sometimes leads to brand-new opportunities.

In this case, simply creating a "promotional shirt" led us to the start of an entirely new division now grossing over $23 million a year.

98

Work that we love is nothing more than serious play.

CHAPTER 13

One Success Leads to Another

THE ONE THING we kept hearing from *Farm Wife News* subscribers was, "My husband loves this magazine, too." That surprised us.

Obviously, farmers were getting a little fed up with the "just the facts" and "just for profit" approach that general farm magazines were now giving them. When most of these publications dropped their Women's Sections, they also dropped all the cartoons, family features, interesting photos and fix-it items.

In fact, one of the major farm publications changed its cover tag line to read, "The Magazine of Farm Management", and another used, "The Business Magazine for Farmers Who Mean Business".

Obviously, farmers missed the less technical features that had long been part of those magazines. As a result, these farm husbands were enjoying the change of pace offered through the chatty exchanges and light-hearted articles their wives were now finding in *Farm Wife News*.

An idea began to surface… It occurred to me that if these macho farmers were so eager to read this kind of material that they were willing to pick up a *women's magazine* to get it, why not turn out a rural lifestyle ad-free magazine for farm *families*?

The more I thought about it, the riper the opportunity became. General farm magazines were now starting to read like textbooks. They no longer served up any salad with the meat and potatoes. They'd become technical journals, telling farmers solely *how to make more profit*. They seemed to have forgotten that farmers farm and ranchers ranch not only to make money, but because *it's a great way of life.*

This new idea had real merit! We'd now proven to ourselves that we could make it without ads. We'd also learned that turning out an ad-free magazine was just so much more…"peaceful". We weren't having to travel and we weren't being bothered by ad managers and agency people; we were dealing solely with *readers*.

For these reasons, the longer I mulled over this new, classy, slick, lifestyle

A boy anxious to mow the lawn is too young to.

99

magazine for farmers and ranchers, the more the concept intrigued me. As an old sage once said, "You can't plow a field by turning it over in your mind." It was time to try it.

We launched *Farm & Ranch Living* in March of 1978. Once again, we didn't just turn out a brochure or promotional package describing the magazine as many other publishers do—we just *did* the Premiere Issue and then tested it by once again sending a sample of it to every 10th name on our *Farm Wife News* list.

It was an *immediate* hit. We quickly rolled out the issue to the balance of the list and also to other farm-oriented lists we were now able to rent. At one point, this new magazine was growing at more than 20,000 new subscriptions a month!

The Premiere Issue told readers right up front that they wouldn't make a penny by reading *Farm & Ranch Living* regularly. Yet, we said, "It will help you enjoy rural living more by emulating the lives of others who share the belief there's no better place to live or work than on a farm or ranch."

Two features made up the heart of that sample copy and remain as the main features today:

First, we have four farm or ranch families in different parts of the country keep a day-by-day "diary" for an entire month, detailing their work, their challenges, their family fun and social activities and even the menus for some of their meals. These four diaries (see sample on page 102), illustrated by multiple color photos, echo our "written by readers" concept.

F&RL's other favorite feature is "The Prettiest Place in the Country" (see sample on page 103), which takes readers on a photo-tour of a different super-scenic farm or ranch in each issue. The copy is written in a first-person format, making it read as though the farm couple is personally "narrating" a walking tour around their farm before inviting the subscriber to sit down to a cup of coffee and homemade cookies at the kitchen table.

Another popular feature in early issues was "The Party Line". We'd hook up two distant farmers by phone and record their chat. We'd connect an Iowa corn farmer with a peanut grower from Georgia, and let them compare crops, weather and growing practices. Readers loved "listening in".

Basically, *Farm & Ranch Living* then and now is filled with easy reading. While other farm magazines deal with crops and livestock, we deal with perspective and attitude—we dig in and find what makes farm families tick. They farm the land; we farm their minds.

This magazine makes farmers and ranchers feel good about themselves. We get their chins up and their chests out and make them proud of who they are and what they do.

Back when we prepared to turn out that first issue, I felt very strongly that this magazine had to be *special* in another way. I wanted this magazine to be of such high quality that people would immediately say *"Wow!"* when they saw it.

I told the printer, "I want the quality of this magazine to even put *National Geographic* to shame. I want to *grab* people's attention and have

We pass this way but once...unless your spouse was reading the road map.

them say, *'I've never seen a magazine like this before!'* I want full color on *every page*, front to back, and I want it to *gleam*."

To achieve that, we chose the *best* paper we could find— thick, heavy, shiny stock.

Next we needed a cover photo that was a real eye-catcher. But what picture could that be??? I thought about that for days, even weeks. Nearly every potential photo I came up with had already been on some magazine. What kind of cover picture would be truly *unique*?

I had a dream... Maybe some of you experience this, too. Sometimes my best ideas surface when I'm not trying to come up with one. Some of my

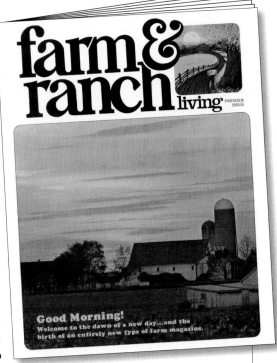

most successful ones, in fact, have occurred to me while I was on vacation and totally tuned out to work. Maybe our minds are freer then.

Anyway, one night during a vacation trip to Atlanta, *I dreamt the cover* that I was pursuing for *Farm & Ranch Living*. I woke up at exactly 3:10 a.m., and I had total recall of the dream and the cover photo.

It was a picture of a farm at the crack of dawn. The farm buildings—a barn, silo, windmill and house—were silhouetted against a *beautiful* orange sky. The sun wasn't quite up yet—just its vivid orange glow provided the backlighting. There was a light on in the farm kitchen; the farmer was likely making his predawn coffee.

I envisioned the logo, *Farm & Ranch Living*, in solid black across the top. I dreamt the copy on the cover, too: Near the bottom, reversed out of the black area below the silhouetted buildings, it stated, *"Good Morning! Welcome to the dawn of a new day...and the birth of an entirely new type of farm magazine."*

What's more, I "saw" that cover sentence typed in Cooper Bold, a font I'd become fond of over the years. The whole thing—the picture, the logo and that bottom call-out copy—was just as clear to me as though it was projected on a screen.

I leapt out of bed, grabbed a notepad and ran to the bathroom so I could turn on a light and write all this down without waking Bobbi. I knew I wouldn't forget the picture, but I wanted to be sure I didn't forget that call-out copy, because it seemed to be the exact statement I wanted (and we later used it verbatim—in Cooper Bold—see above).

When temper talks, composure walks.

A lot of growing up takes place between "it fell" and "I dropped it".

Now, isn't that incredible, that I would dream not only the cover, but the copy and even the type font? Bobbi knows this is exactly how it happened—I showed her my notes when we got up the next morning.

As you'll learn further on in this book, I've dreamt a number of things like that—even plots for complete novels. For many years I never admitted these unusual dreams to friends, because I feared they'd think I was a little weird.

Then I read somewhere that Steve Allen had written several of his hit songs—such as *This Could Be the Start of Something Big*—in his sleep, both the words and the music, and many other songs, too. I felt more comfortable after learning that, figuring if it wasn't weird for Steve, I guess it shouldn't be weird for me.

Several years later, I had the opportunity to meet Steve Allen in person and mentioned this to him. He quickly related he'd written "more than a thousand songs" in his sleep, then began detailing how we only use a portion of our brain by day and it's open to other channels at night, or something like that. I just kept nodding like I knew what he was talking about. But I do believe something like that occurs.

Now we had the concept for the cover picture, but we still didn't have the photo itself. So I wrote to more than 50 of our regular freelance photographers and described in detail the "dawn photo" I had in mind. I asked them to check their files to see if they had one like it.

We received several hundred pictures. None were exactly like the one I dreamt, but I finally chose one that was close to it for that first cover. The Cooper type, on the other hand, turned out just as I'd envisioned it.

Then, to make that cover *gleam* like we wanted, we printed the outside

102

four pages separate from the rest of the issue. Then we had them trucked all the way across Milwaukee to a "laminating plant". There a special varnish-like polish was applied in a heated process.

The finish resulting from this process was incredible—the cover absolutely *glinted* as light hit it from different angles. You could spill hot coffee on it with no effect.

That laminated cover achieved all we'd hoped. We later found that even people who didn't subscribe kept that Premiere Issue around—they just couldn't throw it away. And that resulted in lots of referrals; friends spotted this magazine on a kitchen counter or coffee table, thumbed through it and then subscribed.

Our second winner! Farm and ranch families *loved* this new, "classy" magazine. And they especially appreciated its no-ads approach. Farm women seemed to understand from the beginning why there weren't any ads in *Farm Wife News*, but subscribers to *Farm & Ranch Living* appeared amazed to find no advertising in a magazine of this quality.

The absence of ads and the glossy printing was such a novel thing that readers showed the magazine to their friends. We found they even brought it with them to the local cafe, again helping us spread the word. Some even told us they were tired of "paying for advertising" in other magazines—that is, paying for a subscription and then receiving more advertising than reading material.

We now had two magazines—*Farm Wife News* and *Farm & Ranch Living*—that were so different from others in the field that we really had no *direct* competition. There wasn't (and still isn't) anything quite like them.

We soon learned that going the ad-free route had other benefits, espe-

A kindergarten teacher is someone who loves children and hates zippers.

103

I Drove a Tractor 184 Miles...and Loved It!

SOME STATES have their Harley rides, others have their bike treks, some have jogging marathons. Iowa has the "Great Iowa Tractor Ride".

This year, the sixth for this annual event, 450 old-time tractors purred single file, about 10 mph, along a rural route. Tractors of every make and size strung out for nearly 5 miles.

The winding ride began early on a Monday morning at Spencer, in northwest Iowa, and ended at Jefferson in central Iowa on Wednesday afternoon. In all, the tractors covered 184 miles... and I wish we could have gone further.

As a native Iowa farm boy, I use about every excuse I can to get back to Iowa. This time, when my urban Wisconsin friends heard I was going to drive my car 450 miles to Spencer to then drive a tractor 180 miles for 3 days, they gave me some pretty funny looks.

But you gotta do what you gotta do, and I loved it! A former classmate, Jim Baumhover, who collects old tractors, loaned me a 1953 Farmall M, just like the one we had on our farm.

Humming along on that old tractor brought back all sorts of youthful memories. And the mashed potatoes and gravy served at noon and evening meals brought Mom's cooking to mind, too.

You can see a lot of things at 10 mph from the seat of a tractor you never see from a car. Like butterflies chasing each other...large gardens that are obviously more than a hobby...extra touches to landscaping to make farms unique... and patriotic barn painting.

I particularly liked the way many farm families—right in the midst of their busiest season—decided to take the day off with their kids, to sit at the end of their driveway, watch and wave at this unusual parade of smiling tractor drivers, who all waved back.

I threw lots of candy to the kids... thinking as I did that they had no way of knowing my memories were far sweeter than any of those treats. —*Roy Reiman*

AT LEFT is the column I wrote along with photo I took from my tractor during the "Great Iowa Tractor Ride", a 5-day, 184-mile trek with 400 tractors.

cially with regard to *Farm & Ranch Living*. Here's why:

Farm numbers began to decline drastically in the 1980s. And the circulation of farm magazines began dropping proportionately.

The number of farm *acres* did not decrease, but the number of *farmers* began taking a dive due to big equipment that covered larger tracts of land. A trend had started that has never slowed.

By the mid-1980s, a study showed that *just 2%* of the U.S. population was still directly involved in farming. Yet, at the same time, an article in *Agri-Marketing* magazine revealed there were still *262 farm magazines* being published! This means these *262* farm magazines were all fighting for the same advertising dollars...which were now aimed at reaching *only 2%* of the U.S. population!

Predictably, the remaining farmers and ranchers became inundated with farm publications. A recent survey indicated the average farm family receives *15.2 pieces of mail per day*. That's exclusive of personal mail.

Agricultural firms haven't been blind to this duplication when placing their advertising. They are now demanding much tighter audits, readership surveys and subscriber profiling of these magazines. And they don't want to reach any *retired farmers*; they only want to reach *viable prospects*.

Which leads me to an important point. If there's any "secret" to our success with ad-free magazines, I've just revealed it: Without advertising, *we don't share those concerns about who subscribes*. We cash the check and don't ask questions.

What's more, in the case of *Farm & Ranch Living*, all of those retired farmers—those rejected by other farm magazines because their advertisers don't view them as viable buyers—are prime prospects for us!

These people are also eager subscribers. Just because a farmer's retired doesn't mean he's lost interest in reading about farming. In fact, at this stage of his life it's likely he has *more* time to read...and he may have more discretionary funds for subscriptions than active farmers on pinched budgets.

A personal experience drove this point home. When my dad retired from farming in western Iowa and moved with my mother to a small house in town, he complained to me shortly thereafter, "I don't know what's the matter. I sent my renewal to *Successful Farming*, and they sent it back. Same thing at *Wallace's Farmer* and *Farm Journal*. I want those magazines, but they don't seem to want me."

I said, "Well, Dad, how many John Deeres have you bought lately?" He didn't quite understand that, but that was exactly the point. Since he was no longer a prospective buyer of farm products and services, ad-supported farm magazines could no longer accept my dad's renewal and keep him on their circulation list after he'd filled out their audit forms and honestly indicated he was no longer farming.

While retired farmers still want to read farm magazines, farm magazines won't allow them to subscribe. And perhaps the most ironic point is that, with farm numbers dropping and people living longer, *there are now far more retired farmers in America than active ones.*

So all those retirees became low-hanging fruit for us. We soon found a ripe audience across Canada, too. These ex-farmers readily signed up for *Farm & Ranch Living*, sometimes sending in subscriptions along with their wife's renewal to *Farm Wife News*.

Nor has it been only retired and active farmers who've eagerly subscribed—these magazines appeal to a wide audience of folks who either grew up on a farm or have fond memories of one. My barber, for example, who grew up on a Wisconsin farm, says *Farm & Ranch Living* is easily his favorite magazine because "It takes me back to my youth."

This magazine also resulted in what I feel is the biggest compliment our company ever received. It occurred when the farm economy hit rock bottom in the mid-'80s.

Since *F&RL*—like *FWN*—didn't help their income and didn't pretend to, we feared our circulations might take a dive due to farmers' lack of funds for luxuries. To our surprise and great satisfaction, our circulation not only held its own through this depressed period, we even saw a gradual increase.

We learned why through letters tucked in with renewal checks, such as the one that said, "We're so pinched financially that we can hardly afford this renewal, but yours is the only farm magazine that has a positive viewpoint and reminds us why we live here. You keep our hopes up, and we *need* your magazine now more than ever…" That was nice to hear.

Wrapping up on this magazine, *Farm & Ranch Living* has proven to be one of the easiest publications we do because of its formulaic format. The lengthy diaries and chatty articles appear in pretty much the same place in every 68-page issue. Our magazines don't vary in page numbers like ad-supported magazines, nor do we miss deadlines due to late ads.

What's more, *F&RL* confirmed we were on the right track with reader-written copy. In the beginning, about 80% of each issue came from sub-

"Average farmer now receives 15.2 pieces of mail a day…"

Many children's ailments are cured miraculously as soon as it's too late to go to school.

scribers, much of it handwritten. Today a good deal of the reader material comes in by E-mail as well.

Basically, our editors of both *Farm & Ranch Living* and *Country Woman* (formerly *Farm Wife News*) view themselves as part of a "receiving and distribution station" that allows country people to communicate with each other. We provide readers an opportunity to "talk" with counterparts they'd never otherwise meet.

We're in the middle of that conversation, which makes our jobs highly interesting each day as we select what we feel will be most interesting to readers of the next issue. While we may shorten and "sand off the corners" of some of the material, we try our best to leave it in the writer's language, so that it sounds like them.

Farm & Ranch Living has had a paid circulation as high as 600,000 and still is a steady, profitable magazine today. The heart of each issue is still those four monthly diaries, which—as one subscriber wrote—"makes me feel like I'm *there*, looking over the shoulder of these people or sitting down to a meal with their families. By the end of the month's diary, I feel I *know* them and regard them as friends."

There are three ways to get things done: Do it yourself, hire someone to do it, or forbid your kids to do it.

Talent is a gift you are blessed with.
Skill is how you take care of the gift.

CHAPTER 14

Magazine Born at 30,000 Feet

I WAS FLYING to New York in 1982, reading *The Wall Street Journal*, when I came across something that gave me an idea so exciting, I wanted to unbuckle and pace up and down the aisle.

Any regular *WSJ* reader is aware there's usually a somewhat humorous article about business in the fourth column on the front page. Well, the article I ran across that day may have been intended as humorous, but it wasn't funny to me.

It related how a small Pennsylvania handcrafts firm couldn't handle all the orders for patterns it was offering. Other craft firms were experiencing the same thing. As to why, the folks at the little craft firm made the point that, traditionally, "Whenever the economy goes down, crafts go up."

I hadn't thought of that before, but the logic was obvious. When the economy is weak, women—the primary crafters—stay home more and therefore have more time for crafts. And, being shorter on funds, they make more of the decorative and wearable items that they'd normally purchase.

My reason for rapt interest in this article was twofold:

1. We'd annually designated the February issue of *Farm Wife News* as our "Craft Issue". We'd reasoned that rural women were spending more time indoors at that time of year, so emphasizing crafts then made it a timely topic. We'd announce a national "craft contest" well in advance of the issue, then run the results in February.

Entries to this annual contest poured in by the hundreds, so many that we could fit only some of them in the magazine. So we turned out a couple of craft books with the surplus items.

But it never occurred to me until that airborne moment that we might capitalize on this interest by expanding that craft section into a *separate craft magazine*. And with the economy currently down, the timing would be perfect.

2. My second reason was it had been 4 years since we'd launched a new publication, and we were looking for a new opportunity.

Yes, children are deductible. But they can also be taxing.

Well, here it was. It seemed worth a try, and I began roughing out a format and the approach on a cocktail napkin. By the time the plane landed, I had the concept pretty well in mind.

Back at the office, I discussed it with our staff, and they agreed the idea was worth testing. We could go back to those *Farm Wife News* contest contributors to gather material for the Premiere Issue.

> ### "The concept came from asking for their pet peeves..."

To see what potential subscribers thought of this new type of publication, we sent a questionnaire to a segment of our readers. We happened to include one question that ended up giving the focus and format of how we'd make this craft magazine *different*.

The question: "What are your two pet peeves regarding today's craft magazines?" That was answered with more enthusiasm than anything else. Loud and clear they told us:

1. "We're tired of enlarging patterns from small grids. It's a tedious task that sometimes takes almost as much time as making the project itself. Nor do we like magazines to show us a project, then make us order the full-size pattern and pay an extra fee to get it. We'd like a magazine to have the pattern for *every project* FULL-SIZE, right in the issue."

2. "We're tired of seeing craft projects in black and white. We want them to be *in color*. When it says it's a blue sweater, we want to know what *shade* of blue it is."

Those two things provided our formula for success. We promised subscribers three things: (1) Ours would be the first craft magazine ever *without advertising*. (2) Every craft would be in *full-color*. (3) Each craft would be accompanied by a FULL-SIZE pattern.

We didn't have as good a reason to go the non-ad route on this magazine as we did the others. But we'd now learned that the no-advertising approach had great appeal with readers, and that it would be another aspect that would make this magazine truly *different* from other craft maga-

ANOTHER HIT. Idea that came to me during flight to New York resulted in this craft magazine.

COUNTRY *Handcrafts*

PREMIERE

Featuring **Full-Size** Patterns for Applique • Quilting • Knitting • Crochet • Dolls and Toys • Naturecrafts • Smocking • Christmas Decorating Projects **And Much More...All With Country Flavor!**

Put a Little Country In Your Crafts...With America's First Country Handcrafts Publication!

zines. When you live and die by subscriptions, it's as important that your magazine is *different* as it is to be *better*.

Whatever the reasons, *Country Handcrafts* was another immediate success. Once again we'd come up with the right product at the right time. Our circulation quickly jumped to 200,000, then 300,000, and by 1988 topped a half million!

It's interesting that while I remember that plane flight vividly, and what resulted from it, I can't for the life of me recall what business I did in New York on that trip!

I have 10 more magazine launches to tell you about, but I'm keenly aware that most people—especially those in the publishing industry—are more interested in learning one thing from this book than anything else: *How we've been able to make our ad-free concept work.*

So, I'm going to fast-forward to that, then come back to the rest of our start-ups later—sharing when, why and how we launched *Country, Country EXTRA, Reminisce, Reminisce EXTRA, Birds & Blooms, Country Discoveries, Backyard Living, Quick Cooking, Light & Tasty...*

...and—the star of our stable—*Taste of Home* food magazine, which topped *500,000 subscriptions* before we got the second issue in the mail...hit the *1 million mark* in less than 6 months...and soon became the sixth largest magazine in the U.S. with *5.3 million paid subscribers.*

WHAT COULD BE CUTER than a kitten in the pocket of a farmer's overalls? This picture from a *Farm & Ranch Living* subscriber was irresistible—readers loved it.

Few things that are worth doing are without risk.

Make Them Different, Then Better

I THINK people in the magazine industry—as well as people outside publishing circles—are going to be surprised how *different* our magazines really are. And how hard we've worked and dreamed and schemed to come up with features and contests and events that *readers couldn't find in any other magazine.*

Point is, people don't subscribe just for what a magazine *DOESN'T* have (no ads, in our case). They subscribe primarily for what a magazine *DOES* have.

So, if you're going to succeed with an ad-free magazine, you're really going to have to turn on *a lot* of people (our goal is a *million subscribers* to each ad-free magazine we launch). And to convince that many people to write a check after they scan a copy of it, that magazine *has* to be really *different* and include a lot of things they can't find anywhere else.

I'll get to what some of these differences are in our magazines and describe some of our "off-the-wall promotions" in a bit, but for the moment, consider this:

As I mentioned earlier, when you decide to buy a book—this one or any other—you either pay its *full price*, or you don't get the book. There aren't a bunch of advertisers offsetting *60% or more* of the price of the book (which is the percentage of ads-versus-editorial in most ad-supported magazines) and then you pay the *40% balance.*

Nope. You choose to buy that book because you're convinced it will be so interesting, so entertaining or so informative that you're willing to pay its full price.

The same is true with an ad-free magazine. Someone has to want that magazine so badly that *they're willing to support its entire cost...for a FULL YEAR.*

Now that I have you thinking about it, let me explain why this is so much more difficult to achieve with a magazine than it is with a book.

See, when someone publishes a book, he or she only *hopes* to hit the best-

Those who roll up their sleeves seldom lose their shirts.

111

seller list. Yet, even if the book doesn't result in huge sales, the author can still turn a pretty profit with a high-priced book.

Not so in the magazine world. When you begin publishing an ad-free magazine, hitting the best-seller list is a *must*. You need to aim for the moon—a *million* subscriptions or more! Without a response that at the least tops a half million, you can fuggedaboutit. You're not going to survive.

Here's why: The book publisher can put a healthy price tag on his product. (Let's say in this case the author or publisher is a *guy*—I'd like to be politically correct here and elsewhere in these pages, but the "he/she" thing becomes a pronoun nightmare; so please bear with me.)

Anyway, in today's market, many hardcover books are priced at $20.00 or more. Now think about this: The publisher puts out only *one "issue"* of the book. What's more, if you buy the book by mail, he's going to ask you to pay an extra $3.95 or more to ship it!

Now, compare that to trying to make it with *six issues* of an *ad-free* magazine sent out over 12 months:

First, it's *very difficult* to get someone to pay more than $10.00 for a brand-new magazine. Trust me—we've tested, tested and retested our tests, and any price above the $9.98 range is usually a deal-breaker at launch time.

So, put yourself in our shoes: We get a subscription and have $9.98 in hand for our new magazine, compared to the $20.00 or more John Grisham gets for his latest somebody-done-somebody-legally-wrong book.

But *WE* have to produce, print and mail that subscriber *SIX bimonthly issues* of our magazine, not one "issue" like John does with his book. And *we* will have to pay the *postage* on those six issues, because the postage was *included* in our $9.98 price.

Again, compare that to Grisham, who's sitting over there counting his cash, *ker-ching, ker-ching*. His "postage" *wasn't* included in the $20.00-plus book he sold by mail.

And while John and other highly successful authors may not like me to tell you this, here are the facts:

Actually, that $3.95 "shipping fee" not only covers his postage and handling costs, but—once he gets his book to the reprint stage and rolls off thousands of copies—it likely covers *all* of his printing, paper and other costs as well. That means the price of his book sold by mail can be *net profit*.

I'm not just blowing smoke here. Remember, we're in the book business, too—including both cookbooks and general books, we sell around 5 million a year. When we roll off several hundred thousand copies of a single book, the actual cost to print them can be below $2.00 each, even when it's hardcover and full-color throughout. And it sure doesn't *cost* $3.95 in postage to ship it.

So my analogy that the $3.95 "shipping fee" can actually more than cover *all* the costs of a *very successful* book is a lot closer to fact than fiction. Which means the *cover price* on a book that is purchased *by mail* can be *clear profit*.

That's why so many entrepreneurs crank out books and so few ought-to-know-better gamblers like us try to crank out ad-free magazines.

Now you likely understand how challenging and difficult it is to have a magazine succeed without advertising. And why our goal is always a million subscribers. That kind of circulation is what it takes when you can only ask $9.98 for a 1-year subscription…yet have to pay the postage to ship six issues and have no ads to offset this cost.

Years ago we could make it with a lot fewer paid subscribers. As you learned earlier when I described my first launch back in the '70s, that one was a huge success with 320,000 subscribers.

But those numbers won't cut it anymore. With today's printing, paper and particularly spiraling postage costs, we only look for "home runs".

As I've repeatedly told the staff for years, "A homer and a single only take one swing. So we're only looking for something that'll fly right over the fence."

Here's the rationale for that: The costs are *exactly the same* to prepare a magazine for print whether you're going to run off 10,000 or 10 million copies. Again, that's during the *preparation* stage, before printing.

No matter what the pressrun is, when you get an issue ready to print, you have to gather just as many features and photos, put the same amount of time into design and layout, set just as much type, handle the same amount of color film preparation and all other aspects of pre-press readiness. Ten thousand or 10 million, you go through the very same paces.

Obviously, as the numbers go up, the incremental cost of each printed

> *"A homer and a single only take one swing, so we're only looking for ideas that will fly right over the fence…"*

copy goes down. So, when we prepare to dig in at the plate for our next launch, a "homer" is the only thing on our mind—we're not just looking for something that's going to go between short and second or even bang off the wall. If we're not confident that baby's going to sail right out of the park, then we just pass and wait for our next winning idea.

In contrast, most publishers of ad-supported magazines feel that attracting 250,000 subscribers is an admirable success. That's because their ad sales are offsetting 60% or more of their costs.

Not us. We've actually dropped (ceased publishing) several of our ad-free versions with a circulation of between 300,000 and 400,000 paid subscribers. If any of our magazines ever drops below the half million mark, our bean counters start questioning whether we should continue it.

Again, with today's postage, paper and printing costs, making it with an ad-free magazine is a greater challenge every year. And it's why we have little if any competition (though it occurs to me we may have some in the future after I explain in this book how we do it!).

Okay, I'm finally getting to "the list". I promised I'd detail the things that make our magazines *different*. But I first wanted to emphasize the *need*

The biggest step you can take is when you meet others halfway.

for those differences, as well as the need to have an especially *creative staff*—full of fresh ideas and a zest for trying anything novel—if you intend to survive and thrive with a magazine sans ads.

Again, if anyone thinks they're going to make it in the incredibly competitive magazine world by just telling readers, *"Look, there are no ads in here!"*, they're in for a rude financial awakening.

After all, according to Samir Husni, professor at the University of Mississippi's Magazine Service Journalism Program, there are currently *6,200 magazines* being published in the U.S.

In the month of October 2004 alone, *128 new titles* entered the market, a record high. Worse, Husni predicts a full *60%* of these won't even last through to the end of their first year. Just 51 survivors out of 128!

That's vivid evidence that the magazine field is an incredibly competitive market. Just being "ad-free" isn't unique enough by itself to make a million readers rush to support it by subscriptions alone.

So…here are just a few of the things that make our company's magazines unlike any others in the industry:

● **Readers do the writing.** By now you know that our magazines are basically written by our readers—*real people* who share their views, photos, ideas and suggestions. As I mentioned earlier, we serve as sort of a "receiving and distribution station" that allows people across the country to communicate with each other in a neighborly fashion.

Think about this a minute—don't you find it difficult to turn past the "Letters to the Editor" page in any magazine? Well, if those letters are that interesting to you and other readers, why do most publishers usually limit them to only one page?

We don't. The bulk of each of our issues is based on that type of reader mail. Our editors regularly encourage subscriber response ("Tell us how you improved your backyard"; "What's the best advice you ever got from your parents?"; "Share your top cost-saving shortcut"; "Send a photo of your place"; "How did you meet your spouse?"). Then we pore over piles of reader letters and blend the best of them into articles on these subjects.

One of my daughters once said, "Dad, I have your magazines figured out. It's like going to the mailbox and finding letters from a hundred friendly people."

Yep, that's pretty much our formula. Only it isn't quite that simple— there's a lot of *judgment* required in deciding *which* of several thousand letters will interest our subscribers most.

That means our editors' jobs involve as much reading as writing, and it requires an extremely keen sense of our subscribers' interests. (This also requires editors who can swallow their egos. You don't get many bylines when you're simply "sanding off the corners" of other people's copy.)

I'd like to point out that we started this technique long before it became popular for publications to ask for "reader feedback", as many have begun doing more in recent years. This approach was unheard-of when we began it 30 years ago and it gradually became the trademark of our magazines.

Keep good company and you will be counted among them.

114

A key benefit to "letting the readers do the writing" is that the magazine stays current with what readers find interesting. Some publishers sort of get on a podium and "force-feed" what *they* think should interest their readers. With our approach, *readers* tell us what they and other readers are interested in *now*.

What's more, as you'll learn in the next chapter, the *average cost* PER PAGE of magazines produced the "regular fashion" is between *$7,000 and $10,000*, when freelance and photo costs are added in. In contrast, the copy for our pages is basically free.

This reader-written approach also results in people *talking* about our publications, which was invaluable as we became established.

> *"It's an incredibly competitive field...there are 6,200 magazines in the U.S. alone!"*

The following are a number of other things we've tried over the years in the "seen and heard" world of promotion to draw attention and subscribers to our magazines.

I don't mean to imply that this or any of these ideas or events are world-shaking, but they *worked*. And hopefully they demonstrate that we've tried a good number of outside-the-box things to make our magazines first *different*, then better:

● **"What's that smell?"** When the "scratch 'n' sniff" craze was at its peak, we decided to give subscribers an early "sniff of spring" in *Farm & Ranch Living*. We chose the Feb/March issue because that's when farmers begin itching for the new season in the same way city gardeners start salivating over seed catalogs.

So, we printed a large, beautiful full-color picture of a field of alfalfa at peak bloom across two pages. Then we told readers to scratch one particular blossom in that picture for a harbinger of spring.

There was only one problem: *No one* at the printing firm had any farm background, and they didn't have a clue what "fresh alfalfa" smelled like! So some of us ex-farm kids on the staff had to keep going back and forth to the ink supplier until we got *close* to what we wanted.

Still, the readers *loved* it. They shared the scent and the fun with their family, friends and neighbors.

We got a lot of new subscriptions as a result of that gimmick. The lesson learned: We need to be *different* in any way we can—even if it means *smelling* different.

● **We needle readers.** One evening while mowing my lawn, I was mulling over what we might do next that would set our readers abuzz. They'd gotten to the point that they rather *expected* some new, wild idea every few months. ("We were *wondering* what you folks would come up with next!" was a typical letter.)

Anyway, for whatever reason, Cracker Jack's "surprise" came to mind—I've always thought that was one of the *best* promotional gimmicks ever:

The nicest thing about new friends is they haven't heard your old stories.

COUNTRY COMMENTS
By Roy Reiman, Editor/Publisher

Like Surprises? Then You'll Like This Idea!

I'VE always believed that no one ever really out-grows a Cracker Jack box. The surprise inside, that is.

You always know it isn't going to amount to much—maybe just some little plastic gadget, but you still dig down inside that box to find *what kind* of plastic gadget it is!

For a long time now, I've thought the same should be true of every issue of *Country*. There should be some sort of "surprise" inside each issue that makes readers search through it page by page, just for the fun of seeing if they can find it.

I've been trying to come up with something that carries a high level of excitement, with the aim of making it a part of *every* issue of *Country*.

That's It! That's It!

Finally, I challenged our staff to give some thought to this and then submit their best ideas. This resulted in several novel suggestions, but the out-and-out best one came from one of our youngest staffers, Maudie Selz. I think you'll agree it's a great one.

I wanted the surprise element to be something truly "country"; that is, something that would fit in with our audience and content. And Sharon's suggestion surely is: "Let's take our readers on the famous country hunt in each issue, and have them look for the proverbial 'needle in a haystack'!"

Perfect. That's exactly what we're doing. *Somewhere* in this issue, in *every copy—including the one you're in holding right now*—is a very small sketch of a "needle." You're going to have to look pretty hard to find it—after all, it *is* a needle in a haystack!

It may be used to "underline" a word for emphasis; it may be tucked into a photo, stuck into a drawing or "sewn" into one of the lines bordering a page; it could even be used as an exclamation point at the end of a headline! But it's *there*, somewhere in this issue.

You May Be a Winner!

Now, if you find the needle, you may win a prize! Just use the envelope between pages 50-51 to send us a note

WIN A PIE! If you find our "needle in a haystack" (see details above), we'll have an Amish cook ship a fresh pie to your home!

a second element to it: We're allowing 100 people—just *two* in *each* state—a chance to win another prize!

Once you find the "needle in the haystack" in your issue, closely inspect the margins and other areas of *that same page* and see if you can find the phrase, "Hay, you won!"

We've added that phrase in only *two* of the issues sent to each state—you could be holding one of the *two* right now that we sent to *your state!*

We've recorded the names of the two people randomly selected in each state, so we already know who the potential winners are. But we won't be contacting you—you have to find the phrase and contact us to win.

If you locate the phrase as well as the needle, send us a note that says "I found them both—the needle *and the winning phrase* on page ___."

If your name is on our list, we'll have Elmer Renge of Dixon, Illinois send you a *large package of home-made sausage.* It's delicious! But don't bother to ask Elmer for his personal recipe—he keeps it so secret he won't share it with anyone!

This Should Be Fun!

Now, one more time, just so everyone understands the "rules" here. There are *two* parts to this contest:

1. The sketch of the needle is in *every* copy of this issue, including the one you're reading right now. If you find the needle, send us a note as detailed at left and you'll be included in our drawing for one of the 50 homemade pies. (Write "Attn. Needle" above address on the envelope.)

2. The "winning phrase", which includes the three words stated seven paragraphs back, is included in *just* two copies being mailed to each state. If you find the winning phrase and write in as instructed above, you'll win one of the packages of free sausage.

If readers enjoy this little treasure hunt as much as we think they will, we'll continue doing it in every issue of both *Country* and *Country EXTRA.*

So with that, start "snoopin'" through this issue. See if you're really "country" enough to find a needle in a haystack...and then see if you can find one of those two small "winning phrases" in your state as well!

OUR "NEEDLE IN A HAYSTACK" contest was first announced in my Comments column in August 1990.

Everyone knows that "secret prize" in each box is a cheap little plastic toy, but you still wonder *what kind* of cheap little toy it is, so you eagerly dig down in that box. (It would be interesting to know what percentage of buyers have bought Cracker Jack over the years for the secret prize as much as for the snack.)

So, I began thinking as I continued to mow (I've always found lawn-mowing a good time to *think*—you can't hear the phone or the kids or the dog…you're moving, and there are few distractions to occupy your mind). I thought, *Wouldn't it be fun to do something similar to Cracker Jack with our magazines—to have a "surprise" in each issue …something "hidden" in them?*

That's it! We'll HIDE something in each copy and then give prizes to the readers who find it!

By the time I finished the lawn, I decided to start this new concept in *Country*, which I was personally editing at the time. (You'll learn all about *Country* and our other magazines in the chapters ahead.) I wanted the hidden item to be something very *rural* to tie in with that magazine.

A tiny mailbox came to mind, but I knew that wasn't it. If we made the hidden mailbox small enough to be difficult to find, it would be hard to identify. If we made it large enough to be easily identified, it would be too easy to find.

So the next morning at the office, I did what I've always done when I needed creative help: I held a "$100 contest".

I gathered a group of our most creative people, explained the concept and what I was looking for—something other than a mailbox that was very "country" that we could hide in each issue. Then I tossed a $100 bill on the table: "Best idea by noon gets the hundred bucks."

It wasn't even a half hour before one of them, Sharon Selz, stuck her head in my office and said, "How about hiding a 'needle in a haystack'?" *Perfect!*

We've done it in every issue of *Country* since. The small, straight-line drawing of a needle is easy to hide (somewhere inside a photo, underlining a word, as a small exclamation point, laying in a margin). We've hidden it everywhere over the years—we once sneaked it on our front cover!

Success is hanging on after others let go.

Searching for the needle quickly became so much fun for readers (and their children and grandchildren—we hear of "family contests" to see who finds it in the least time) that subscribers soon urged us to hide something in our other magazines, too.

We took their suggestion and now hide "Hattie's Hatpin" in *Reminisce*, "Ted's Toothpick" in *Taste of Home*, an oven mitt in *Quick Cooking*, a tiny acorn in *Birds & Blooms* and "M-itch" the mosquito in *Backyard Living*.

Many subscribers say the search is the first thing they look forward to when each issue arrives. I'll describe the unusual prizes we give to "finders" of these hidden items in a later chapter.

● *A pot of gold!* Several years ago, we were in the final stages of an issue that featured a beautiful color photo of a rainbow, spread across two pages from margin to margin. I'd just finished writing a caption for it on a Saturday morning and was driving home when it occurred to me, *What if somehow a few of our readers could find a "pot of gold" at the end of that rainbow?*

Suddenly I had it! I made a U-turn, headed back to the office and rewrote the caption (the issue was headed to the printer over the weekend). I told the readers that, to add a little fun, we were inserting a brand-new *$100 bill*—a "Pot of Gold"—in that rainbow spread in just ONE copy in each of the 50 states and in each province of Canada.

When my CFO, Norb Whittle, got to work on Monday and I told him what I'd done, he had a fit. "One in each state? That's *$5,000 in cash!*" he nearly shouted (that was big money to us then).

"Well…it's actually more than that, Norb. I promised one for each province of Canada, too." Sharing that with him didn't have any kind of calming effect.

"Oh, man! How are you going to keep that money from falling out of the issues in the mail?" he asked.

I pointed out that wouldn't be a problem. To protect the high quality of our issues, we seal each copy in plastic shrink-wrap, so there was no way the bills would drop out.

But Norb being Norb, he didn't trust any printer with that much cash. So I assured him that I, personally—or he could send one of his staffers—would be at the printer to insert the money at 2 o'clock in the morning or whenever. Then I tried to console him by telling him how much our readers were going to "talk about this" and how many more subscriptions we might get.

I could tell he wasn't buying it, but he backed off. He'd always said, "You make the money, I manage it. As long as you try 'small' things, okay. Just don't ever bet the farm." This time he didn't really have much choice—the type for that rainbow spread was already headed to the printer.

When the presses began rolling, we randomly pulled a single copy off the line that was headed to each state and province, and tucked in the bills.

As we lifted off each copy, we jotted down the names and addresses

The best way to appreciate your job is to imagine yourself without it.

of each of those winners. That way we'd know later whether any of these people had "missed the money", and we could then notify them to take a closer look.

Finding the money surely didn't prove to be a problem with our readers! We quickly heard by mail or phone from all of those excited winners...except one. After an appropriate waiting period, we contacted that subscriber, and she said she definitely hadn't found any $100 bill.

We didn't know what happened to it until nearly a year later. That same subscriber said her granddaughter was paging through some of her old magazines in the attic and suddenly came running, shouting that she'd found MONEY! It was our $100 bill.

Still, we got a lot of mileage from this effort right after we did it. As soon as each finder called us, we sent a news release to newspapers and radio stations in the surrounding area of each winner, detailing how so-and-so from their community had won a "Pot of Gold" from *Country* magazine.

Those releases got widespread use and brought in more new subscriptions. Enough to even make Norb happy.

• **Reek of class.** I mentioned the *quality* of our magazines earlier. People who have never seen a copy of any of our company publications often assume that an "ad-free magazine" is on a very tight budget, and therefore is likely filled with black-and-white photos printed on cheap, thin paper.

They'll find they're wrong on all three counts when they see one of our magazines. We print on the *best* paper we can find and use *full-color* photos throughout.

Readers also notice other differences about our magazines. For one, without ads, there are never any "jumps", as they're called in the industry; that is, no "continued on page __" as in other magazines, which sometimes force you to skip through 10 pages of ads to read the rest of the story. Once any of our articles begin, they're *continuous* on the following pages to the finish. Our readers like that.

There are other quality items that make our magazines easy to read. For example, we try to keep paragraphs from being more than seven or eight lines long. (You'll note I'm generally following that practice in this book as well.)

With our older audience, that's important. Other publications often have 20 or more lines in a paragraph, which results in large blocks of "gray" copy that makes it difficult to detect where one line ends and the next begins.

We even "square the captions" below photos, meaning the last line of the caption ends at lower right flush with the previous line. This results in a crisp, straight edge that lines up with the right side of the photo, giving the page a neat, clean appearance. (You'll see what I mean if you note the square photo captions in this book.)

There are many other little extras. We try to treat each page the way an ad agency would treat a single-page ad. For example, our headlines are

Making a marriage work is like operating a farm—you have to start all over again each morning.

seldom more than seven words long (an editor at my first job once told me any head longer than that was a *sentence*, not a headline).

We break up copy with bold subheads about every five paragraphs (not only for reading ease, but these "mini headlines" alert you to what's ahead and keep you reading). We put "call-outs" here and there throughout longer articles—italicized quotes of interesting phrases from the story to draw readers to it. (You'll note those practices in this book as well—such as the quote at right.) Finally, another difference is what we call our "seasonal issues". See, the first annual issue of all other bimonthly magazines is the Jan/Feb issue...the second issue is March/April, then May/June, followed by July/Aug, Sept/Oct and Nov/Dec.

> *"We publish on a seasonal basis—ad-supported magazines can't do that..."*

Why? Because that is the schedule their *advertisers* prefer and have become accustomed to. But if you think about it, it doesn't make sense on a *seasonal* basis.

Their Nov/Dec issue—mailed out in late September or early October—becomes their "holiday issue", which arrives well before their readers are ready to think about the holiday season. Then their Jan/Feb issue, mailed in late November, carries features about the New Year ahead—long before the readers have even celebrated Christmas. That trend continues throughout the year, with each issue arriving well ahead of each seasonal activity.

Since we have no advertisers, we can *time* our issues to arrive to better fit the seasons. So, our first issue of the year is a Dec/Jan issue, which is perfect for a "Holiday Issue"—it arrives just as readers are *in* the holiday spirit and eager to read nostalgic articles, decorating suggestions and festive recipes.

The next is Feb/March, which fits nicely as a "Winter Issue" with a lot of outdoor snow and indoor fireplace scenes. That's followed by an April/May "Spring Issue", a June/July "Summer Issue", then an Aug/Sept "Autumn Issue" and finally an Oct/Nov "Late Fall Issue". Again, each of these issues arrive when readers are enjoying that particular time of year, which enhances their enjoyment.

Note I mentioned both "Autumn" and "Late Fall" issues. We have a reason for that, too. Since our magazines feature an abundance of beautiful color pictures, and the August through November months are by far the prettiest for outdoor photography, this gives us "two shots" at the autumn/fall season.

There's another benefit to our offbeat schedule: Our magazines arrive on that month *in between* the arrival of all other publishers' bimonthly magazines, making ours more welcome and likely better-read due to less competition when they reach readers' homes.

• Readers love our "sayings". One day I was studying our pages, wondering what else we could do that no other magazine had done. It sud-

Is the opportunity fraught with difficulty or the difficulty fraught with opportunity?

denly struck me that the broad, white margins along the outside edge of each page amounted to "wasted space" (we've always been bent on giving our subscribers their money's worth and then some).

Since I'm a big collector of sayings and one-sentence philosophies, it occurred to me: Why not put one of those humorous or inspirational sayings in small type *vertically* along the side of each page? We started doing it, and readers liked that, too. Some subscribers soon told us they'd begun copying down their favorites and were posting them on their refrigerators.

And then many of them began sending us *their* favorite sayings for future issues. After a couple of years, they asked us to assemble the best of those into a book, which we did. Amazingly, we sold tens of thousands of copies of that little booklet called *601 Sayings To Make You Smile.*

Since we were the first people to put those "marginal notes", as we call them, in a magazine, I also decided to be the first (to my knowledge) to put them in a book. So you'll find some of my favorites listed in the outside margins throughout these pages as well (as the one at left here).

● **That's only the beginning.** We do and have done a LOT of unusual promotional things to draw attention to our magazines. That's *invaluable,* because with postage going up steadily, the more people we can draw to our magazines without having to mail a sample issue or a promotional piece, the more it saves us in marketing costs.

Here are just a few examples of how, during those early years, we got rural women to learn about *Farm Wife News*:

✓ We decided a special month should be set aside to honor and recognize the nation's farm women. So we contacted Secretary of Agriculture Earl Butz, and he readily signed a special proclamation designating November as "National Farm Wife Month". Subscribers were very appreciative and our magazine received a great deal of exposure.

✓ We tucked a color *I'm Proud to Be a Farm Wife* bumper sticker in the center of one issue. Subscribers quickly put it to use (see photo above), which resulted in great exposure to the *Farm Wife News* logo prominent at the bottom of the sticker.

✓ We started an annual "National Farm Wife Forum" in Kansas City, Missouri that featured sessions on farm taxes, estate planning, cooking and decorating, along with speakers such as Charles Kuralt. More than 2,000 women showed up!

Fully aware that many of their husbands would show up as well, we had an experienced tax attorney and several rural bankers lead sessions for them in a separate room, discussing farm finances and estate planning. Then in the evening, everyone had *fun.*

We put together an "Agri-Sports Night" that attracted more participants

If you think you can't do something, you probably can't. But when you think you can, one way or another you get it done.

OVER 2,000 WOMEN attended first "National Farm Wife Forum" in Kansas City.

than we could handle and absolutely delighted the hundreds who watched them. Held in a large arena, the affair was supposed to begin at 6:30 and end at 10:30, but no one wanted to leave! It was near midnight when arena officials flashed the lights and cleared the building.

These rural "olympic" events included everything from husband-calling and nail-driving contests to grain shoveling and wheelbarrow races. A hay-mow free throw shooting contest was popular, too.

The crowd's favorite events were "Mechanical Calf Roping" (where a wife on a garden tractor drove for her husband, seated on a trailer with a lasso in pursuit of a mechanical calf; and "Backseat Driving" (which put a blindfolded husband on a garden tractor with his wife in the trailer behind, *shouting* directions to guide her spouse through an obstacle course).

Perhaps the overall favorite was the "Tractor-Trike Races". We painted

121

PARTICIPANTS in our Agri-Sports Night competed in "Mechanical Calf Roping" (above), a "Husband-Calling Contest" (at right) and even a not-too-serious arm wrestling event (below).

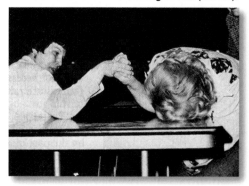

tricycles to look like tractors, with John Deere, Farmall, Case decals, etc., then had participants race in a lap around the arena. To add to the difficulty, at mid-course they had to stop and don long johns—suspended from a clothesline across the track—then remount and pedal to the finish! To hear the yelling from supporters, you'd have thought it was the Kentucky Derby.

Back then, it was amazing to see how *brand loyal* farmers were. If they owned a John Deere back home, *no way* would they get on a red "Farmall" tricycle! Even if the line was only half as long behind one of the other brand of trikes, they would stand there and wait until one of *their* type of tiny tractors became available.

That Agri-Sports Night was such a hit, it's a shame something like that isn't held in rural areas across the country every winter, just to have some unique farm-type fun and chase away February blues.

✓ For several years, we shaped the logo of *Farm Wife News* on the front cover of each issue in some unique way that grabbed attention.

We had a subscriber cross-stitch it in a colorful pattern…had a Minnesota farmer disk it in his field, then photographed it from the air…asked a Wisconsin creamery to shape our logo in butter…drew it in dew on the side of a tractor…formed it in fruit jars at the start of canning season…lined

TRACTOR-TRIKE RACES were a highlight, as was the "Backseat Driving Contest" (right). A grain shoveling event was a big hit, too.

up 227 students to shape our logo and shot it from the top of a crane (see photo on the next page)...and formed it in kernels of seed corn at the beginning of planting season.

Then one day we saw the Goodyear blimp fly over some event with an electronic message flashing on its side. "Would Goodyear actually do that with our logo?" we wondered. "Well, we won't know till we ask."

We called Akron, Ohio and were routed to someone in charge of "airship public relations". He heard us out (we didn't miss mentioning that the average farmer owns 100 tires on his implements, tractors, pickup, wagons and cars). Then he surprised us by saying, "That sounds challenging. We'll give it a try."

And Goodyear did it—*free*. We learned later it took them 4 hours to program the logo and 7,560 lights to spell out *Farm Wife News*. It turned out the Mayflower blimp at Akron didn't have enough lights to handle it, so they shipped the magnetic tape to Los Angeles for use on the larger Columbia blimp stationed there. Then one of their photographers spent an

A cheerful friend is like a sunny day.

227 STUDENTS lined up to shape the *Farm Wife News* logo for cover of our September back-to-school issue. At left, logo was shaped in watermelon seeds.

hour shooting progressive shots as the sky darkened.

A week later, we got a whole stack of pictures to choose from. Again, Goodyear didn't charge us a penny. Best of all, we could just hear all those puzzled people in Los Angeles, looking up at that blimp circling overhead for an hour, asking, "What on earth is *Farm Wife News*?"

✓ We sponsored a "National Pop-Off Contest", with subscribers sending us samples of their home-grown popcorn. The eventual winner, "Cousin Willie" from Indiana, became so well-known that he began marketing his product through supermarkets across the Midwest. He probably still does.

As we launched more magazines, we continued coming up with ways to draw attention to these new publications, get people talking about them and curious enough to subscribe. For example:

✓ In 1993 we bought a beautiful six-horse hitch of Belgians. We named them "*Country's Reminisce* Hitch" (combining the names of our *Country* and *Reminisce* magazines), and set out on a cross-country trek from Maine to California. The in-no-hurry trip took over 16 months.

We had a professional crew drive them over a preset rural route from Kennebunkport to San Diego, stopping at senior centers all along the way. My wife and I and various editors took turns joining the hitch crew regularly so we could *personally* thank thousands of our subscribers for supporting our ad-free magazines over the years.

In all, *over 50,000* appreciative seniors enjoyed a ride on the custom-

TEAM—Together Each Accomplishes More.

made wagon as it made frequent stops and welcomed them aboard. The trip garnered TV and newspaper coverage all along the route, and resulted in a book and video that covered part of the costs. (See photo of this hitch on page 128 and much more about it in Chapter 37.)

✓ We "partnered" with the Case tractor company in Racine, Wisconsin. We succeeded in getting Case officials to send a letter (which we wrote for them) to the wives of their 280,000 rural customers.

The letter told these women if they convinced their husbands to come to a Case dealership and sit in the seat of a new Case tractor, they'd receive a *free* subscription to *Farm Wife News*.

We received *thousands* of subscriptions from this program, all paid for by the Case marketing department for the opportunity to get those farmers (and their wives) in their dealerships to hear a sales pitch while sitting comfortably in their air-conditioned tractor cabs.

LOGO OVER LOS ANGELES! These photos, top to bottom, show timed sequence of *Farm Wife News* logo that Goodyear folks created on their blimp with 7,560 lights.

The most handicapped person in the world is a negative thinker.

125

SHAPING OUR LOGO differently on each cover of *Farm Wife News* was a challenge for our staff and a delight to our readers. We shaped it in ice cream cones (top) in June, in canning jars in August, in needlepoint in July and chicken feed in March.

We never learned how many of their $80,000 tractors Case sold as a result, but the promotion must have been awfully successful—they asked us to repeat the program with their combines in the fall!

For us, that fall program resulted in several thousand more subscriptions that didn't cost us a promotional penny, since Case printed the letter, paid the postage and supplied the mailing list of their 280,000 customers.

✓ We sponsored a rural golf tournament and gave away a car on a par-3 hole. Except our contest was different: We bought an old clunker at a used car lot for $150, and the hacker whose ball landed *farthest* from the hole *had* to take it!

Nobody wanted to be that embarrassed, and it appeared most of the golfers tried harder on that shot than if they'd had a chance to win a new car for a hole in one. (The pro bought the car from the winner to do it again!)

✓ We announced we were going to make our small headquarters town of Greendale the "Daffo*dale* Capital of the Country". "If you'd like to help in this effort so you can say *you* helped create the 'Daffo*dale* Capital'," we told readers, "we'd appreciate it if you'd consider sending us a couple bulbs of your own."

In less than a month, we received *over 54,000 bulbs* from our subscribers! And now thousands of them come to Greendale each spring to see the beauty they had a hand in creating. More on this in a later chapter.

✓ We had a tomato growing contest, and from this developed and patented a unique "Tomato Booster" device. We've now sold over *3 million* of these units by mail over the past 14 years. We now also sell a Hot House and "Maxi-Mix" fertilizer as well.

✓ We launched a "Rent a Cow" program right before Christmas, allowing *Country* subscribers to give a really unique gift to friends. Every month through the following year, each recipient received a new picture of their cow and a letter from the dairy farm operator telling how "Bessie" was doing. They also received a small gift each month, such as a sample of cheese made from her milk, a sample of the hay she was eating, the straw she was sleeping on, etc.

This program was so successful that the next year we added more unique rental gifts, including "Rent a Pig", "Rent a Horse", "Rent a Lamb", "Rent a Country Acre" and more.

✓ We held a national limerick contest in *Reminisce* magazine ("They have to be the type you can tell your mother or your minister," we warned), and followed that with a series urging readers to recall their favorite Burma-Shave rhymes. We received such a great response, we concluded those old signs were a slice of early Americana that ought to be brought back.

So we selected the best rhymes, put them on sequential road signs just as they were way back when, then offered just *one* set of these signs to readers in each state. We emphasized this would make their community something special, having the *only* new/old Burma-Shave-type signs in their entire state.

The chamber of commerce in many towns across the country *cam-

Begin each day with a purpose; end each day with an accomplishment.

paigned to get that single set, which resulted in our magazines being discussed in those meetings and in good coverage in the local newspapers.

We eventually made our selections, and a set of those signs is now standing in *43 states* across the country. They look just like the old Burma-Shave signs did, except for one major change:

The last sign doesn't say "Burma-Shave". It says "*Reminisce* Magazine". Those signs continue to provide that magazine billboard-type exposure free in those 43 states.

✓ Now, here's an idea that we *didn't* do: I decided to print just one issue *horizontal* instead of *vertical*. Just picture turning a magazine "sideways" and you'll see what I mean. Instead of it being the usual 8-1/2" wide by 11" *high*, the magazine would be 8-1/2" high by 11" *wide*…and would open to *22 inches wide*.

Why would we want to do that? Well, first of all, it would again be something *different* that would catch readers' attention. Second, *no other magazine could do that*. Their advertisers—all who prepare vertical ads—wouldn't allow them to do it. So once more we'd be breaking the rules.

Third, I planned to do this with *Country*, because when you think about it, almost everything in the country is *horizontal*—barns, cows, covered bridges, etc. About the only thing vertical in rural America is a silo.

So in just this one issue, we'd be able to turn out some incredibly long, *wide* panoramic pictures (such as the one below). The photo across a spread could run *22 inches* in width! Those pictures would show up not only on refrigerators, but likely in wall frames as "country art" .

We were excited about the idea until the printer screamed, "No! *No!*" And he was right. With a large pressrun, our magazine is printed on a web

The best prize that life offers is the chance to work hard at work worth doing.

OCEAN-TO-OCEAN TRIP by our six-horse hitch was made official when the team splashed in Atlantic near Kennebunkport and did same in Pacific 16 months later.

MAGAZINE WAS GROWING—LITERALLY!
When we shaped logo in corn seed, we were surprised to discover later seed had grown!

press, which has the binding equipment right at the end of the line. And the machinery is set up only to staple magazines the vertical "normal way". To do it any other way would require having it done at a separate bindery at a huge expense.

We did do something else highly unusual later, though—and neither the printer nor our readers knew it until we told them. We printed the cover of one of our magazines *upside down.*

The cover photo was an incredibly sharp picture of a farmstead reflected in a mirror-like pond. The reflection was so spot-on that you had to look closely to see whether you had the photo right side up.

So we printed it upside down, then put a small boxed item inside that asked, "Did You Notice? We Flipped!" and then told readers what we'd done. Our subscribers loved this continual teasing and our "playing with them" like that.

They also looked forward to our April Fools' pictures and pranks in our April issues, and some were

> *"I was going to buy 1 acre of land in each state... but then I backed off REAL fast!"*

real doozies (we retouched a photo to make it look like cows were eating their way down from the top of a full silo, for example, and another that showed a manure spreader suspended below a helicopter so the farmer could spread when the ground was too wet for his tractor, and more).

✓ Here's one more idea that we *definitely* didn't pursue: Mulling over what we might do next to "get our readers talking", I decided to buy *1 acre of land* in each of the 50 states, then "deed" *1 square inch* in each state to each *Country* subscriber.

Every subscriber would be able to proudly state to friends, "I own land in every state in the country!" We'd give each of them a "land ownership certificate" to display, plus a wallet card to carry as evidence.

I'd already begun looking into the 1-acre purchases when CFO Norb Whittle again called me off. He was adamant this time—he said if we

Any child knows that the real purpose of a middle name is so he can tell when he's really in trouble.

owned land in every state, we might have to pay *state taxes* in every state for *every subscription we sold*. When I heard that, I backed off real fast! But our subscribers would have *loved* that program.

✓ The national "Adopt a Highway" program has helped clean up the nation's major roads, but not much had ever been done to clean up rural roads…until we started our annual "Great *Country* Cleanup" each spring.

To get our millions of subscribers involved, we had our *Country* field editors hide *10 wooden needles* somewhere in each state and each Canadian province! Finding each needle, we announced, was worth *$100.00*.

We emphasized that this "needle search" was simply aimed at adding some fun and intrigue to the "Great *Country* Cleanup". The real purpose was to clean up rural roads, and for that reason they should be sure to take a garbage bag along to pick up litter while they looked for the needles.

The program worked so well that we received letters from small-town mayors. They told us how much they appreciated the program, since they'd observed groups of families walking along rural roads on Sunday afternoons, then later hauling pickup loads of garbage to the local dump.

Amazingly, more than *half* of those wooden needles were *found* by our deadline! The needles were inside clear biodegradable packets with instructions inside for the finders.

The second year of this cleanup program, we urged our millions of readers to "Pitch a Dollar in the Ditch!" to add momentum to the program. If readers tossed a few $1 bills along rural roads, we asked them to tell the local newspaper about it, so community people would know there was *money* in area ditches.

> ## "Subscribers helped 'Pitch a Dollar in the Ditch!' "

Yep, many subscribers did just that (in fact, one subscriber tossed 50 new $1 bills along rural roadways), and locals had all the more reason to get involved in our "Great *Country* Cleanup". And *Country* magazine cleaned up with more exposure.

Again, the activities described above are only a few of the continuous flow of ideas and promotions we've used over the years to get our magazines "noticed", talked about and subscribed to. (Yes, Mrs. Kluever, I *know* I just used a preposition at the end of that sentence, but it's just more conversational that way.)

I'll share more of these ideas—and how they played a big part in the success of each magazine's launch (as well as details of our incredible "Cookie of All Cookies" contest) in the chapters ahead.

But first I want to tell you why industry experts and even a lot of regular folks often find it difficult to believe we're for real.

We find comfort among those who agree with us
—growth among those who don't.

Life shrinks or expands in proportion to one's courage.

CHAPTER 16

Even Experts Can't Believe It

I BET I've received this letter a hundred times over the years. It goes something like this:

"Roy, I received a sample copy of your magazine, with its color photos and expensive paper. But there are no ads in it. And since you say you have no intention of accepting advertising, I don't see any way that your magazine can survive.

"Yet, when I read your introductory copy on page 2, you seemed *so firmly convinced* you were going to make it on subscriptions alone, I decided to subscribe just to see how long you'll last."

That kind of letter has shown up in my in-basket again and again and again. In 90% of the cases, these letters are written by men, who seem to have far more difficulty believing in our no-ads approach than women do.

I received this kind of letter so often, I eventually turned out a stock answer: "Well, if you're subscribing 'just to see how long I last', you're going to be watching for a *long* time. We now publish a dozen *ad-free* magazines, and one of them has been around—*without ads*—for more than 30 years. So we're not only surviving, we're thriving."

People who are unfamiliar with our company just *cannot believe* anyone can publish a magazine without advertising. And that's not just the Average Joe. It's true among so-called publishing experts as well.

Despite the fact that we've been around for over 30 years and have become one of the country's largest publishers, there are people in the print industry who still have no idea our company exists.

Here's an example of what I mean: Several years ago, I was at an MPA (Magazine Publishers of America) meeting in Naples, Florida. The keynote speech was delivered by an executive who was then head of magazine publishing at Time, Inc.

He gave a rousing "I have a dream" type presentation, inspiring his audience to improve the caliber of their publications. He ended his talk by saying it was his hope, his dream, his vision, that one day, "We'll discover the knack of publishing magazines that are so unique, so interesting and in such demand that we'll be able to make it on *subscriptions alone*...and the profit from the ad pages will simply be 'frosting on the cake'."

Jim Autry, who at the time was President of the magazine division at Meredith in Des Moines, knew our company well. He was sitting about five rows ahead of me, and at this point Jim turned all the way around in his chair toward me—his eyes wide open, his arms spread apart and palms up—in a gesture that said, *Where has this guy been?*

Yet Jim and I were obviously the exception, not the rule, in that audience, because when the speaker finished, those gathered leaped to their feet to give him a standing ovation.

> ## *"I'm subscribing just to see how long you last!"*

I went to the podium and tried to get a brief moment with the speaker. But he was so busy shaking hands and accepting congratulations on his motivating talk that, when I said, "Here are several copies of our ad-free magazines—we've been doing exactly what you're advocating for over 15 years," he just took the issues, laid them aside and went on with the handshaking.

I don't know if he even took them to his room. At least I never heard from him. To me, if he was *serious* about what he was recommending to his audience, and that he felt it was actually possible for publications to make it "on subscriptions alone", he would have been *eager* to see that such magazines *already existed*. And he would have called me to chat about them.

I've had many similar experiences in the publishing fraternity over the years. Early on, when folks in the industry heard about our sans-ads approach, it seemed they either pictured our publications as simply newsletters, or that we were having some mediocre success that surely wouldn't be long lasting.

It's still happening. As recently as 2003, the head of a major New York magazine company was quoted in *FOLIO* (a magazine for magazine publishers—yep, there's a magazine for these people, too). He flatly stated, "Advertising is still the key to publishing success. You simply cannot survive without it."

Really?

Some of my favorite phone calls over the years have been those I've fielded from potential advertisers. The calls go like this:

They: "This is so-and-so of such-and-such advertising agency, and we'd like to consider your *Country Woman* magazine for a client of ours in the coming year...are you still publishing that magazine?"

Me: "We certainly are. Its circulation is well over 2 million and growing steadily."

They: "Really! ...Well, then how come I can't find a listing for the magazine in Standard Rate & Data Service?" (SRDS is a national marketing service that lists circulation and ad rates for all U.S. magazines that carry advertising.)

Me: "That's because we don't accept advertising in that magazine or any of our magazines."

(At this point there's usually a long pause; I can *see* the puzzled look on their face right through the phone.)

They: "You...you *don't accept advertising?*"

Me: "That's right."

They: "Well...how long do you think you're going to be able to do that?"

Me: "Well, been doing it now for over 30 years. Actually we publish 12 national magazines on the same basis. All of them make it on subscriptions alone."

They: "That's...*amazing*. What kind of circulation do you have to those magazines?"

Me: "Over 16 million."

They: *"16 million???"*

Me: "That's right. Again, those are all paid subscribers; that's the only way they get any of our magazines."

As the incredulous silence on the other end continues, I usually can't resist adding:

"I'm proud to say that one of these magazines—*Taste of Home*—is now the sixth largest magazine in America. In fact, at 5.3 million subscribers, it's far bigger than either *Sports Illustrated* or *TIME*."

About then the call ends pretty quickly. They either figure some guy in Wisconsin is blowing smoke in their ear, or whatever it is we're doing can't possibly fit their marketing plan anyway. *Click.*

We've been below the radar for years. It's still true today. Main reason? *The lack of advertising in our magazines.* That more than anything else has kept us in the closet of the publishing world.

Despite our numbers—12 national magazines, 16 million subscribers, every 10th home in America receiving at least one of our magazines, sales of 5 million books a year—we often find people in our own industry who haven't heard of Reiman Publications. Here's why:

By contrast, ad-supported magazines—even small ones—are "heard of" in a hurry. That's because their promotion department trumpets their existence at every opportunity. The more notoriety they can gain, the more advertising they hope to attract.

"Wining and dining advertisers can prove very costly..."

So even before their Premiere Issue is off the press, they send out press releases...put ad reps on the road...assure a prominent presence wherever potential marketers gather...sponsor golf outings...send out clever premiums...hire specialty firms to construct impressive exhibit booths at conventions...and wine and dine. And they wine and dine and they wine and dine.

At one marketing convention I attended in Phoenix several years back, I counted <u>32</u> matching gold jackets. Those jackets were the uniform of the

You get more than you give when you give more than you get.

133

day for the ad reps representing just one magazine. Those gold-hued merchants were sprinkled about in all parts of the auditorium, checking out name tags and glad-handing prepicked prospects.

Later, I found several large groups at tables in the most expensive steak house in town, each being hosted by one or more of the gold jackets. Can you imagine what the total cost was to have those 32 sales reps work that convention?

Surely they'd held several meetings in advance to discuss the approach, who would pursue whom, and the sales strategy once they cornered a prospect. Then they'd had all of them flown there, plus the cost of hotels, cabs, meals and tips. For total expenses, we're talking a bundle.

Now let's compare that approach to ours: Since we don't sell ads, our only "clients" are our 16 million subscribers. We don't wine and dine any of them. We don't take them to steak houses; we don't even treat them to a brown-bag lunch. (My apologies to any longtime subscribers reading this who never thought of that before. Come to our company Visitor Center in Greendale and we'll offer you a large cookie from our test kitchen...for just 50¢.)

Instead of ferreting out ad managers and entertaining them, we put all of our time and effort into the *product we're delivering* to our subscribers—to make sure they get their money's worth.

> ## *"We put our money into our product instead of sales pitches..."*

Instead of wine, we deliver recipes; instead of dining, we deliver food for thought; instead of sales pitches, we deliver fascinating features that subscribers can read quietly on their own, with no one urging them to agree to some ad contract.

We've learned that if we do that job well enough, subscribers will renew and also tell their friends about our unique, full-color, "conversational" magazines.

Yet, without ads—rather, without all the public clamor and promotional efforts surrounding the sale of magazine advertising—we continue to be "the silent company" in the publishing world. Even among some who *should* think of us as "competition".

For example, about 5 years ago, *FOLIO* magazine interviewed one of the top executives at *Bon Appetit*. He was asked whether he was familiar with our *Taste of Home* magazine. No, he said, he hadn't heard of it.

Think about that: We then had *over 5 million subscribers* to a magazine in <u>*his field*</u>, the food industry, and *he hadn't heard of us*. By comparison, his *Bon Appetit* magazine had a circulation of 1.8 million.

When the reporter pointed out our food magazine had over 5 million subscribers, and that this should surely be regarded as competition in his field, he responded:

"Really? Well, they're probably just reaching all those people in the C and D counties."

Now, let me explain what he meant. The publishing world is fond of breaking audiences down into A, B, C and D counties, based on population density. An "A" county designation refers to people in major cities—like New York, Chicago, Atlanta, Los Angeles. "B" county people would be those in less populous cities, such as Buffalo, Sacramento, Topeka, Salt Lake City and Charleston.

In turn, "C" people would be from counties with still smaller cities—Peoria, Ill.; Madison, Wis.; Reading, Pa.; and Palm Springs, Calif.

And "D's"? Now we're talking about little bitty burgs like my hometown of Auburn, Iowa, and other Hooterville towns such as Duckwater, Nevada...Rolling Fork, Mississippi...Marked Tree, Arkansas...and West Overshoe, Nebraska (okay, I made up that last one, but the first three are for real). Anyway, the "D's" include people in these tiny rural towns plus all the country folks located in the rural areas around them.

> ### *"His gesture asked, 'Where has this guy been?' "*

So, again, just 5 years ago: (1) This publisher of a major food magazine didn't even know our food magazine *existed!* (2) At that very moment, our 5 million circulation of *Taste of Home* was more than *double* the 1.8 million of his *Bon Appetit*. (3) He *assumed* all or most of our subscribers were, as he said, "probably just people in C and D counties."

Well, first, he should have kept in mind that those rural people eat, too. Sure, not all of them eat fancy meals with stuffed mushrooms, but some do. There are some pretty classy people among the *thousands* who in recent years have chosen to escape the city for the peace of the country.

But what he really missed is this: *More than half* of the 5 million-plus subscribers to *Taste of Home* were then—and still are—in *A and B counties*, the very counties he thought he still owned.

So, our food magazine was reaching far more of *Bon Appetit's* targeted audience than he was. Yet he admitted he didn't know our *Taste of Home* even existed!

Sometimes it appears we're not just below the radar, we're even below the limbo bar of people who are in the same game. And we're often their direct opponents at that.

While we may not be a threat to *Bon Appetit* for advertising, seems to me that publisher should have recognized and been concerned about the revenue we were pulling from him in subscriptions and renewals. There's only so much subscription money going around and readers have the opportunity to make choices.

Yet, this doesn't surprise me much either because, for eons, the publishing industry has looked to *ADVERTISING INCOME* as its first and main source of revenue, while putting subscription income a distant second.

I'm about to tell you why I feel that's been a major mistake for far too long, and how—with the ad market now tightening—other publishers are gradually beginning to appreciate and look at things from our point of view.

The world is full of willing people—some willing to work, the others willing to let them. —Robert Frost

*Too many people go to their grave
with their music still inside them.*

CHAPTER 17

I Think They Have It Backwards

IN THE FALL of 2003, John Mack Carter asked me to come to New York to speak at a Publishers Forum luncheon. I'd become friends with John years earlier when we were both at Capper Publications in Topeka—he was Editor of *Household* magazine, and I was Managing Editor of *Capper's Farmer* magazine.

Back then John and I would sometimes meet during the noon hour in a large empty room on the second floor where we had set up a Ping-Pong table. I'd enjoyed the game and thought I was half good at it...until John kept waxing me and I went back to my office not only defeated but in need of deodorant.

I didn't learn till later that John had reigned as the Ping-Pong champion of Meredith when he'd been in Des Moines. Thank goodness I played him for exercise instead of money.

Anyway, John and I stayed in touch over the years as he moved on to edit several magazines, including *Good Housekeeping*, and became highly regarded in the industry.

John had followed my path, too, from the basement to the boardroom, and after he saw the piece in *The Wall Street Journal* about our company having been resold by Madison Dearborn Partners to Reader's Digest, he called me. Not just to congratulate me, but to ask if I'd talk at one of the monthly luncheons he hosts for a group of 30 or more Manhattan media friends.

I finally fit a trip to New York into my schedule and addressed his group. From experience, I wasn't surprised to find there were people in the group who still had never heard of Reiman Publications. And shortly after I got started, they had trouble believing what they were hearing.

Bobbi, who was with me, told me later she saw jaws go slack as these execs heard about our 12 national magazines...our 16 million paid subscribers...that we sold over 5 million books a year...that one of our magazines, *Taste of Home*, with 5.3 million subscribers, was currently the

Patience is the quality you admire in the driver behind you and scorn in the one ahead of you.

137

sixth largest magazine in America, etc.

And we were doing all this with…*no advertising???*

When I finished and opened to questions, predictably the first one was: "I have to admit I'm flabbergasted by what I've heard here today. Can you explain how you can possibly launch a new magazine without advertising?"

I responded: "Actually, I've gotten to the point where I often wonder how you can afford to launch a national magazine *with* advertising. Let me tell you why."

Then I explained why I sometimes think other publishers have it *backwards*…that to me it can actually be *easier* and far less costly to launch a subscription-supported magazine than one supported wholly or primarily by advertising.

Compare their way of doing it to our way. The group began squinting their eyes, paying close attention and taking notes as I ran through a fictional-though-factual analysis of the two totally opposite ways of launching a national magazine.

"First, let's look at the 'usual way' of doing it…let's take a new national magazine that's going to be primarily supported by advertising," I began. "There can be exceptions or different versions of the sequence I'm about to describe—particularly for small regional or trade magazines—but in most cases here's pretty much how things unfold when a new national magazine is launched:

"Usually, the basic idea for a new publication comes from one person. He or she either wakes up one morning with this incredible concept, or it's an idea that's been simmering on the back burner for some time and it just *has* to be tried. (As is stated in the quote above the Chapter 2 heading, "You can't plow a field by turning it over in your mind.")

"Whatever way it came about, this new magazine in most cases is primarily one person's idea. It's his dream, his vision, and it consumes him—he can almost smell the ink before he prints the first issue.

"So he gathers his ad staff around him, and he scribbles and sketches as he excitedly extols the wonders of this *entirely new concept*, a magazine like no other before, and how readers—and *advertisers*—are going to go absolutely bonkers about this new title. This magazine is going to make him, the company and everyone else involved *a fortune*.

> *"In contrast, I sometimes wonder how others can afford to launch a magazine WITH advertising…"*

"After this incredible presentation to his ad staff—let's say it's 10 people—they are then asked to fan out across the country to pursue (again, wine and dine) potential advertisers.

"They're each equipped with a lavish press kit and a chronological presentation guide. They may even have an expensive video or PowerPoint presentation. These 10 people in turn may also be asked to recruit 10 or more additional ad reps in each regional area, all the more to help con-

Your assumptions are your windows to the world. Scrub them off every once in a while or the light won't come in.

138

vince marketers to come on board," I explained to the group.

"And each time this sales message is handed down to others, it's diluted. Not one of those first 10 ad salesmen or the subsequent ones can possibly convey the vision and enthusiasm as the magazine's originator. It's not *their* idea; it's *his* idea.

"**And that dilution is going to get greater** and the presentation weaker every time it goes down to another level. Worse, those 'levels' have just begun.

"Unless these ad reps really have some 'connections', seldom will any of them get the opportunity to talk directly to the Marketing Manager, the Advertising Manager or whomever is the actual buyer of these ads.

"In most cases they'll only get the opportunity to talk to some media person at an ad agency or company, whose job it is to screen off the multiple presentations being pursued by dozens if not hundreds of similar salespeople representing other publications, who are all equally excited about *their* magazine, whether new or old."

I asked the group: "When you were in grade school, did you ever play 'Telephone'? That was when the teacher whispered a sentence in the ear of a student in the front desk, and it was passed at a whisper to everyone in the room *without repeating*. Then everyone got a big laugh at how screwed up the message was at the end.

"Well, that's about how jumbled this sales message can get when it's passed along, filtered down and diluted through the multi-levels of salespeople before it eventually reaches these media reps.

"It's about to get worse because, remember, it's likely going to be one of these media reps—not one of the magazine's salespeople—who in turn is going to describe this new publication to the real decision maker.

"I often think that if the guy or gal who had the 'vision' for this new magazine could hear one of these presentations and how diluted it gets this far down the road, he'd run for a window or she'd head for her hair salon for a new do!

"So now, okay, despite all this, let's say this new magazine catches the interest of the media screeners, is taken to the decision maker and is duly considered by the actual buyer. Even then, in most cases, that advertiser will be offered a 'deal', one that's commonly referred to in the industry as a 'two-fer' or 'three-fer' agreement.

"What that means is the advertiser will be given *two ads* for the *price of one*, or in the 'three-fer', three ads for the price of two.

"In either case, the *first* ad is usually given *free* to the advertiser, because the publisher wants that Premiere Issue plump with advertising, not only to portray instant success and attract other advertisers ("Hey, our competitor's in there; we better get in there, too!"), but because he wants to accurately portray to readers what kind of magazine can be expected with future issues.

"He can't go without ads in the first issue and then shock subscribers with a fistful of ads in subsequent issues. So, any advertisers signing on to

A father is someone who carries snapshots where his money used to be.

the 'two-fer' type deal will be given that first ad *free* in the Premiere Issue…with the agreement that—*after* and *IF* that first issue is a success—they'll commit ads to the second and possibly third issue and pay for them at the full rate.

"If the magazine is an immediate flop and there is no second issue, the advertiser isn't billed. That's what makes these offers pretty enticing to a marketer who feels this new publication, while untested, is reaching part of his targeted audience…there is *no cost* to him if there is no second issue.

"On the other hand, there's some sort of stigma in the advertising industry about being part of any publication that fails. They don't want to be in the 'last issue' of *any* magazine, whether it's a new one being launched, or an old one that's been around for years but doesn't have good legs under it anymore.

"These marketers seem to feel it reflects negatively on their judgment, and this very fear of being in the last issue sometimes results in it *being* the last issue.

"But for now, let's go back to this 'new launch' we've been describing: **"Think of the costs racked up so far!** Ad schedules of most companies are pretty much planned a year in advance. So this crew of ad salespeople will be crisscrossing the country for 6 to 12 months, calling on and cozying up to marketers and media reps, trying to convince them to include the new magazine on *next year's* schedule.

"That means it's likely going to be a full year and a half before ANY income comes in. All this travel, all the salaries for the ad sales staff, all this wining and dining, all the office rent and equipment, all the paper purchases and film preparation, all this and more has to be fully financed for the *first 18 months* with *no income* to offset it.

"Here's why it will take that long to expect any checks from advertisers in the mail: Let's say the idea for this magazine comes up in November or December (winter's a good time to *think*). And the visionary gets his or her ad force ready to hit the road in January, with the goal of selling ads for the debut of the new magazine in January of the *following* year.

"Meanwhile, an entire editorial staff has been assembled. And they were likely paid premium salaries to leave secure jobs in return for taking the risk of the new launch. These editors, too, will be flitting about the country for most of the coming year, gathering features and photos and lining up freelancers.

"They're not just gathering and preparing articles for the first issue, they're working much farther ahead as well. A good deal of magazine content is prepared months or even a year in advance; for example, next July, when they need a snow picture and feature for the Holiday Issue they're working on, they can't run out and shoot a Rockwell-type snow scene.

"Therefore many seasonal features are done and put 'in the can' a full 12 months ahead of time. So all the costs of gathering these advance features and photos have to be covered for a magazine that hasn't even been printed or tested yet.

"According to industry expert John Klingel, the average cost per editorial page in the launch of a large consumer magazine is in the $7,000 to $10,000 range. Again, that's *per page*, and publishers like to include a lot of pages to make their Premiere Issue impressive. So if you have a 100-page issue, do the math.

"And it doesn't stop with that first issue. Someone at Meredith Publishing once told me that when they launched *Midwest Living*, the staff had pretty much assembled enough features to fill the issues for most of the first year before the Premiere Issue was put to bed. Again, think of the *cost* of that, all done in advance for a magazine that may not go beyond the first issue if the response sputters.

"What's more, in most cases this publisher is going to have to *guarantee* he's going to print and mail a minimum of 250,000 copies or even 500,000 of that first issue. Today's major advertisers don't much want to bother with audiences smaller than that. Again, think of the *cost* of the paper, printing and today's *postage* rates to mail out that many copies of that new magazine.

"Okay, let's say the first issue is now designed, filled with features and thick with ads, fresh off the press and is put in the mail in January of the *second year* after editorial and sales efforts began.

"Any money coming in from all those advertisers yet? Nope. Remember, all those ads in that first issue were free.

"That means the publisher will have to wait until the *second* issue is printed in March if it's a bimonthly (many magazines launch as bimonthlies; they can always go to a monthly basis later, but it's a lot more difficult to start as a monthly, then cut back to every other month).

"So now the March issue goes in the mail. Any advertising money coming in now after 14 months of covering the costs? Nope.

"That's because while the advertisers are finally billed for their ads after that second issue is mailed, almost all ad bills state 'Payable in 60 days'. So, most marketers are going to wait that full 2-month term to pay those bills. That means the

> *"Publishers won't see any ad dollars for a year and a half…"*

publisher can expect the *first* ad payments to arrive sometime in *May*.

"Let's go back over this sequence: From conception of the magazine in November or December of one year…to May of the following year…this means the publishing company had to bankroll this new publication for a full *year and a half*.

"It covered the salaries of a management staff, an ad sales staff, an editorial staff, all the travel expenses of both staffs, the office rent, the paper and printing of the first two issues, the postage to mail them, etc., etc. etc. It's easy to see how this cost can run into many *millions*.

"As an example, John Klingel—mentioned earlier—was involved in the launch of *Science 80* magazine, and he feels the cost of that start-up was

141

a bargain at $3 million. As evidence, he compares that to what he says Time, Inc. spent—*over $20 million*—to launch *Discover* magazine in 1980.

(By the way, both *Science 80* and *Discover* eventually reached 800,000 in circulation. By comparison, we topped 1 million paid subscribers to two of our magazines in less than 6 months.)

"Wait! Wait! Wait! All of what I just described is the 'upside'. This is the kind of start-up costs you're looking at *if the magazine makes it*. That is, if it's a success, and if both advertising and subscriptions begin coming in at a respectable level high enough to encourage printing subsequent issues.

"But what if this new national magazine fails?

"What if subscriptions come in far below expectations, and advertisers (who are going to be asking regularly about reader reaction) learn the response isn't meeting projections and decide to put their ads elsewhere. After all, that next issue could be that dreaded *last issue* and the sky might fall.

"If the response looks bad, the publisher—even with these cold facts right there in front of him—is going to find it difficult to shut it down. Again, this has been *his* idea of all ideas, his dream, his vision. His macho and professional reputation are on the line. All these things tug at his heart and linger like a morning moon.

"If he gives up, he's going to be regarded a 'loser', and it could affect his future in the industry. If it's not his own money, it's almost sure he's going to try to convince his company's management to go ahead with at least *one more issue*.

"And if it is his own money, he may be even more likely to stay with the ship. After all, now he's not only fighting for his image, but it's his only chance at getting back all that money, some of which may have been loaned to him by family and friends!

"I've seen this happen again and again in this industry, people hanging on to a magazine long after they should have yelled 'Stop the presses!' I was guilty of it myself in the middle of my career. Even though I'd experienced my first major magazine failure from my basement, I went ahead and published several issues of a new launch named *Country Kids* long after I should have pulled the plug.

"It was the second magazine failure I'd experienced and I should have known better. This second failure happened in mid-career after we'd had a number of successes, but I still didn't like being bucked off that horse the second time any more than the first.

"So I hung on for three more issues of *Country Kids*—which turned out to be three hard jumps before hitting the ground with more pain than needed. I should have used good sense and read the writing on the wall much earlier.

"But 'good sense' is often hard to come by for any driven person when the cards aren't good. That's probably more true in the magazine business than any other industry. If a guy comes up with a new mouse trap or a whiz-bang trailer hitch, and it falls flat on its keister, that doesn't reflect on him

Avoid picking a quarrel...even when it's ripe.

in the kind of personal way it does for someone who launches a magazine.

"When a guy conceives and launches 'his' magazine, so much of *himself* is wrapped up in it. It's far more than just a 'magazine' to him. It's so much a part of him, it's almost like giving birth. It's his baby; it contains his beliefs and interests; it details what he enjoys and finds entertaining. It's an extension of his personality. In many ways, it's *who he is.*

"And for that 'dream magazine' to fail, for people not to support his beliefs and values, for thousands of them to say, 'Sorry, I didn't like it...', that's such a kick in the stomach that it can lead to major depression.

"He thinks *everyone* who knows him is zeroing in on his failure. It's like the old saying 'There's nothing like a hanging to focus one's attention.'

"He takes it very personally, and that's why he doesn't give up easily. He's more than willing to throw money at the problem for as long as there's at least a glimmer of hope that he was *right* all along.

"**So, when a magazine fails,** there's emotional stress in addition to the financial stress. Bad enough, but there's more: Even after the millions of dollars of loss for a failed national launch of an ad-supported magazine is somehow paid, the problems are far from over.

"First, the publisher has to return the subscription money to all those people who did respond. The physical handling of this, cutting all those checks, the mailing and the postage of accomplishing this can be significant.

"Secondly, what about all those staffers who joined the team and bet on the dream? A responsible publisher will feel compelled to give them some severance pay and help them find other jobs, again running up the cost of this failure.

"Thirdly, what about all those extra features and photos that were gathered for those future issues that are now not going to be printed? They've already been paid for, but what's he going to do with them? Sell them to a competing magazine? Hardly. They already hate his guts for trying to take them on.

"There's great emotional stress when a magazine fails..."

"Remember earlier in this discussion when I was asked, *'How can you launch a magazine without advertising?'*, and I countered with, *'I sometimes wonder how you can afford to launch a national magazine with advertising.'*

"Now you see what I mean. And hopefully you can understand why I think launching an ad-supported magazine can be *incredibly costly* as well as *incredibly risky.* You can lose *millions* of dollars, and mess with lots of people's lives in the process.

"In contrast, that's not the case when you do it my way. I contend you can test an ad-free magazine for as little as $50,000 to $100,000. And that instead of waiting a year or 18 months to see if it has wings, you'll know whether it's 'go' or 'no go' within a month or so after the launch.

"Yes, I still contend most publishers do it backwards."

Kindness is the oil that takes the friction out of life.

143

If everyone is thinking alike, then somebody isn't thinking.
—*General George S. Patton*

CHAPTER 18

Why It's Easier 'My Way'

MY TALK to the New York group was followed by an extensive question session. Here are some other things I covered:

Some people would liken the launch of an ad-free magazine to a journey to the moon. Trust me—it's not that difficult.

If this ad-free approach, or if publishing as a whole was that intricately complicated, I wouldn't have excelled at it. I'm a lot like my dad. He was an Iowa farmer who never went beyond grade school, but I always felt he had an advanced degree in common sense.

In contrast, I have a college degree in journalism. But what I'm about to explain basically involves a good deal of plain old common sense.

In the previous chapter, I detailed how and why the risk and challenge is tremendous with the launch of any ad-supported national magazine. It can take about a year and a half to learn whether you have a winner…it can affect the careers of dozens of people…and it can costs *millions* of dollars, none of which are recovered if it's a loser.

By comparison, to try it my way, all you need is a typewriter. Well, that's the way it was when I started. Upgrade that now to a computer. That's all it takes. Got the computer…plug it in…you're set to try your "dream" magazine. All the outside services you'll need are readily available for a fee.

You can turn out the whole magazine yourself. Or, you can do it with the help of freelance writers and photographers. Point is, you don't need to hire a staff and uproot people from solid careers to take a leap of faith along with you. You can wait to gather that staff later if/when you know you have something and want to continue.

Nor do you need to hire a bunch of ad salespeople and cover their expenses while you sic 'em across the country for a year. Don't need to rent a bunch of offices and fill them with fancy furniture, either.

You just spend whatever time it takes you to create that first issue and make it as *perfect* as you can possibly make it. Then you mail a sample of it to a percentage of your targeted audience to test it. And wait.

What will doing it this way cost? Around $50,000. Maybe $100,000. Or even as high as $250,000 if you want to do a bigger, quicker, more thorough test.

How long will it be before you know if you really have something? Not a year and a half as with an ad-supported magazine. With this method, in about a month you'll pretty much know whether it's go or no go.

How can the cost be *that low* to test your dream magazine?

Well, first of all, you don't have to print 250,000 or 500,000 copies of your "test" issue; that print-run is pretty much required for those who launch national ad-supported magazines, because most major advertisers don't want to "bother" with a circulation smaller than a half million.

Second, your Premiere Edition doesn't have to be 150 pages or more thick. Each issue of our magazines is 68 pages. Which may seem small until you consider that *all* 68 pages are *solid reading.*

In an ad-supported magazine it would take *170 pages* to deliver the same amount of editorial material. That's because most ad-supported magazines are run on a 60/40 basis—60% ads, 40% editorial. So our 68-page issue provides the same amount of reading as a 170-page issue with a 60/40 mix.

Some publishers of ad-supported magazines never really do that math. Nor do they give any thought to how much it costs them in paper, printing and postage to basically print and mail all those ad pages!

So, now we're up to here: Again, you don't have to hire a staff or ad salespeople, and you don't have to pay for the paper, printing and postage to send out a half million or million copies of a fat first issue.

How many copies *should* you print and mail to test your new ad-free publication? Well, that depends on your budget, and how widely or thoroughly you want to "test" your Premiere Issue.

It's likely much higher today, but early on it cost us a total of 50¢ a copy to produce, print and mail a sample of one of our 68-page issues. So, even if it's now $1 each, you can send your Premiere Issue to 50,000 people for $50,000.

There's no doubt that the larger your test, the more accurate the "reading". What you'll learn by sending it to 100,000 potential subscribers will be a far better indicator than if you send it to 50,000.

You can also select from more *targeted* mailing lists now. Today, list rental agencies offer lists of names so segmented that they allow you to target almost *any* kind of audience—broken down by age, profession, income, interest or whatever.

If you're short of funds, you can test your new magazine in "stages". If 500,000 names are available to you, you can first test 50,000 (every 10th name). If that looks good, you can go deeper, testing another 50,000 or even 100,000 if the first response looked good.

But whatever amount you sample, it's important that you have your printer "at the ready" so you're prepared to follow any test *quickly.* The more time that passes between the test mailing and the rollout, the less your follow-up mailing will match the original.

Why? A lot of things can happen in a short time—moods can change …national holidays or elections can prove distracting…the economy can suddenly change…or a national crisis can occur. Any of these, especially the latter, can have a serious effect on response.

For example, when President John Kennedy was shot in Dallas in 1963, several national magazines had made major drops of promotional mailings a few days earlier. Predictably, the results to the mailing were a catastrophe. It was as though they had put nothing in the mail, because the publishers received almost nothing in return. The shock and depression of the public was so great that no one was in the mood to subscribe to a new magazine.

Understandably, this was a *huge* financial loss—in the millions—for those magazines. But it was another indication of how important it is to follow any test as *quickly as possible*

> *"You haven't really sold a subscription till you've sold your first renewal. That's a mouthful!"*

with an added test or rollout, so that your potential customers receive it while they're still in the same frame of mind as those who received the first mailing.

Send a sample issue or a brochure? Some people in the industry recommend sending a brochure or flyer or postcard that describes your potential magazine. Obviously this greatly reduces costs as compared to sending a 68-page sample issue.

In fact, at one New York publishing seminar I attended years ago, a leading industry consultant strongly recommended a brochure rather than a sample copy for these reasons:

"First of all, you're looking for a quick response," he said. "And if you send the sample issue, the recipients are not likely going to subscribe until they've had a chance to review the whole magazine. Surely they're going to be interrupted by something—the phone's going to ring, the kids will need attention or the cows will get out—before they finish, so the magazine's put aside and they don't respond.

"What's more," he emphasized, "I feel it's best to let potential subscribers 'dream a little', so that they 'envision the magazine as they'd hope it to be'. You can accomplish that with a brochure that only hypes its highlights. But if you send them the entire issue, you risk the chance of their not liking a few of the features and thereby deciding not to subscribe."

Well, I *strongly disagree* with both of these points! First of all, I don't think this guy shows a lot of confidence in his magazine if he thinks readers are going to get distracted, put it aside and forget it.

Hey, when I send out a sample issue that I've sweated over and perfected to the best of my ability, I don't care if the whole herd of cows plus all the chickens get out! My mindset is that any reader is going to be so interested in my new magazine that he or she will make an effort to get back to

Vacations would be a lot more fun if you could stop the lawn along with the paper and mail.

it as soon as their schedule allows. Firmly *believing* that is a key to success.

Secondly, I don't want my prospects to subscribe to a "dream", or to "the magazine they *hope* it will be". I want them to know exactly the kind of magazine this is, so that they'll not only subscribe, but they'll *renew when that first year is up.* (Another consultant once said, "You haven't really sold a subscription until you've sold your first renewal." *That*, I feel, is a mouthful.)

In contrast, if readers subscribe to the magazine for what they *envision* the magazine will be, and later it turns out to be something else, they're not going to renew.

Which means that, with the "dream brochure" approach, you may get a great initial response, have high hopes and spend a lot to staff up. But then at the end of the year, you may be facing a failure after all, and have to hand a lot of pink slips to a staff that—like you—has been grossly misled.

> *"Clearly, believing is more than half of achieving…"*

So, while sending out an actual copy of the Premiere Issue is certainly far more costly than sending a brochure, you have a far better idea whether that subscriber's going to be there for you after the initial subscription expires. That way, what they see is what they're going to get…not something they envisioned.

Since I'd much rather know if I have a magazine with *staying power* right out of the box, I highly recommend the sample issue approach if you can afford it.

You "talk directly" to each prospect. Remember in the previous chapter I explained how the originator's message is "diluted" again and again with an ad-supported magazine as his vision is passed along through a series of assorted ad salespeople, media reps and ad buyers?

Well, that doesn't happen when you turn out your Premiere Issue of an ad-free magazine. *You* are talking—with all the initial excitement and energy of your big idea—*directly* to *every single potential subscriber.*

Recall, too, I mentioned earlier the letter I'd received from hundreds of subscribers over the years? The one that begins, "Roy, I received a sample copy of your magazine. It's beautiful, but there are no ads in it. So I don't see any way that your magazine can survive.

"Yet, when I read your introductory copy on page 2, you seemed *so firmly convinced* you were going to make it on subscriptions alone, I decided to subscribe just to see how long you last…"

See??? I had the chance to "talk" *directly* to each of those people. There was no dilution of my message. It went on a straight line from visionary to prospect. *That*, in my opinion, is one of the greatest benefits of launching an ad-free magazine with a sample issue.

Plus, I think subscribers feel they "know" you. And they sort of "root" for you; people tend to pull for an underdog. (An admission: I still rent Avis cars. That "We're No. 2. We have to try harder" slogan of theirs appealed to me from the outset, and I've stuck with them ever since.)

People rather enjoy seeing or learning that someone has the guts to take a risk by trying something new and different. They *want* you to make it. And if you succeed, they feel they were a small part of your success.

I think those people who wrote "I'm subscribing just to see how long you last..." were indirectly admitting they were caught up in my venture. More than likely they were not only *hoping* I'd make it, but wanted to *help* me make it. They noted how strongly I believed in that magazine, and they wanted to believe with me.

Our staff knows how often I've said this during my career: *"Believing is more than half of achieving."* There is so much truth in that—with a magazine launch in particular and life in general.

So when you write that introductory copy near the front of your new magazine, you have the opportunity to pass along that *strong belief* of your vision directly to each prospect. I think that's the reason so many people wrote, "...but you seemed *so firmly convinced* you were going to make it, I decided to subscribe..."

To summarize this chapter: By using no more than a computer and contracting for outside services, you can turn out your Premiere Issue, sample about 50,000 potential subscribers for around $50,000 and know in about a month whether your "baby" has a future.

Easy, huh? Wait—maybe you better read the next chapter before you buy the computer and start typing.

The exclamation point is becoming obsolete. No one is surprised by anything anymore.

*The future belongs to those who see possibilities
before they become obvious.*

CHAPTER 19

It's Not Quite That Simple...But Close

EVERYTHING I've said up to now about launching an ad-free magazine is true, based on my experience. But I need to add a caveat that's terribly important: You better have a *terrific idea.* You can't make it without ads with an ordinary magazine. You have to do something *extraordinary.*

As I said earlier, the ad-free gimmick on its own isn't going to do it. People don't subscribe to a magazine for what it *doesn't* have (e.g., no ads). They subscribe for what it *does* have. And whatever that is, *it better be something they can't readily find anywhere else.*

In other words, your magazine better be *different.* No, make that *DIF-FERENT.* Remember, there are an estimated 6,200 magazines currently being published in the United States. And there were 128 new titles launched in October 2004 alone. That means you have a *lot* of competition.

On the other hand, you can take a positive view of these figures: This means thousands of other publishers *have succeeded.* So why can't you? That's why you often see four gas stations at an intersection; one did so well, other operators wanted a piece of the action. Same is true in publishing; if others can make it, you can!

Still, your new magazine needs to be *unique.* It has to be so different from anything else available, in fact, that it can attract at least a half million subscribers at a reasonable rate. (*Pssst!* In the next chapter, I'll tell you how you *might* be able to get by with 350,000 subscribers by coming up with some supplemental income sources.) But with today's postage and paper costs, you'll need to shoot for high numbers to survive and thrive.

Don't be discouraged by this! If you have a concept for a new magazine that has real potential in appealing to a national audience, attracting a *half million* subscribers from among a U.S. population of *over 290 million* people shouldn't be that difficult.

Do the math. It only takes a small percentage of an audience that large. If you don't think you can achieve that, well, maybe your idea isn't that terrific after all.

A laugh is a smile that bursts.

151

This challenge has never discouraged us. Our company has now achieved that goal *12 times*. In almost every case, we've repeatedly topped that half million mark in a matter of months.

As this is written, six of our dozen magazines are in the top 100 of paid circulation magazines in the U.S., with each of them supported by well over a million subscribers.

So, if we can do that, so can you…IF you have a *terrific idea* for a new national magazine. But wait—even with your "idea of all ideas", there are two other things you're going to need to succeed with an ad-free magazine:

First, creativity. Better put that in all caps, too: *CREATIVITY.* Either you have to be highly creative, or you need to find and hire someone who can keep your magazine *interesting* with a steady flow of *exciting features*— the kind that readers enjoy anticipating…and not available elsewhere.

Some people think a fresh design or a "new look" is enough to make a magazine different and appealing. Likewise, too many publishers feel that a logo change or a different design and more white space are the cure for existing magazines when readership and renewals tail off.

Some also turn to shouting out features with large type on the cover, believing it will have an effect on readership and renewals. (Subscribers already know what to expect inside—why ruin a pretty cover?)

> *"Even with your 'idea of all ideas', there are other things you'll need to succeed…"*

Some also begin shouting "command" headlines, such as "LOOK INSIDE!" A respected copywriter taught me long ago that readers don't like to be *told* what to do in any heading, whether it's on the cover or at the top of a page. If your magazine is of interest to them, readers will likely "look inside" without being told.

To me, just redesigning a magazine that's in trouble is like having a house on the market that isn't selling. So, to make it more appealing, you decide to repaint it, both inside and out.

That's likely not gonna sell it—it's still the same house.

In order to make this house "different", you're likely going to have to go inside and tear down some walls, put in the kitchen of all kitchens, jazz up the front entrance, maybe add a pool and a patio…and then come up with the deal-closer: Spend as much creative time as it takes for you to come up with something truly unique that *no other house in the neighborhood has.*

When you come up with that, the house will likely sell quickly. What's more, everyone who visits it will decide *they* want a house like that, too.

Same is true with a magazine. Redesigning or repainting isn't going to do the trick. That isn't going to make it *different* enough from others. It's the copy between the covers that counts. You have to keep coming up with new, fresh ideas and features that keep the magazine exciting for readers.

Just coming up with new graphics alone won't do. Your magazine has to have a "mission" or a "soul"; otherwise it isn't going to be much more than a bunch of features and photos with a cover wrapped around them.

Each of the magazines we've launched has some of this element about them. There's something special or unrivaled about them. They're bent on offering something you can't get from other magazines. They have a "culture"; they have a "soul aspect".

At least that's what we strive for. And that takes *creativity*.

As for the magazines of others, I think Oprah's magazine does it as well as any. Her magazine has a *mission*; it encourages self-betterment, and it does it well. Martha Stewart achieved that in her magazine in its early stages, too, but then—in my opinion—it gradually went far too upscale and lost a good deal of what was special about it.

As a whole, though, we never wasted time subscribing to and studying other magazines. We didn't *want* to look like them.

Instead, we just kept listening to our readers and giving them what they wanted, along with a steady flow of new features, reader contests and enough wild ideas to keep them wondering, "What will they think of next?"

Instead of studying the competition, we figured—with our steady growth—the competition would be studying us. And they did.

On several occasions, a group of our subscribers informed us they'd been invited to the headquarters of a Midwest publishing firm to be part of a "panel". There the editors spent the day going over our magazines page by page, asking our subscribers what it was that they liked best about our publications and taking extensive notes.

We received detailed letters from a few of these panelists in which they said the editors openly admitted they wanted to learn how to "Reimanize" their magazines. We'd never heard that term before. But later we heard it from another publishing firm as well.

Being imitated is supposed to be flattering, but…

At any rate, the point here is that you will need lots of ideas and a great deal of *creativity* to make your magazine *unique*—so unique, in fact, that the competition will be studying you rather than the other way around.

That's what it's going to take if your magazine is going to be ad-free and attract a half million or more subscribers. It will have to offer *something* readers can't find anywhere else, whether that's quality, content or networking.

I'm convinced entrepreneurs are born, not made. Some people have the innate ability to simply *know* that anything is possible and achievable. They merely have to dream and create it. Your chances of success are better if you're fortunate to be one of these people.

Second, you need a large universe. That is, your new magazine has to have a HUGE potential audience.

If, for example, you plan to launch an ad-free magazine for left-handed drag race drivers, and you learn there are only 10,000 of those in the country, that universe isn't big enough for you to make it.

On the other hand, if you come up with a magazine for left-handed golfers, and your research shows there are over 10 million of them,

Between each dawn and setting sun, set aside some time for fun.

153

around the country, that universe may have potential.

(Hmmm… Hmmm…a magazine for left-handed golfers…you know, that's not a bad idea; that just might fly. Okay, I thought of it first, but you can have it; I have three other ideas I'm working on.)

I'm sure you get my point, that you need a *large* potential audience to reach your half million goal. And it's important that you check that out in advance. I'm speaking from experience here. Bad experience. We made this "oops, universe-too-small" mistake about 5 years ago.

We found there were over 30 million military veterans in the U.S., and we decided this was a huge untapped audience for a magazine just for them. Not a publication about blood and bombs and the horrors of war, but one filled with the "fond memories" that many veterans have— they love to recall the camaraderie, the travel, the "buddies", the days on KP, the banter and the humor of their days in service. This magazine would be sort of a Sergeant Bilko or Beetle Bailey version of the armed forces.

We named it *As You Were*. I liked that title—it was readily recognizable as the military term to stand "at ease", yet also connoted the magazine's collection of memories "as you were" in earlier military years.

We turned out a sample issue to a small test list, and the response was excellent. We were getting ready to roll out with a larger mailing…and that's when we learned we hadn't done adequate advance research on our "universe".

We *assumed* we would be able to rent the vast mailing lists of the American Legion and the Veterans of Foreign Wars (the American Legion alone had the names and addresses of over 27 million veterans at the time, which was a huge universe).

But when we requested the Legion's list, they refused to rent it to us! Then the Veterans Administration backed off, too, even though local groups of both the Legion and the VFW had been highly enthusiastic about the magazine and assured us that attaining the national list shouldn't be any problem. (After all, we learned that General Motors had recently made a mailing to the entire Legion list.)

The top dogs at both these organizations seemed concerned that our new magazine would compete with their membership publications. While we felt that was far-fetched (their magazines were pretty much all fact and no fun), it was their opinion, not ours, that mattered. As they say, if life was fair, horses would ride half the time.

Without access to those key mailing lists, we didn't have a chance at reaching our "homer" goal of a million subscribers. So we folded the magazine quickly and started an "As You Were" section in our *Reminisce* magazine. It's still running there and is very popular with veterans.

But if we'd done our homework earlier, we wouldn't have lost a great deal of time and a good deal of money by trying a launch without first learning more about our audience and its accessibility. You shouldn't, either.

Remember the three key things you need to make it with an ad-free magazine: A *terrific idea*, a great deal of *creativity* and a *huge universe*.

*Excellence can be attained if you
care more than others think is wise,
risk more than others think is safe,
dream more than others think is practical
and expect more than others think is possible.*

CHAPTER 20

Better Really Know Your Audience

UP TO THIS POINT I've emphasized that with today's costs of the "Three P's" (printing, paper and postage), you need to set a target of a half million paid subs to make it with an ad-free magazine.

Well, maybe not. Maybe not, that is, if you can come up with *other ways* to substantially supplement the subscription income to your magazine. I'm about to share some of the ancillary income approaches that have worked for us.

They should work for you, too, for this reason: Anyone who has the creativity to start a magazine is likely to be inventive in other ways as well.

Yet, to succeed with an ad-free magazine, and also with related endeavors, *you really need to know your audience* and what your readers' interests are. If you don't, you're doomed before the ink is wet on your first issue.

Being really *into* your audience is key to success with any magazine. That's *especially* important with one hoping to making it on subscriptions alone.

As an example, I'm an avid golfer, so I have often heard the expression "Be the ball!" Frankly, I've always thought that was a pretty stupid saying, but I understand its intent: You should be so focused on your game that it's as though you are the ball itself.

In line with this, I've often advised our staff, "Be the subscriber!" The point being, if you're going to be successful with a magazine, you need to *totally relate* to the subscribers.

You have to immerse yourself among them—know what excites them, what they need, desire and enjoy. You not only have to "be just like them", you really need to become *one of them.*

One of my strengths in our early launches of farm and country-oriented magazines was that, as an ex-Iowa farm kid, I really *knew* that audience and what their interests were. I knew what interested them and what they enjoyed reading.

155

I was able to talk to them in their language. I knew a bale of straw from a bale of hay even if it was shown in a black-and-white picture (in color it's easy—straw's gold, hay's green). And I could pretty much tell a heifer from a bull just by seeing its head. Still can.

These things are important to readers. I brought up the hay and straw example because I'm still wincing from it. One of our young hires—who didn't grow up with as much manure on his shoes as the rest of us—once wrote a caption for a photo in one of our magazines and made the mistake of identifying a load of straw as a load of hay. I bet we got a hundred letters from readers who caught the mistake.

A small mistake to you, maybe, but not in the eyes of our farm readers. I'm sure they lost just a bit of respect for us. They probably wondered whether we were a bunch of city folks after all, rather than the "been there, done that" ex-farmers we'd presented ourselves to be.

I've always felt this ability to relate to readers was extremely important. I already gave you an example in Chapter 9 of how, when I launched *Farm Building News*, I put on a hard hat and spent a full day on a construction site between each issue. I worked right alongside those builders so I could more closely relate to them, then wrote a "diary" of my day's experience later so I could share it with the entire audience.

Now, I'm not suggesting that you go to the length I did to relate to my readers. But you *do* need to have a deep understanding of your audience and establish a strong relationship with them. Being "part of them" should be innate. You shouldn't need a *survey* to find what their interests are.

"Phooey on surveys." I don't put much stock in formal surveys or focus groups. Never have. I don't care what field you're in, if you don't know your customers well enough without doing a *survey*, maybe you should get in some other field.

Besides, I think surveys can often be misleading. Why? Because I don't think enough of your *average* or "mainstream" customers or subscribers respond to them. As a result, the feedback can lead to false conclusions.

Fact is, certain people are just too *busy* to fill out a survey. And it's often those very people you really want to hear from. They're likely the heart of your audience, and the ones who can best afford your subscription or renewal price. If you're not delivering what they want, these busy people are likely to be the first ones who *won't* renew.

In my own case, when I receive one of those surveys with a fresh dollar bill tucked inside to "reward you for your time", I just stick the buck in my pocket and vow to put it in the collection next Sunday. I'm too occupied to fill out a lengthy survey, and my time is worth more than a dollar. Yet, I may be the "average" reader whose opinion the publisher is particularly seeking.

Instead, the magazine gets responses from people who have more time on their hands, who may be retired and looking for something to do. Those folks may fill out the form, resulting in a response that may not be

156

at all representative of the magazine's typical readers.

Here's another way surveys can be misleading: Magazine companies—even ours after I sold and handed the control to others—send out surveys asking subscribers to rank various features. So, the survey form lists about a dozen or more well-known features and asks the respondent to rate each one "Excellent", "Good" or "Poor".

Well, I've scanned the feedback from this kind of survey. Predictably, the first three features are rated "Excellent". Maybe even the first four or five will get high ratings.

But then it's obvious the subscriber is saying to herself or himself, "Gee, I can't rate *everything* 'Excellent'. They want me to help them here." So, they begin taking the role of a movie critic who can't write "Loved it!" about every film.

And from that point on, the rating of the list of features tapers off. I've seen some of our most popular regular features get poor ratings in these surveys because they were near the bottom of the list. Yet, I know if we dropped some of those features, the majority of our readers would be upset.

"If you don't know your customers well enough without doing a survey, maybe you should get in some other field..."

How do I *know* that? Because I read the mail. A *lot* of mail. I do so because I think the mail (now including E-mail) is the best indicator of what readers honestly like and dislike in your magazine.

We've always received a slew of letters from readers. Our staff will vouch for the delivery of several hundred letters in a single day for a single magazine. In our case, that mail is our lifeline, because a major portion of our magazines is "reader written".

So we peruse and read as much of that mail as possible. After all, the better part of our next issue may be among those letters. But just as importantly, that mail registers the pulse of our readers. It tells us what they're thinking...what they like best about our magazine...and what they'd like to see in future issues.

Those letters offer a much better take on our audience than a survey. Especially since we respond to a good deal of those letters. For most of my career, I've spent nearly every Saturday morning at the office, writing personal letters to people who took the time to write to us.

Even when we got bigger and published multiple magazines, I thought this was an important part of my job and urged the other editors to do likewise. I still do it today—by "regular mail" to make it more personal.

If you just read the mail, that's one thing; but if you write back, you learn more from the "exchange". You really have to *think* about their letter and their comments, and that results in knowing your audience better.

Over the years this has also resulted in hundreds of nice follow-up notes I've received from subscribers saying, "It was so nice that you took the time to answer personally..." (I even receive over 100 Christmas

Three essentials of happiness are something to do, someone to love and something to hope for.

ONE SOURCE of ancillary income for us has been our annual "Food Expo". It attracted over 10,000 people and more than 40 exhibitors for the 2-day cooking event.

cards from subscribers every year, and I proudly line them up on my credenza; these people feel they know me well enough to include me on their holiday list. How many other publishers get a hundred Christmas cards from subscribers, with warm, friendly notes besides?)

So again, *be confident you know your audience.* I think you'll learn a lot more by reading the mail from *average* subscribers who write on their own accord rather than from readers who were urged to respond to a survey with a dollar bill or "a chance of winning a free TV if you fill out our questionnaire".

Now, about making "ancillary money"…enough so that you may not need to top that half million or even the 350,000 paid subscription mark.

As I said at the start of this chapter, if you're creative enough to start your own magazine, you're likely creative in other ways as well. And that can be the key to providing an extra source of income that will help you survive and thrive without a huge circulation.

The best way I can describe this approach is to briefly detail some of the related profit areas we've struck on over the years:

Books. I've already mentioned that we now sell around 5 million books a year. But we didn't start out that way; that is, we surely didn't sell that many the first year. Still, the idea was triggered then.

Our first book was the result of a "cookie recipe contest" we held among our subscribers the year we began publishing *Farm Wife News.*

"What readers send you is what they want in return…"

Several weeks after the contest, I walked past the office of one of our editors and noticed a cluster of cardboard boxes behind her desk that were overflowing with mail.

When I asked about them, she said, "Oh, those are all the leftovers from the cookie contest. We got a couple thousand entries, but we only have space for about a half dozen of the best ones in each issue."

I said, "Gee, let's do a cookie book!" (Usually you can tell what kind of book your readers will eagerly buy from their response to an appeal for input. If you only get 50 entries to a broccoli contest, you won't sell many broccoli books. But when you get a couple thousand cookie recipes, you'll likely sell a couple thousand cookie books. What readers *send you* is what they *want in return.*)

So, that was our first book, and we sold a bundle of 'em. In fact, we more than quadrupled the response when we put a small flyer in with the magazine's renewal statements, telling readers, "You can order the book for $1 less if you do it while renewing." That was a bonanza!

Another example: In an issue of *Reminisce*, we asked readers to tell us "How did you meet your spouse?" We expected enough responses to start a series in future issues.

But we were *flooded* with hundreds of very personal, poignant stories that just cried out to be *shared.* So we turned out a book entitled, *How I Met*

My Spouse, and sold several thousand copies.

You can do the same with your magazine. If you encourage input from your subscribers and start a subject that strikes a chord with them, you may want to turn it into a book. I've already covered how *profitable* books can be if you sell a batch of them.

Conventions. If you're starting a national ad-free magazine, it's assumed that you're tapping into an audience of people who have something in common.

And it's a fact that people of common interest like to "gather". That's why *over 250,000* Harley-Davidson owners revved their "Hogs" from all corners of the U.S. to gather in Milwaukee for the motorcycle company's 100th anniversary in the summer of 2003.

So, consider holding a convention for your audience, with speakers and exhibitors that will interest your subscribers. We've done that successfully a number of times.

I already shared how, early on, through our *Farm Wife News* magazine, we held a "National Farm Wife Forum" in Kansas City, Missouri. We attracted over 2,000 people who paid $25 each for the convention and several meals. We not only got a number of companies to pay a good dollar for booths at the event, we convinced them to sponsor the meals as well. Proved very profitable.

We're still doing those types of things today. For the last 3 years, we've sponsored the *"Taste of Home's* Food Expo" in Milwaukee. Each year over 10,000 people from across North America flew or drove to attend the 2-day run at $10 each. (See photos on page 158.)

Products. If you really know your audience, you may be able to come up with proprietary products that can be sold to them…even if it's only a T-shirt with your magazine's name on it. With that, you win twice—first with the profit and second with the exposure.

I previously described how turning out a single "I'm Proud to Be a Farm Wife" sweatshirt eventually blossomed into an entire catalog mail-order business for us. I've also mentioned our success with selling over *3 million* "Tomato Boosters". Later in these pages, I'll tell you more about that Booster and other products we've developed.

I've always had three rules, though, for products we originate and offer to our readers: (1) Is it something novel or new that readers can't get anywhere else? (2) Do we feel good about selling it—will it *benefit* our readers? (3) Will it add to our bottom line?

If we could answer "yes" to the first two, the third one pretty much always took care of itself.

Tours. People with a common interest are likely interested not only in "gathering", but in visiting or seeing the same things.

As you'll see in Chapter 23, when we learned our readers were "looking up" people we'd featured in our magazines and then stopping in to visit, uninvited, we decided to start a tour business that allowed groups of people to have this same opportunity, albeit *invited*.

Contentment is contagious.

160

STAFF'S ALL DECKED OUT to escort one of our annual winter tours to Hawaii.

Today our "World Wide Country Tours" division has hosted as many as 6,000 people a year on group tours, traveling domestically and to many parts of the world.

You likewise may be able to do one or all of these things for your audience—offering books, conventions, products and tours that can add substantial income to your bottom line. We actually had one case where the ancillary income of one of our magazines exceeded the profit of the magazine itself!

As you consider sales of related items to your market, keep this in mind: All the promotion for any of these "house products"—books, conventions, products, tours—is *free* in your own magazine. And you can do it editorially, by simply "talking to your readers". In most cases, that's far more persuasive than doing it in the form of "advertisements".

Having said all of the above in favor of ad-free magazines, I need to—in all fairness—make this point in favor of ad-supported magazines:

IF an individual or a corporation can afford the millions of dollars—plus the staffing, the travel, the promotion, etc., etc. connected with an ad-based magazine launch—such a magazine can be *incredibly* profitable. Take, for example, women's magazines such as *Glamour*, *Vanity Fair* and *Bazaar*, which lean to-

> *"Highly successful ad-supported magazines are literally cash cows..."*

ward "ad nausea" with *over 80% advertising*. With their large circulations, these magazines are literally cash cows.

Readers pay high subscription prices (some in the $20 and over range) or high newsstand prices ($4.95 or more) for a 200-page magazine that's

Some people get up, go to the window and shout, "Good morning, Lord!" Others pull the sheet over their heads and say, "Good Lord, it's morning!"

161

filled with 160 pages or more of advertising. What's more, all these ads are likewise sold at high rates—often over $50,000 per page. Wait—did you want that ad in color? Add another 10 grand!

Readers of magazines like these are literally "buying advertising". But that's apparently what they want, and when this combination works, it's akin to running a Vegas casino with half the hassle.

Again, the risk is high and the stakes are even higher for an ad-supported launch of this type for all the reasons I've detailed in the last few chapters. Not many *individuals* ready to launch their "magazine of all magazines" will be able to pull together the kind of funds necessary to carry such a gamble for more than a year with no return on the investment—even if it's successful.

For that individual visionary, I still contend that going the ad-free route as I've outlined it is by far the safest way to go. Not only is there much less risk, but by using the test methods I've suggested, you'll know in a month or two whether you really "have something". Plus, importantly, you won't hurt a lot of staffers, friends, relatives and other investors who may be betting on *your* dream.

Then, if you're successful with an ad-free launch, you can always consider opening it up to ads later. Remember, that's what *Reader's Digest* did successfully several years back after going for decades without advertising.

While I hope that will never be the case with our company's publications—being "ad-free" is what our magazines and our firm have become particularly noted for—that's still something you could consider for your magazine somewhere down the line.

Candidly Country...Through the Years

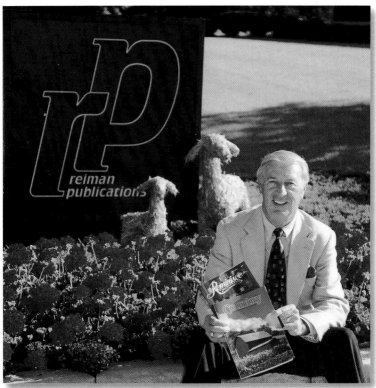

THOUGHT I was having fun, but change in hair color makes me wonder!

SMILING with Bobbi...and clowning around with Mike Beno, our Editorial Director.

An error is like a leak in the roof—the amount of damage it can do depends on how fast you fix it.

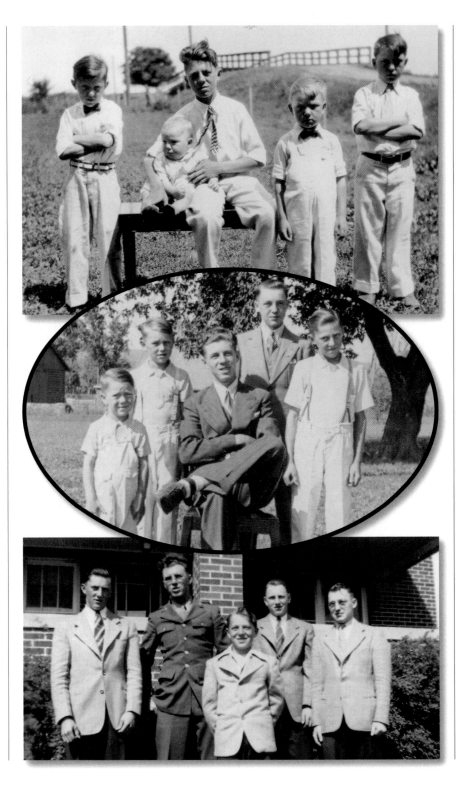

Family and friends are chocolate chips in the cookie of life.

GROWING UP the youngest of five boys on an Iowa farm provided me a good appetite for hard work. I'm the baby in that photo at upper left, 14 years younger than my oldest brother, Al, who's keeping me from falling off the bench. That's Vern on the left, then Orv, then Ray at far right. The complete family picture at top includes our parents, Christina and Ed. The photo directly above was taken when we five "Reiman boys" took a fishing trip to Canada a few years back. Left to right, that's Al, me, Vern, Orv and Ray. I'm pretty sure that those only *look* like beer glasses on the table.

165

MY FAVORITE FAMILY PHOTO has always been this one taken some years ago at a park. The photographer said, "One last picture—why don't you all go, '*Ta-daa!*'" From left, our hamming-it-up kids are Cindi, Joni, Lori, Scott, Juli and in front, Terri.

SAY "CHEESE". Most of our kids and grandchildren gathered for this 2003 photo.

166

Courage is contagious.
When a brave man takes a stand,
the spines of others are often stiffened.
—Billy Graham

CHAPTER 21

Why We Veered from Farm to Country

OKAY, now that you have my "thesis" on the launching of magazines without advertising, it's time to "rewind" a bit here and get back to describing the when, why and how of our various start-ups over the years.

By late 1985, our growth had flattened out. We were still doing well, profit-wise, but it seemed we'd reached a plateau. We could have just stayed there and ridden it out, but as it's said, "Business is like a bicycle—if you don't keep pedaling, it'll fall over."

I'd learned to enjoy the ad-free approach so much that I'd sold off *Farm Building News* in 1980, and now, with *Farm Wife News*, *Farm & Ranch Living* and *Country Handcrafts*, we basically had all of our eggs in the "farm" basket. This became a growing concern, because the farm economy continued on a sour note, and since we were primarily dependent on the farm audience, that hurting economy was hurting our growth.

Once we got people to subscribe, they stayed with us through thick and thin, as we'd learned with *Farm & Ranch Living*. The problem, though, in this weak economy was in finding *new* subscribers who didn't know us.

Everyone kept telling us that the farm economy was turning around. "It's coming back soon, and it's coming back strong," we kept hearing. But I personally couldn't see any signs of it.

And then something happened that brought that situation into even clearer focus. One of my four brothers, an Iowa farmer, suddenly got caught in the financial bind.

Up to this point he'd experienced a good deal of success—he'd taken on more acres and was feeding over 7,000 hogs a year. To finance this expansion, he—like many other farmers—had taken out some large, long-term loans. But when the downward spiral of farm prices hit in the mid-'80s, it became impossible for him to meet the repayment schedule.

When I heard about his quandary, I chartered a small plane and flew with my attorney to a tiny airport near his farm to see if we could help him. But after most of a day studying his records at his kitchen table, we could see there was no hope, and he was forced off the farm. It was a very sad day.

That experience had a very sobering effect on me. If operators as good as my brother weren't making it, what kind of shape were all those other farmers really in?

I felt if we didn't look to other areas to broaden our base, our firm could go the way of the farm economy. A growing number of farmers weren't "retired"; they were simply being forced off the farm, and like my brother, they didn't have a lot of loose change lying around for luxuries.

I use the word "luxuries" because, when you think about it, that's what our three magazines were. They weren't "how-to" magazines that told farmers how to make or save money, nor did they give them insights into running a business. While we may have felt that they helped people's *spirits* and gave them a positive attitude, when you're short of money, those things aren't an easy sell.

Still, I didn't want to stray too far by attempting a publication for an industry or an area that we knew little about. Ideally, we needed to do something on the fringe of agriculture, where we could combine our solid rural backgrounds with the little bit of city sophistication we'd picked up since we'd switched from bib overalls to sport coats.

> ## "That experience had a very sobering effect on me..."

Thinking on that, the first thing we decided to do was change the name of *Farm Wife News* to *Country Woman*. Experience had shown us that a *farm magazine* sells best only to a farmer or ex-farmer.

For example, I have a sister-in-law who lives in a small town in Iowa, right in the heart of some of the best farm country in America. But if you ever called her a "farm woman", you'd likely have a fight on your hands!

I'd sent her a free subscription to *Farm Wife News* from the beginning, but while she enjoyed reading it, I got the impression she'd prefer not to have it displayed on her coffee table. Yet, I didn't feel she would have a problem if you referred to her as a "country woman".

I was certain there were thousands of other small-town women who felt the same, and for that reason if we changed the name of *Farm Wife News* to *Country Woman*, it could substantially broaden our base. We would be able to pursue every small-town woman in America, and that would offer us a *huge* potential new audience.

Actually, we were at the point where we had to do something about the name anyway. *Farm Wife News* was an acceptable name that worked well when we'd launched this publication in the early 1970s.

But by the mid-'80s, rural women as well as other women deservedly wanted their own identity, and we began receiving some letters objecting to our title. (I personally thought the best "shot" we got was from a woman whose letter I pinned on our bulletin board by the coffee machine: "You wouldn't call a magazine 'Farm *Husband* News', would you?" she wrote. "So why do you call yours 'Farm Wife News'?")

The harder you work, the luckier you get.

We agreed it was time for a change…but the change was scary. Major changes to names or logos are frightening with any kind of magazine. Subscribers become comfortable with a name, so it's risky to change it quickly, if at all. Our concern was even greater because many farm folks are conservative and resist change of any kind.

Being more isolated and having less contact with other people than urban folks do, farmers tend to be even more dependent on magazines than their city counterparts.

A magazine becomes somewhat of a "friend" who comes to visit them regularly. And they don't want this friend to suddenly show up one month wearing sandals, a beard, a headband and a guitar slung over the shoulder! If the friend changes that drastically, they may not invite him back.

With this concern in mind, we wanted to move toward the name *Country Woman*, but we didn't want to leap into it. So, we first gradually phased the name of *Farm Wife News* to *Farm Woman News*.

The first two words had always been dominant in the logo design anyway, so we also phased out the word "News" by making it just a tad smaller in each issue until it "melted away".

By the end of 1985, we'd successfully phased out "News" and only *Farm Wife* appeared on our cover. Now we were ready for the next "gradual" switch. In January of 1986, making sure to use the very *same type* in our logo, we

CAREFULLY using exactly the *same type*, we slowly changed title from *Farm Wife News* to *Farm Woman* and then to *Country Woman*, broadening the appeal from 325,000 to *2.3 million* subscribers!

changed the cover from *Farm Wife* to *Farm Woman*.

Some readers told us later they didn't even notice the name change until we mentioned it inside, where we *briefly* explained our reasons for the change—that we wanted to keep in step with society and address women on their own instead of as "the wife of someone". They obviously agreed.

We stayed with *Farm Woman* through the 12 months of 1986. Then, in the January 1987 issue, we once again used the exact same logo type and this time changed the word "Farm" to "Country" on our cover, thereby completing our switch from *Farm Woman* to *Country Woman*.

We were much more concerned about this second change than the first. We now knew farm women understood our reason for changing our title from "wife" to "woman", but we were afraid that our subscriber base of what was now a half million farm women would feel we'd somehow turned our backs on them.

We carefully prepared our rationale. We pointed out that this would give us the opportunity to explain the current farmers' plight to urban women. Plus, we had now switched to a full-color *magazine* format, with *more pages* per issue, *more food pages* featuring cutout "recipe cards" and a number of other new features and improvements.

"We'd sold ourselves short... Country Woman peaked at 2.3 million subscribers!"

Our readers seemed to understand, and it worked—big time! While we suffered a little attrition, it was more than offset by a great number of new subscriptions from all those small-town women and country folks we knew were out there.

Actually, we found we'd sold ourselves short—we soon learned by testing more mailing lists that we could even attract subscribers in large *metropolitan areas* as well!

This was about the time when Barbara Mandrell came out with her hit song, *I Was Country When Country Wasn't Cool*. So maybe a lot of urban women thought being a little "country" was cool, too.

Whatever the reason, our circulation immediately grew by leaps and bounds...first by a full 100,000, then another 100,000, then another. It kept booming year after year, until in 1997, *Country Woman's* paid circulation peaked at *2.3 million!*

The primary reason appeared to be the name change—which is always a risky move in the publishing business. By *listening* to our readers and *gradually* changing the magazine's content as well as its title over a 2-year period, we had increased our circulation *seven times*—from 325,000 subscribers to *Farm Wife News* to 2.3 million to *Country Woman*.

Country Woman still fares well with a huge audience after *34 ad-free years*. Yet there are people in the magazine industry who adamantly contend a magazine can't survive without advertising. As I said earlier, we must be slow learners!

You think pennies, you get pennies.
You think dollars, you get dollars.
—From the movie "Ray"

CHAPTER 22

Country's Where It's At

THE INCREDIBLE GROWTH of *Country Woman* hadn't begun to happen as yet when, back there in the mid-1980s, we'd flattened out and were looking for new opportunities. We had no idea then that *CW* would—in the next 10 years—soar to more than *2 million* subscribers. That wasn't even a gleam in our eyes at the time.

But with early indications resulting from the name change of *Farm Woman* to *Country Woman*, we were convinced that veering more toward "country" was a good direction for us. The farm economy was still in the doldrums, and there was plenty of evidence that we could attract a large number of small-town and even big-city subscribers with country-oriented publications. I already had a new one in mind.

I'd found a study by the *Milwaukee Journal* of particular interest. It showed that, given the choice, nearly 50% of the people living in Milwaukee would prefer to live in the country or in a small town.

It appeared that many metropolitan people were beginning to feel a bit of concrete claustrophobia, brought on by the crowds, traffic, noise and pollution of urban living. Yet, the majority just didn't have the choice of moving to "the country".

Well, the magazine I had in mind would take them there...vicariously.

Little things sometimes sway your thinking once you start leaning in a certain direction. For example, in addition to what that study indicated, I'd begun noticing the locations chosen to film television commercials. It's still true today. Whether they're selling cars, insurance, refreshments or beauty products, many advertisers use a *country setting* to enhance the product's appeal.

It appears they're selling an "escape" along with the product. If they can portray the product in a way that will give viewers the sense they're "out there", free in the wide-open spaces, that adds to the product's appeal. To me, this offered more evidence of people's appreciation of "country scenery".

I'd also watched with interest the success of *Country Living* magazine.

Opportunities take now for an answer.

171

Country

PREMIERE ISSUE

Good Morning!

Welcome to the dawn of an entirely new type of magazine...
for those who live in or long for the country.

I concluded if the Hearst company could successfully produce a country-oriented magazine in midtown Manhattan, just think what we could do out here in America's Heartland.

By now, all indicators and our focus were on "Go" with this new country-oriented publication. We set a launch date for late in 1986 and started clearing a name for it.

We were amazed when our trademark search showed that publishers had come up with everything from *Country Living* to *Country Journal* and from *Country People* to *Country Place*...but no one had used just plain *Country!*

That's exactly what we wanted; that one word said it all. And that's what we used.

Yet, there's no doubt the tag line we later added below the title helped a great deal in quickly establishing our focus with readers. That tag line still appears below the logo on each cover today: *For those who live in or long for the country.*

Obviously, the second part of that phrase is a mouthful and meaningful—it broadened our market by appealing to people who live in the condos of Pittsburgh and the Loop of Chicago, plus all those transplanted Northerners who retired and relocated across the Sun Belt and the Southwest.

(In fact, we've since gotten letters from subscribers in office towers in New York City who tell us they enjoy reading *Country* while having lunch at their desks. And the state with *Country's* largest number of subscribers by far? California.)

Once again, we gave the magazine a heavy, *glistening*, laminated cover. We printed it on the highest quality paper we could find. We used full-color photos on every page, screening as many as 5,000 photos to select 100 for a single issue. Then we used what had become our unique formula—we had the readers write it for us.

We spent a good deal of creative time making this new magazine totally different from any of our others. Its leadoff article was an eye-catching piece entitled, *"This* Is God's Country!" It was a glorious 10-page photo essay "narrated" by a reader who contended *his* area of the country is by far the most scenic. This is still the leadoff feature today, with different readers contending *their* region is prettiest each time.

Other regular articles include the "Country Primer", teaching readers various country facts and folklore; "The View from Our Place", in which readers share pictures of scenery near their rural homes (such as covered bridge below and mountain view on next page); "Can You Help Me?", which allows readers to ask for help in finding, fixing or restoring certain items.

Other popular features: "A Taste of the Country"—readers from four different regions of the country share recipes for their favorite foods; "Country People", describing some real country "characters"; "My Most Embarrassing Moment"—usually about someone new to the country who did something neighbors found laughable; "Little Humor"—readers share funny things their young children have said.

And finally we included a little item that proved to be a great conversation piece: "A Needle in a Haystack", involving a tiny needle hidden in each issue, and a country-oriented prize for 50 of the readers who found it. (I've already detailed this popular needle search in Chapter 15.)

The cover of the Premiere Issue was a real eye-grabber, too. We used a beautiful sunrise scene (at left) that was similar to the one that had been so successful with the launch of *Farm & Ranch Living*.

We were all pretty proud of this first issue of *Country*. It looked very good front to back, and we were highly optimistic as we put it in the mail in the hope of broadening our audience from farms to small towns, cities and beyond.

Again, we didn't promote this magazine with a letter or a brochure—we sent a free copy of the actual Premiere Issue of *Country* to a test list of 100,000 prospects. Then, once more, we waited.

Another winner! I hope you don't tire of hearing this; we likely never will. The launch of *Country* was better than anything we'd experienced

One nice thing about egotists. They don't talk about other people.

173

before! Subscriptions *poured* in, and we quickly put several hundred thousand more samples in the mail to a larger list of prospects.

By now we'd gotten pretty calloused to the kind of response that would blow other publishers away. As mentioned earlier, the goal for most mailings such as this is normally a 2% response. With *Country*, we received an _18%_ response to the first 100,000 copies! That kind of response had never been heard of in the magazine industry.

We kept putting more sample issues in the mail, and by the end of the first year, we had topped a *half million subscribers*. What's more, a high percentage of those folks had paid for *2 years* right off the bat.

Why was this new magazine so "hot" from the start? We gave that some thought and came to several possible conclusions:

Maybe it was because a high percentage of our society is only one or two generations away from Grandpa's farm, and in today's fast-paced world they long to go back there now and then, to the way things were in those happy, uncomplicated days of their youth. *Country* takes them "home" again, each issue offering a 2-hour escape from the realities of their lives.

That or something like it must have been the appeal, because we soon found we could sell this magazine to cosmopolitan people as readily as to rural residents. Urbanites who weren't a tad "country" were finding it chic to *appear* country by having this classy magazine on their coffee table.

Again, our timing was good. Just after this launch, President Bush (the first one) openly expressed his love for country music, fishing, hunting, the outdoors and the unsophisticated things in life.

It wasn't long after that a lot of "country" folks began coming out of the closet, apparently figuring, "Hey, if it's all right for the President of the United States to admit he loves these things, there's no harm in admitting that I'm a little 'country', too."

We don't know all the reasons this magazine became such a quick hit. What we do know is that *Country*, by topping a half million paid subscribers, turned a *good profit* in its first year!

Any student of the publishing industry knows that, historically, you'd have to search long and hard to find any magazines that dug themselves out of debt in their first year. And when you factor in the fact that *Country* achieved this *without accepting advertising*, it's even more amazing.

Some publishing people will find that and what follows hard to believe, but we have the financial records to prove it (and have since duplicated this feat with several more ad-free magazines launched since then).

> **"Country received an 18% paid response!"**

Our early mailings of *Country* gave us an immediate idea of how "ready" the general public was for this type of publication: After receiving more than an *18% response* with our first test mailing to 100,000 prospects, we averaged *13.8%* with the first rollout.

Now, here's what makes this even more impressive: We got this kind of response with a *cash only* offer! Most magazines accept "credit orders" (subscribe now, pay later), and then normally get a 50% pay-up. Which means even if they achieve the 2% response that is normally their goal, this actually converts to only 1% if only half of them pay up when they later receive the invoice.

In our case, since we accepted only check or credit card payments *up front*, this means our 13.8% response to a cash offer is akin to getting a *27.6% response* to a credit offer.

There is even more that makes this response astounding: Our final tally showed that *over 25%* of these original subscriptions to *Country* were for *2 years or more*.

When we stopped reeling from this initial reception and did our quantitative analysis, we knew—with this new magazine in this broader market, which obviously appealed to urban as well as rural people —we were onto something *big*.

Very few wishes come true by themselves.

Again, we'd broken the rules by sending a copy of the Premiere Issue to each prospect. Most direct-mail promotional packages promise more than they deliver. By comparison, we felt such a mailing wouldn't promise as *much* as we were going to deliver. People would have to *see* this new magazine to fully appreciate its high quality.

For example, *Country's* laminated cover was even heavier and more beautiful than the one we'd used on *Farm & Ranch Living*. But if we described this new cover as being "laminated", what would that have meant back then to the average person who read it in a direct-mail piece?

Once more, we felt people had to see and *feel* this magazine's quality to fully appreciate it. How else would people know how good this paper stock was, and how well color photos would reproduce on it, by just reading a *description* of it? And how were they going to understand what we meant by the magazine being "full-color throughout"?

And, with *no advertising???* Who was going to believe that without seeing it? Remember, while that had become a staple in *Country Woman* and *Farm & Ranch Living*, we were now branching out into a whole new audience of urbanites who were totally unfamiliar with our company or our previous no-ad successes.

With its rocket-like growth, *Country* quickly became the company's flagship in its second year and soon became our first *million-plus* circulation magazine. More importantly, it appeared we hadn't even begun to tap the full potential of this magazine.

> *"Subscribers in New York City tell us they enjoy reading Country at their desks during lunch..."*

We came to that conclusion when we digested a statement made by the Secretary of Agriculture in spring of 1987. He'd stated that *27%* of the U.S. population were living in rural America...yet only 2% of that 27% were still involved in farming.

To us, that meant a huge market: Since *Country* had proven appealing to rural people who *weren't* engaged in farming, that 25% of the nation's population—those living there but not farming—were prime prospects for this country lifestyle magazine.

In plain numbers, that 25% computed to over *57 million people* who we could consider as ripe targets for *Country*. Faulty math or not, we were staggered and salivating at the potential.

Whatever was behind it, circulation kept soaring. Subscribers liked *Country* so much that they gave well over 100,000 gift subscriptions to friends at Christmastime at the end of its first year.

The pace didn't slow. Those gift numbers, as well as subscriptions and renewals, just kept coming in the years that followed.

At the end of 1991, its fifth year, *Country* hit a circulation of 1.7 million and grossed $17.6 million. It didn't stop there. In February of 1993—after we finished tallying an even bigger holiday gift subscription response—the circulation of *Country* reached *2,264,000.*

Better to ask twice than to go wrong once.

As that Russian comedian, Yakov Smirnoff, in Branson, Missouri says, "What a country!" In this case, what a *Country*.

Monthly, or Bimonthly? Our company is probably the only publishing firm in the world that publishes the same magazine in two different frequencies. Yes, you can get *Country* monthly…or every other month, whichever you choose. Here's how that came about.

We'd launched *Country* like each of our other publications, as a bimonthly (six times a year). But soon after we got *Country* well under way, we repeatedly heard this kind of comment from subscribers again and again: "The only thing wrong with *Country* is that it doesn't come often enough. Please go monthly!"

Problem was, we didn't know *how many* readers felt that way. When a magazine is supported by advertising, the publisher may be able to double the frequency without changing the subscription price. That's because the potential of doubling the ad sales will support those six extra issues.

But with a magazine like ours, which is supported solely by subscriptions, the only way we could double the number of issues would be by also doubling the subscription price.

So we were very reluctant to make this mass move. For some people, receiving a lighthearted magazine like this every other month is often enough. If we doubled the frequency and doubled the price, we just might kill the golden goose—the majority of our subscribers may not be willing to pay twice as much. Yet, there was obviously a public of some size out there begging to be served.

My wife and I were in Pasadena when I came up with the solution. Some friends invited us to go to the Rose Bowl that year. We were staying at a hotel downtown near the parade route, and being an early riser, with a 2-hour time change, I had difficulty sleeping in.

So I was out walking the street one morning, thinking on this monthly/bimonthly issue, and the solution suddenly occurred to me clear as a bell: *Why not give them a choice?* Would they like it

"REFRIGERATOR COVERS." That's what readers call our covers. Unlike other magazines that have multiple bold headlines shouting about what's inside, ours have "clean covers", which subscribers like so much that they post them on their refrigerators.

The best remedy for a short temper is a long walk.

177

monthly—for twice the price? Well, let's ask them.

I pretty much wrote the approach to this on a cocktail napkin on the plane on the way back (I've made big use of those napkins over the years). We used it in the next issue:

"If you're satisfied with *Country* arriving every other month, fine. You don't have to read any more of this announcement—just go on and enjoy the rest of the issue.

"But if you're one of the people who has been pleading with us to 'go monthly', keep reading. We're now offering you an opportunity to get six extra issues—one on the months *in between* each issue of *Country*—for an additional $9.98.

"We're calling those six extra issues *Country EXTRA*. So, you can now receive this kind of magazine *every month* for an extra $9.98 by filling out the form below..."

It worked. We soon had 448,000 subscribers to *CX*. And the cost of getting these *CX* subscriptions was pretty much zero, since the offer and explanation was spelled out right in the pages of *Country*.

So again, we may be the only firm anywhere that offers two different frequencies of the same magazine—you can get it monthly or bimonthly. Later, you'll learn we offered this same choice of frequencies to another of our magazines...and it worked again.

It doesn't always rain on weekends; sometimes it's just cold.

*There's nothing more exciting
than an idea whose time has come.*

CHAPTER 23

Traveling in a Different Direction

WITH FIVE MAGAZINES in the country field, we felt we had that market pretty well saturated. Any future growth for one of these five could eventually be at the expense of the other. If our company was to continue to grow, it would have to be *outside* the country market.

As we considered that, we became increasingly aware of just how big the senior market had become, and how it was continuing to grow by leaps and bounds as people began taking better care of themselves, exercising, eating smarter and, as a result, living longer.

What's more, while editing *Country*, we noticed a pulse beat of fond memories flowing in. It appeared our older readers were eager to share these nostalgic stories, and we began receiving far more than we could print.

Hmmm…what if we launched a whole magazine filled with these fond memories of the good old days?

Paying closer attention, we found basically only one magazine, *Modern Maturity*, serving the 50-plus market. Then, and now, it isn't really a "subscription" magazine. It's distributed as a benefit to AARP membership. Yet, its circulation was amazing—*34.6 million* at the time!

Again, little things you hear or see often catch your interest once you're tuned in to something—like the quote I saw back then that stated, "Every 8 seconds someone turns 50 years old in the U.S."

We noted other facts published by AARP and other "Aging of America" sources: "There are more people turning 65 today than babies being born." "In 5 years, 50% of the U.S. population will be over 50 years old." "By 2010, one out of every five Americans will be 65 or older." "People turning 65 will double to 70 million in the next 30 years."

This senior audience obviously offered us a *huge* universe of potential for a magazine, and it was growing by the minute.

We began taking a closer look and found other publishers had shown little interest in pursuing this market. The main reason: They'd found it extremely difficult to sell ads aimed at seniors.

Never miss an opportunity to make someone happy.

179

Welcome!

Yes, welcome to an entirely different type of magazine (no ads!)...that brings back the good times...by taking you on a walk down memory lane.

Most advertisers prefer to target people in the 35 to 50 age bracket. They don't view the senior market as big spenders.

(Yet, a *Forbes* article a few years ago indicated 68% of the country's money is in the hands of people over 60 years of age—they just don't spend it as readily as younger folks do.)

We also learned that several ad-supported magazines had been tried in this senior market and eventually folded due to the difficulty of selling ads.

That may have discouraged some publishers. On the contrary, it actually *encouraged* us to go ahead.

Why? We didn't plan to sell ads anyway. And because ad-supported magazines had failed in this market, this would likely *discourage* other publishers from competing with us. So if we succeeded with a magazine here, we could *own* a good deal of the senior market.

With this huge potential before us, we launched *Reminisce* magazine in January of 1991. (That's the cover of the Premiere Issue above.)

By the way, Bobbi named that magazine. We were flying somewhere and I was describing this new nostalgia magazine to her, when she asked me what I was going to name it.

"I'm thinking about calling it *Memories*," I said.

"I don't think that's such a good name," she responded. "You can have bad memories as well as good memories. I think you need a title that's more obviously positive."

"And what might that be?" I asked.

In about 10 seconds she said, "Reminisce".

I knew in an instant that was the perfect title. But I couldn't resist needling her. "Couldn't you have made this appear to be a little more difficult? We've been throwing around names for several weeks now!"

I had our Art Director, Jim Sibilski, work up the logo as soon as I got back, and the nostalgic flair he gave that *Reminisce* title (see above) looked great.

We combined it with the tag line *The Magazine That Brings Back the Good Times.* On the contents page is this thought: "Nostalgia is like a grammar lesson...you find the present tense and the past perfect."

Each of our consecutive magazine launches just seemed to be better than the previous one, and *Reminisce* was no exception. Within 11 months of that January '91 launch, we found this new/old magazine wasn't just a hit, it was a homer!

This nostalgia-oriented magazine was our first magazine to top 1 million subscribers in its first year! In fact, it hit the million mark on Nov. 22, 1991 and was at *1.2 million* by the end of its first year!

There was a maze of mailing lists available for the senior market, and we kept at it with good success. *Reminisce's* paid circulation hit *2,158,000* in January 1995. Again, gift subscriptions contributed greatly to that growth.

Soon we heard the same thing we heard when we launched *Country*: "Please go monthly." This time we immediately knew how to respond. We don't learn fast, but we remember well.

We offered six issues of *Reminisce EXTRA* on the "in-between months" for an extra $9.98 and quickly added 393,000 subscribers who wanted the extra edition.

Both *Reminisce* and *Reminisce EXTRA* continue to be a great nostalgic success. Now, on to another surprise success.

Hitting the road with readers. Our Travel Division became a reality shortly after our subscribers began showing a keen interest in visiting other people's farms. Rural folks we'd featured often told us that some of our readers made special trips to stop in at these farms or ranches.

But there was one letter in particular from a Southern farmer that triggered my thinking about offering group tours. He related that after we'd featured him in one of our magazines, he kept getting visitors—by the *dozens.*

"They're all nice people, but it's taking up way too much of my

> *"Nostalgia is like a grammar lesson...you find the present tense and the past perfect."*

time," he wrote. "People who saw that article just keep showing up at my place. I get rid of four, and an hour later two or four more show up, day after day. Can you run some sort of 'retraction' or something to keep all these people from just driving in?"

Well, since the issue we were working on wouldn't come out for a couple of months, we couldn't do much to help this poor fellow. But it did occur to me that if that many people were interested enough to show up at this farm *uninvited*, how many of them might show up if we *invited* them to join us on a "group tour" to *several* farms we'd featured in our magazines?

We'd recently featured two Hawaiian operations—a pineapple farm, and a 1,000-cow dairy farm where they milked three times a day to serve the tourist trade. It occurred to me that, with winter coming, what could be a better place to start...than with a "farm tour of Hawaii in January"?

As a result, Bobbi's and my first trip to Hawaii was a business trip. We spent a week there checking out sites we felt our readers would enjoy...asking for suggestions from University of Hawaii personnel...getting approvals from the Parker Ranch and various farms for group visits (including small

Life is made up of three age groups—youth, middle age and "You're looking good!"

extras such as picnic lunches or coffee and cookies on their front porch).

Then we stumbled upon something really special: On the island of Kauai, we happened upon a retired farmer from Perry, Iowa who had practiced no-tillage for 2 years back home before moving here, and was now itching for something to do. (No-tillage refers to planting corn or soybeans without plowing—the planter puts the seed, fertilizer, weed and insecticide chemicals down in a single pass, cutting costs and erosion as well.)

This new minimum-tillage practice was catching on across the country, and many farmers were curious to see how it was done, firsthand. So the idea occurred to me, if we could have a *field demonstration* of no-tillage as part of our tour, we'd *really* have something to attract our readers!

> ## *"Imagine that—a tax-deductible tour for farmers!"*

Why, that might even make part of it *tax deductible* for farmers wanting to check out this technique.

Convinced this would be a big draw, I rented 12 acres of farmland in Kauai near this ex-Iowan's home and worked out an agreement with him for planting and caring for it. Later—since we still had a good relationship with Allis-Chalmers—I arranged to have one of their new no-till planters shipped over (which they did free for the exposure it offered).

I told the farmer to time the crop for our January visit, and that once we gave him the go-ahead, we wanted him to plant just 16 rows of corn every 2 weeks. These 16-row segments would allow our tour members to see the crop at all stages of growth, from just coming out of the ground to maturity. This would add a great deal to their learning experience.

Back home, with everything finally arranged, we started promoting the "Hawaii Farm Tour" in our magazines. We were surprised at first how well this tour sold through *Farm Wife News*...until we thought back to our farm background and remembered that farmers always think they're *too busy* to get away until their wives convince them they're not!

During our advance trip, we'd taken numerous color pictures of our rented land in Hawaii to use in our promotion. Plus, we asked the Iowa/Hawaii farmer to take and send us photos every other week to keep us up to date ...and we shared these in our magazines, too.

This whole project proved to be an exhilarating challenge to us. We'd never run a tour before, anywhere. We had absolutely no experience at this, nor had we ever offered such an opportunity to our readers before. Of course, no other farm magazine had offered any kind of trip before, either. We were the pioneers, and we had no idea what to expect.

We were overwhelmed! You've seen that expression several times before in this book, but we just kept hitting homers when we sometimes didn't know for sure whether we were even going to get a turn at bat.

Actually, "overwhelmed" is even putting it mildly. In the first 3 weeks, *over 500 people* had sent in their reservation forms with $100 down payments attached!

The tour operator in Chicago handling the bookings had trouble believing us when gave him updates by phone. So he kept coming up to our Wisconsin offices to see for himself. Then he'd race back to Chicago and spend long hours on the phone with airlines and Hawaii hotels, frantically trying to keep pace with us as even more reservations kept coming in.

There's so much more to tell about the early stages of this Hawaii tour, but too much to describe here. The wrap-up is this: The tour operator could only get airline and hotel space for _864_ people the first week. So we quickly offered a carbon copy of the same tour the following week and soon had _480_ more confirmed reservations on that one!

We turned away at least a hundred more—additional space just couldn't be found. Our company books validate all this. And we paid taxes based on these audited figures of _1,544 travelers_.

With planeloads of farmers heading to Hawaii (the vast majority of whom had never been there before, and some who had _never been on a plane before_) from a number of different airports, we hurried there ahead of them to get ready to greet them and make preparations for conducting daily seminars and tours.

To assure we packed as much information as possible into the seminars—both to give farmers their money's worth and to satisfy the IRS for those planning to deduct part of the trip—we gave 15 no-tillage experts and their wives a free trip in exchange for their participation in our programs.

They conducted seminars, made slide presentations, answered questions and facilitated the demonstrations in the field. We broke the tour members into three smaller groups, then alternated them so only one group at a time would be at the lectures while the other groups were making field visits.

The first day our motorcoaches came over the hill and the 12 acres of no-till corn came into view, the farmers on the bus just let out a _whoop_! Here it was, the middle of January, and they were seeing _green corn_. What's more, it was in all stages of growth, from just emerging from the soil to 10 feet high, all in adjacent 16-row segments. Likely, none of them had ever seen corn in that many different stages at one time, and they found it quite a sight.

> "The farmers on the bus just let out a whoop!"

We urged the farmers to get on the tractor for a few minutes to run one of the planters, or participate in other ways when we were in the field. We also encouraged their wives to take pictures of them involved in the tillage demonstrations to show their tax man later, providing photo evidence that this was a working vacation.

Because of the two separate weeklong programs running back-to-back, it proved to be an _exhausting_ 2 weeks for our dozen staffers. I emceed all the programs while Bobbi and the others were at the seminar registration desk, answering questions, directing people, helping in any way they could.

183

If it is bright and sunny after two cold and rainy days, it's probably Monday.

FARMERS RELAXED but learned during our Hawaii tours. They operated corn planters, toured dairies, watched sugarcane harvest and attended tillage seminars.

Bobbi and I were often up late having dinner with the next day's group of speakers (I had to make notes to properly introduce them), and most days began at 4 a.m. to be sure everything was ready when this large group showed up at the regular 7 a.m. opening sessions.

Actually, the fact that these tour groups were this *large* made many things run rather smoothly. With 864 people that first week, we filled *every room* in the Sheraton Waikiki and part of the Royal Palms hotel next door as well. And when you have these kind of numbers, the hotel is eager to respond to any requests on behalf of the group.

For example, our farm couples were used to getting up early at home. In Hawaii, with the 3- to 4-hour time change, they were up well before dawn. So when we asked the hotel to begin serving breakfast at 5:30 a.m., they said, "No problem." They didn't want all those farmers to go down the street and eat somewhere else.

Our people loved it! We readily saw how eager rural people were to travel and experience *our* kind of country-oriented tours—which offered them not only beautiful scenery but interesting information and knowledge they could *use* when they got back home.

During this Hawaii tour, for example, in addition to the no-tillage plots, we arranged for all these people to tour a 1,000-cow dairy farm near Makaha…a pineapple farm (we picked several, sliced them up and passed the sweet pieces to everyone on the bus)…and a sugarcane farm, where we watched them harvest. We also had University of Hawaii agricultural extension people address the group on other phases of local agriculture.

"An estate planning expert answered questions each afternoon..."

And finally, we brought along an attorney who was an expert in estate planning. Each afternoon after our scheduled no-till sessions were finished, he addressed the group and answered personal questions. Many of these farmers had achieved considerable success, but their small-town attorney hadn't been able to provide the financial direction they needed. As a result, many of these farmers never headed to the beach; they just stayed inside from 3:30 to 5 each afternoon to listen and learn.

We continued these no-tillage trips for the following 5 years, conducting *17 separate tours* there in all. Some years we ran two in January and two in March to meet the demand. Our staff got to know Hawaii like a second home, and we learned a *great deal* about the travel industry in general.

Using this newly acquired moxie, we soon branched out into tours of Alaska in July, then finally to various parts of Europe and South America. Of all these, Switzerland turned out to be an especially popular destination for our audience.

We first offered the Swiss tour in late autumn, then in spring and finally in midsummer as well. In 1985, we had our best year in travel up to that

One of the hardest lessons to learn is where your business ends and somebody else's begins.

point, with our tours to Switzerland alone accounting for nearly 1,100 people. We beefed up our travel staff, and we were really rolling...

...Then terrorism hit.

It literally "bombed" our Travel Division. Our tour business went from the top of the rock to rock bottom with a thud.

Rural people are more conservative than urban people, and when they heard and read about terrorism and hijacked planes, they weren't about to climb on any plane that was headed to Europe! As a result, we went from 1,094 people to Switzerland alone in 1985 to only 376 people to all of Europe in 1986.

We didn't know what to do. We couldn't just fire the people who were handling our tours—we were confident that the business would come back in a year or so when the fears subsided. But what were we to do in the meantime?

As stated earlier, "Every problem offers you an opportunity if you come up with the right solution." We proved the truth of that once more when we decided to give a domestic tour a try.

We knew by now that our subscribers had a penchant for traveling, especially if offered our country-oriented type of tour. We needed to take them somewhere *that didn't require flying over an ocean*. We needed an intriguing destination right here in the States.

So...what if we offered our readers a chance to take a winter trip to the Deep South, visiting some of the farms and country people we'd featured in our magazines over the past 3 years or so?

We'd give Northern farmers an opportunity to see firsthand how crops such as peanuts, peaches and tobacco were grown...we'd have these Southern farmers give them a walking tour of their place and answer all their questions. We'd even have farmers from the area on the microphone, describing their crops and points of interest as our bus moved along.

> *"Hi, Bill! Hi, Mary!*
> *I just read about you and*
> *I feel like I know you..."*

With this idea in mind, we went through back issues and pinpointed farms we'd featured in four states—Georgia, Alabama, Louisiana and Mississippi. We were amazed how many farms and families we'd covered in just a few years.

We roughed out a circular route, from Atlanta through Alabama, Louisiana and Mississippi, then back to Atlanta. That way our travelers could get to the departure point any way they wanted—by car, train, plane or motor home—and return to that point 7 days later.

I wrote to a selected group of farmers along this route; I told them Bobbi and I were coming for a brief visit to discuss this potential tour. With that, she and I drove the route and mapped out the trip, choosing farmers and sites we felt our subscribers would find interesting.

Our selection included a peach grower and an Amish farm in Georgia...peanut and pecan growers in Alabama, as well as a trip to a

Expecting success without hard work is like trying to harvest where you haven't planted.

Kindness, like a boomerang, always returns.

OUR DOMESTIC TOURS have proved popular, offering subscribers group trips to Kentucky horse country, the Great Northwest, and New England in late autumn.

AMISH TOUR reminds older tour members of their earlier farming days. Some even tried their hand at shocking oats.

peanut processing plant…a large cattle feeding operation, plus a tour of the beautiful Bellingrath Gardens in Mobile…a tour of New Orleans and lunch on a paddle wheeler while cruising past huge ships in the bay.

It also included a stay-over in Baton Rouge and a tour of plantations near Natchez (one of which at one time had 900 working mules) …a tour of the Civil War battlegrounds at Vicksburg (where we were amazed to learn that Union and Confederate soldiers had sometimes met after dark—smoked, chatted and exchanged letters from relatives—then resumed the fight in the morning!)…and a fascinating stop at a catfish farm in northern Mississippi, where our buses could drive out on the dike separating two large ponds with 90,000 fish each.

We told these Southern farm hosts if more than two buses (84 people) signed up, we would start the second tour a day behind the first, and any additional tours would each be a day behind the previous one. We agreed to a fee per bus with these hosts, and said each group visit would take about a half hour.

With all things in order, we offered our first "Deep South Tour" to readers that winter of 1986, promising them that a Southern farm couple would ride the entire route to narrate the tour between farms, answer their questions and provide local knowledge. We timed the trip for February, the slow month for Northern farmers, when they'd likely get the "February blues" and be itching to go someplace warm.

I don't know why we're continually surprised by the responsiveness of our country-oriented audience, but our readers amazed us again. We quickly sold out _nine back-to-back tours_ of 84 people each!

Our tour members walked out in fields and watched Southern farmers harvest pecans, peaches, huge fields of carrots and vegetables, cotton and peanuts. (We learned some Northerners thought peanuts were grown above ground like grapes on a vine!)

They also watched fish farmers spread feed on ponds, then saw thou-

188

sands of hungry fish "boiling the water" as they fought for the granules. A few minutes later, the group sat down to a picnic fish fry at the farm.

Once more, we'd struck on something with potential—homeland tours—and knew we needed to set up more.

So we flew to California and organized an "Imperial Valley to Napa Valley Tour". It included a tour through California's rich agricultural heartland, with stops at date, strawberry and vegetable farms (including one place with a square-mile *section* of carrots!), tours of vineyards and wineries, then a drive down the coast back to San Diego on famous Highway 1.

When that California tour began selling well, and when we sold out *13 more* of the Deep South Tours the following winter, we got more serious than ever about our tour division as a major profit center. We hired an experienced Tour Manager and began positioning our publications as "The magazines that allow you to visit the people you read about."

We fulfilled that promise by making an even greater effort to include farm families we'd featured among the stops on each trip. As a result, we often observed how tour members would step down from the bus, shake hands with the hosts and

> *"Some tours include homemade cookies on host's front porch..."*

say, "Hi, Bill! Hi, Mary! I just finished reading about you again in the magazine last night and I feel like I know you..."

In 1987, the concern over terrorism lifted somewhat, and the interna-

OUR ALASKA TOUR each summer allows subscribers to see Mt. McKinley and agricultural wonders—such as strawberries that won't fit into the mouth of a pint jar!

We make a living by what we earn; we make a life by what we do for others.

tional portion of our tour business began coming back. Now we were hitting on both cylinders, foreign and domestic, and we promoted the division as "World Wide Country Tours".

As we added magazines, each resulted in new audiences, which helped build tour numbers. We kept adding different domestic tours ("The Great Northwest", "Alaska and the Yukon", "Autumn in New England", "Amish Farm Tour", "Canadian Rockies", "The Grand Canyon/Great Southwest"), and also continued offering foreign tours (to many European countries as well as to Africa, Australia/New Zealand and Mexico).

By 2003, we were offering a choice of 62 different tours—40 to various U.S. destinations and 22 to international destinations. We've now hosted as many as 6,137 travelers in a single year and since the outset of our tour division have hosted *44,788 travelers.*

Many of these have become "repeat travelers" who obviously enjoy our special kind of see-and-learn country-oriented tours. Our records show that 2,066 people have traveled with us five times or more, and that three people have each taken *40 separate tours* with us over the years!

We're now trying several "theme" tours—cooking tours, craft tours and nostalgia tours to tie in with each of our magazines. And a growing percentage of our tour members are now urban people, who are looking for something different in the form of travel.

Our rural tours provide them that outlet, since no one in the travel industry offers the "down-home farm visits" that make up the heart of our tours. What's more, these tours help build our magazines' circulation, because when our tour members return home, they talk excitedly not only about the trip, but about the magazines that host them.

Slow down—the thing you're rushing to may not be as important as the thing you're passing by.

*God gave us two ears and one mouth
so we'd listen twice as much as we talk.*

CHAPTER 24

Now We're Cookin'?

IN 1992, we started thinking about launching a cooking magazine for a number of reasons…but to be quite honest, I think we were just getting "itchy" to try another new magazine.

By now we had experienced six solid no-ad successes—*Farm Wife News*, *Farm & Ranch Living*, *Country Handcrafts*, *Country*, *Country EXTRA* and *Reminisce*.

The one thing we'd learned by now was to be good "listeners". We always made a point to read all the mail, to see what subscribers were saying about our magazines—it was important for us to know what they liked most, what they wanted more of.

It was for this very reason we began considering a pure "food magazine". Throughout 1992 and even before, we kept receiving mail from our subscribers asking for "More food!" and "More recipes!"

They liked our "down-home and hearty" recipes. And they especially liked the way we printed our recipes in a "recipe-card format" that they could cut out and insert right into their kitchen files.

Before I go on, I'd like to comment on those "recipe cards". It has been my experience that sometimes a little ignorance is a wonderful thing, and this is a good example:

Way back when we were putting together the first issue of *Country* (there's nothing more creatively stimulating than having 68 blank pages in front of you and having the challenge of deciding what to put on each of those pages, with no one looking over your shoulder saying "You can't do that!"), I decided we needed to include some food features and have about a dozen good recipes in that magazine.

Now, I don't know squat about cooking. I can make eggs and toast for breakfast and I can turn out a steak on a grill that doesn't taste like a two-bit porterhouse. But I am no "cook".

So, when deciding what type of format to use for these recipes, I thought, *Why not just put 'em in the same size and shape as a recipe card so peo-*

ple can just clip them out and slip them right into their recipe file? With that in mind, I took a card from Bobbi's recipe box, handed it to the art director and said, "Let's do it like this."

Maybe I should have looked at some other food magazines first, to see how *they* did it. Fortunately I didn't. Had I done so, I likely would have concluded there was a reason for *not* doing it that way. But with my ignorance-is-bliss approach, we designed this "Clip & Keep Recipe Card Section" using that card format, with a little scissors sketched along a dotted "cut" line around each card.

Subscribers immediately told us how much they *loved* those recipe cards, and how handy it was to cut them out and slip them into their file box. While we weren't watching other magazines, it became obvious later they were watching us—because there are now several large food magazines that are duplicating our card-size format for their recipes.

Anyway...late in 1992, we began to seriously consider responding to all those subscribers who were pleading for "more food, more recipes". We couldn't satisfy that request within our current magazines, because—with our consistent 68 pages in each issue—if we added more food, it would mean deleting other favorite features that readers would miss.

> **"I've learned that a little ignorance is sometimes a wonderful thing..."**

A new magazine featuring *only* food could be the answer, and it just might be a huge success.

Still, we had some trepidation about going this route: Doing so might cost us some of our subscribers to *Country* and especially *Country Woman*, which had always carried a good-size food section.

Offsetting this was our optimistic viewpoint that the gain could greatly exceed the loss. If we lost 100,000 subscribers collectively from those magazines but garnered a million subscribers to this new one, we'd still be way ahead.

What supported this thinking is this had been the case with each of our subsequent launches. Predictably, we'd lose a number of subscribers via the migration from one of our "old" magazines to each new one, but the huge influx of new subscribers was always more than enough to offset it.

There was still another concern that gave us pause: Up to now, we'd made our living in "niches"; we'd launched magazines by defining voids and filling them. This time it would be different. By moving into the food field, we'd be taking a bold step away from our proven niche approach.

And maybe not, since we felt there was a niche for *our* kind of recipes. Still, there was already a buffet of food magazines out there, and launching a cooking magazine of our own meant we'd be taking on the "big boys", the *Bon Appetits* and *Cooking Lights* published by Conde Nast and the *TIME* magazine group.

We gave that a lot of thought, but eventually it was that very *challenge* of moving up to the majors that stirred our creative juices on a whole new

THIS IS MY DOODLING as I started thinking about a food magazine, then began sketching out topics and pages for the first issue. Many of these features are still regulars today in what became *Taste of Home* magazine, our biggest success ever.

level! We felt we could make our food magazine *different* enough to stand out from the crowd through five unique approaches:

1. This new food magazine would be sort of a "magabook". That is, it would be a magazine and cookbook in one. The "cookbook" would be a center section of *32 pages* of recipes in our recipe-card format. Then it would have 36 "magazine pages" wrapped around it to make up the 68-page issue.

That center section of recipe cards would be a "Pullout Section" that could be easily removed. (We later told potential subscribers, "With a 1-year subscription, you can combine these recipe sections and turn them into a 192-page cookbook.")

2. We would concentrate on "down-home comfort foods" gathered from great country cooks, in contrast to the diet-conscious and "trendy" recipes featured in other food magazines, which often seemed better suited for company than family. What's more, the magazine would basically provide a "recipe exchange for good home cooks". Again, we'd view our role as selling a service, not a product.

3. We would promise readers the kind of recipes that can be prepared with readily available ingredients. "You'll likely already have these items in your house; no need to drive to a specialty store for exotic ingredients."

4. Every issue would offer *menus* rather than a bunch of isolated recipes.

Collector's Edition

COUNTRY
Home
Cooking

THE MAGAZINE EDITED BY A THOUSAND COUNTRY COOKS!

Oh, No, It Isn't!
"Just another food magazine?"
No way! See why inside.

Get a FREE COOKIE
from one of the cooks!
(Details on page 2.)

SORRY! Yes, I spilled coffee on this cover I doodled for first issue. The name was changed later, but the ladle and tag line became part of the cover design (as you'll see when you turn to the photo on page 196).

We'd already learned from our audience that when a recipe for a certain dish is offered, cooks want to know what other things to serve with it.

We also knew they liked our "Quick and Easy" and "Meals in Minutes" sections in our other magazines, so we decided to give those a much greater play in this new food magazine.

5. Finally, we knew our success to date had been in producing "people" magazines. That is, magazines "written for people by people". By now we practically had a patent on producing publications filled with material gathered from hundreds of folksy, friendly, chatty reader letters, many of them handwritten.

(One subscriber hit it right on the head when she wrote, "Yours isn't a magazine, it's a *conversation*. Each issue is like sitting down at the kitchen table with a cup of coffee for a friendly chat with people just like me from all across the country.")

So, with this background, we decided this new one would be more than just a food magazine; it would be a *people magazine* as well. It would feature people with one thing in common—the love of cooking good, down-home food.

Instead of simply running a series of recipes like most other food magazines do, we would give the *story* behind each recipe; we would tell how "This recipe came from my Aunt Helen, who made it every time I visited her house, and Helen in turn got it from her mother, who lived on a ranch in Montana..." or "This recipe was handed down by my Norwegian grandmother" and so on.

This would add meaning and appeal to each recipe; we'd make these recipes come alive by explaining their roots. The recipes would exude warm feelings and sort of take readers on a "trip" as they pictured this same food being prepared in that Montana ranch kitchen.

But...how would we gather these stories behind each recipe for the

Treat arguments like weeds—nip them in the bud.

194

Premiere Issue? In fact, how would we get those kinds of "grass roots" recipes, period, from cooks across rural America?

After more thought, we felt that would be no problem. We knew we had the names and addresses of several thousand great country cooks in our files who had previously sent us recipes, food preparation tips and kitchen time-savers. We would simply write to them, tell them what we had in mind and ask for their best recipe along with the story behind it.

Then we came up with an even better idea: What if we asked some of these great country cooks to be our "Field Editors"? What if we selected one cook in *each state* so we would have broad representation?

Wait—why stop there? Why limit it to one—what if we selected two from each state? That way we'd have a *hundred* editors in the field! And why not also include one from each province of Canada as well?

Wait again—why not think *really* big? What if we asked _1,000_ of these rural cooks to be our Field Editors? *No other magazine* has ever had a "staff" that large!

Yes! We'd list every one of them on our masthead. That listing would likely take up two pages of the issue, but it'd be worth it. Readers would find it interesting to check for the names of the field staffers in their state.

And this would allow us to use the tag line *The magazine edited by a thousand country cooks.* (This still appears on the cover of each issue today.) This tag line would surely catch readers' attention and set us apart.

The excitement grew from this unique idea—we'd really put these Field Editors to work for us. We'd send each of them a newsletter prior to each issue, called "The Newsletter for Field Editors Only".

This little publication would make them feel special and "exclusive",

> *"No other magazine has a thousand field editors!"*

plus it would have a purpose: We'd announce our "theme" for the next issue, then tell them what type of recipes, food tips and kitchen shortcuts we were looking for to fit in with that theme.

With this concept in mind, we sent a letter to 1,400 of the country cooks we had on file, describing this new food magazine we were about to launch and asked if they'd be willing to be one of our "1,000 Field Editors". We explained that if they consented, they would receive no direct fee, but there would be two benefits:

First, they would have the honor of being listed on our masthead as one of our magazine's staffers from their state.

Secondly, since they'd receive this newsletter far in advance of each issue, they would have the chance to fill our needs well before the general public. While we don't pay for small items or mentions, we pointed out, we do pay modest freelance rates for sizable pieces.

Again, the response amazed us. We *hoped* we'd get 1,000 of these 1,400 cooks to agree to this "Field Editor" arrangement. We needn't have worried—we quickly received a "Yes" from over 1,200!

So many were eager to sign on, in fact, that we were able to screen them and base our final decisions on their cooking ability, where they lived and their interest in really helping with the magazine rather than simply being listed on our masthead.

We eventually selected 1,000, then told the extras that we would hold them in "reserve" until if and when any others dropped out.

A New Englander named it. When a new magazine is launched, there are hundreds of things to consider. What approach will make it unique…what features will make it interesting…what kind of picture should be used on the cover, etc.

We already had most of those answers in mind. But we still hadn't made one of the most important decisions—*what should the magazine be called?*

The name of any publication is a key to succeeding because—whatever it is—just seeing or hearing that name will conjure up a certain image and make a certain impression on potential subscribers.

For these reasons, we'd been giving the name for this new magazine a *lot* of thought. Not unlike a couple expecting a new baby, we came up with dozens of names…pondered them…discussed them…and even argued about them.

We wanted a name that immediately projected the hearty but healthy, "homey", practical type of food magazine we had in mind. So the staff suggested names such as *Country Home Cooking…Country Cooks…Dinner Bell…Taste of the Country…What's Cooking…Country Flavor…Country Tastes*…and many more.

When, after a month, we still hadn't settled on *the* name, we decided to seek the opinion of the 1,000 great country cooks who had now agreed to join our staff. The Field Editors took this first assignment to heart and responded with a great many suggestions.

But among all these, one letter and one name for the magazine stood out. It came from Janet Siciak, a great cook from Bernardston, Massachusetts.

"I studied the names you are considering," she wrote, "but I find most of the country-oriented ones ambiguous—they suggest nothing extraordinary or unusual to set your magazine apart from the myriad of food magazines already on the market.

"I'm sure you want the title to conjure up the kind of expectant anticipation you get when you're offered a peek into a dear friend's heirloom recipe collection; a title that suggests food that is authentic, is kid- and husband-approved and practical enough not to call for exotic ingredients.

"The homey feeling you want to instill in readers is, *'What's in the pot on the stove that smells so good?'* With that in mind, the title I think conjures up those feelings is *'A Taste of Home'*."

PERFECT! That's it! Our staff agreed immediately that title was right on the money. That's *exactly* the kind of image we wanted to project with this new magazine.

We soon got the go-ahead from our trademark attorney, then gave the title to our art department. Our Art Director, Jim Sibilski, decided to work a soup ladle into the design to achieve the desired down-home, "pot on the stove" type feeling. After several tries, he came up with a logo we all liked.

We called Janet Siciak to tell her we'd chosen her suggested name for the magazine, congratulated her and informed her that, in appreciation, we'd arranged for her to receive a special food treat from one of our subscribers every month for the following year.

She was delighted to hear all this, and during our chat mentioned several things she liked about the two of our company's magazines she was al-

No matter how serious life requires you to be, everyone needs a friend to act goofy with.

RECIPES are turned "sideways" on pages and are designed to fit into recipe boxes.

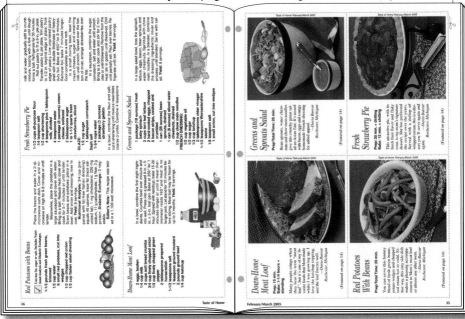

197

ready receiving.

"I like your tried-and-true recipes," Janet said, "and I particularly like the way your magazines offer a method of networking, tying people together across the country.

"I appreciate the fact that your magazines are very positive and uplifting and aren't 'demanding'—they never tell me and other readers to 'Lose 10 pounds before Christmas!' They just let readers be themselves."

No wonder Janet came up with the perfect name for our new food magazine. She pretty much described our publishing approach to a T.

More ways to make it unique. With its title now firmed up, we worked hard on putting together the Premiere Issue of *Taste of Home*. We were well aware we were taking on some stiff competition in an already crowded field, and this magazine had to be *different* in as many ways as we could come up with. Here are a few ways we accomplished that:

"By our fifth issue, it became the highest circulated food magazine in America!"

We did indeed list every one of those Field Editors on a two-page masthead inside headlined, "Meet the 1,000 Cooks Who Help Edit This Magazine!" We included a map of the U.S. and Canada, with a "dot" in each state and each province to show the location of at least one of these Field Editors.

We did a full-fledged article on one of these cooks, entitled, "Here's One of Our 1,000 Editors…and Here's Her Favorite Meal". Plus, we ran pictures and a short background piece on six of these people and promised to do the same with others in future issues.

Another feature was "Taking a Trip With Food". Part of the fun of taking a trip to another area of the country is enjoying the local foods and the special ways they're prepared. So this regular feature, we explained, would vicariously take readers to Virginia to show how the locals prepare Virginia ham…to Mississippi to show how cooks there prepare Mississippi catfish…to Idaho to show new ways to prepare potatoes…and so on.

Other features included, "How I Get My Kids to Cook"…"What's Cooking Across the Country?" (using our network of 1,000 editors to tell what's current in their kitchens, gardens and produce markets)…"My Mom's Best Meal"…"Getting to Know Herb"…"Cooking for a Crowd"…"What I Add to Make _____ Special" (how to make ordinary foods extraordinary, such as my wife's trick of adding 3 tablespoons of cinnamon red-hots to her peach pie filling)…and "How I Got My Kids to Eat…Broccoli" (with a different food in each issue).

The Premiere also promised a "National Recipe Contest" in every issue, featuring a different category each time. The Grand Prize? "A dinner for eight…cooked by one of our Field Editors..*in your home!"*

There were a lot more features in this first issue likely never seen in a food magazine before, such as "Our Family's Favorite Grace"…"How to Publish Your Own Cookbook"…"Cooking Up a Home Business"

Having a child fall asleep in your arms is one of the best feelings in the world.

198

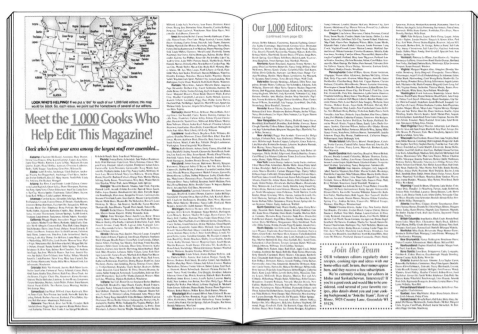

…"Shortcuts Worth Sharing"…and even an irresistible full-page pullout picture titled, "Refrigerator Poster of the Month".

Inside the back cover was "Lifting the Lid on Our Next Issue…", which previewed an even wider variety of articles to come. Plus, we promised to send a FREE COOKIE baked by our food staff to 1,000 of our new subscribers who found *something hidden* in the issue—"Ted's toothpick".

For the cover, we took a picture in our company test kitchen, showing some of our staff baking those cookies so readers could "meet us", then gave it our usual high-gloss finish. With all this and more, we finally went to press and printed 250,000 sample issues.

While we'd tested with fewer than 250,000 copies in the early years when we (1) couldn't afford more and (2) weren't sure what response we could expect, we were now getting much more optimistic and aggressive by sending out far more copies at the test stage—and were "at the ready" to turn out thousands more copies if and when the test looked good.

By now we'd also learned the *best time* to launch a new magazine: in January. The response is best then, perhaps because it's the beginning of the new year and people want something new in their lives…or because people in Northern states are more housebound then and are eager for something different to read…or whatever. No one's really sure; it just works.

So we began putting the quarter million copies of *Taste of Home's* Premiere Issue in the mail on December 26. Since this time we were competing with some of the "giants" of the publishing industry, we were admittedly a little more anxious than ever before.

A person who takes responsibility on his shoulder isn't likely to have a chip there.

…We shouldn't have worried.

This time we were ASTOUNDED! While the response to some of our other magazines had amazed us, nothing came close to what we received with the launch of *Taste of Home*. It was simply incredible!

We kept pumping out more and more samples of the Premiere Issue, 250,000 at a crack, to additional mailing lists as fast as we could. And before we got our second issue in the mail, we had already topped *500,000 paid subscriptions*.

That was just the beginning. We hit *1 million subscribers* on June 23, in less than 6 months!

The pace picked up rather than tapered off—cooks were talking about this new type of food magazine and the word was spreading beyond our mailings. Many orders were referrals—that is, one cook showing another her copy of *Taste of Home*.

Subscription orders kept streaming in, and by the time we put our fifth issue (Aug/Sept) in the mail, we'd passed *Bon Appetit* and became the highest circulated food magazine in America with *1.7 million* subscribers! Again, that was in just 10 months, in November of our first year.

During *Taste of Home's* second year, it grew by an average of 28,000 new subscribers per month. Its circulation soon passed that of *Sports Illustrated*, *TIME*, *Woman's Day* and many other majors that had been published for years.

By February of 2000, *Taste of Home* had *5.3 million* subscribers, making it the *sixth largest magazine in America*. Here's another way to put that in perspective: At that point, *TOH* had a larger circulation than either *Sports Illustrated* (3.2 million) or *TIME* (4.1 million).

This huge growth had many additional benefits we hadn't anticipated. For one, we could now draw on multiple new mailing lists—ranging from *Better Homes & Gardens* to *Sunset* and even food catalog lists. These lists hadn't worked with our previous publications, but they did now—because people, no matter what their interests, *eat every day*.

> *"Food in any photo has been prepared three times…"*

Taste of Home's success brought a whole new audience to our door. We began publishing a wide series of cookbooks to meet the demand, which led to doubling the size of our food staff and tripling the size of our test kitchen. Our book division soon became incredibly successful.

Overall, since 1996, we have sold and shipped over 27 million books, accounting for over half a billion in gross dollar sales.

With this growth, our costs have soared, staff-wise and grocery-wise. We buy *lots* of groceries. With all the food testing we now do for *Taste of Home* and all these cookbooks, maybe we should have started our own grocery store! We now receive and screen about *65,000 recipes* per year.

Each of our recipe contests draws up to 10,000 entries, and testing the best of these takes an endless supply of groceries. Especially when you're

People who do things that count don't stop to count them.

My Mom's Best Meal

Her mother's home-cooked meals fostered full stomachs, fond memories and enduring family ties.

What's Cooking Across the Country?

Readers share food news and views from their communities.

MONTANA—"Our church's Women's | with turkey and
Ministries

Our Family's Favorite Grace

Odessa, Texas. *Father, we th
sends us all that's good. Gi
love and serve Thee day by*
 • "I wrote this table pray
it frequently," says Marge
*Thank You for this food. Th
for our family and friends,
this land of ours, where we
You, Lord, for everything, w*
 • Adalene Palke of Omah
a farm in Nebraska, and our

SAYING GRACE is as much a part of the holiday meal as
the main course. Many of the prayers shared here by readers

Men Who Run the Range

Kitchen Clatter Is Music to His Ears

WHEN Tom Guenther (below left) of

aroma that was as much a part of the
season as Santa Claus," he remembers.
 Tom also has developed his own
recipes, including Chocolate Celebration Cake and Bear Meat Chili. "It's

Ted Dropped His Toothpick— Can You Spot It?

*Find the hidden toothpick drawing in this issue...
and you might win a great prize!*

THIS MONTAGE shows some of regular features *Taste of Home* subscribers love.

ANOTHER PACKED HOUSE, top photo, listens attentively at one of our cooking schools in Fargo, North Dakota. Above, our professionals who conduct schools.

mindful of this: *Any time you see a photo of food in any of our magazines or cookbooks, that food was prepared at least twice, and maybe more.* Here's why:

We never feature a recipe our home economists haven't actually tried and tasted in our test kitchens. So when it's first prepared for testing, that's once. If it's then selected to be published in one of our books or magazines, that recipe is prepared again later to be photographed in color. That's twice.

But setting up that picture in our photo department "just right" may take a good deal of time, and the food—from being under bright lights— may no longer appear fresh. So, that's when the *third* preparation comes in.

This latest version of the recipe is called "the hero" by our photography staff. When everything's finally ready for the shot, they call, "Bring in the hero!", and that third preparation replaces the second in exactly the same position. If the staff later decides the photo isn't "perfect", stages two and

202

three may be repeated again.

And *that's* why every food you see in our magazines has likely been prepared at least two, three or even four times.

I asked Janaan Cunningham, the head of our still-growing food staff, to estimate how many recipes are prepared in our three large, modern test kitchens each year. She did some figuring and came up with *12,000 to 14,000!*

As I said, we buy a LOT of groceries.

About now you're probably asking, "Who eats all this food?"

Well, our company "test team" consumes some during their regular taste trials. And our kitchen staff of about 30 (home economists, dietitians, assistants, plus five food stylists and two photographers) takes the leftovers to their families. While these take-homes are a nice bonus for the food group, they also help us select recipes that are "kid- and spouse-approved".

Taste of Home, with its 5.3 million subscribers, not only became our new flagship, it singularly changed the direction of our company. It led us to other huge opportunities in the food field and other fields as well.

More importantly, it taught us that we no longer had to limit ourselves to small "niches" or "voids" with new magazine launches. We now knew we could invade occupied territories and succeed by using our unique, people-oriented, no-advertising, conversational approach.

In fact, we eventually did that four more times with additional launches. In the next chapter I'll tell you how and why we went for a second helping in the food category…and while *Taste of Home* remained the main course, the second one turned out to be a surprisingly great dessert.

But first, I want to tell you about an acquisition we made.

We bought a "school". I've never been very big on mergers and acquisitions. I know about all those so-called economies of scale gained by joining two companies—you have only one accounting department, one HR department, one computer department, etc.

But then there's the downside. There's often confusion of who does what, who reports to whom, the need for long meetings to reorganize, an increase in bureaucracy…and always some people with hurt feelings because their position at the new company is different than it was at the old one.

To my way of thinking, it's sometimes a little like buying a used car. You buy the problems that were behind the previous owner's decision to sell. Better, I've always felt, to start from scratch and build the company from

No one gets dizzy from doing good turns.

within rather than look for growth from outside.

Yet, with all that said, and those beliefs growing even stronger over the years, I kept casting a wistful eye at this little company over in Madison, Wisconsin. It was called Homemaker Schools, and it had been hosting "cooking schools" throughout the Midwest for several decades. With the steady growth of our food department, doing something like that seemed a perfect fit for us.

I considered just starting up a series of cooking clinics like theirs on our own. But this company already had the formula, the experience, the home economists who "taught" at these schools, plus the necessary contacts with a group of food companies that were sponsoring these schools.

All this, and then in 1995 I learned the owner was ready to retire and interested in selling. We negotiated, then closed the sale quickly.

We moved their staff into our offices and pretty much gave them a free hand, since they knew this business far better than we did. What we added were two things—we changed the name to *"Taste of Home Cooking Schools"* and began promoting them to our millions of subscribers, offering far wider exposure than these schools ever had before.

The growth was immediate and huge. The schools are sponsored by firms such as Crisco, Nestle, Campbell's Soup, Reynolds and Kikkoman.

Anyone who has ever attended one of these schools will agree that the professional home economists who conduct these programs are *entertainers* as well as great cooks. Attendees have a great deal of *fun* at these events and travel great distances to be on hand for the laughs and the learning.

They enjoy the freebies, too. Recipes are prepared on stage using each sponsor's products, and each person in attendance is given a "goody bag" containing coupons for and samples of the food products demonstrated on stage.

This acquisition of Homemaker Schools proved to be an excellent move. The schools have continued to grow over the years—we now host more than 300 of these cooking schools in 48 states (all but Hawaii and Alaska). With an average attendance of over 800, we now greet and teach more than 250,000 "country cooks" annually.

The schools are a perfect partner for us. First our magazines keep you supplied with a variety of great recipes…then once a year our trained home economists come to your state to *show* you how to prepare them.

The difficulties of life can make us bitter…or better.

204

Even if you're on the right track,
you'll get run over if you just sit there.
—Will Rogers

CHAPTER 25

Hmmm...Anyone for Seconds?

AFTER *Taste of Home* was off and flying, it happened again—readers kept pleading with us once again to "Go monthly", just as they had with *Country* and *Reminisce*.

But even though both *EXTRAS* had been easily sold and handsomely profitable, this time we gave it a good deal of thought before moving ahead with a second food magazine on the in-between months. We concluded we weren't going to make this one just another *EXTRA*.

We'd now learned that each of these *EXTRAS* delivered only a *portion* of the "parent's" circulation. For example, *Country EXTRA* delivered only a quarter of *Country's* circulation; that is, only 25% of the original subscribers—one of every four—had shown they were willing to double their subscription price to receive six extra issues.

By 1997, *Taste of Home* already had over 3 million subscribers. So coming out on the in-between months with a new one called *Taste of Home EXTRA* would have been the easy way to go.

We could likely have attracted a quarter of those subscribers—again with very little promotional cost—and had ourselves an additional magazine with 750,000 subscribers. Most publishers would likely lick their chops at that kind of easy profit potential.

Instead, we decided to shoot much higher...so high, in fact, that if we succeeded, we just might have another success as great as *Taste of Home*. To do so, we decided to aim at a whole new, *younger* market.

Our mail has always been our pipeline to what our subscribers are thinking. Scanning it has repeatedly steered us in the right direction. Through these letters, we had become increasingly aware of the *pressure* being put on today's young cooks.

In many cases, both parents work away from home, and when they return each evening, they're stressed to put a good, nutritious meal on the table *fast*. This, we decided, was a new, ripe market for us. These young people could make great use of a magazine featuring "meals in minutes".

Sharing your time is showing your friendship.

Taste of Home's

QUICK COOKING

Rapid Recipes with Homemade Taste

*Satisfying soups...freshly baked breads...
and prize-winning stovetop suppers.*

We had another reason for thinking the timing was right for this type of magazine. We'd noted a growing concern among our older subscribers regarding their married children and their grandchildren; they worried that these young families weren't getting enough wholesome, home-cooked meals.

Many of these older letter writers emphasized that the evening meal was more than just about food; the evening meal had been special to their families for other reasons as well. "It's when we all gathered to talk over our day and catch up with what was really happening in our lives," one wrote. "Now they're all darting in different directions to fast-food outlets..."

We knew from these letters that a growing segment of our society was experiencing a problem with this aspect of modern family life. We felt that our older subscribers would give thousands of *gift subscriptions* for this new magazine, since it would tout "Home-cooked meals that you can have on the table as fast as you can pick up fast food and rewarm it!"

We were sure *Taste of Home* "moms" would order it for their sons and daughters in the hope of encouraging them to have those "sit-down-to-gether-as-a-family" evening meals they'd championed.

The more we studied and discussed it, the more convinced we were that this younger, working audience was <u>HUGE</u>. So, instead of offering another *EXTRA*, we'd publish an entirely *different* food magazine. Yet because it would be mailed on the months "in between" each issue of *Taste of Home*, it would still allow that *TOH* audience to get a *monthly* food magazine.

A lot of our staffers contributed ideas, but Coleen Martin of our test kitchen staff came up with the basic concept for this new magazine that would offer *quick* recipes for *busy* families.

A busy young mother herself, she wrote, "It'll be filled with rapid recipes, the kind that help time-pressed cooks turn out a whole meal from start to table in *30 minutes*, including dessert. In fact, many of the recipes will take only 10 minutes or less. And all will be easy to prepare."

With this concept firmly in hand, we held another "reader naming contest" (the winner got a free trip to our offices to help put together the first issue!). From hundreds of entries, we chose *Quick Cooking* and launched

The only thing most people get on a silver platter is tarnish.

206

it in January of 1998. Once again, we'd read the market right and it took off in a flash. We received *over 500,000* subscriptions in the first *3 months* of 1998!

And we'd guessed right about the gift subscriptions—we received a pantry-full of them from our other magazines' older audiences. In fact, the response and growth of *Quick Cooking* in its early stages was even faster than what *Taste of Home's* had been in the same period! *QC* also quickly passed *Bon Appetit* and all other food magazines, and in its *first year* it became the country's *second largest food magazine*!

> ## *"We received over 500,000 subscriptions in the first 3 months!"*

One thing for sure, launching *Quick Cooking* instead of producing another *EXTRA*—to allow *Taste of Home* subscribers to go monthly—proved to be the right decision. Again, based on past experience, the *EXTRA* would have likely yielded 25% of the "parent's" circulation—i.e., 750,000 new subscribers.

By comparison, in January of 2001—once more thanks to thousands of gift subscriptions over the holiday season—*Quick Cooking*, with its "*quick* recipes for *busy* families", hit its peak circulation of *3,054,000* paid subscriptions.

It's tapered off a bit since then, partly due to the dilution caused by the launch of our third food magazine, *Light & Tasty*, in 2001. We started the latter to satisfy requests from diet-conscious cooks, and it's another solid success. The circulation of *L&T* is 1.5 million as this is written.

This one's for the birds. Because it was easier for me to tell how one food magazine led to another, I skipped over a very successful launch in January of 1995. Again alert to potential new markets, we'd noted the incredible increase in bird feeding across the country.

George Harrison, a well-known wildlife author, brought to our attention a study by the U.S. Fish and Wildlife Service that showed *82.5 million Americans* had fed birds in their backyard in the past year. We found that extremely interesting, since it's one thing for people to *talk* about a hobby and quite another for people

to reach for their wallets to satisfy that interest.

We likewise noted a growing interest in flower gardening, pun fully intended. Gardening had become—and still is—the No. 1 hobby across America. What's more, we became aware that many people purposely grow certain types of flowers to attract certain types of birds.

So...it occurred to us, what if we put these two interest areas together and launched...*Birds & Blooms*?

We thought the topic would pair well with our passion for full-color layouts and high-quality printing. The birds and flowers would allow us to do color at its best. On that part we were certainly right—of all of our magazines, even our staffers feel it's easily the *prettiest* one.

Although we never tire of these one-success-after-another stories, I fear you might tire of hearing them here. So I'll simply tell you that *Birds & Blooms* also caught on quickly and topped the *2 million* subscriptions mark in December of 2000—thanks to another year-end burst of holiday gift subscriptions.

I do, though, want to give our staff complete credit for the success of *Birds & Blooms*. Mike Beno, our Editorial Director, initiated the idea for the magazine. I came up with the concept and the title. Then Tom Curl, our President, along with other editors and the art staff turned the idea into reality, from format to finish, with very little of my input.

As you know by now, I'm a collector of "sayings", and one that applies to our talented staff came from Teddy Roosevelt: "The best executive is the one who has sense enough to pick good people to do what he wants done, and the self-restraint to keep from meddling with them while they do it." In other words, stand back and let them do their thing.

Over the years I've carefully chosen and hired some excellent people— good, honest, talented, hardworking, creative editors and artists—who share my passion for turning out "different" magazines...magazines so unique that they can survive and thrive on subscriptions alone. This crew of ours is such an excitable, energetic bunch that I've sometimes had to pull back the reins...but I wouldn't want it any other way.

I'll wrap up the launches of our current 12 magazines here by first mentioning *Country Discoveries*. Launched in 1999, it's a travel-oriented magazine designed to help readers find backroads places and little-known rural sites they'd never find on their own.

It now has a half million sub-scribers and is growing steadily but slowly. That circulation may be highly satisfying to some publishers but is admittedly below what we've come to expect. See, we're not al-ways hugely successful.

> ### *"We sold 200,000 subscriptions before we printed the first issue!"*

Still, we're highly optimistic about our most recent launch, *Backyard Living*, which came out in January of 2004.

The "why" and the opportunity behind *Backyard Living*? It's our feel-ing that most of the large gardening magazines have gone far too upscale. As Mike Beno aptly put it—"They've been Martha Stewarted to death."

In other words, most renovation projects in those magazines look as though the homeowner called in a professional landscaper, plopped down $25,000 to $50,000, then eased into his lawn chair to watch it happen.

By contrast, *Backyard Living* is filled with "Here's what I did to my back-yard and you can do to yours" stories…weekend projects…answers to plant questions…backyard blunders you shouldn't repeat, and so on.

As mentioned earlier, once you have a single success, it's much easier and far less costly to have subsequent successes with "sister" magazines. That's because you can announce and promote those new ones *free* right in your existing publications.

Backyard Living is a great ex-ample of that. According to the magazine's Editor, Jeff Nowak, we sold *200,000* subscriptions *before we printed the first issue*!

Yes, that's how many of our "regular" subscribers signed up for this new magazine before any of them had even seen a sample issue.

We simply described it, an-nounced we were going to launch it and gave them a chance to subscribe in advance so they could be sure they'd receive a copy of the Premiere Issue…and 200,000 people quickly sent in checks.

Actually, we've sometimes received letters from subscrib-

Admit you're wrong when you're wrong and you'll be all right.

ers stating, "We like your magazines so well, when you launch a new one, just send us an invoice!" That's what can result once you establish a loyal following and the trust of your readers.

At any rate, *Backyard Living* got off to another good start with 700,000 paid subscribers near the end of its first year. What, you're probably asking, this newest magazine didn't have a million subscribers in the first 6 months? What a bummer!

No, but *Backyard Living* is growing steadily and we feel it has an extremely bright future. We feel just as optimistic about our fourth food magazine, *Cooking for 2*, which is just coming out of the blocks as this is written. It's not just for empty nesters; it's also aimed at serving young couples just getting started. Combined, those two groups offer a *huge* potential audience.

In all, 12 successes out of 14 tries with ad-free magazines isn't bad. Especially when you consider facts like this: According to Samir Husni of the University of Mississippi, there were *789* new magazines started in 1993, and only *77* of those are still being published today.

In this business, new magazines fall like privates under Custer.

Letting go of something you love isn't easy...
but sometimes it's better for everyone involved.

CHAPTER 26

Toughest Decision Yet...When to Sell

BY NOW you've noted that above each chapter heading in this book, I chose some quote that seemed to fit the content of that chapter. Some are from famous people. The source of others is unknown.

The one above is my own. I just now came up with it, because it fits the emotions of what I'm about to describe.

I don't know if there's ever a right time to sell a company. I do know that if the founder is as intricately involved as I've been with this one, that decision will not be easy. Painful is a better description.

But, after more than 30 years at the helm of this company—seeing it grow from that typewriter in the basement of our home to over 500 employees and 16 million subscribers—I was being urged by my trusted financial adviser, Norb Whittle, to consider selling.

What he told me made sense on a monetary basis. He repeatedly pointed out, "Roy, you have all your eggs in one basket. I hate to be morbid, but if your plane goes down, this company won't be worth nearly as much without you. You're so intricately involved that its value will take a dive if you're no longer around."

I listened to him, but the reasons he was giving me—wholly financial—weren't making much of an impression. As he well knew, the money part of the business was never the main motivator for me.

While I find business challenging, am aware that success is often measured by profits and am human enough to enjoy financial growth, what I always enjoyed most was the creativity and excitement of blazing new trails in an industry that hadn't seen many new ideas since Mr. Curtis started *The Saturday Evening Post*.

Jokingly, I often told Norb, "Just let me know if we're still solvent and growing." Honestly, I seldom even knew what my salary was—my paychecks went directly to the bank.

For me, it was always enough that we were doing well, I had a good marriage, a healthy family and a job I greatly enjoyed. It seemed most of our

Some people are like blisters—they show up after the work is done.

211

employees felt pretty much the same way—they were part of an extended family and were all faring well.

That being the case, what began to bother me about what he was telling me wasn't the financial loss if something happened to me...it was what might happen to our more than 500 employees...and our 16 million subscribers as well.

I was now in my 60s, and I began to agree that it was time to work on a succession plan. Since I was still uncertain as to *when* I'd make the decision to sell, though, I decided to keep the matter entirely to myself.

I quietly and steadily began preparing for it. I already had a strong, talented Executive Team in place and had promoted one of them, Tom Curl, to President, while I moved up to CEO. (This title was a little strange to me, because we were never much into titles; I'd always signed my letters as just Roy Reiman, Editor. That's how I always viewed myself.)

But now I needed the staff to recognize Tom as their new leader, and giving him the deserved title of President helped achieve that. There wasn't much other choice than to bump myself up to CEO.

The Exec Team had recently worked with me to select a "Leadership Team" of about 30 staffers. This proved to be an excellent idea. This group was made up of key staffers who we'd carefully chosen from every different part of the company. We let this group know they were our "executives of the future".

We scheduled quarterly dinners with this Leadership Team, during which we shared details of our plans, programs and problems. To make these gatherings a little special, we held them at a nearby private country club. We always promised everyone would be home by 8 o'clock.

As I began looking ahead, part of my succession plan was a little thing I started doing in meetings. When the staff asked me questions, I responded with, "What do you think?" I urged them to make more of their own decisions, and they did.

I re-emphasized the need to peruse subscriber letters carefully and listen closely to what the readers want. And I continually pointed out that— to be truly creative—you have to be *flexible*, *daring* and *responsive*. The fun of creativity is not knowing where those next surprises and opportunities are going to come from.

> **"I started answering questions with, 'What do you think?' "**

Within a year, a good deal of the succession plan was in place. We now had a great group of employees, top to bottom, which I was confident would keep us headed in the same direction with the character, culture and enthusiasm that had carried us this far.

Even so, I vacillated. I just couldn't pull the plug. A hundred times I must have decided to completely discard the sell plan and just continue down the road and see what happened.

And a hundred times I decided, "No, you need to get this done *now* while

Just when some parents retire, they find the birds who left the nest are homing pigeons.

you're here and can be on hand to direct a smooth transition."

What made this decision even tougher was that it was one of the few things I didn't share with Bobbi. I felt I had to make this decision alone.

I kept changing my mind, and I didn't want her to ride that same roller coaster— "Maybe"…"Maybe not"…"Yes, I'm going to do it now"…"No, I think I'll wait awhile"…"Definitely yes"…"Definitely no". I just kept making those *final* decisions day to day and week to week.

At one point I tried the method Bobbi's taught me to use when you're facing a tough decision: You make a list of the pros and the cons. You list all the positives on one side and all the negatives on the other, then see which list is longer.

Well, I did that, and got up to 14. But it was still even—I had 14 pros on one side and 14 cons on the other!

This company had become such a part of me, I just couldn't let go of it. I was there at its birth…I'd nurtured it from basement to boardroom. And almost to the Board of Trade.

For me it was like putting up a kid for adoption. You wouldn't ever want to do something like that until

> *"I kept making the final decision…day to day, week to week…"*

you absolutely *had* to, and there were days when I felt I didn't *have* to make this decision now. No one was forcing me to do it.

Yet, there were so many reasons why it was the right thing to do and the right time to do it. It's simply a fact that no one can work or continue doing the same thing forever…so hanging on and leaving things as they are can actually be a selfish thing to do.

Some individuals hang on to their company too long; they don't pass the gavel early enough to allow them to be around to advise and supervise the people who are taking over. Then one day something happens and the transition of authority is far from smooth.

So the battle in my brain went on. And on. And on. If it was just me, I'd likely just keep doing this the rest of my life…because this is what I do, this is what I'm good at, and I've loved every minute of it.

But I realized it wasn't just me who was involved. This was no longer just *my* company. This was now our *employees'* company and even our *subscribers'* company.

All this came into even sharper focus when I noted a *Wall Street Journal* article about David Packard, co-founder of the huge Hewlett-Packard conglomerate. He'd died very suddenly and had no type of succession plan in place. It proved to be a nightmare not only for the company, but his kids, none of whom had taken an active part or interest in the company. I didn't want something like that to happen to my family, or to my extended family at the company.

Once all these things became clear to me, the decision came easier. I finally reached a conclusion one Saturday afternoon as I took a long walk

If you watch a game, it's fun. If you play it, it's recreation. If you work at it, it's golf. —Bob Hope

through the woods behind our house. It just suddenly became very clear to me: "It's time. I'm going to go ahead with the sale."

Interestingly, while it had taken me a *long* time to get there, I never wavered from that point on. In a way, I felt a sense of relief. Months of turmoil and uneasy sleep were finally over.

That evening I told Bobbi about it, and shared all my reasons for finally coming to that conclusion. This time—unlike that evening way back when I told her "I'm quitting my job"—she didn't respond with, "Let's talk it over after the kids are in bed."

This time the kids were gone; we were empty nesters. She was very calm about it. She said she knew the decision was difficult for me, but that she was completely comfortable with it. She agreed it was time to do it.

We then talked about more travel, more golf, more visits to the grandchildren, etc. But I warned her the months immediately ahead weren't going to be easy. I now had the *if* and *when* part taken care of. The next difficult part would be the *whom*.

Who would we trust to take over this company? Who could we find who would be willing to put the word AUTONOMOUS in all capital letters…and let us just keep doing our thing?

My assumptions about the long selling process and it not being easy were accurate. The process was downright stressful. Yet it gave me the opportunity to meet some incredibly interesting, highly successful people.

That—and how we spared our employees the usual, "Oh, my gosh, we're gonna be sold!" anxiety before and after the sale—is a story in itself.

*Those who fear the future
are likely to fumble the present.*

CHAPTER 27

'Fix Roof While Sun Is Shining'

THE CHALLENGE I was facing now was how I would prepare our employees for the sale of our company and avoid a panic mode.

We'd always done things "out in the open" at our company, and I didn't want to start sneaking around now. I wanted our people to learn about the potential sale from *me* before there was a chance they might hear whispers or rumors of it from anyone else.

I've always contended that I type better than I talk, so I turned out a lengthy memo and distributed it to *all* employees, even the part-timers working back in the warehouse and on the shipping dock. I worked up to the sale part gradually in the memo, so they wouldn't be shocked, then explained that, after many months of consideration, I'd decided this was a good time for me to consider a "transition of ownership".

I described how much fun I'd had in starting and growing this company, and that in many ways, "I've been dreaming with my eyes open," I wrote. "Yet, as much as I still enjoy what I do, and plan to continue to do much more of it, no one can work or continue doing the same thing forever.

" 'Better you should fix your roof while the sun is shining,' it's said, and it's time for me to do just that," I explained. "It's far better to do something that's wisely planned and completely thought through than having to make sudden decisions based on need.

"I owe my family—and all of you—the comfort and security of having the transition of ownership fully settled while I'm still healthy and vigorous enough to be a part of the process—a process hopefully so smooth that you and our subscribers will scarcely notice any change has taken place."

As I began writing this chapter now, I looked for but couldn't find that memo in my files. I needed it to recall those quotes above. But when I asked about it, several employees readily provided copies of it, so apparently they'd found it meaningful enough to be saved.

The memo promised—so they'd have it in writing—that I would do four

Happiness is making a mistake when there's no one around to notice.

215

things as we searched for an acquisition firm:

1. I will never sell the company to anyone who would plan to move it from Greendale.

2. I will be extremely sensitive to how all of our employees and subscribers are taken care of. My name will still be on the door, and how employees and subscribers are treated will continue to reflect on me and my family. That will be as important to me as the price.

3. When I sell the company, *I'll still be here*. I'm still enjoying this "work" far too much to retire. I hope to gradually draw back and spend more time out of the office, but I'll continue to be involved from the creative, editing and supervision standpoint.

4. We will partner up only with a firm that will assure that we can continue operating as independently as possible, allowing us the freedom to pursue the same creative route that has brought us success to date.

Then I added the coup de grace: I described to them the "bonus of all bonus programs", which assured each of our employees that *there would be no cutbacks or layoffs or major changes for at least 3 years after the sale.* (This part could be the reason why staffers found the memo worth saving.)

Here's why I included and spelled out this unique bonus package that, to my knowledge, had never been offered by any company before in connection with a sale:

I was well aware that even though our employees trusted *me*, they may not be as ready to trust the *buyer*. It's common knowledge that when companies are sold, bold promises are often made that "Nothing will change". Then a few months later 20 people are let go here, a department is eliminated there, and a different direction is charted.

> *"Everyone's heard, 'The company's being sold...but there'll be no changes...' "*

I feared if I didn't address this situation in my memo or in person, there would be a great deal of *anxiety* in our ranks during the weeks and months ahead. I didn't want that to happen with our staff. I wanted to come up with a way of eliminating that stress and concern...and I finally did.

So, I shared with them what was sure to be *good news*: I promised, again in writing, a *sizable bonus* that each of them would receive a few days after the closing...and that each of them would receive the very same bonus *again* 3 years later on the anniversary of the sale. Here's how that part of the memo went:

"Bobbi and I have pondered at length about how we can say 'thank you' to every employee who has helped this company grow to its unbelievable size and success. We gave a lot of thought to some tangible way of expressing our appreciation and eventually came up with a system of awarding *cash bonuses* shortly after the sale of the company is complete.

"Our goal was to create a bonus program that would (1) be fair to everyone and (2) be easily understood by everyone. I feel we've accomplished that in this manner:

"We decided to base these cash bonuses on *tenure*, since the longer any person has been employed here, the longer they've contributed to our success. Therefore, here is what will happen at the time of the actual closing:

You will receive $100.00 for every month
(or part of a month) that you worked here.

"That comes to a cash bonus of $1,200.00 per year for each full-time employee. For example, a full-timer who started here 10 years prior to the sale date will receive $12,000.00 (10 years times $1,200). Part-time employees will receive proportionate shares of the $100.00 per month based on the number of hours worked.

"We have many long-term employees—some who have been here more than 25 years—so this will mean some sizable bonuses to them, which is only fair since they've contributed more to our growth. Likewise, it's fair because every employee—regardless of status or position in the company—is being treated *exactly the same.*

"WAIT! THERE'S MORE!" the memo continued. "We want this company to stay just like it is, with the same people and the same philosophy, after the sale. To assure you this is our intent, and to encourage all of you to remain part of our company 'family' and collectively help our continued growth, here's the second bonus program:

We're going to give each of you this exact same
bonus again if you're still with us in 3 years!

"That's right. You have it here in writing. Bobbi and I will set aside enough of the proceeds of the sale so that those of you who are employed here on the closing date of the sale and are still here 3 years from that date will receive *the same bonus again* at that time.

"So, in the example of the 10-year employee used earlier who receives $12,000.00 at the closing, that employee will receive a *second bonus* of $12,000.00 if he or she is still employed here 3 years from that date.

"Now, we know there will be some special situations. For instance, if an employee should die or become permanently disabled, we'd still pay the entire bonus amount. But if any employee leaves the company for any of the usual reasons (quits, moves, terminated), no portion of the second bonus would then be paid. This should encourage everyone to stay on board, keep our culture the same and spur our growth."

That memo, that promise, that program *worked*. It did exactly what I'd hoped: It eliminated most, if not all, of the *anxiety* regarding the projected sale.

Every employee now knew three important things: That after the sale (1) We *wanted them to stay*. (2) They would *be paid to stay*. (3) All their fellow staffers would be staying as well *for at least 3 years*.

So collectively they were assured that little if anything about the company would change in the foreseeable future. Everyone was now on the same page as we prepared for the upcoming "previews" of the sales process.

If you stay up with the owls at night, you can't soar with the eagles in the morning.

This way they'd all know what was up when a stream of executives from various potential acquirers started touring our offices. What's more, they'd likely be more patient and tolerant as these "suits" came through and asked a lot of questions.

Actually, with that "double bonus carrot" now on their minds, some staffers may have welcomed those interruptions! Seriously, I could detect little if any stress among our people; in fact, it seemed everyone was genuinely upbeat.

Think about it: How many cases can you recall where that kind of attitude prevailed in the hallways of a company about to be sold?

While that was the case inside our offices, I did get a few jabs from CEO friends at other companies when they heard about our unique we'll-pay-you-to-stay 3-year bonus program. "Thanks for raising the bar for all of us, Roy," one said with only a hint of humor.

So, our company and our employees were set to begin the sale process. Now the big job was ahead of us: To choose that perfect buyer.

Again, we'd seek out that acquirer "who could spell AUTONOMOUS in all caps"…one that would help us make a transition so smooth, our subscribers wouldn't be aware any change of ownership had taken place…and one that we felt would keep our employees content and smiling long after they'd collected those big, fat bonuses.

The greatest tragedy in life is people
who have sight but no vision.
—Helen Keller

CHAPTER 28

Screening Buyers Starts with People

AS WE BEGAN meeting with possible buyers, I was reminded of a conversation I had with our only son, Scott, when he was a few months into his sophomore year at the University of Wisconsin-Whitewater. That chat likely set the course for the rest of his life.

I'd always told the kids, "Look, I'll pay your college tuition, but every time you come home, I'm going to ask you, 'What are you going to do when you graduate?' You can change your mind and your answer as you go along, but I want you to continually think about that question as you pursue your studies."

I was basing that condition on my own experience. I'd seen far too many students who were just "going to college", without really deciding on a major or an eventual career. I felt that was a waste of time and tuition. I think you get so much more out of your studies—and give more thought to *which courses* you'll take—when you have a goal or an envisioned job in mind.

Frankly, I thought that was one of the real benefits of Iowa State when I went there. The administration insisted that you commit to your major at the beginning of your sophomore year. So you already started *thinking* about that pending decision all during your freshman year.

I contend that has merit, because nearly everyone will put off a big decision as long as they're allowed. Even small decisions. If you give me till next Friday to decide something…I'll wait till Friday.

Same way with college. If students are allowed to put off deciding on a major for as long as they'd like, most of them won't give that decision serious thought until they're forced to. They can just keep taking liberal arts for as long as Dad and Mom continue to pick up the tab.

(And, you know what? I think some universities don't *mind* that too much; if this student waits until the third or fourth year to finally decide to go in a different direction, it then means that student has to spend another year or two on campus… I also find it more than coincidence that at many colleges today, certain required courses are filled up quickly, thereby

When you live in an old house, the only thing that works is you.

forcing students to spend more than 4 years to get a degree. 'Nuff said.)

Anyway, back to Scott and then to just what all this has to do with our choosing a buyer for the company.

Scott came home for a weekend in the fall of his sophomore year and we went out to a Friday night fish fry. (Almost *nobody* in Milwaukee eats at home on Friday nights; fish fries are a strong carryover from the days when many in this predominantly Catholic city couldn't eat meat on Fridays. Still today, even taverns that don't serve food all week will offer a fish fry on Friday night and be packed to the walls.)

So, even before we ordered, Scott said, "Dad, I know you're going to ask me what I'm going to be when I graduate, and I don't have an answer! I know I want to go into some sort of business, but right now I don't have a clue what *type* of business."

We talked about that a bit, and I finally asked, "How would you like to spend some time with a few business friends of mine, shadowing them for a day to see what they do, and get an idea of whether their type of work would interest you?" He liked that idea a lot.

So, next day while I was spending my usual Saturday morning at the office "catching up", I wrote a letter and sent it to about 30 of my business friends. The letter went something like this:

"How would you like to be a 'college professor' for one day? The reason I ask is, since my son, Scott, can't decide on the career he'd like to pursue, I'm suggesting that he drop out of college for the upcoming semester and instead take a 'Crash Course in American Business'.

"And I'm asking *you* to consider being one of his instructors for just one day. The pay won't be too great, but it will be twofold: First of all, Scott will take you to lunch at the restaurant of your choice. Don't even think of picking up the tab, because none of his professors at Whitewater have bought him any lunches to date.

> *"How would you like to be a 'professor' for one day?"*

"Secondly, look at the enclosed list of other friends who are receiving this letter. At the end of each day, Scott will write a complete report of what he learned during the time with his mentor, and whether he feels that would be something he'd like to consider as a career.

"That report will then be sent back to each 'professor' not only so it can be checked for accuracy, but so anything that might be confidential can be deleted. That could be important because here's the second part of the 'payment': You can request a copy of any or all of Scott's reports written after his days with the other mentors. You might find it interesting to learn the intricacies of their jobs, as well as what Scott concludes about that profession as a possible course in life."

I then emphasized that, if Scott's shadowing them for a day would be any inconvenience or not permissible for any reason, I would fully understand and it wouldn't harm our relationship in the least if they said no. On the oth-

A study of economics usually reveals that the best time to buy anything is last year.

er hand, if they would like to suggest some other business friends who might be interested in allowing Scott to spend time with them for this career pursuit program, it would be appreciated.

The response was touching. I had no idea I had such good friends! Only two turned me down, yet even they along with the others suggested more "professors" who might enjoy showing Scott the ropes. (I've learned that most people who love their job—and that includes me—enjoy detailing it to others. They're likely to drop everything to give a tour of their facilities…especially someone who is considering that path for a career.)

Scott ended up with *43 mentors*. Once the schedule of on-site visits was set, he did indeed drop out of college for the next semester to take this "Crash Course in American Business" instead.

These friends went the extra mile to give Scott *quality* time and a chance to really *experience* their line of work. In fact, one of them who was an executive at United Airlines took Scott to the airport on his day off! He said he wouldn't be able to give Scott the time and attention needed on a "normal day".

> *"Scott seemed surprised that all these executives were such nice people…"*

So that day, Scott shadowed the United agents behind the ticket counter, sat in on a meeting in the airport manager's office, spent an hour in the control tower—he even got to see where those conveyors tote off your luggage and how it's sorted back there in the bowels of the terminal. (I envied the latter; I've always wanted to see how that works.)

Scott spent a day with one of my best friends, Don Massa, the CFO of Journal Communications, which publishes Milwaukee's daily newspaper. He tagged behind Don at meetings, toured the facility, then went out with an ad rep to help sell an ad that appeared in the next day's paper.

He spent a day at WTMJ-TV and accompanied a rep who sold "airtime", then stood behind the camera during that evening's 10 o'clock news. He spent a day with several different bankers…with an insurance adjuster…with an express delivery executive…with a construction foreman…with a travel agent…with an investment officer…he even spent a day at the Chicago Board of Trade. And much more.

Each evening Scott wrote up his report, describing the executive's job and whether it held interest as a possible career. And each day he'd come home and tell me how *nice* these people had been, not just to him but to others as well, that they were just genuinely good, kind, honest people.

That seemed to surprise him. And in discussing it with him, I learned that he—like a lot of college students—held the opinion that really successful executives probably *aren't* "nice people". They assume such business leaders tend to be arrogant, demanding and maybe a tad dishonest.

That's when I told him that he had it *100% wrong*. "Most people who are successful over the long term are usually very *good people*," I said. "That's not only how they got that way, more importantly that's how they

Children are a great comfort in old age. And sometimes they help you get there faster.

221

stay that way. They're also usually self-assured; they have less to prove.

"Sure, there are the 'new rich' and quick successes who get a little big for their britches and become demanding due to their supposed stature, but those people *don't last*. It doesn't take long for others to spot those traits, and no one wants to work for or with a jerk. So, in the long run, most really successful people are extremely *good* people. They're honest and trustworthy, and it's likely they're charismatic and interesting to be around."

Scott's told me several times since then that I was definitely right on that point, and that he enjoys being around successful people for all those very reasons.

As a side note, I might add that this "Crash Course" was invaluable to Scott—based on what he learned, he decided he wanted to go to one of the best financial colleges in the country (he chose the University of Denver), that he wanted to learn the stock trade first (his first job was with Dean Witter) and then he'd like to eventually run his own investment firm (he now does; it's called Hexagon Investments, a name derived from his being one of six children).

Now, just what the dickens does all this have to do with the sale of our company? It's that I was continually reminded of that years-earlier discussion with Scott when we began meeting the individuals at large companies who showed an interest in acquiring us. One by one, they proved to be *very good people.*

They were incredibly successful, each had been that way for a long time, yet they were personable, sensitive, had a great sense of humor and obviously enjoyed life. At the same time, they were extremely intelligent, motivated, energetic and charismatic—sparks just flew off some of these individuals.

We began the sale process by contracting with a broker. We chose A.G. Edwards of St. Louis after we found them to be a group of up-front, likable people who listened well. They made a concerted effort to learn what our company was all about…what made us unique…and came to understand the specific kind of buyer we were looking for.

We told them the relationship with this buyer was going to be as important as the price. In fact, we would be willing to accept less if the fit was right. If we were going to sell this special kind of company, it had to be to a special kind of buyer.

> *"The relationship with the buyer was as important as the price…"*

With that, we compiled our "Offering Memorandum", or what is often referred to as a "Prospectus". Either way, it's the complete story and details of a company's history.

Frankly, our five top execs and I drove the Edwards people nuts with our editing of this lengthy document. The Edwards group had never worked with a publishing company before, so they'd never experienced people so picky about little things like semicolons, quotes, punctuation, spelling and

An expert is somebody who is more than 50 miles from home and has no responsibility for implementing the advice he gives.

phrasing. It likely wasn't a coincidence later that several of the prospects commented that, if nothing more, it was "the best *written* memorandum I've ever seen!"

This Offering Memorandum was sent to over 50 potential acquirers selected by the Edwards people. We were proud to learn these prospects were so impressed that *20* of the 50 bid in the first round. Two out of every five. That's unheard-of, we were told. And even some of the ones who didn't bid said, "It sure was well written!"

From there, we carefully weeded out more than half of the 20 that we didn't think would work out for this reason or that. After a week of discussions, we selected *seven* of these potential buyers that we felt were a good fit.

…And then the tension really began, with multiple meetings, company tours, PowerPoint presentations, lengthy discussions and a lot of late-night dinners. Sometimes the conversation was so intense, I later didn't remember what I'd eaten.

You'll never lead the band if you're not willing to face the music.

We judge ourselves by what we are capable of doing;
others judge us by what we have already done.

CHAPTER 29

Which Suitor Suits Us Best?

WE INVITED EXECUTIVES from these seven firms to meet with us, but prior to their coming, we required each of them to sign a confidentiality agreement.

We didn't want the fact that we were considering a sale to become public. What if later we determined *none* of these firms was a fit for us and changed our mind? We'd have subscribers and others upset for nothing.

With that, the get-acquainted sessions began. We began confidential presentations to these groups of dark suits one at a time, each taking up a full day. All these meetings took place at the law offices of Quarles & Brady, one of Milwaukee's top law firms.

We made lengthy presentations with charts, graphs and samples. I led off describing the company's background:

"If you came here today thinking that you're going to hear and learn about a company that's prosperous and predictable, we don't fit the mold of the latter.

"But if you came here to learn about a company that's grown by leaps and bounds and launches…a company whose people enjoy doing things *differently* and, better yet, doing things that haven't been tried by anyone else before…a company with a 'You wanna *bet*?' attitude…then you should find the next few hours pretty exciting. Hopefully what you'll hear and see today will get your adrenaline going, just like it gets ours going every day when we show up for work.

"Doing things differently is where we live. Our goal is to provide customers with products they can't find anywhere else, whether it's magazines without ads…group tours to backroads places that aren't on any map…or proprietary products from our Country Store division that have never been in anyone else's catalog or even our own before.

"Our goal is to publish high-quality magazines and books that resonate *class*. Through our publications that are lighthearted and upbeat, we try to get people's chins up and their chests out, and make them proud of who they

Progress always involves risk—you can't steal second and keep your foot on first.

are and what they do."

Then I explained my reasons for deciding to sell at this time (along the lines of what I detailed in Chapter 26).

Tom Curl, our President, followed by detailing where the company was at present and its future potential...John LeBrun gave an in-depth view of our circulation...Mike Kuzma gave an overview of our book marketing efforts...and then Norb Whittle and Jeff Anderson wrapped up with the financial picture. (I noted the prospects always seemed to lean a little closer when looking at Norb and Jeff's financial charts.)

After each of these 8 a.m.-to-noon presentations, we held afternoon break-out sessions, allowing these potential acquirers to sit down personally with a few key editors, as well as with top people from Circulation, Book Marketing, our Country Store catalog division and our Travel Division.

I can't tell you how often I sat in these meetings with a lump in my throat...and how *proud* I was of our people. They were repeatedly asked tough questions...and they never once sounded defensive. They answered eagerly and excitedly, almost as though, "I'm glad you asked that, because you're going to love what I have to tell you!"

I sat there day after day, meeting after meeting, and said to myself, "Man, we really do have a *great* company! What a tremendous *team* we've put together." It made my heart swell every time I watched them perform.

These sessions took up a *lot* of our time, especially for the lead people in our Finance Department, who often spent nights and weekends to come up with infinitely detailed figures and projections requested for the next go-round with the prospective buyers.

But while time-consuming, there was a hidden benefit to all of us presenters: We got to know each other better. We gained an even greater respect for one another.

Being forced to go into this much detail, we learned things about our company we didn't know before. And we surprised ourselves by coming up with new ideas and new potentials right in the midst of these meetings when we learned what some of these newfound capabilities were. Better than anything, we all became even closer friends.

And then there were the dinners. Night after night, we went out to dinner with these various groups, sometimes with the same group for the second and third time. In order to keep these negotiations confidential, we couldn't go to public places. We held them at private clubs, and we had access to only two of them.

So we had all these dinners in the backroom dining areas of the University Club and the Milwaukee Club. It wasn't long before we knew the menu by heart. And got tired of everything on it.

I asked Bobbi to join us at every one of these dinners. She had an assignment—she was in charge of reading "body language". Actually, she'd been doing this same thing for me for years whenever we'd hired somebody for a key management position.

I've learned over the years that Bobbi, and actually all women, are much more intuitive than men. They're more sensitive and tuned in to personality quirks. We guys say, "Hey, he seems bright, he hits a good ball, he tells a good story, he seems okay to me."

And your wife will say, "*Wellll*...I'm not so sure about that. I noticed something that bothered me a bit..." By nature, women have their defense at the ready and their antennae up; they tend to detect characteristics that fly right over most guys. So Bobbi would give me a "reading" every night as we headed home from these back-to-back dinners.

Sometimes I'd sit there at these gatherings and think to myself, *Did I already tell these people this or that? Or was that last night's group?* I didn't want to look stupid by repeating the same fact or clever phrase...yet it was important that they knew some of these things that might enhance their regard for us.

While going through this was highly strenuous for all of us involved, it was also an incredibly rewarding experience. It was exhausting but exhilarating...frustrating but fascinating...arduous but uplifting.

These potential buyers were some *tremendous* people. Obviously, anyone who could afford to buy our company had already achieved a great deal of personal success. People don't reach this level of success by being unscrupulous or by

> *"She had an assignment—she was in charge of reading 'body language'..."*

specializing in the "Find 'em, fleece 'em and forget 'em" approach. Success for that kind of person is normally short-lived.

As I emphasized earlier, people who are hugely successful normally attain that status by being forthright and up-front. It's this reputation that opens doors to future opportunities and fuels their growth. And those were the kind of people we met among these seven groups—smart, ethical, honest, likable people.

One of the unforgettable ones was Teddy Forstmann. His name was already familiar to me through extensive media exposure—he shows up at the same events as Donald Trump, plays in the Pebble Beach golf tournament each year with Vijay Singh (who is sponsored on the PGA tour by Forstmann's firm) and gets a lot of ink for his keen ability to buy and sell companies.

He's exhibited great management moxie as well. Several years ago, he spent mega-millions to buy Gulfstream, the corporate jet firm, with the plan to quickly repackage and resell it. But when he found no buyers, he decided to become its CEO and began operating it himself.

And it's doing well. He let us know in the first few minutes that he'd flown out here in his own G-4...also made a point of letting us know that he doesn't often personally go out to check out a potential acquisition...but that he was impressed enough with ours that he decided to do so.

Near the end of our dinner with Mr. Forstmann, he leaned toward me and asked privately whether just the two of us could go to a side room, or maybe someplace where we could shoot a game of pool. He said that's what he'd

If you lend someone $20 and never see that person again, it was probably worth it.

done effectively during one of his other acquisitions. If we could do that, he said, "I think we could cut a deal in 30 minutes or so."

I told him that it had taken me 30 years to build this company, and that I wasn't inclined to make a decision this important in 30 minutes.

Yet, despite his aggressive business approach, I found him to be personable and a generous, philanthropic man. For example, I learned he felt so strongly about the education needs of young children that he'd contributed over *$100 million* for tuition assistance at private schools for low-income families…despite the fact that he was single and had no children of his own.

And much later, after the sale was finalized, he was one of the people who was kind enough to write a personal letter congratulating me, even though we hadn't chosen his firm.

We finally narrowed down the choice to three bidders after multiple meetings and discussions. Those three were *The Washington Post*, Willis Stein & Partners and Madison Dearborn Partners. The last two are investment firms in Chicago.

Honestly, we probably would have been happy with any one of these three. To begin with, we simply *liked* them, which I feel is the first and most important thing in any business or personal dealings.

> *"It was exhausting but exhilarating… frustrating but fascinating… arduous but uplifting…"*

In fact, we gained such respect for the people from these three firms that we felt badly when we had to turn two of them down. We could closely *relate* to them.

John Willis of Willis Stein, for example, has a country home in rural Illinois that he and his family drive to each weekend, so I related strongly to him and his "country ways". His partner, Avy Stein, was so gracious that he called and invited me to play golf *after* we'd made the decision to sell to one of the other two.

The Washington Post people were especially warm and genuine. They provided a particularly memorable experience for Bobbi. Coincidentally, she was reading Katharine Graham's thick book on the history of *The Post* at the time of their visit. That provided good conversation when we had their three top executives—the President, the Vice President and the CEO, Don Graham, Katharine's son—come to our house for lunch.

Despite their stature, all three were congenial down-to-earth folks. I learned that day that when Don Graham finished his military service, he decided to first take some other job in Washington; he wanted to "know the territory" before going to work for *The Post*. So he joined the D.C. police force and became a beat cop for 18 months. What a great way to learn about a city!

Also, after learning that Bobbi was reading his mom's book, Don graciously sent her a handwritten note that was delivered to our home the

When you invite trouble, it's usually quick to accept.

very next day. It was attached to a hardcover copy of the book in which his mother had written a personal note to Bobbi and signed her autograph.

Now and then we pinched ourselves. "Think of it," I told Bobbi that night, "I'm from a rented farm near the tiny town of Auburn, Iowa, and you're from a little town in Kansas. Last night we had dinner with Teddy Forstmann, and today Katharine Graham's son was at our house for lunch!"

Admirably, Don Graham has stayed in touch since, dropping more hand-written notes now and then, along with invitations to stop in for a visit whenever I'm in D.C. (I did so while in the capital city just a few weeks before writing this, and was warmly received by Don and key members of his editorial staff.)

After all that, we finally chose Madison Dearborn. For me, it actually came down to two—Madison Dearborn and *The Washington Post*. The benefit of *The Post* was that they already understood publishing—they'd be on third base ready to score while the Madison people would still be in the locker room listening to a lengthy chalk talk.

Yet, as much as we liked those *Post* people, the concern we had with selling to another publishing company was the fear that somewhere down the line they might step in and ask us to do it *their* way, accepting ads, etc.

By contrast, the Madison Dearborn people kept pointing out that their *lack* of publishing experience would be a *benefit* to us. It would be the main reason they *wouldn't* be prone to interfere with us.

The one thing they said repeatedly that impressed us was, "We're investors, not advisers. You just keep doing your thing, and we'll leave you alone." And they looked us in the eye when they said it.

Again, a major plus was that we *liked* this group of people from Madison Dearborn as soon as we met them. For whatever reason, they were simply "our kind of people". We had a lot of laughs with them during our meetings, and fun has to be part of business. If it isn't fun, you shouldn't do it.

A key question I asked them more than once was, "How soon might you resell us?"

I asked that because a friend of mine had a really bad experience when he sold his group of radio stations. He chose one firm over the other, even though the price was lower, because he didn't think his people would like to work with the management of the second firm. *Would you believe it*—a few weeks after he sold it to the first firm, that firm sold the stations to the second firm for the higher price!

I didn't want that to happen to us. Paul Finnegan, a Madison Dearborn VP and the "lead guy" in the acquisition, said they usually didn't turn over a company for at least 2 years, most often 3. And with the way we were growing, he saw no reason to veer from that schedule.

With all this in place, we okayed the deal with Madison Dearborn and got ready for the closing near the end of November 1998.

By now I was comfortable with all the details, but I still got emotional as we gathered in Chicago for "the signing". I was actually aware of the hair standing up on my arms as we sat down at this huge table, with lawyers and accountants filling all the chairs. It was just extremely difficult to sign that first paper finalizing the deal.

This was it—I was finally putting our company up for "adoption". Though I knew it was the right thing to do for all the right reasons, I sat there for a full minute before I could pen my signature on that contract. And then it was done.

The sale price was mind-boggling: *$640 million!* Who would have ever thought that something we started in our basement would one day carry that kind of price tag? And who would have thought that when I left Dad's rented farm in Iowa that this kind of life would unfold.

It had been quite a year and quite an experience. It had been challenging and stimulating and rewarding. But more than anything, it had been *very emotional.*

Yet, there was also a sense of relief. It was over. That difficult chapter was behind us. When we went to bed that night, I said to Bobbi, "Well, honey, now we're ready to live the rest of our lives."

THE SIGNING. It was an emotional moment when it came to signing the sales contract, with CFO Norb Whittle (left), Bobbi and a host of lawyers on hand.

There is no limit to how much good you can do
if you don't care who gets the credit.

CHAPTER 30

And Then What Happened...

IMMEDIATELY after the sale, Bobbi and I followed through on our written promise—we paid each employee that cash bonus of $100.00 for every month they'd worked at our company.

Some of these bonuses were quite sizable. After all, we had a lot of people who had been with us 20 years, and at least three for 30 years. As I explained earlier, these bonuses—along with our guarantee that we'd *duplicate* those same bonuses again 3 years from the sale date—accomplished exactly what we hoped.

It eliminated the *anxiety* that is often pervasive when a company is sold. All our people now knew we *wanted* them to stay…we were going to *pay* them to stay…and everyone was being made the *same offer*…so all the others would be staying as well.

Bobbi stopped in at our offices a couple weeks after the sale and that evening she mentioned how many *smiles* she'd noted in the hallways. I couldn't help but comment, "I'd bet it'd be hard to find that kind of atmosphere in most companies that have just been sold."

Again, this assurance—that things weren't going to change for at least 3 years—had the calming effect we'd hoped for. But one of the nicest things resulting from those bonuses was a big bound "book" the employees put together on their own and presented to us. It was filled with their personal letters and handwritten notes of thanks.

Most told what they planned to do with the bonus money, and some of those comments were extremely heartwarming. They ranged from, "We've been needing a new furnace the last two winters" to "Our three married sons haven't been home for Christmas in 5 years—we were able to send airline tickets for their entire families", and even "We've been wanting to adopt a little girl for a long time…now we can." Others just as touching are too private to share here.

I still have that thick book of letters on my credenza, and I occasionally pick it up and page through it just for the lift it provides. But I want to share

I used to be indecisive. Now I'm not so sure.

one thing that wasn't in that book that meant a great deal to me:

We had one warehouse employee who had a severe speech impediment. He was dependable and did his job. While I've always known and greeted all our employees by first name, he never responded when I said hi to him. I was pretty sure he could speak very little, if at all.

But 2 days after the bonuses were distributed, I met him in a hallway back by the warehouse. This time he stopped me, put out his hand and, with some difficulty, said, "Th-anks, Woy."

That just plain got to me. I went back to my office and closed the door for a few minutes. It meant as much as any of those nice letters.

These people kept their word. Just as they'd promised, Madison Dearborn (MDP) basically left us alone. It was a business marriage made in heaven. Paul Finnegan and his MDP people would drive up from Chicago to our offices four times a year, for quarterly meetings. Beyond those updating sessions, it was pretty much business as usual.

While the stock market slumped during that period and slowed virtually all business growth elsewhere, we were still growing, and they saw no reason to change anything. On several occasions they suggested acquisitions of small firms they felt would partner well, but when we decided against them, they said okay and didn't push it.

> *"After all, I hadn't worked for anyone else for more than 30 years..."*

Things really were pretty much the same as prior to the sale. For me, it was even more enjoyable because a good deal of the administration was now off my shoulders. As the company President, Tom Curl maintained most of the contact with MDP and handled the bulk of management of our staff.

Just the same, the first year after the sale, I put in even more hours than before. In fact, one of my people asked why I was no longer playing golf on most Wednesday afternoons, as I had for the last couple of years.

Well, I explained, I hadn't worked for anyone else for more than 30 years, and now I felt compelled—since I was now on *their* payroll—to give the MDP people their money's worth. Also, I wanted to show my staff I was true to my word, that I hadn't changed, nor had my work habits.

Besides, there was plenty of growth opportunity in front of us and plenty to do to accomplish it. We ex-farm kids don't drop the shovel and leave an unfinished job for someone else.

Add to that the fact that I'm extremely sensitive to my image. I didn't want MDP, my staffers or my subscribers to think I'm the kind of guy who takes the money and runs.

And finally, I wanted the company to continue to grow so the MDP people could see my word was good on another level—that this company had great future potential, both immediate and far-reaching.

For all these reasons, I put in a busy 12 months after the sale. But by the second year, I wanted to cut back to what had been my pre-sale rou-

THE WALL STREET JOURNAL.

WEDNESDAY, AUGUST 23, 2000   © 2000 Dow Jones & Company, Inc. All Rights Reserved.

Cash Cows

A Magazine Publisher Finds Fertile Ground For Profits in Farmland

Reiman's Homespun Titles Belie Aggressive Strategy: Direct Mail and No Ads

'Stumpy, the 3-Legged Ewe'

By PAULETTE THOMAS
Staff Reporter of THE WALL STREET JOURNAL

GREENDALE, Wis. — Sitting in the audience at a publishers' convention a few years ago, Roy Reiman heard a speaker describe his industry's impossible dream: that one fine day, a magazine might be so beloved by its readers that it could survive without selling advertising.

Mr. Reiman could only turn to an acquaintance and shrug. The 11 magazines in his stable carry no outside advertising. Yet they will pull in $300 million this year in revenue. With a combined circulation of roughly 15 million, Reiman's homespun titles include the nation's sixth-best-selling consumer magazine, Taste of Home, with five million subscribers, as well as Country Woman, Birds & Blooms, Farm & Ranch Living, and Reminisce.

Roy Reiman

The silver-haired Midwesterner has built one of the country's quirkiest and most successful publishing businesses by employing tactics most of the mainstream wouldn't dare try. Rather than competing for the hot demographic of urban baby boomers and Generation X'ers, Reiman Publications LLC focuses on the underserved market that is older, rural America. Instead of relying on advertisers, Reiman depends for the bulk of its income on subscribers lured with aggressive direct-mail campaigns.

And perhaps most crucially, long before "interactive" became the buzzword of the publishing elite, Reiman hit upon a way to engage its customers in a continuing relationship. Reader contributions account for as much as 80% of the content of some of the Reiman magazines. Patriotic reminiscences, embarrassing moments, recipes for raspberry pie — and photos along the lines of "Stumpy, the ewe with three legs" — fill the 64 glossy pages that constitute the Reiman standard format. Mr. Reiman's readers, in short, are also his writers.

"I know that audience," says the 65-year-old Mr. Reiman, founder of the company, who grew up on an Iowa farm. "We are filling a need."

When readers offer up more on a particular topic than the fanmazbly magazines can use (such as the time 14,000 cookie recipes rained down on editors), the company simply pours the contributions into its growing catalog of books. This year, Reiman expects to sell 3.7 million volumes with such titles as "Motorin' Along" and "America's Classic Farm Tractors."

Reiman also runs a tour operation, traveling cooking shows, and a mail-order business with $35 million in annual sales. (Big news with $35 million is self-embarrassment, sellers include a sweatshirt emblazoned, "I'm proud to be a farm wife.") In an era when many traditional magazine publishers are struggling to define their future, Mr. Reiman two years ago sold the bulk of his business to a group of Chicago investors for $635 million. Executives familiar with closely held Reiman predict this year's earnings before interest, taxes, depreciation and amortization will top $70 million.

Pilgrimages to Milwaukee

"They are like a cult, in a positive way," says Samir Husni, a professor of journalism at the University of Mississippi in Oxford. "You get the magazine and you believe it." Last year, 52,000 people toured the Reiman Visitor Center, located near the company's sprawling office complex in this Milwaukee suburb, to take in oil paintings of Mr. Reiman and his wife, Bobbi, and to sample Reiman dishes test kitchens.

In person, Mr. Reiman looks like a craggier Paul Newman. All the toisy, chit-chat-over-coffee tone that all of his publications and promotional materials adopt. He believes that a sizable part of America hungers for a voice that isn't profane or ironic, and he directs editors to "stay out of politics, the bathroom and the bedroom." Mr. Reiman once killed an editor's first-person account of an exciting canoe trip, believing it would make a homebound rural woman envious. Discussing Farm & Ranch Living, he says: "We make farmers feel good about themselves."

The sawbucks content belies a business strategy that targets potential subscribers — and competitors — with smart-bomb accuracy. Reiman deploys a database of 30 million names, and last year blitzed the American heartland with 275 million pieces of direct mail. In a pricey departure from standard industry practice, Reiman dispatches unsolicited copies of rival publications to subscribers of rival publications, as act as Good Housekeeping. "It works for us because we give people a product that they aren't aware exists," says John LeBrun, Reiman's senior vice president for circulation. A year's subscription typically costs $17.98.

Many media companies wouldn't dream of launching a new magazine without first conducting months of market research. Mr. Reiman prefers a hit-or-miss approach. He doesn't believe in focus groups — mostly because he observed one years ago in Chicago, and was struck by how the room's responses became surlier through the day.

When it comes to assessing how his personally don't put much stock in readers' studies, but the company does conduct them sparatically. He prefers to rely on the 200 to 700 letters from readers each magazine receives weekly. And imagines how his absent-in-law and other relatives would react to each feature. "Would they like it?" he asks himself. "If not, kill it."

Mr. Reiman got his start four decades ago by dabbling in magazine publishing and working as a free-lance writer. In 1970, he noticed that two farming magazines had eliminated their soft "women's features," and he sensed opportunity. He devised a prototype for a magazine called Farm Wife News. Worried that he might have trouble attracting advertisers, Mr. Reiman borrowed a mailing list of 400,000 farmers from an agricultural company and sent a test copy to a tenth of them, offering six issues for $3. The response was so great that he abandoned his test and cranked out the full run of 400,000 magazines.

Along with their checks and $3 bills, readers piled on their thanks for the no-ad approach. Mr. Reiman was even happier than they were. Production was efficient; he didn't have to wait for late ads, as he had in the past, and he could lay out similar features on the same page in each issue. Best of turns on the same page in each issue. Best of all, he didn't have to low-row to advertisers over rates, or ply them with the expected game and wine late into the evening. "I'm a family man," says Mr. Reiman, who now has five grown children. "I just hated that."

That early prototype evolved into Country Woman, which today has a paid circulation of 1.8 million — more than either Vogue or In Style.

Other Reiman titles followed over the years. Farm & Ranch Living, a sort of male version of Country Woman, launched in 1978, and Crafting Traditions came in 1992. In 1997, Mr. Reiman started Country, "for people who live in or long for the country." In the latest issue, readers Ray and Ruth Wegman

(over please)

---

tine. Even more, I wanted to travel more frequently to see the kids and grandkids.

To do so, I needed to relieve myself of the "guilt complex" I still harbored when putting in fewer hours. I've always had a problem with asking anyone to put in more hours than I do at something that benefits me.

After giving it some thought, I came up with a way to fix it: The first year after the sale, the MDP people had continued my old salary, which wasn't any higher than that of our other top execs. Just prior to the second year, I met with Paul Finnegan to discuss changing that.

"Look, I don't want to feel *obligated* to put in a certain number of hours anymore," I told him. "So here's my suggested arrangement—I'd like you to pay me just $2,000 a month and continue all my benefits. Then we'll sit down at the end of the year and you tell me what you think I was worth."

I said I would be like Ted Williams (the only ballplayer who ever asked that his salary be *reduced* after he'd had a bad year). "If I don't hit my average, then we'll agree to something lower. On the other hand, if I come up with several ideas that prove to be homers, we'll discuss something higher. Okay?"

That system worked well. I quickly became the lowest-paid exec in the company, and I've continued under that same arrangement ever since. I believe this has been to the company's benefit in ways beyond financial, because I often come up with my best ideas when I'm away from the office. It allows me time to finally slow down and *think*.

Thinking time is extremely important in a creative company like ours. Some of our biggest successes have come from pouncing on an opportunity that we didn't know existed at the beginning of the year. As we've often said with pride around our place, "We have ideas we haven't even thought of yet!"

That's what always made this company exciting. We have a bunch of truly creative people in our ranks. Sometimes we all go to work on a Monday morning thinking, *I wonder what wild, wonderful, off-the-wall thing we're going to come up with this week!*

Anyway, this new "Just pay me what you think I'm worth" salary basis yielded a personal benefit—as my hours went down, so did my golf hand-

People never say "It's only a game" when they're winning.

233

icap. In fact, I got it to a single digit for the first time in my life—albeit only for a short time—and also recorded my *first hole in one*.

Amazingly, that golf highlight happened on the very same day, August 23, 2000, that an article about our company appeared on the front page of *The Wall Street Journal* ("Magazine Publisher Finds Fertile Ground for Profits in Farmland; Homespun Titles Belie Aggressive Strategy: Direct Mail and No Ads"—see previous page).

For me, there was no doubt which of the two was by far most memorable. That's how I remember the date—August 23, the day of my first and only hole in one!

And life moves on. True to their word, Madison Dearborn held onto the company for 3-1/2 years, then sold it to The Reader's Digest Association in 2002. True to our word, the company had continued its steady growth over those 42 months.

That was evidenced by what the Digest people paid for it—*$760 million!* A gain of $120 million in 3-1/2 years.

As this is written, the merger of Reader's Digest and our company is still being played out, but it appears to have great potential. Many things about our two companies are similar. For beginners, the *Digest* was published without advertising for many years, and RD's management has vowed to keep our existing publications ad-free for the foreseeable future.

To me, that makes good sense. While our 16 million subscribers continually comment on our beautiful photos and enviable color reproduction, what they mention more often than anything else is "Yours are the only magazines with no ads." That single trait is still what makes us most unique in the industry.

As I've continually told our staff over the years, "First we make them *different*, then we make them *better*." Our ad-free approach has a great deal to do with that difference, and I hope it will never change.

I'm confident our editors will continue our aim of affecting millions of readers in a positive way. Our goal is to publish only uplifting stories about upbeat people in the hope our subscribers will enhance their own lives by emulating those they read about.

Our readers not only trust us, they *relate* to us. As evidence, their letters address me and most of our editors by first name. They regard us as friends, people "just like them" with similar backgrounds.

I've always believed that a large part of America hungers for a voice that isn't profane, ironic or cynical. So we've made it a policy to stay out of politics, the bathroom and the bedroom.

Basically, we're "The good news company". That's how a subscriber once described us, and we gladly accept that description.

Now that you know *all* about what makes our magazines different, I'm about to describe something else that's made us different over all these years—our management style.

You'll likely find some of these methods unusual…some actually surprising…and some that make you say, "Gee, maybe we should try that."

Everyone needs encouragement to dream big dreams.
I like to think I can help them do just that.
—Tiger Woods

CHAPTER 31

Things I Learned Along the Way...

HOW MANY COMPANIES have a starting time of 7:45 a.m., begin their noon break at 11:45, then call it a day at 4:30 p.m.? Ours has done it this way for decades.

Why? Years ago I asked our employees to "vote" on our working hours, and that's what they came up with. We only had a dozen or so people then, and I told them as long as they put in the usual 8 hours, I didn't care what times they chose. That's when they came up with the 7:45 to 4:30 bracket, with a 45-minute noon break. Over the years, we never saw any reason to change it.

For one, our people are on their way to the office 15 minutes ahead of heavy morning traffic. The fact that roads get much more congested between 7:45 and 8 a.m. doesn't concern our staffers—they're already at their desks by then.

Same way at lunchtime. We now have a company cafeteria, but in the days when many of us went out for lunch, beginning our noon break at 11:45 resulted in getting our staffers a table or booth ahead of the crowd. And that earlier, quicker service helped make our 45-minute lunch break much more manageable.

Likewise, heading for the door at 4:30 p.m. has a variety of benefits. Again, it puts our people on the road ahead of the 5 o'clock traffic…it allows parents to pick up kids at school earlier or watch an extra half hour of the kids' sporting events…and it allows our managers and others meeting deadlines a little more quiet time at the end of the day. (Our key people get a lot of wrap-up work done between 4:30 and 5:30.)

We also made a point not to take ourselves too seriously. To add a little levity during those early years, we played a recording of a rooster crowing over the PA to start each day at 7:45. And at 11:45, we had the receptionist announce, "It's…lunchtime!", because it was a fact that our people often became so engrossed in what they were doing that they'd forget what time it was. These unusual office hours are only a small part of what

Being kind is more important than being right.

235

OUR CORPORATE OFFICES are set within 9 acres of landscaped grounds, which include winding paths, flower beds, a gazebo and a fountain in "Ponderin' Pond".

we've done differently management-wise over the years. Another is our well-known "The earlier you get here, the closer you park" policy.

I mentioned in a preceding chapter that we've never had reserved space for anyone in our company parking lot. There's only one sign in the entire lot, right next to our entrance. It reads, *"Reserved for the First Person Here"*.

Why? Well, I was once an "underling" myself at another company, and it had always bugged me to see those choice "executive spaces" go unused on cold or rainy days. Executives travel a good deal, so those preferred spots right in

OUR FRONT ENTRANCE lined with flowers.

front of the building are often wasted. That can become an irritant for those walking by those empty spaces on rainy, cold, blustery days.

I vowed if I ever had a say in something like that, we'd treat everyone alike and reward those who got there earliest with the best spaces.

I didn't realize till later that I'd unwittingly come up with a motivational way to get people to work even earlier during inclement weather. People show up so much ahead of our regular starting time on lousy days—just to park closer to the front door—that I once jokingly said we should consider hiring a "rainmaker" on good days; we'd cover the costs with the extra hours and productivity!

Little things like no reserved parking mean a lot to employees. We never had a lot of company turnover, so we must have been doing something right. We tried to make everyone feel an intricate part of our team. We paid them well, we treated them fairly and we provided modern offices, state-of-the-art equipment and pleasant surroundings.

As for the latter, our corporate offices are set within a 9-acre "campus" that includes colorful flower beds, a pond and fountain, a gazebo, hanging flower baskets, and an abundance of trees, bushes and benches. A path winds through these grounds, measured so employees know the distance they've covered during walking breaks. We even have "Silver Anniversary Row", where a tree is planted to commemorate each 25-year employee.

The pond was named "Ponderin' Pond" by employees, because it's where our creative staff often ponders new ideas. On the north edge of the grounds is 3 acres of thick woods (that's where my home is located; I walk a curving path through the woods to the office each day).

An apology is the superglue of life; it can repair just about anything.

237

DURING THE HOLIDAYS, our company grounds are flooded with colorful lights.

Colorful displays are set up in keeping with major holidays, but nothing tops the efforts of our grounds crew at Christmastime. Over 100,000 lights cover the trees and buildings, a miniature church is perched on the hill above the pond, lighted reindeer and doves adorn the corners of the property, and more. A local TV station sends out a helicopter each December to share an aerial view with its audience.

In essence, we try to make our offices a pleasant environment, a place where our people *enjoy* coming to work each day. And, since we regularly feature attractive rural settings in our magazines, it seems only fitting that we emulate those places at the site where these magazines are published.

In addition to liking our grounds and offices, it's obvious that our employees like each other. And that's incredibly important.

I made it a policy early on to never hire anyone I didn't like, no matter what their potential. When you think about it, you spend more waking hours with the people you work with than the ones you live with. So you might as well spend that time around people you enjoy.

I recall years ago when CFO Norb Whittle and I interviewed a young man we were considering to head up our Travel Division. In addition to being bright and aggressive, this fellow had the kind of experience we needed. Still, I decided to sleep on it before making a decision.

The next morning I stepped into Norb's office and said, "I'm not going to hire him." Norb seemed surprised; he said this guy would likely do a great job and make us a lot of money, then asked why I'd decided not to hire him.

I responded, "Because there were some things about his personality that bothered me...I just didn't like him."

"You know," Norb said, "he was a little arrogant—I didn't like him that well, either."

We agreed to continue our policy of "If you don't like 'em, don't hire 'em." As a result, we've ended up with a lot of good, kindhearted people who get along and enjoy each other's company.

A measure of the latter is how often your employees get together *after* work. We find our employees gather often, for visits, dinners, summer picnics, bowling, ball games, exchanging baby-sitting, whatever.

We don't do business with people we don't like, either. That's another "policy" we've had from the get-go. I still advise our production and purchasing people never to buy anything from someone they don't like, no matter the price.

"If you don't like them, there's obviously something wrong with the chemistry, and it's going to come back to bite you eventually," I contend. "So you might as well deal with it right from the outset by not dealing with them, period."

Maybe it's a bit of my Iowa past, but there are two other reasons I don't want to do business with people I don't like: I don't want them to make any money off me. And I wouldn't feel right about making money off them.

As a result of this practice, we have terrific suppliers who have become good friends. We know they'll go the extra mile if and whenever needed; they've delivered urgent jobs right to my home on a Sunday evening so I'd have it in time for a Monday morning flight.

It's also been gratifying to see these suppliers grow along with us. Some of these firms have been with us way back to my basement days and have deservedly become highly successful.

Our "Friday Memo" boosts a "family feeling". For decades we've turned out a weekly memo, which is distributed to each employee as they leave for the weekend. Sometimes this folksy piece is eight pages long!

If you keep saying things are going to be bad, you have a good chance of being a prophet.

Each Friday Memo begins with a motivational saying, then details projects that are going through the company, describes new launches or books being planned, announces staff promotions, spells out new employee benefits, details plans for company gatherings and more.

But it also lists lighthearted, newsy things, such as employees' birthdays…who joined the company how many years ago this very week…who got married…who just had a baby, including name and weight…who had a high bowling score or low golf score…who won a prize at the state fair. Then it ends up with a "classified section" that allows employees to sell or buy furniture, adopt a kitty or whatever they'd like to exchange.

> *"What if it doesn't work out?*
> *How you gonna fire*
> *your own mother?"*

This Friday Memo is so popular, we don't hand it out before quitting time; we've learned employees will stop everything and read it immediately like "a letter from home". On the other hand, on a few occasions we've had a problem with printing it (eight pages for over 500 employees is no minor printing task) and employees have actually waited a few extra minutes until it was finished!

There's a twofold reason we hand out the memo at our exits: So they'll read it on their own time…and so they'll take it home and share it with their families. That way the spouse and the kids are tuned in to what's happening at the office, and they become part of our "extended family".

There's a third reason as well: We've never discouraged nepotism at our company. We just make sure family members don't work in the same department. While nepotism is a no-no at many companies, we've found many benefits to hiring people from the same family. Such as:

1. If one family member was good enough for us to hire, hopefully another member of that family will have some of those same positive traits.

2. That second person likely already knows a good deal about our company and will hit the ground running, having learned it from the first member.

3. That second person will likely come in with a positive attitude, having heard enough good things about the company from the first member.

As a result, we have sisters, sisters-in-laws, spouses, mothers, adult children and about every other combination in our ranks. Again, we make certain they do not work in the same department or even in similar jobs. That can lead to salary comparisons and other potential problems.

Before I move on to other things, I can't resist including this one "nepotism story":

Ann Kaiser has now worked with me for over 30 years. During her second year with the company, she told me she needed to hire a secretary to handle all of her mail (she was then Editor of *Farm Wife News*).

I said fine, go hire one. She came in a week later and said she'd decided on a secretary and would like to talk to me about it. I asked why—she should be able to make that decision on her own.

MORE THAN 30,000 FLOWERS are planted on our company grounds each spring.

"Because I decided I want to hire my mother," she responded.

"*What?* Ann, sit down, we'd better talk about this!" I almost shouted. "What if it doesn't work out? How you gonna fire your own mother?"

Ann said she was sure it would never come to that…that her mom was her best friend…that she was perfect for the job because she was an excellent cook and would be able to sort through the recipes to be tested…and a lot of other good reasons.

I said I still thought it was awfully risky, but if that's what she wanted to do, maybe she should tell her mother (Nettie Golke) that "We'll both give this a try for just 1 month, okay?" so no feelings would be hurt.

Well, that "month-long trial" went on for over 20 years. Nettie not only screened the mail and handled all sorts of correspondence, but she became everyone's "mom" at the company.

I recall going to her one day to have her dig a sliver out of my finger. Nettie *listened* to people and helped them mentally as well as physically. Every company needs a "mom" like Nettie in their ranks.

"Don't ask to take time off." That's what I advised people after they'd been with us long enough to know they were trustworthy.

"This isn't a 'permission company'," I'd explain. "If you need time off to take care of a kid or close on a new house, or to watch the school Christmas program, just let us know in advance when you're not going to be here.

"If you're *our kind of people*, we know you won't take advantage of us. You'll still get your job done and make up the time if it's needed. We want you to enjoy your job and your life."

I found people appreciated being respected like that. In return they often put in extra hours to be sure we'd continue that policy.

> ## "It's a beautiful spring day—we're closing early this afternoon..."

It may sound a bit paternalistic, but that's the way you'd treat a member of your family, and that's the way we wanted staffers to feel as part of our company. They'd soon tell others how fairly they were treated, and that led to more good people joining our ranks.

Also, we annually switched to "summer hours" from Memorial Day to Labor Day. During these summer months, we put in an extra half hour per day Monday through Thursday, starting office hours 15 minutes earlier and ending 15 minutes later. Then we closed at noon on Friday so everybody could have a long weekend. We still do that today.

We did impulsive things, too, that employees seemed to appreciate. For example, winters are pretty harsh in Wisconsin. So, in early spring when that first really perfect warm, sunny day occurred, we'd have the receptionist announce in mid-afternoon, "We're going to close early today so that everyone can enjoy more of this beautiful spring day with their family."

It was just an hour or two, but obviously appreciated. So much so, in fact, that Judy Larson—one of our retired art directors who is designing this book—remembered it and suggested I include this item about it.

"It was sort of a celebration of spring after a long winter," Judy says. "That was always special and appreciated by all of us."

Sometimes it's the little things that are remembered most.

Which brings me to this final thought: Turnover is the most expensive problem for a company in any industry. Once you find good employees, do whatever it takes to keep them.

*If you had to identify, in one word,
the reason why the human race has not achieved
and will never achieve its full potential,
that one word would be "meetings".*
—*W.B. Grace*

CHAPTER 32

Okay, Okay...I Wasn't Always Right

AS OUR COMPANY GREW, *managing people* became one of my biggest challenges. I was ill prepared.

I had no training or background in being a "boss", supervising a staff or running a company. I was basically a writer, no more, no less, albeit one with a lot of wild ideas and dreams of what could be.

As an employee at other firms, I didn't pay particularly close attention to how managers went about their roles—after the first 5 minutes in most meetings, my mind was already drifting; I just wanted the session to be over as soon as possible so I could get back to my typewriter.

Over the years, I learned that condition wasn't limited to me. The same is true for almost every other writer, editor, artist or other creative type. They just want to be left alone to "do their thing", not tell others how to do it.

For that very reason, it is very difficult for a publishing company like ours to grow. Here's what I mean:

If a friend said to you, "I'm looking for someone to manage and run my company," and you gave it some thought, then responded, "I have this artist friend you might want to consider."

"An *artist*?" your friend would say. "You gotta be kidding. Artists are known to be temperamental, unpredictable, moody and impulsive. They may be good at design, but they're not *managers*."

He could be right. But what a lot of people don't recognize is, writers are artists, too—we just paint with words instead of pictures. So all those traits can be attributed to writers as well as artists. Including me.

And that's what makes it hard for a company like ours to grow. Most artists don't want to be promoted to Art Director if it means managing other artists. Most writers don't want to become Managing Editor if it means managing other writers. Artists just want to design; writers just want to write.

Yet, in a company like ours, if you go to your company's Finance Department—made up of people who know a lot about *business*—they don't necessarily make good managers of creative people, either.

Pain and suffering is inevitable; misery is optional.

243

Why? Because they don't understand "the creative animal" and what makes them tick. They have difficulty relating to the quirks of writers and artists. Financial people and creative people just don't talk and think on the same terms. Both groups get frustrated.

I think that's why CFOs don't always make good CEOs. Managing people is far different from managing finances and requires far different skills and attributes. In fairness, most CEOs aren't equipped to be good CFOs, either.

I had no choice but to learn on the go as we grew. As much as possible, I tried to hire people a lot like me—people who just wanted to be told what their job was, then be left alone to do it.

That's why we seldom held any formal meetings. We talked things over—in the hallways, over lunch, on the way to the car—but we rarely sat down for the purpose of lengthy discussions. The few times we did, it wasn't long before I shared the itchiness of the others around the table—we all just wanted to get back to work instead of talking about it!

> *"Writers are artists, too—*
> *we just paint with words*
> *instead of pictures…"*

For that reason I allowed our staffers to work as independently as possible, rather than have them spend their time supervising others. It was obvious the majority of them didn't want to manage anyone; they just wanted to "bring it" themselves. Bottom line, we resisted bureaucracy in every form.

Part of this was based on a "chart" that my friend Clancy Strock once drew for me in pencil on a yellow legal pad. At top left he put "Employee A", then wrote "Excellent employee, 100% productive" under him.

Next he gave "A" one person to supervise. "A" now was "90% productive", since he spent 10% of his time supervising. Clancy kept adding on people for "A" to supervise, until he got to 10. Then under "A" he jotted, "0 productivity, 100% supervising."

I never forgot that penciled chart and the point it made, that the best, most experienced person on the staff was now producing *nothing*, while spending all of his time supervising people of lesser talent!

I still see that same thing happening in a big way in large companies. The *best qualified*, the *most experienced* and the *highest paid* people get promoted to management positions…and from that point on they produce little if anything that's billable. They just hold meetings, supervise others, hold meetings, set strategy, plan budgets, hold meetings, study profit/loss charts and…conduct more meetings. (Some companies should consider adding "The Meeting Place" under their corporate name.)

These executives also travel a good deal, regularly attending national conferences to "learn what's new" (while also privately networking with other industry execs in case a better job surfaces elsewhere).

Too many of these highly paid people don't directly produce anything themselves; they just supervise, manage and count what others produce. I

244

once read this: "Management doesn't make anything or sell anything. When overdone, top people work themselves out of a job."

I've seen that happen again and again. Often the top people just plan what *other* people are going to do. They do none of it themselves.

I never wanted that to happen at our company with our best writers and artists. Most of all I didn't want it to happen to me—I was a *writer* and that's what I wanted to remain as we grew. And I did.

I can't recall a day that I didn't do something billable—I'd either write or edit something or come up with a new idea that had potential for our growth. I worked at staying *productive* while heading up a company that eventually grew to over 500 employees during my tenure.

As a whole, I urged our managers to take the same approach, to keep productive while supervising, and they did. For example, while Mike Beno was our Editorial Director—supervising a staff that eventually grew to over 100—he continued developing new magazines, edited books and churned out copy every day. He kept *producing*.

In this fashion and others, I gradually developed my own approach to management, and most of it seemed to work.

Yet I was far from infallible. Early on, I think I expected too much of our people. I thought everyone should care as much as I did and should be willing to put in the same number of hours. That's not realistic in any entrepreneurial firm headed by someone driven with a vision.

Perhaps I was even a little "Scrooge-like" in my early management style. If something distracted me and curbed my productivity, I assumed it hindered others as well. Like I didn't want anyone to have a radio in their office or cubicle.

I found a radio to be a major distraction, especially if the station included news, commercials or vocals. If you have radios in adjacent cubicles tuned in to three or four different stations, it soon sounds like a mariachi band playing in a courtyard! How can anyone work *creatively* in that environment?

One particular experience really turned me against office radios. I went into our art department and asked "Teresa" to come to the conference room; there was something I wanted her opinion on. She hesitated and said, "Wait—I want to hear the answer to this question first."

That really bothered me. It wasn't that she didn't value my time—if she'd said, "Just let me finish this last bit and I'll be there," I would have been fine with it. But it occurred to me that if she was reluctant to leave her art cubicle *this* particular time because she wanted to hear some answer on a daytime quiz show, how many *other* times were there that she let that radio dictate her work activities?

Soon after that incident, we installed Muzak. While some people refer to it as "elevator music", it is in fact programmed for productivity. I was shown how it plays "spirited" music at the start of the day to get people going, as well as "peppy" music in early afternoon when post-lunch fatigue hits. The reason most Muzak programming doesn't include vocals, I

Nothing is impossible for the person who doesn't have to do it.

learned, is because they've found workers tend to listen to and learn the lyrics. While all those reasons seem plausible, some employees still turn our Muzak down to where it's inaudible.

Another peeve of mine was people who tended to short the company at the beginning and end of each day. I always had a thing about people putting in a full 8 hours.

So much so that I once included a paragraph in our Friday Memo, pointing out that employees were expected to be "at your workstation at 7:45 a.m. and be ready to work...not *arrive* at 7:45 a.m., then get ready to work." Likewise "you're to *work until 4:30 p.m.* and *then* prepare to leave, not prepare to leave at 4:15 so you can leave exactly at 4:30."

> ### *"One of my peeves is people who short the company at the beginning and end of each day..."*

I wince a little as I reread that now, but I still think that's fair. I don't have a problem if, now and then, people leave exactly at our 4:30 quitting time for a specific reason. But I do have a problem when the *same people* leave *every day* at *exactly 4:30*. There's little doubt those people were "preparing to leave" for that last 15 minutes or so; for sure they didn't start any *new projects* while they were "winding down".

People who are really into their jobs are often so absorbed that they're unaware what time it is. They only become aware it's quitting time when others start bidding them good-bye. Those are *our* kind of employees.

It likewise bothered me when we had a time clock for hourly people back in the warehouse. I repeatedly noticed that for some, the very *first* thing they did when they came in each morning was to punch in on that time clock. Then they took their time to take off their coat, hang it in the closet and stop to visit and discuss last night's TV shows before eventually going to their workstation.

At the end of the day, they reversed the procedure—they left their workstation, chatted with cohorts, went to the closet, put on their coat and then the very *last* thing they did before heading for the door was to punch out at the time clock.

When 100 or more hourly people do that every day, and you multiply 100 by an average of, say, 15 minutes of unproductive time each day, that kind of work habit can become very costly for a company.

Again, this sense of fairness in work hours is likely rooted in my rural background. When I worked at that summer construction job during college, we were expected to have the shovel in our hand when the beginning bell rang, not get there when the bell rang and then go search for a shovel. Likewise, we weren't to put it down until *after* our 8 hours were complete. Then we got ready to go home.

"Hours" were even less heeded on the farm; there weren't really any hours or time schedule. We seldom looked at a clock—we just worked until each job was *finished*.

Oh, and I also think employees should eat breakfast and *then* come to work, not come to work and then have breakfast. In the past year I noticed one supervisor who went to our cafeteria about 8:30 each morning, ordered bacon, eggs and toast, stood and waited for them to be prepared, then sat down and enjoyed the meal while reading the morning paper.

That's *not* a good example for others who notice and soon conclude that they should be able to do the same. I don't have a problem with people having a granola bar or someone's birthday treat with their coffee at mid-morning, but if a full-fledged "breakfast" better fits your needs, that's something you should have before you come to work.

Again, I think all employees should basically be treated alike, top to bottom, when it comes to a sense of *fairness*. These time issues bothered me more early on than they do today. I gradually learned to soften on some of these expectations and likely became less demanding.

Just the same, the people who got promotions at our place were the obviously dedicated workers—you just *know* who these people are after working with them awhile. They're the ones who feel the mission, who are willing to do what it takes for as long as it is needed to simply get things done on time and done *right*.

I was "down" on smoking, too, long before efforts to curb it became a national campaign. In fact, our company has been smoke-free now for nearly 10 years—not just inside our company, but *outside* as well.

I got the idea from a newspaper item while Bobbi and I were visiting Phoenix one winter. An article about Motorola's large facility there with 1,100 employees detailed how the company had successfully enacted a firm no-smoking policy inside their buildings and *anywhere on their premises as well*.

I figured if they could do it with 1,100 employees, we could do it with less than half that many. So I talked it over with our key people and we went ahead with it. No other company in Milwaukee or the Midwest—to our knowledge—had tried such a program back then.

In July we announced our plan to go smoke-free on our entire grounds by January 1. This gave people 6 months to prepare for it. We offered to cover the cost of any smoking-cessation classes or methods by reimbursing employees the cost *after* they had successfully completed such a program.

Understandably, the idea wasn't popular with some people at the outset. But we stuck to our guns, and it's paid off. We take great pride in the appearance of our corporate grounds. We no longer have to deal with cigarette butts being scattered about and fuzzed up by our lawn mowers.

Another positive: We've actually had people show more interest in joining our company after they heard about our smoke-free policy. And something I recently noticed in our Call Center made me smile: Some of the crew there had taken our policy to another level on their own. Over the wide closet door was a sign stating, "Smokers' coats" on one side and "Non-smokers' coats" on the other!

Best of all, some employees have told us our smoke-free policy was

Treat your friends as you do pictures and place them in their best light.

247

just the motivation they'd needed to quit for good. I'm sure it's why our "Wellness Program" works so well—we give anyone who hasn't taken a sick day in the first 6 months of the year an extra day of vacation. Then we repeat that program during the second 6 months.

Our records show our employees have taken a lot fewer sick days than they used to...and that more of them are enjoying bonus "vacation days" with their families instead.

Like the Studebaker, we've often been ahead of our time. Sometimes we've been wrong, but on smoking, we were right.

MY ART DIRECTOR wanted to add these extra pictures of our grounds—so here.

The best things in life are not things.

There are two kinds of people—takers and givers.
The takers sometimes eat better,
but the givers always sleep better.
—Danny Thomas

CHAPTER 33

My Top 10 Management Rules

ABOUT A YEAR AGO, I was asked to give a talk to Milwaukee's "Young Presidents Club". The idea was for me to share my best management tips.

I decided to turn it into my own version of a David Letterman's "Top 10 List". I told the group this wasn't "The Gospel of Running a Company …from the Book of Roy", and that I wasn't the brightest bulb in the closet. But these are simply things that have worked for me over the years:

1. Keep meetings to a minimum. Meetings have become the absolute curse of modern business. A meeting set every Tuesday morning at 8 a.m. becomes a meeting for meeting's sake.

Instead, call people together only when necessary, and end the session as soon as possible. Consider scheduling meetings an hour or half hour before lunch; they're self-policing. Or consider my friend Michael Cudahy's rule of meetings: "Either have it in a room with no chairs or in the parking lot."

Seriously, sometime take a few minutes to total up the "salary per hour" of everyone in a meeting; it will encourage you to keep the next one shorter. Remember, while staffers are meeting, they're not producing.

2. Don't run a company by committee. Listen to people, get their views, then make a decision. Someone has to call the shots. Procrastination is very costly in a company. So is making decisions by consensus.

The "leader" must have a gut feeling for what best suits the company and its customers. As sort of a benevolent dictator, that leader needs to set the direction and *sail.*

3. Don't make organizational charts. That categorizes people and sets them apart from the *team.* It puts parameters on people; suddenly certain things "aren't my job". It makes some smug and others mad.

Don't get hung up on strict budgets, either. The biggest chill to creativity is calculated planning. Decide if it's a good idea, then decide if you can afford to go ahead with it.

4. Promote from within. Go outside only when necessary. No one understands the company better than those who work there, and they're most deserving of promotion. They'll not only continue your "culture", but doing so will show other staffers they have a future here rather than elsewhere.

5. Never hire anyone you don't like. (I covered reasons for this in Chapter 31.) You spend more time with the people you work with than the people you live with, so you might as well make your days pleasant. For the same reason, don't buy anything from a supplier you don't like.

6. Surround yourself with people you trust. Business is a little like a marriage—its cornerstone is *trust*. You don't want a bunch of yes-men or kiss-up people around you. When you ask for financial or response figures, you want *honest* answers even if they hurt. Choose management people you'd want to be in a *foxhole* with.

7. Seek people who know what you don't know. No manager can know everything about everything, and you need people to fill those voids. That's when *trust* comes to the fore again, because they may talk in terms you don't totally understand. In computer jargon, you may not know how the "firewall" works, but you better trust the person who's in charge of it! Surround yourself with these kinds of people.

8. Don't be a big shot. No reserved parking, no big cars, no fancy offices, no thicker carpeting…and get your own coffee. Don't put yourself above anyone, know everyone by first name and insist they call you by yours. Let people understand they work *with* you, not *for* you.

Walk around your place now and then, chat with people, ask about their kids. And phooey on being politically correct—give 'em a hug when they deserve it. If they trust you, they'll know your intent.

9. First be *different*, then be *better*. You want your company to be "unique" in as many ways as possible, to make it a *special* place to work. If you succeed, your employees will tell others and help with recruitment.

10. Keep business *FUN*. At all costs, preserve your sense of humor. Times can sometimes be tough, but you have to allow for levity. Employees need to look forward to coming to work, and a few laughs each day can aid that important element.

This last rule has been well applied at our company. Busy as we've been, we've always taken fun seriously and had time for pranks involving our co-workers. Crazy posters, a humorous "Thought for the Day" posted by the coffee machine, sticking "Sold" signs on the furniture of someone out of the office for a week…all these were never discouraged. It's possible to be serious and humorous at the same time.

One of the sayings that's been posted on my office wall for years states, "The day this isn't fun, I quit." I never had to. We found things to laugh about every day—sometimes our mistakes.

AFTER I ran through this list of Management Rules with these young execs, we discussed the whys of a few of them. Then I expanded by sharing a few other management suggestions based on personal experiences:

• *Encourage employees to admit their mistakes.* Mistakes just happen in a business. I told the group about "Patti", a young woman who came into my office about 5:15 one day. She worked in the Production Department and had only been with the company 6 months or so. That's likely why she didn't address me by first name.

"Mr. Reiman, I feel I need to tell you something," she began in a tight, shaky voice. "You see, I made a mistake…it was my fault." She then described what she'd done, and why we would need to reprint the piece, at a cost of over $10,000.

"This is really difficult for me to do," she continued, "but my dad always said that if you make a mistake, it's best to be the first to 'fess up to it, before someone else points it out."

Boy, had that girl's dad taught her a lesson in life! I surely wasn't happy about the mistake—$10,000 was a lot of money then, not that it isn't now—but what she didn't realize is she'd just turned a lemon into lemonade. I knew we could *trust* Patti, and that made her management material down the line.

I calmed her by thanking her for her honesty and told her—in effect—what I sometimes tell irate subscribers when they phone and want to talk to *no one* but the publisher:

"We have a lot of good people working here, but the problem is they're all human. And humans sometimes make mistakes. Obviously that's the case with your account. But we have many conscientious people here who are going to fix it, and I'm personally going to see to that."

Encouraging your employees to immediately admit to mistakes will save you money, because the faster they're discovered, the sooner they can be corrected.

• *Ready, FIRE, Aim!* I'm well aware that some companies look at this phrase negatively—they feel it refers to the practice of acting before adequately thinking things through. Conversely, I think some people and companies think too much.

If you aim too long, the target might move and you'll miss the opportunity. So if you're confident you know your audience and it feels right in your gut, *go for it!*

> *"Indecision is sometimes worse than the wrong decision…"*

Indecision is sometimes worse than the wrong decision. You're far better off keeping things *moving*, even if it means learning from mistakes. So, as long as you're not betting the farm, *Ready, FIRE, Aim!*

Truly, we've often come to the office with an idea on Monday, typed it on Tuesday, had it designed and typeset on Wednesday, printed it on Thursday and mailed it on Friday to a "test audience" of 10,000 random households across the country.

That sure beats what many companies do. They hold multiple meetings, have lengthy discussions, work up potential budgets, rehash the concept, rethink the approach, look at the downside, then…hold more meetings. Valuable time goes by—sometimes months—as they discuss what *they*

Advice is what some give by the bushel but take by the grain.

think without knowing what the *public* thinks.

Instead, we regularly "ran it up the flagpole" by checking what 10,000 *real people* thought of the idea. Within a week to 10 days, we pretty much knew whether we had a "boom" or a "bomb".

If it was the former, we pursued it further. If it was the latter, we hadn't wasted a lot of productive time; we just tossed it in the wastebasket and started thinking about our next great idea.

- *Don't ever forget that the leader sets the pace.* If you get to the office late in the morning, the people you supervise will do likewise…because you're not there to see and appreciate their promptness.

It's true in other areas. You fly first class, they'll fly first class. You stay in suites, they'll stay in suites. You take long lunches, they'll take long lunches. You order expensive wine at dinner, they'll order name brands, too. If all that's okay with you, fine; just know it's going to happen.

Bottom line, there are two ways to lead—you either set the pace or kick 'em in the butt. The former is always better.

- *Always take the worst job.* That way no one can complain. Jump in the backseat of a waiting car…take the seat farther back in the plane…park farther back in the company lot. Don't treat yourself special; let them know you're part of the team, willing to do anything they do.

- *When in doubt, leave it out.* That applies to many things. It's always been our policy with copy in our magazines; over the years we've left out some really *funny* items on the slight chance they might offend someone.

The same is true when you're writing a speech, a memo to staffers, or deciding whether a joke you've heard is acceptable to tell in a meeting or the hallway. When in doubt, leave it out.

- *When you get a call from the media, don't respond immediately.* Remember, that reporter's pen is ready. If you shoot from the hip, you may be super sorry later.

Instead, say you're busy at the moment and that you'll get back in a few minutes. But ask what, in general, does he/she want to know?

Then hang up, gather your thoughts and *write them out.* Now you're ready to call back. Better yet, *fax* your comments back to the reporter and state this is all you have to say. You're not likely to be misquoted when the reporter knows you have a copy of your comments in writing.

- *Take your business home to your spouse.* Talking it over will not only keep your spouse in the loop and thereby result in sharing an interest in your job, but you may well come to conclusions on your own while explaining a problem or challenge.

- *Consider developing a "telephone code" with your spouse.* There are times when someone is in your office, your spouse calls, and for whatever reason you'd just as soon not have that person know who's calling.

So come up with some little "code" to alert your spouse that you're tied up…and that you'd rather not take down a list of groceries right at the moment. For example, here's the one Bobbi and I have used for years:

Some time before we met, she worked for a sheriff's department in

Kansas, and often communicated with officers by radio. Whenever an officer said "10-12" on the radio, it alerted her or any listener that the officer "couldn't speak freely" at the moment; there was someone within earshot.

She's never forgotten that code. Neither have I. So...whenever she calls me at the office or anywhere and I'm in a situation where I don't want to be short or curt without her wondering why, I just use "10-12" somewhere in my conversation. I may say, "Ten to twelve would be okay...", or "Ten, twelve, whatever..."

When she hears that, she immediately *knows* what's up, and that I'll call her back as soon as I'm finished. Plus, it's sort of our little "secret" we share that makes us both grin. (Well...I guess it's no secret anymore.)

That just-between-us code has become such a thing for us that she even has it on her license plate. I'm sure a lot of folks see that plate and wonder what those simple numbers are all about. Now *you* know, so if in the future you see a Wisconsin plate with "10-12" on it, wave—that's Bobbi.

> ## *"Develop a 'secret code' with your spouse..."*

- *Never give in to "shotgun raises".* That is, learning someone is quitting, then attempting to convince them to stay by giving them an immediate good-size raise.

I described my reasons for this earlier, when within 5 minutes of telling my boss I was leaving, I was offered a series of raises until my salary would have been increased by 20%! Hey, if I had that kind of value to the company, why hadn't I been paid that all along?

I never forgot that, and I figured others would feel the same way. So when someone I valued highly informed me they were thinking about leaving, I methodically spelled out their *future* with the company if they stayed on board. But I never adjusted their salary at the moment.

Keep in mind that employees (or ex-employees) share information like this. If you do it once and word spreads, one or more of your people might simply threaten to leave, just to see how you might respond "shotgun-wise".

- *Catch people doing something right.* That's the premise of the original *One-Minute Manager* book. I've encouraged our managers to read it every 6 months; I do myself. It only takes a half hour.

Its basic point is that you make a concerted effort to *compliment* people again and again when they do a good job.

That's doubly important in our kind of business. I've often said that, with creative people, you could attach a mechanical hand-patter on their back, turn it on, and they'd never get sore. Just make sure the battery doesn't wear out; they'll never get too much of it.

I've even given out "Attaboy" and "Attagirl" awards when I hear someone's done something special. No plaque, no bonus, just a verbal "Way to go!" is always appreciated.

And when you hear about one of these achievements, try this: Tell every-

When someone else blows your horn, the sounds carries twice as far.

one present that when they meet Jeff or Juli or whoever it is in the hallway, they're to stop, tell that person what they heard and extend congratulations. I've personally seen in employees' eyes how much this means to them—"Those executives were talking about *me!*"

One of the main benefits of "catching people doing something right" and lauding them immediately is that it also allows you to correct them immediately when they've done something wrong.

If employees are only singled out when they make a mistake (like a football lineman during a televised game), they'll find criticism hard to take. But if it's mixed in among multiple compliments, you can be much more direct, not dillydally around and get things *fixed*, right now.

● *Keep your receptionist's voice fresh and friendly.* How your receptionist answers your phone is incredibly important to the image of your company. That's the *only* contact hundreds of people will ever have, and they'll form an opinion of your firm in just those brief moments.

A personal example: A number of years ago, I was in New Orleans and called our office late in the afternoon. After hearing Mary's voice, I said, "Mary, you sound tired."

She said, "Well, I *am* tired—it's been a long day."

I thought, *Well, you can't <u>sound</u> tired; being upbeat, perky and having "Glad you called!" in your voice is part of your job.* But I didn't tell her that. I fixed it another way.

After I got back, we began switching receptionists at noon each day, to keep a fresh voice on the phone. Later, when both our business and incoming calls doubled, we changed that person three times a day.

Now we're at four. That's how important we think it is to have a voice paint a positive picture of us, and that there's a good bunch of friendly people beyond that receptionist's desk.

> *"My job is to have you smiling before you get off the phone..."*

● *Empower your people to make small decisions on behalf of the company.* An example, when a customer phones and is really irate (it happens; we screw up sometimes), we train the operators in our Call Center to do a number of things:

(A) Write down the person's *first name* as soon as you hear it. (B) Let the person *vent.* (C) As you respond, use that first name immediately and repeatedly for two reasons—the caller will appreciate your caring enough to have noted their first name; secondly, it's likely to defuse an irate caller because he or she no longer feels they're a stranger—"This person on the other end of the line *knows* me because she keeps using my first name."

We also instruct our phone crew to begin by saying, "Bill, I'm sorry, but I want you to know that part of my job is to *have you smiling before you get off the phone.* You may find that hard to believe at this minute, but you just wait and see if I don't succeed..."

Then we empower our operators by allowing them, without checking with a supervisor, to *give away whatever it takes to make that irate caller happy*—an extra year's subscription, a full replacement of their catalog order, a free cookbook or whatever. Give it away, make 'em happy and get off the phone!

Numerous times new Call Center employees have asked me, "Roy, how can we afford to give away all this stuff?"

"Well," I explain, "a company our size would normally have a $100,000 budget for public relations. We don't have a public relations department— you're it. So use these 'giveaways' when appropriate to make that customer happy.

"Think about it," I add, "what are you going to gain by *proving that person on the phone is wrong*, even when you're pretty sure that's the case?

"Most of our customers are honest people, and they're not trying to cheat us. It's more likely that something they received from us just wasn't what they expected. So give them whatever they want and *get off the phone*.

"The longer you stay on the line, arguing with them, the more time you're tying up the phone and likely missing new callers trying to get through to order something else.

"If they're forced to wait too long and then hang up, we've lost that customer and now have another person a little irate. What's more, if we have to hire more people to handle those calls, that increases our costs, too.

"So, it's far better to do whatever it takes, give away what's necessary and get off the phone. Plus, if that irate customer ends up smiling like you promised, they're going to tell others, and that can lead to more new customers. No one puts more stock in what they hear from their neighbors than people who live in rural America."

After examples like this, I shared with the Young Presidents group a few other tidbits I've learned along the way:

- *Don't hire a person until you need a person and a half.*
- *Look for people who share your passion, who have a "fire in the belly".* Rate enthusiasm over talent and degrees—people with high energy get more out of what they have to offer.
- *Fight bureaucracy at every turn; do real work instead of paperwork.*
- *Avoid multiple memos rehashing the same problem.*
- *Remember this rule: Compliment publicly, criticize privately.*
- *Forget the rule about never hiring friends.* If they're the right people, they'll soon become your friends anyway, and if the day comes when you have to terminate them, it will be no easier than if they were friends before you hired them.
- *Always sign your letters in a different color of ink than they're typed.* That way the recipient will know you took the time to personally sign it, that it's not a form letter.
- *If you run your own company, stop looking for another you.* If a person has as much talent and ability as you, he's likely already on his own.
- *If you're not in a technical field, be careful about hiring people who have a Master's Degree.* Sometimes this is an indicator of an indecisive per-

Nothing great was ever achieved without enthusiasm.

son who simply "stayed on campus" longer than necessary. People who are driven, have a specific talent and *know* what they want to do can't wait to grab their diploma and get on with their life.

Then, concerned I may have offended members of this group with advanced degrees, I explained I feel the latter is particularly true in my field, journalism. Many would agree that good writers are born, not taught.

A Master's in journalism is worthwhile if you plan to *teach* journalism. Otherwise, I think, articles written by those with advanced degrees tend to be less "conversational". They too often try to impress their readers rather than just inform them; they use the 50¢ word when the nickel word would keep the copy moving more fluidly.

- *Never underestimate the ability of someone without a formal education.* Sometimes there's a downside to education—it tends to restrict thinking and tells inventive people what can't be done. A lot of well-known entreprenuers—Thomas Edison, for example—had very little education and they did just fine. Truly inventive people—no matter what their background—don't give up easily; they just grit their teeth and get it done.

- *When you go to a convention, listen more than you talk.* Keep what you know close to your chest. Try to learn how other companies do things rather than reveal how you do them. And don't tell people your business is great; it will only motivate them to go back home and try harder to compete with you. A convention is a good place to remember why God gave you two ears and one mouth.

- *When you manage people, it's usually better to "blend in" rather than set yourself apart*—by how you dress, act and even what you drive. You'll get more of a team effort if you're regarded as one of them. There's a big difference between living well and conspicuous consumption.

- *When you get a bright idea, don't tell too many people.* Chances are they'll try to talk you out of it, no matter how good it is. Go with your gut; take the time to think it through and *write it out* before sharing it too broadly. Putting things in writing helps clarify them in your own mind. You'll likely come up with even more ideas while you're writing it!

- *If your career takes off like a meteorite, don't forget the people who helped you get there.* Because if you ever come back down, you may need those people to vouch for you as you pursue another job.

- *When you experience financial success, don't wait till later to support local charities.* An old saying that makes sense is "Give while you live so you know where it goes." Plus, you'll meet some fine, successful people in charitable organizations. They're there because they want to give back to their community; you should, too.

…I wrapped up the session with the Young Presidents by emphasizing that the things I'd covered were just my opinions—no more, no less— then answered their questions.

For me, the best part of this session was noticing these young execs frantically jotted notes all the while I talked. Even better, one called me a month later and said some of these things actually *worked*.

The smallest gift can give the largest lift.

You can tell if a man is clever by his answers.
You can tell if a man is wise by his questions.

CHAPTER 34

You Get Bigger, You Get Dumber

A NUMBER OF YEARS AGO, I belonged to a group called "The Publishers' Forum". It was conceived and organized by a friend of mine, Barry Mano, who edits *Referee Magazine*. Yes, there's a magazine for sports officials, too, and Barry has made it very successful.

Anyway, there were about 15 of us publishers located in Wisconsin, and since none of us produced competing magazines, we were quite open in sharing "secrets" and successes at our quarterly dinner gatherings.

The year Barry was president of the group, he asked each of us to come to the next meeting and describe "the biggest success you've had since the last meeting".

The following year I was president, and I asked each member to describe "the biggest *mistake* you made since the last meeting". I think we got more out of that approach—you always learn more from mistakes than you do successes.

To urge everyone to 'fess up to some really stupid mistakes, I offered to pick up the dinner tab for "the biggest *bomb* of the night". Then, in December, I had the group vote on "The Dumbest Mistake of the Year!"

I won.

I'm still a little embarrassed to share this story, but I'm going to because it's vivid evidence that, as you get bigger, you get dumber. That is, as you add on more people, you don't have time to personally interview all new staffers nor explain the "culture" of your company...what your goals are and what simply makes good "business sense". As a result, your philosophy gets diluted as it's passed down through the ranks.

Okay, here's the year's winner: As you know by now, I have a penchant for hiding things in our magazines to add fun for readers. A month after each issue is out, we draw 50 names from among the responders who have correctly identified the page number of the hidden item, and we send those 50 people a prize.

Well, at this particular time, we'd only been hiding "a needle in a

Promises may get you friends, but it's performance that keeps them.

haystack" in *Country*. But we were receiving such a great response (averaging *125,000* "finders" an issue!), that when we began *Reminisce*, I decided to hide something in that new magazine as well ("Hattie's Hatpin", which has also become a hit).

Within days after I'd made that decision, "Arlene" (I'm not using her real name for obvious reasons), who worked in our mail collection area, showed up in the door of my office.

She put her hand on her hip and said, "Well! I heard you now plan to hide something in this new magazine."

I said yes, I did.

"Really? Do you have any idea how many more people you're going to have to hire to handle that?"

That puzzled me. "What do you mean?"

"Look," she said, "we have three people working pretty much full-time now just to screen all the responses to the needle contest for *Country*. You're going to have to hire that many more to handle the contest in *Reminisce*."

By now I was out of my chair: "What do you mean—we have *three people* handling the needle contest???"

"Well, that's what it takes to carefully screen more than 100,000 letters each month."

"Why…why are you *screening* all that mail?" I asked.

"Well, Roy, you always say this is an honest company. So we first have to read through all those letters to be sure they have the correct page number of the needle before we do the drawing for the 50 winners."

Now I was walking toward her: "No! *No!* You don't mean you've been reading all that mail just to see if they have the right page number! You just walk up to the pile of mail and randomly *select 50 letters*."

> **"Think of it—
> they'd wasted $460,800
> on three empty buildings!"**

"You can't do that," she said. "What if seven of those letters you draw have the wrong page number?"

"Then you draw seven more!" I almost shouted.

Her eyes opened wide as she suddenly realized how simple the solution would have been. Then she turned and nearly ran down the hallway. I had to resist the urge to chase after her!

After I calmed down, I checked with the mail room, and sure enough, that was exactly what they'd been doing…screening and reading through *over 100,000* letters an issue to check for the correct page number!

It gets worse. They'd been doing it that way for a *year and a half*.

We quickly put a stop to it. From that day on, one person took about 5 minutes to walk up to the responses to randomly pluck out 50 letters from different levels of the pile. Then those 50 were quickly checked to see if the reader had correctly identified the page where the needle was hidden.

See, you get bigger, you get dumber.

Think that's bad? Try this one. The grounds and buildings where

258

our corporate offices are located were previously owned by the Allis-Chalmers company. At one point, over 500 people were employed at this facility, working on a large government contract.

Eventually, A-C lost the contract, phased out that part of their business, and the staff was dispersed. Then the three large buildings sat vacant for over 8 years until we came along and decided this would be a good site for our growing business. We could use the administration building for our editorial and marketing divisions, and the large warehouse would be perfect for our growing catalog business.

After we completed the purchase from Allis-Chalmers, we didn't move our staff there for some time—a good deal of renovation work was needed. But the first month after the deal was closed, even though we hadn't moved in, we got a bill from the power company…for *$4,800.*

Thinking there must be some mistake, Norb Whittle, our CFO, called the utility company to check on it. Nope, he was told, that's the correct monthly bill.

"*What?*" asked Norb. "How can that be? How could you bill *$4,800* a month for three *empty buildings?*"

"Sorry, nobody told us they were empty," was the reply from the power rep. "Allis-Chalmers was working on this high-tech government program, and they required an expensive 'booster backup' program, just in case their power ever went down."

"So you've been billing Allis-Chalmers $4,800 a month for the last 8 years?" asked Norb.

"That's right. And they've been paying it," was the response.

Someone in A-C's billing department obviously hadn't been paying attention and simply continued to pay the monthly bills for *8 years* after the facility was shut down!

Following an on-site visit and discussions, the amount was adjusted and we received the correct monthly bill for the empty facility—around $300. Is that an example of a large company financial nightmare or what?

Norb loves fiddling with figures, and here's what he came up with:

A-C had been paying $4,800 for 96 months, which came to a total of *$460,800.* When compounded at 6% interest annually, the loss came to *$543,148!* That was the total electrical bill that had been paid for three empty buildings that hadn't had a lightbulb turned on in 8 years.

I guess I don't have to mention that the large Allis-Chalmers corporation went out of business about 15 years ago. Maybe other people were surprised when it happened. Norb and I weren't.

Little things soon become big things. As evidenced by these two examples, as a company gets larger, it's important to still "think small". If you don't, a lax attitude becomes pervasive and things start adding up.

It bothers me when I see small, wasteful habits of our employees. I still put the cap on a felt-tip pen between *paragraphs* when I'm writing. Yet I see these same pens scattered about on other desks, caps off, through the noon hour and even overnight. Those pens are 78¢ apiece, and they last

If you want to stay youthful, stay useful.

twice as long if you keep the tip from drying out.

I still recycle paper in my computer printer—might as well use the blank side—and I jot notes on the back of scraps. Yet employees sometimes send me notes on our *two-color company stationery*…and route it inside our freshly printed *company envelopes.*

Those things *bother* me, not just because I recall how we had to watch costs and "get by" in the early days, but because that casual regard soon leads to a "The company can afford it" attitude in more costly areas.

I was once in an employee's home and noticed some of our company pens on the kitchen counter, our small company flag notes being used for grocery lists and several of our notepads being used for kids' homework. That employee isn't with us anymore for other reasons, but the "seed" was planted right there.

> ## *"There's sometimes a thin line between theft and entitlement…"*

That employee also used to turn in a rental car *after* the weekend. These are all examples of how small things can lead to bigger things; it becomes a mindset.

There's sometimes a very thin line between employee "theft" and what some regard as employee "entitlement", but it's certainly something to watch for. A national study 2 years ago confirmed that employee theft amounts to major costs at many companies.

Fortunately, we have great employees, and I've seen few problems of this type over the years. Perhaps it's because of the way I dealt with it one time when we only had about 30 employees; maybe the memory of that episode lingers for those who were in our ranks then.

We were growing fast and had just hired a couple of new editors, who were scheduled to come on board the following week. An assistant in charge of supplies came into my office and told me we'd be needing two more typewriters (shows how long ago this was).

"How can that be?" I asked, knowing just a few months prior we'd bought several typewriters, calculators and dictating machines from a nearby business that had closed down.

We started checking, and sure enough, not one of those typewriters was in our storage area. Neither were a couple of the calculators, at least one of the dictating units and some other equipment.

So, I simply posted this sign by the coffee machine:

"It has come to my attention that several typewriters and other office equipment items are missing. If any of these were taken home, they need to be returned immediately. These are company items, not personal items.

"As you know, I'm normally here at work by 7 a.m. Tomorrow morning I won't be coming in until 8 a.m. I want all of this equipment returned by then. I'm not interested in who took it or who has it, I only want it returned. I want it placed on the conference table before 8 a.m."

The next morning when I came in, the conference table was so loaded with equipment, it made me laugh out loud! There were a half dozen type-writers, various calculators, dictating units, staplers, staple removers, pack-ets of typing paper, notepads, boxes of pens and a whole lot more! People weren't taking any chances—they brought *everything* back.

A half hour later, one of our ad salesmen (we were still publishing *Farm Building News*, an ad-supported magazine then) ambled into my of-fice and said, "Well, Chief, you got a lot of stuff back, huh?"

After I expressed my amazement, he said, "I have to admit—I had two of the typewriters."

"Really, Don...you don't even *type*."

"I know," he said, "but my two daughters are taking typing in high school and they were using them to practice. Actually, I had one of the dictating machines, too."

"How were you using *that*?"

"Well, my wife and I are going to sing in the church variety show, and we were using it for practice to hear how we were doing."

Suddenly I felt like "Scrooge" again. I told him if he wanted to quietly take the unit home until the church show was over, to go ahead; but taking something after having it cleared is a lot different than just taking it.

We had to send out a good deal of that equipment for repairs after kids and others had given it a good ride at home. But this is an example of how far "entitlement" can go if you don't clarify the rules and stick to them.

Nipped in the bud. Fortunately, Norb Whittle joined the company soon after that to head up our Finance Department. *Nothing* got by Norb. The day I hired him, I gave him this simple marching order: "Spend every dollar like it's your own."

Norb really took that to heart. He scrutinized every bill and noted when any supplier's rate increased. Here's just one of his "catches" that saved the company a bundle:

We were having all of our food photography and pictures for our cata-log items taken by a photographer in downtown Milwaukee. We were be-ing billed a set rate per issue of each magazine. But when we started our eighth magazine, Norb noticed the photographer's bill for the first issue of this new one was a good deal higher than the others and men-tioned it to me.

> *"Marching order: 'Spend every dollar like it's your own...'"*

One of our food staff was head-ed downtown that day, and I asked her to question that increase. I couldn't believe the response she got: "Well, you're now doing eight magazines and I felt you could afford a little more."

That irritated me. When did *he* become part of our growth and success? You're supposed to round prices *down* with volume, not *up*. I started check-ing, and found that by now we were doing over $860,000 a year with this photographer!

I met with Norb and asked, "At this rate and with our growth, wouldn't

261

we be better off hiring our own photographer and buying all the necessary equipment? We could set it up in that extra space in the warehouse."

We did the math and it made sense, but we didn't know anything about what equipment we'd need or its fair price. Good salesmen can take advantage of novices. We needed an expert's input.

I'd played golf several times with a photographer named Ron Bates, who ran his own photo processing business. I knew he was trustworthy—you learn a lot about people playing golf; Ron always gave his honest score after each hole, even though we played for quarters. (As an aside, that's all we ever wager on golf—I have this theory that you should never play any game for so much that it can cost you a friend. You never lose a friend over quarters. But, boy, do we keep track of those quarters!)

Anyway, I asked Ron whether he would—for a fee—be willing to advise us in choosing and buying all this equipment. He agreed to do it and he saved us a *bundle*. He knew exactly what we needed for our operation, and he knew exactly what each item was worth. He also knew several good photographer candidates and about what salary would be appropriate.

> *"Pays to bring in an expert rather than proceeding blindly on your own…"*

This is an example of how it's sometimes worth paying a fee to an outside expert rather than going ahead blindly on your own. It's also an example of how you can lose a good account—one worth $860,000—by getting a little greedy and "rounding up" because a growing firm may not notice. Norb noticed.

My favorite "Norb story". Norb gained quite a reputation among our suppliers, who would often complain to me how *tough* he was when it came to prices.

I'd ask, "Is he *fair*?" They'd begrudgingly respond, "Yes, he is," and then some would add, "and I wish he worked for me!"

I'd also told Norb early on, "Let's just pay our bills and pay our taxes. Let's not take time looking for any tax shelters or loopholes or outside investments—let's just concentrate on growing this business and stay squeaky clean ethically, okay?"

That worked for us. Later we became so profitable that the IRS would audit us regularly. That IRS guy would sit in a small office in the Finance Department for more than a month, drinking our coffee and taking up our time with a lot of questions. But he *never once* found anything wrong with our books.

After Norb retired and I watched the Tycos, Enrons and other companies go through their problems and have their names muddied, I wrote Norb a brief thank you note for having kept us *honest* through all the years.

As I've often told our kids, "It takes a lifetime to build character, but you can lose it in a minute with just one wrong deed."

Anyway, back to my favorite Norb story: By now we were in the travel business big time, taking more than 5,000 people a year on various group trips to a variety of destinations. We were working with a good travel agent, Brian Mosey, out of Chicago.

Brian handled many details of our European trips for a fee per person. One day he plopped down in my office for a brief chat after he'd just finished another price-haggling session with Norb. As usual, he complained about how *tough* Norb had been and how he'd been so "squeezed down" in his fees that it was hard for him to make a profit, etc.

As Brian talked, I could tell he was distracted by something he'd observed out the window behind me, so I glanced back. There was a huge machine at work in our front lawn, digging a long, deep trench in preparation for our new irrigation system.

"What's going on out there with all that digging?" Brian asked.

With a straight face I responded, "Oh, Norb dropped a quarter out there last week and they're looking for it."

Brian exploded with laughter! He never forgot that, and every time we meet to this day, he retells that quarter story and laughs all over again.

While funny, that pretty much described how Norb Whittle scrutinized everything we spent over the years. There's *no way* he would have paid that $4,800 monthly utility bill for an empty facility like that Allis-Chalmers employee did. Hey, he even noticed one time when the price of the weekly flowers for our receptionist's desk went up $5!

Appropriately, at Norb's retirement party, someone toasted him by saying, "For all these years, Norb spent every dollar like it was his own. After he's gone, we're going to spend every dollar like it's Norb's!" Hear, hear!

You need someone overseeing *your* finance department who spends every dollar like it's their own. Or even like it's Norb's.

Being patient during one minute of anger may save a hundred days of sorrow.

CHAPTER 35

'Wince Factor' and Other Quirks

FOR YEARS I've referred to it as the "wince factor" when we discussed prices of items we were selling at the company.

I always contended that you have to raise your price until somebody winces. If no one is wincing, you're giving away profits. You have to get to the level where there's some resistance.

That's why we tested and tried different levels of subscription prices. We learned that some buyers equate quality with price—they may even respond better at a higher price due to the perception of receiving a better, "classier" product.

So my wince factor saying was tossed around a lot at our offices, and it was applied in small ways as well as large ways. Here's an example of a small way:

For every magazine subscription and every item in our Country Store catalog, our prices for several years ended with "95¢". Whether it was $3.95 or $13.95, those last two digits were always 95¢.

One morning I stopped in Norb's office and said I was thinking of something last night: "What if we changed that 95¢ on each item to 98¢? I can't see that we'd lose any customers for that 3¢ difference. Yet, with our volume, that 3¢ could add up in a hurry. So, how much difference would that make for us over a year's time?"

Norb's eyebrows went up and he reached for his calculator. With over 6 million subscribers by then and several million catalog orders per year, that little 3¢ per order added up to *thousands* of dollars per year. We adjusted immediately, and nobody seemed to notice. Or wince.

Speaking of pennies, are you game for a little trivia at this point? Most people know that J.C. Penney is the person given credit for starting "99¢" prices. But most people *think* he did it to make the prices sound lower and more appealing.

Not the case. Several years ago, I read a long dissertation about J.C. (I love reading about early entrepreneurs) and learned he began the 99¢

265

thing solely to keep his clerks from cheating. He'd found that if something was priced at an even dollar figure, the clerk could slip the folding money in his pocket after the customer left.

But if the clerk had to give the customer 1¢ in *change*, he had to ring up the cash register to get that penny. Ol' J.C. was one smart cookie! He not only curbed cheating, but his prices seemed lower at the same time.

Now here's a juicier example. We had just put together our first tour of the Deep South, which would take our groups on a 7-day route through farms and scenic spots in Georgia, Alabama, Louisiana and Mississippi. It was the first domestic trip we'd ever offered, and Norb and I spent some time discussing what kind of markup would fly with our audience. We finally settled on $100 per person.

Next morning when I came in, I went directly to Norb's door (he *always* beat me to work) and said, "I was thinking about this last night. I think we should mark up these tours by $200."

> ## *"Ol' J.C. Penney was one smart cookie!"*

"What? *$200?*" Norb reacted. "Why, that could cut the response in half!"

"Exactly," I answered, "but we'd still make exactly the same amount of money with half as many people and half as many staff escorts."

We decided to go with it…and we sold out *13 tours* of 90 people each (two motorcoaches per trip) back-to-back! There's *no way* we would have been able to handle twice as many people on 26 trips. Even if we had, it would have yielded the same amount of profit.

Plus, people loved the tour and lauded its value. Apparently we still had not reached the "wince factor".

There's another aspect worth noting in this. We hadn't taken the time to do a market study before making this decision about the tour price. Sometimes you just have to know your audience and go by gut feel. You don't always have *time* for checking the pulse of your audience. It's another example of our company's standard philosophy of "Ready, *FIRE*, Aim!"

Sometimes it isn't good to pay too much attention to what's happened in the past, either. It can be a mistake to overanalyze. Instead of coming up with new, creative ways to increase sales, some people keep wringing the juice out of what already happened. Move on!

Speaking of creativity, it's my opinion you shouldn't give a creative person too many negative facts. One time I was discussing some wild ideas with Norb and a few other people in Finance. I was highly excited about them, but for every idea I ran past them, they came up with reasons why it wouldn't work.

Finally I got exasperated. I said, "Guys, look—I'm your three-point shooter. If you keep coming up with reasons why this and that won't work, you're going to put doubts in my mind before I take the next shot. Even worse, next time I might decide not to shoot at all."

Certain things worry a boss…like when the finance department orders three pencils and a dozen erasers.

Norb never forgot that, and often thereafter he referred to me as "The Shooter". He would still give me his honest opinion, which I wanted and respected, but he'd always add, "Of course, in fairness, I would never have started the first magazine without ads, either!"

These things have worked for us. This about wraps up some of the management and marketing practices that have paid dividends at our company. But here are a few tail-enders for what they're worth:

• When you're interviewing someone who's applying for a job, note how fast they walk. I've learned slow walkers are slow workers. Just observe, sometime, how briskly people walk down the hall when they're really *interested* in what they're doing. They can't *wait* to finish it.

By contrast, I've noticed some of the part-time warehouse help we hire during the holiday season—they *amble* down the hall, obviously bored with their job and life in general. I once told Bobbi those guys walk so slowly that I passed two of them on the way to the rest room and met the same two when I came out! That was an exaggeration, but only slightly.

While discussing this "fast walker" theory with my golf foursome one day, one said after he interviews someone, he makes a point to walk them out to their car to thank them for their time. But what he's *really* doing is looking inside their car. "If they have junk all over in their car, they're not going to care about their work as much as I'd like," he says.

Another said he checks the back of an interviewee's shoes for the same reason. "If they only shine the toes, they're not likely to care about work details." Hmmmm. "And if they're chewing gum, they're gone!" he added.

While I might question those interview techniques, all four of us agreed we always appreciate a firm handshake of an applicant, even if it's a woman...along with looking you right in the eye as they do so.

One final thing I always note during an interview over lunch or just judging people in general: A person who is nice to you, but rude to a waiter, is not a nice person. Never fails.

• When giving small bonuses to employees for "going the extra mile" on this or that, consider giving unique *items* instead of *cash*. If you give someone a $100 or $200 "thank you" check, that cash will go home and just melt right into the grocery money. The family won't notice, so no big deal.

> *"Give unique bonus gifts instead of cash..."*

But if you send a huge gift basket, filled with candy, nuts, cookies and fruit ("For the fruits of your labor"), that package will cause a real stir. When your employee arrives home, the whole family will ask, "What did you *do*, Dad (or Mom)?" This kind of bonus may cost less and be appreciated far more.

I've given bonuses such as baseball tickets for the whole family ("For keeping your eye on the ball"), sent a magician to their home ("Keep working your magic") and once gave tailored suits to three guys when they wrapped up a big project ("Your effort suits us fine").

It pays to go out on a limb. That's where all the fruit is. —Will Rogers

267

And once my wife and I took the top five members of our Exec Team out to lunch just prior to the holidays. For dessert we handed each of them a box of Cracker Jack. The hidden "prize" was more than they anticipated—we'd slipped in ten $100 bills as their Christmas bonus.

- Watch the "cents" aspect when you list prices in your literature. It's a small thing I learned years ago in a publishing seminar that's stuck with me because of the "cents" it makes.

Here's what I mean: If you're listing the price of something you're *SELLING*, take the zeros off it like this: *$5* rather than $5.00. But if you're showing how much your customers will be *SAVING*, add the zeros: *$5.00* rather than $5. The zeros add to the perception either way.

- Don't EVER forget to add *"Please PRINT"* on the first line of *every* order form you ever print. If you get responders to print their name on the first line, they'll likely print everything else requested on the form.

Without that reminder, a high percentage of people will just *handwrite* (in cursive, i.e.) rather than print…and you'll have a problem. Many people's penmanship is difficult to decipher, yet people are very fussy about having their names spelled right. You get it wrong, they're unhappy. Worse, if you can't make out the address and their order doesn't reach them, they're even more unhappy.

So, at our offices, we established a scary penalty for anyone who forgets to add PRINT on any order form: First, we sneak up behind them when they least expect it and *SCREAM* at the top of our lungs!

But that's not half as bad as what follows—we send them to our fulfillment center for a day and have them try their darnedest to decipher the scribbling of hundreds of responders. The scream may be the easier penalty of the two.

> *"Don't ever forget to add 'Please PRINT' on order forms…"*

Okay, I'm kidding about both of these penalties, of course, but we're dead serious about all the *time* that's wasted and the *money* that's lost from misdirected and returned packages. All because of two little missing words, *"Please PRINT"*. Never turn out an order form without them.

- Don't ask why some things work…if they work, just go with the flow. A good example of this is the "blow-in cards" that fall out when you pick up one of our magazines or anyone else's.

Drive you crazy, don't they? Me, too.

Problem is, those cards *work* so well that we and other publishers can't afford to stop using them. Here's why: They're called "blow-in cards" because they're literally blown into the magazine as it speeds along the press. This system is now so refined that you can choose specifically where you want each card in the issue, between certain pages; the air pressure can be adjusted to separate the pages and pop a card in there.

Well, while those cards are likely a pain to readers, we and other publishers continue to use them because they're incredibly *effective*. For example, the large subscription form that we bind into the issue costs *eight times* as much as one of those little cards. But the response is exactly the opposite—we receive *eight times* the response from any of those blow-in cards as we do the bind-in form!

Why? Maybe because when those pesky cards fall out of the magazine, they force the reader to pick them up and read them. On the other hand, maybe it's because readers are reluctant to tear the bind-in out of their magazine. We really don't know. We just know the results, which makes the why less important.

> **"When interviewing someone, note how fast they walk..."**

• I almost always stand up when someone enters my office. It's a time-saver. If I stay sitting, the person is more apt to sit down and make themselves comfortable. If I stay standing, they'll stay standing, and it allows me a minute to get an idea of whether what they want to discuss is worth a longer "sitting session". I can then make that decision and ask them to take a seat.

I once mentioned this in a management roundtable, and a woman said, "That's about the rudest thing I've ever heard!"

I responded, "Which is more rude—later standing up while the person is still seated, sort of 'urging them to leave'? Or continuing to stand in the first place while—unknown to the visitor—you're deciding whether to ask them to take a seat?"

Standing discussions are *always* shorter than sitting discussions. And time management at the executive level is important.

• Be careful how many college interns you take on for summer jobs. While it's admirable to give these students some real work experience and tuition funds, be aware they can cost more than they contribute.

For example, if you assign them to jobs that take considerable training, their 3-month session is pretty much over just as you get them up to speed. And all that training takes productive time away from one or more of your high-paid people.

The best use of college interns, I've found, is to select students who are between their junior and senior years. That way, if they're really good, you can consider hiring them after they graduate. This provides you a "3-month interview" period to see how well they can perform on the job, plus they're partially trained if they later come on board full time.

• Treat your suppliers as well as you do your clients. Your success is based on both. We have such a high regard for our suppliers that we invite over 200 of them to a Milwaukee Brewers baseball game each summer. We call it our "BB&BBB Night" (Beer, Brats and Brewer Baseball).

We don't invite only the "brass" at these companies—we concentrate on the people who are on the line doing the *work*. We want the main-line people who run the presses, buy our paper, handle bookings for our tours and even those who clean our offices.

This annual BB&BBB party has grown bigger every year—now up to

Nothing lasts forever...even your troubles.

269

250—from our supply firms. We give each of them a name tag, and our management staff personally meets as many as possible, shakes their hands and thanks them for what they do.

Each year at this event we present "The Workhorse Award", naming the firm we feel did the most during the past year to improve our quality, cut our costs or boost our profits.

While this annual event runs up a tab of several thousand dollars, we feel it's money well spent. For example, when our magazines go to print, those pressmen know that pressrun is for our company and likely say, "We know these people." We think it makes them more attentive to going the extra mile and getting it *right*. Same applies to cleaning our building or whatever. You treat suppliers right, they'll treat you right.

• We discourage gifts at Christmas. We send a letter to all of our suppliers around Thanksgiving each year, asking them *not* to send or bring us any gifts during the upcoming holiday season.

"Your quality work is already all the gift we expect," the letter says in part, and adds if they still insist on giving something, we'd prefer they give it to the United Way campaign or some other local charity rather than to anyone at our company.

Why? Gifts can cause dissension in the ranks. If the head buyer gets numerous gift items from multiple suppliers, his crew envies those gifts because they received nothing. If he or she is generous and shares all those gifts—chocolates, fruit baskets, assorted nuts, candy, caramel popcorn—you have a staff with sticky hands who find it hard to work and hard to diet.

Suppliers often privately thank us for this policy. They admit it gets more difficult for them to decide on a "proper gift" each year. And local charities benefit from those suppliers who still insist on giving "scale" to each client.

For whatever reasons, these are some of the management practices that have worked well for us over the years.

270

Attitude and aptitude are blood brothers.

CHAPTER 36

Can Casual Become Too Casual?

A LOT OF YOU reading this book—including some at our own company—will likely disagree with me on this one, but I think today's casual wear policies have gotten out of hand.

I never minded "Casual Fridays" during my term at the helm—people had worked hard all week, and by Friday it was time to taper off a bit. Still, it's said "You are what you wear", and I often noticed on Fridays there was a less serious attitude and more levity in the hallways. But for that one day it was okay.

Not long after our company was sold, my successor made casual business wear pretty much the standard attire. And I now detect more of a casual attitude all week long.

Frankly, I miss "dressing up for work". I grew up on a farm and never had nice clothes; now that I have them, I enjoy wearing them.

For me, putting on a dress shirt and a tie is a bit like putting on a "uniform". I'm then in my "work mode", I feel more professional, and a certain amount of business decorum tends to go with the clothes.

Apparently I'm not alone in my thinking; according to *The Wall Street Journal*, suits are selling again as a growing number of companies have started "Dress-Up Thursdays". In some firms this Thursday thing is intended as a way of phasing out casual attire and getting back to more professional wear.

These companies are finding that many people just don't know where the limit on "casual" is. Wrinkled khakis, faded blue jeans and well-worn tennis shoes give their company an unprofessional image. As one company exec was quoted, "How you dress shows the world what you think of yourself."

I'm reminded of when one of our daughters was a high school senior and asked if she could host a party of nearly *100 classmates* at our house after a prom. I sorta panicked and called the principal. I was more than a little concerned about the behavior of that many kids in our home.

Next time someone shows you a kindness…pass it on.

I'll never forget his response: "Mr. Reiman, I don't think you need to be concerned. These kids are all going to be dressed up; they'll be in formal dresses and rented tuxes. My experience is this: When kids dress up, they don't act up."

He was absolutely right. We had zero problems—those kids "minded their manners" and handled themselves incredibly well that night. Now, I'm not putting that situation on the same basis as an office environment, but it does make a statement for the fact that, at any age, "Attire and attitude go hand in hand."

I, for one, would like to see casual wear fade away like some of those faded blue jeans, and I'd welcome back the days of dressing professionally for work. Besides, I have some great ties that just aren't seeing the light of day simply because I don't want to be the only uppity one at the office.

I'm not a fan of "flex time", either. For those of you unfamiliar with this growing trend, flex time requires employees to put in the usual 8 hours a day, but gives them flexibility as to when those hours are.

Our company's flex program, which was started after I handed over the reins, calls for 7 "core hours" per day—from 8:30 a.m. to 3:30 p.m. (minus lunch hour)—when everyone has to be there.

But beyond those 6 hours, staffers can put in the other 2 hours whenever they want. So we now have about half of our people coming in at 6:30 and leaving at 3:30, and the other half coming in at 8:30 and leaving at 5:30. To me, that's a problem—this means there are *4 hours per day* that certain "team" members are unable to work together. It's sometimes like trying to run an engine with a few gears missing.

Another negative is it made our salaried employees "time conscious". They now tend to think in strict 8-hour brackets instead of coming in a little early or leaving a little late as they often did before. The morning group now comes in *exactly* at 6:30 a.m. primarily because it allows them to leave *exactly* at 3:30 p.m.

So, while they're on hand at 6:30, there may not be a good deal for some of them to do because part of the needed *team* is missing. Then they leave right at 3:30, which is in the heart of the afternoon for those working the 8:30-5:30 shift. Having all those people walking out in the middle of the afternoon is a distraction in a creatively inclined company.

Flex time may work well in some companies, but in cases where projects require a great deal of interaction, I feel it cuts productivity. I know I'm not alone in that view—I recently talked with an exec at a major company who said he gave flex time a *trial* for a month to see how it would work at his firm, and he couldn't *wait* for the month to be over!

Now, I *totally understand* why most employees love a flex-time program for many good, personal reasons. Conversely, I hope they'll understand why

There are few greater loans than a sympathetic ear.

I and other managers might have a different view.

Running a company is not a popularity contest. You'd like it to be…you'd like all the employees to love you…but that's not always what's best for you, or them.

Business is sometimes like football. Offense is much more exciting, but defense is what wins games.

Likewise, flex-time hours, abundant benefits, multiple meetings and liberal vacation days are sure to help employees love their leader. But they won't love him or her down the line when this standard operating procedure begins cutting deeply into the company's profits.

What generally follows then is laying off key people, staff restructuring and other major changes. Given the choice, most people would rank job security over job benefits.

Again, I fully understand why the majority of our employees appreciate the flex-time program. I hope they in turn will understand why, from a management standpoint, I might view it otherwise.

As it's said in a marriage and life in general, "If two people agree on everything, one isn't needed."

*If you could kick the person who
causes you the most problems,
you couldn't sit down for a month.*

CHAPTER 37

Promotional Stunts That Worked

WHEN you buy a six-horse hitch of Belgians and have them driven along a rural route from Maine to California in a trip that takes over 16 months, you could write a book about it.

And we did. It was called *The Mane Event*, and it described in detail this one-of-a-kind trek by *Country's Reminisce* Hitch (which combined the names of the trip's sponsoring magazines, *Country* and *Reminisce*). Of all the promotional things we did to draw attention to our publications, this one probably heads the list.

I'd been a horse lover since the days when Dad would sometimes hand me the lines. ("Lines" are used for *driving* a horse, "reins" are used for *riding* a horse. Isn't this book just incredibly educational??)

I'd also been a fan of Dick Sparrow's famed 40-horse hitch. Dick even let me drive that mammoth team briefly on two occasions, which was quite a thrill—how many people in the world can say that they drove 40 horses at one time?

I'd owned several Belgians over the years, too. That started when Bobbi asked me one fall day what I'd like for Christmas, and I glibly replied, "A Belgian mare." The more I thought about it, the more I wanted it, and that's what I got, "*F&RL* Maggie", named for *Farm & Ranch Living* magazine. I'll tell you more about Maggie later.

After that, for some reason I became intrigued with buying a six-horse hitch and having it driven across the country—partly because no one had done that before, either. But I needed a *reason* for it—just being a promotional trip for our magazines seemed too self-serving.

Then an item appeared in the paper that provided us with a "mission". This was in 1993, and I learned it was the 50th anniversary of the very first senior center in the U.S.

That's it! We would paint "We Salute Seniors" on the side of the wagon and stop at every senior center along the route!

And we did. We knew we had many readers of our magazines at those

275

A hint is something we often drop but seldom pick up.

VIKKI AND DAVID HELMUTH were the "wagon masters" of our coast-to-coast trip over the route at right.

senior facilities; this cross-country trip would give those people something to look forward to when the hitch came by.

"We bought this team with your subscription fees," we told subscribers as we announced the trip, "so these are *your* horses." We learned later they really took that sense of ownership to heart. As the hitch approached, we'd hear people say, "Here comes *our* team" and "Here come *my* horses!"

These Belgians were easy to be proud of—this was one of the top hitches in America. They'd won a host of awards at national draft horse shows. They were *beautiful* and behaved wonderfully all along the route.

The trip was purposely unhurried—the team covered no more than 10 miles a day and rested every Sunday. These huge horses seemed to enjoy the trip; they were six proud prima donnas, tossing their heads and prancing whenever people appeared along the route.

To make it officially an "ocean-to-ocean" trip, the team was driven in the Atlantic surf near Kennebunkport, Maine (at left—President George H.W. Bush's summer home is clearly visible in the background of some of the other photos taken that day), and we did the same thing in the Pacific surf when the team reached San Diego.

My wife and I and various editors took turns joining the hitch crew regularly so we could *personally* thank thousands of our subscribers for supporting our ad-free magazines over the years. These experiences were often extremely heartwarming.

We published a map of the route in our magazines, then updated the hitch's progress in each issue over the 16 months. Subscribers could also get updates every week via a toll-free phone service. (The star of the team was "Firestone", and one of our staffers added fun to these recordings now and then by providing the info in a "horse's voice"; he made Firestone sound like "Mr. Ed", and the callers loved it.)

Subscribers would line roadsides out in the middle of nowhere to see *their* team and smile and wave. We had the gleaming red wagon custom-

Clearing away cobwebs does no good unless you get the spider.

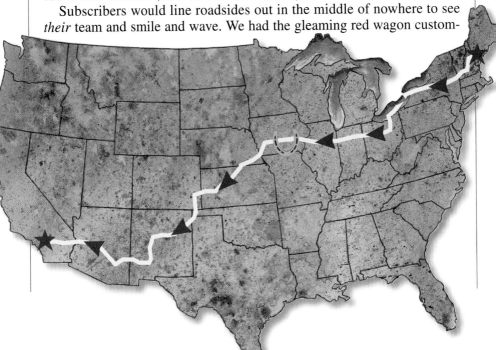

RESIDENTS of senior centers all across the country eagerly awaited arrival of *their* hitch.

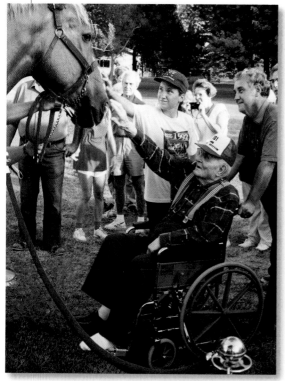

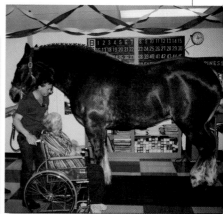

made by a Canadian firm, and it was equipped so 12 people could ride at a time.

We'd stop, pick up a dozen, haul 'em a half mile, then pick up another load. To give you an idea of how often that was done, we had the riders sign an insurance form as they boarded. We tallied these names later and found more than *50,000 people* had the opportunity to ride this historic wagon during the trip. We still get letters from subscribers saying, "I was one of the riders!"

When we neared a small town, you'd have thought the circus was coming. Most of the community would be waiting, often joined at the town's bandstand by the mayor and dignitaries.

10 MILES A DAY were covered in slow walk by the hitch. A truck with flashing light (out of view in this photo) followed behind to warn traffic. Not a single accident occurred during the trip.

But what I always liked seeing were the grandpas holding children high on their shoulders to show the kind of horses *they* used to drive. I noticed some of these grandpas looked 10 years younger while beaming as the team passed by.

When we arrived at the senior centers, it often got emotional for us. *Hundreds* of elderly people who had waited weeks and even months for the arrival of this team would be on the front steps, on the front lawn (many in wheelchairs) and waving out of the windows.

Probably the most memorable stop for me was the rainy day we stopped at a Massachusetts senior center. Because it wasn't feasible for the hitch to be driven near the facility, and residents couldn't come several blocks to see the hitch, David Helmuth, our driver, walked Firestone to the circular drive at the front of the building, along with "Barron", our dalmatian.

"Bring him in," said the activities director.

"You mean the dog, right?" asked David.

"No, the horse—bring him in."

We were a little shocked. "You mean you want me to bring this 2,200-pound Belgian inside your center?" David asked.

"Yes, I do. I have over 400 people here who have been eagerly waiting months for the day your hitch would arrive, and I'm not going to let the weather disappoint them. Whatever that horse dirties up, we'll clean up. Bring him inside!"

So we did (see middle photo at left). David led Firestone right through

Laughing is good exercise. It's like jogging on the inside.

279

CROWDS gathered in rural towns when the hitch arrived. These photos show the turnout in Centerville, Iowa.

the double entry door and into the lobby. This horse was enormous to begin with, but he looked even larger in there. His metal shoes *clonked* on that tile floor. Firestone was always kind of a character, and he didn't disappoint this time, either.

Just as he got near the information desk, he swung his head and put his nose right in the guest book! We have a video of that moment to prove it.

The residents were *jammed* along the walls of that lobby, and they stepped forward one by one to pet and hug that huge horse. Firestone, always the puppy, just seemed to *know* how much it meant to them and patiently soaked up every minute of it.

That same activities director then surprised us again. "Take him down the halls," she said. "I don't want the people who can't leave their rooms

THAT MAKES IT OFFICIAL. Team splashes in Pacific surf at San Diego to culminate its ocean-to-ocean trek honoring seniors. Note the yacht in the background.

to miss this, either."

So David led that huge Belgian *clonking* down the hall, while I ran ahead yelling, *"Horse in the hall! Horse in the hall!"* I was afraid otherwise some of these folks would think they were hallucinating—that they'd imagined they'd just seen a huge *Belgian* walk by!

Another memorable moment for me occurred at another senior center, where an elderly farmer in a wheel-chair was petting Firestone, who predictably held his head down so the man could reach him (see photo on page 278).

> *"We kept hearing people say, 'Here comes our team!'"*

As he stroked Firestone's face, the man turned to me and said, "I've been in here 12 years, and what I miss most is horses. You can see them in movies, you can read books about them and you can look at pictures of them…but you can't smell them."

Then tears ran down his cheek. And soon mine, too.

There are so many similar stories to tell that I can't include here. The trip, which officially ended Aug. 12, 1994, garnered TV and newspaper coverage all along the route; it literally did put our magazines on the map.

Quadruplets—four crying out loud.

281

Again and again, we concluded that whether it resulted in good promotion or not, it had been more than worth doing by allowing us to give back something to thousands of our subscribers—especially all those appreciative people in senior centers along the route.

Many of them vicariously took the entire 16-month trip with us, bumping along on that beautiful wagon. They did so through the two lengthy videos we produced, as well as the photo-filled book, which included a diary of the trip "narrated" by Firestone.

Through *Country's Reminisce* Hitch, we got more than we gave.

We've dreamed and schemed for years for ways to bring our magazines to the attention of potential subscribers, because promoting and selling subscriptions solely by mail is an expensive route that gets more costly every year.

Basically, we've tried to incorporate things into our magazines that make people *talk* about them. I've already mentioned hiding needles and other items in our pages. We've learned many families have a timed "race" to see how long it takes to find the item. Some even call relatives long-distance to see if *they* found it. That kind of conversation among readers and potential readers is *golden*.

> *"We once discovered 11 families were sharing a single subscription..."*

We also learned to deal with "pass-alongs" in a positive way. By that I mean the practice of one person subscribing, then passing on the magazine to someone else when finished. (We once discovered that a single subscription to our *Country Woman* magazine in Iowa was being shared by *11 families*.)

Now, when you live and die solely by subscriptions as we do, you'd like to find a way to encourage each of these people to get their *own* subscription. And we've come up with a number of ways to do that.

For one, we often try to encourage people to "cut out" things. That way the pass-along reader finds things missing.

Secondly, we like to put a tight deadline on contests. That way it may be too late for the "hitchhiker" to respond.

But the *best* idea came from some of our readers, who kept complaining about these pass-alongs.

"Can you do something to encourage my friend to get her own subscription to your magazine?" they'd write. "She knows about when each issue arrives, then lets me know she's *waiting* for it. So I not only have to hurry, but I have to *copy down the recipes* before I pass it along to her.

"That doesn't seem fair because I'm the one paying for it! I think you should urge everyone to get their *own* subscription."

So...we started running an item in each issue headlined, *"Is This YOUR Issue You're Reading?"* The type below it read:

"If the issue you're presently reading isn't your own, but is a copy that some subscriber passed on to you, perhaps you'd like to use this form to order your own personal subscription.

"That way you won't have to wait until your generous friend is finished reading each issue. And, it just could be that—while she doesn't want to tell you—she'd prefer to *keep* each issue so she can refer back to it later for its recipes and other features…"

That approach not only resulted in many new subscriptions, but we received a raft of "Thank yous!" This pass-along problem was obviously bugging more subscribers than we'd thought.

The post office didn't appreciate it, but we also came up with a way of curbing our renewal costs. We'd found, to our chagrin, that only a small percentage of subscribers responded to the first renewal notice. We usually had to send multiple mailings to finally pull that renewal payment out of them.

I learned one day that we were mailing up to *nine renewal notices* before we gave up. That's costly when you figure not only the postage, but the envelopes, addressing them, and printing the letters and the renewal forms for each of those mailings.

We gave some thought to this reluctant response and came up with two possible reasons: Some people look at the date of the expiration and feel there's no need to hurry. Conversely, we're trying to get that payment processed on our time schedule so they won't miss an issue.

The other likely reason is that they've noticed the renewal fee of *other* publishers' magazines is sometimes reduced if they wait and don't respond right away. (That's because ad-supported magazines have a "rate base"—i.e., a certain circulation number they've guaranteed their advertisers—and they sometimes eventually lower their renewal rate just to keep people on board.)

With these conclusions, we came up with a fix-it, when microwave ovens were all the rage. Every busy cook wanted one, but not all of them could afford one.

Knowing that, we ran an item headlined, *"YOU Can Win a FREE Microwave Oven!"*

The article simply explained our problem and the high cost of sending multiple renewal notices. We pointed out that if they were hoping our renewal rate might eventually drop like other magazines', that wouldn't ever happen with ours.

"Respond to the first renewal, and we'll put your name in the cracker barrel…"

"We don't have to assure a certain circulation for advertisers, so our rate will stay the same whether you renew early or late," we stated. "Plus, we don't feel charging late responders a lower fee would be fair to those who responded earlier."

What's more, we said, if we are forced to continue sending multiple renewals, the cost of doing so may force us to raise our subscription rates. Which was true.

283

"So," the article explained, "this is what we're going to do. To encourage subscribers to respond to our FIRST renewal notice, we're going to collect the names of those people who respond to that first notice *within 10 days after receiving it.*

"We're going to put those names into a large cracker barrel. Then we're going to have one of our staff draw a name and award that subscriber a *FREE Litton Microwave Oven!* Those who wait for the second or subsequent notices won't be in on the drawing."

You guessed it. The response to our first renewals *jumped immediately,* saving us thousands of dollars in postage alone. We continued the program for a long time, showing the picture of each winner—with the oven—to add credibility. That exposure seemed to increase the response even more; it wasn't just a chance to win a free microwave, but to have your picture in a national magazine!

What's more, again people *talked about* this little Greendale, Wisconsin magazine publishing company that was "giving away a microwave oven every month".

Recently, while talking to Bobbi, I reminisced about this years-ago microwave giveaway and wondered whether we should try something like that again. I said a microwave might not be a good enough "draw" today. With our current circulation, the prize would likely have to be something much bigger.

"Like a Volkswagen Beetle!" I suddenly blurted.

Just as quickly, she came back with, "Yes, you could tell readers, 'Respond within 10 days and we won't 'Bug' you anymore!'"

That's the way we've worked for years—I came up with the concept, then she often came up with the idea that made it work.

Don't go around saying the world owes you a living.
The world owes you nothing. It was here first.
—Mark Twain

CHAPTER 38

Sales Methods That Opened Doors

AS YOU KNOW BY NOW, my first publishing success was the ad-supported *Farm Building News*. Before that, our fledgling company turned out product promotion pieces and catalogs and handled public relations for a number of companies.

It's sometimes difficult to get the doors of potential clients opened before you're established, well known and have some working capital. So here are a few of the things that were effective for us during those early years:

• When I was still operating out of my basement, I was *dying* to get a chance with Allis-Chalmers, which was located in a suburb of Milwaukee and was still one of the largest farm equipment companies in the country. I felt if I could find a way to do just one promotional piece for them, it might lead to a lot more.

I knew the name of the advertising manager there, but despite several attempted contacts, couldn't get an appointment with him. Then I heard from one of their engineers that A-C had just developed a new no-till planter.

He said what made it especially unique was that the farmer—by adding whatever attachments he wanted—could basically build his own planter; he could make it a two-, four- or six-row planter, along with choosing his own accessories.

I thought about it, then sent a short note to the ad manager: "I have an idea that I am convinced will sell more than a hundred of your new No-Till planters. I'll share it with you free if you'll call me."

He called.

His name was Dean Carpenter, and we eventually became good friends. When he asked "Okay, what's your idea?", I described an experience I once had. I'd gotten into the passenger seat of somebody's Buick and was highly impressed with a little silver plate attached to the glove compartment. It said, "This car was specifically manufactured for (name of owner)." Pretty classy.

So…I told Dean, with all the options available for this new planter, what if they called it "The Personalized Planter"? And then, to make it really special, they attached a little silver plate like that to each planter: "This planter was specifically designed for (name of owner)."

He liked it. With that door opened, I said I also had an idea for the brochure that could be used to sell it. It would fold sort of like an accordion, and the farmer could keep folding it to show pictures of a different number of planter units and accessories against that tool bar. This would help him visualize the type of planter that would best suit his needs.

Dean liked that idea, too, and told me to give it a try. I worked with a great Art Director, Bob Blaser, and the accordion-type gimmick worked even better than we thought. Allis-Chalmers ended up selling hundreds of those planters, which had a great deal to do with starting the whole no-tillage trend that began sweeping across the nation's agriculture.

> **_"Sure you get a lot of mail...but how many people send you the mailbox?"_**

How much that personalized plate and the "accordion brochure" had to do with that success, I don't know. But I do know that as a result of that door opener, we ended up writing and producing as many as 30 catalogs and brochures each year for A-C. What's more, it led to our eventually landing Allis-Chalmers' advertising account—we became their sole ad agency, creating and placing more than $1.3 million of advertising annually.

- **Color and creativity sell.** Whenever Allis-Chalmers or other clients asked me to bid against several other suppliers on a black-and-white or two-color brochure, I always showed up with a four-color layout instead. I found that had two benefits:

(A) Once they saw it in full-color, it was hard to resist. And if they went with it, I had no one bidding against me—the other suppliers had bid on a b/w or two-color basis.

(B) Even if they found the full-color version too costly, they were impressed with the creativity and willingness to deliver more than they'd asked for. Either way, my chances of landing the job were improved.

- **Getting to the "Big Guy".** When we were selling advertising for *Farm Building News*, I often found it particularly tough to arrange a personal meeting with top execs at big companies.

For example, I needed to reach the Marketing Manager of General Motors truck division. The average farm builder owned a half dozen or more trucks, yet I couldn't get GM's ad agency interested in advertising. Our ad rates were low, and on a 15% commission basis, ad agencies didn't view them as very profitable. Especially an agency serving an account as large as General Motors.

Yet, I felt if I could talk *directly* to GM's Marketing Manager, I'd be able to convince him ours was not only a magazine he should advertise in, but he should also be exhibiting at our National Farm Builder Show.

I finally came up with an idea that resulted in a personal meeting: I

When a hypochondriac has measles, he tells you how many.

286

went out and bought the *largest* mailbox I could find—one of those big, expensive things that, parked at the end of your drive, will hold large packages along with letters. Then I shipped this huge mailbox to him inside a carton the size of an oven. We taped a handwritten note to the front of the mailbox: "Personal letter for (his name) inside."

The letter inside began: "Sure, you receive a lot of mail…but how many people send you the mailbox with it? That's how important I feel it is for you to give me just 10 minutes to describe a way I feel will sell a lot of your trucks…"

The letter further pointed out that he was going to receive something from me *every single day* until he called me. The second day I sent him an extra-large T-shirt, with my entire letter printed on the shirt. (We were also printing shirts and turning out other promotional merchandise then.)

I can't recall what I sent him on the third and fourth days, but I well remember that I overdid it on Friday, the fifth day, when his secretary called to tell me—lightheartedly—that "You scared us so badly, we considered calling in the bomb squad!"

See, I'd gone to the hardware store the previous weekend to test flashlights; I wanted to be sure one would last for more than 24 hours, so it would still be on after I overnighted it to Detroit. The outside of that box said, "The Switch Is On!" That was to tie in with the accompanying letter, which explained a lot of advertisers were *switching* to *Farm Building News.*

I never anticipated their *bomb* interpretation! Nevertheless, she said the GM exec had been lining up those daily items of mine on his credenza, showing them off and chatting about them with co-workers. She then suggested several dates for me to come in and meet with him.

I did, and he became an advertiser. It all started with a mailbox…an idea that almost "bombed".

● **Golf balls can be "letter openers".** It doesn't always take something as big as a mailbox to get your letter read by a bigwig. But you do need to come up with a way of getting that letter past his assistant.

The exec may have made clear he doesn't want to be bothered with anything that looks like a solicitation. So if you simply send a naked letter, chances are it won't get beyond that assistant's desk (or wastebasket).

So, when we were still soliciting new business in those early years, I learned to put something of *value* with a letter, so the assistant might feel a little guilty if it didn't get passed along.

Examples of things that accomplished this: A sleeve of Titleist golf balls with a letter that began, "You could be playing more golf if we handled your account…"

Fishing lures: "If you're fishing for a new agency, we'd like to talk to you…"

Sunglasses: "You could be spending more time in the Sun Belt this time of year if you turned things over to us…"

Packet of lightbulbs: "We have some bright ideas we'd like to share with you…"

Time flies when you're paying a baby-sitter.

Corny? Maybe. Bottom line, attention-getters like this worked. We'd keep sending these promos to arrive every Monday morning, sometimes for more than a month, until we got a call. Our success with this approach just might validate the old saying "Don't scorn corn."

• **Cocktail parties are costly.** During the time we were selling ads for *Farm Building News*, there was one big convention each year hosted by the NAMA, the National Agricultural Marketing Association. Almost all the farm magazines sponsored evening hospitality suites at this event in hopes of luring in advertising agencies and advertising managers.

Personally, I never felt those cocktail affairs were very effective. It was far too noisy in those crowded rooms for good conversation, it was more of a party than a business-like atmosphere, and all that booze was incredibly costly in a fancy hotel. Yet, we needed to make contact with many of these ad decision makers.

So…the year this convention was held in San Francisco, my five staffers and I circulated among these cocktail parties dressed like "medics", wearing white shirts, white pants, white shoes and red jackets. On our lapels we had large name tags that read, "The Reiman Rescue Squad".

We then handed out "prescription cards" to attendees, inviting them to come to "The Recovery Room" between 6 and 8 a.m. the following morning for "Hot coffee, juice, bagels and aspirins". I'd noticed in previous years at this convention there were long lines at the restaurant, when in fact all that most people wanted was some coffee, juice and a pastry.

Next morning, we could hardly handle the traffic! We had a young woman at the door, dressed in a nurse's outfit, who collected the business card of everyone who came in (so we could contact them later). As compared to the standing-only cocktail party, we had soft chairs for them…we had a quiet, business-like atmosphere…and the room was well lit so we could display sales materials.

"The Recovery Room" was so effective, we used the same approach again the following year…again at likely a tenth or less the cost of one of those cocktail parties.

• **Our year at the "Masters".** After a couple years of the Rescue approach, we came up with an even less costly way to "corner" key prospects at this convention. Back then we were so cheap, it bothered us that a lot of the people coming in our Recovery Room weren't potential clients—even competitors were coming in for the coffee and freebies!

Recognizing that many people in advertising are golf enthusiasts, we requested an advance copy of the "Who's attending" list and then carefully selected only those people we *really* wanted to talk to. The list came to about 40 people out of the 1,500 or more who'd be there.

A week before the convention, we sent these 40 prospects a letter inviting them to be "part of the Masters". We told them we wanted to have a brief, private chat with them. To urge them to do so, we taped a *broken golf tee* to the top of the letter…which surely caught their attention.

We told them to put that tee in their pocket and bring it to the convention. Then, if they spotted any of us—"We'll be the ones wearing the 'Masters Green Jackets' "—they should stop us to see if that broken tee of theirs matched the other half of the broken ones the five of us were carrying in our pockets.

"If yours is a match, you'll win a complete set of golf clubs *worth* $700.00!" That sentence popped off the page in bold.

It worked wonderfully. We didn't even know some of these people on sight, but it didn't matter—they sought us out, pulled the tee from their pocket and checked if they had a match. In fact, I was sitting 10 rows from the back during one seminar, and this guy tapped me on the shoulder and beckoned me to the back of the room to check out his tee!

> *"The broken tees worked so well, prospects came to us!"*

This Masters approach was our lowest cost idea yet. It also had the added benefit of being such a novelty that each conversation with these prospects started on an upbeat basis.

● **Tees weren't all we broke.** The broken tee gimmick led to a similar promotion we used at our exhibit booth during the national FFA (Future Farmers of America) convention in Kansas City.

We wanted to lure FFA advisers to our booth to convince them to have their students sell our calendars for fund-raising projects. (We produce more than a dozen country-oriented calendars each year, and this FFA sales program has since been quite successful for us.)

But how could we screen out just the advisers from thousands of attendees and get them to come to our booth, which was *way* at the back of the exhibit hall? We managed to do so. This time we broke pencils.

We stationed young ladies at the top of the main escalator that brought participants up to the exhibit floor. We directed these young women to study name tags, which revealed which ones were FFA advisers. That proved pretty easy—their tags were color coded.

Then they offered these advisers a broken pencil with an attached note, which explained if they came to our booth, and if that half pencil matched the broken half in our booth, they'd win *$100.00 cash.*

Worked again. We had one of those GIANT pencils in our booth to tie in with the gimmick. Plus, we knew whether the pencil they brought in was a "match" the second they handed it to us: The winning pencils were a slightly different color, gold instead of yellow.

Every few hours, we'd "plant" another potential winning pencil. It was amazing how many of these advisers made the effort to come to our booth, where we had our full line of calendars on display. This proved very effective in convincing them to try our program.

Again, the broken pencils provided a lighthearted conversation opener.

● **Looking for another "lure"?** At still another advertising convention, we used a "Pair Up for Prizes" gimmick.

As people came to our booth, we handed them an attractive little stick-

A good reputation is easier to maintain than rebuild.

er that had our company name on it along with a LARGE NUMBER. We urged them to wear the sticker on their lapel or pocket.

Why were they willing to wear these stickers? Because if they spotted the exact same number on some other attendee—and the two of them then came to our booth—we'd give each of them their choice of prizes, from a small radio to a large umbrella. Thus, "Pair Up for Prizes".

This was highly effective, too, and had the added advantage of having our company's name displayed by everyone wearing those stickers.

• **Short 'em on chairs.** This is sort of unrelated, but it's such a cool idea I can't resist passing it along. Because we'd begun hosting a number of conventions (Builder Show, Farm Wife Forum, Cooking Expo, etc.), I once attended a "Seminar on Conventions". It offered advice on how to run them.

One of their tips was this: If you don't know exactly how many people are going to attend your function, it's better to put out *too few* chairs than *too many*. Here's why:

Let's say you're expecting 100 people and you set up 100 chairs. Then only 75 show up. After the show, someone asks an attendee, "Was it well attended?"

Answer: "Not really…I saw a lot of empty chairs."

Conversely, you feel you *might* have 100 people, but you're not sure, so you set up 75 chairs. A hundred show up. Later someone asks an attendee, "Was it well attended?"

Answer: "Sure was! They even had to stop the program to set up extra chairs!"

Success at anything is often based on perception rather than facts. Even when it's measured by chairs.

*I wouldn't like to have
lived my life without ever
having disturbed someone.*
—Will Rogers

CHAPTER 39

And Some Things That Didn't Work

YOU'D THINK by reading the previous chapter that everything we tried actually worked. Sorry, that's not the case. We had a lot of ideas that *we* thought were good…but others obviously didn't. And their opinion mattered far more than ours.

I've already mentioned that I failed with two of the magazines I launched. Failed badly, in fact. The first one—the magazine for teenagers that I started in our basement—hurt the most, for two reasons:

Being the first, it hurt my confidence and ego because I didn't have any successes to fall back on. Worse, while we "only" lost $10,000 on that one, it was everything we had at the time.

The second failure was *Country Kids* magazine, and while I lost over $100,000 on that one, it didn't hurt as much because by then it *wasn't* every cent we had, and by then I had four other successful launches to boost my confidence.

While I mentioned those two failures earlier, I didn't explain *why* that second one, *Country Kids*, failed. Basically, it was because I didn't give its marketing enough advance thought.

Here's what I mean. If you start a magazine for farmers, you can just secure a mailing list of farmers and make a sample mailing. But this new magazine of mine was for *farm kids*, between the ages of 6 and 12.

Now, how on God's green earth would anyone know *which* of the farmers on any mailing list had children between the ages of 6 and 12? *That's* what I should have thought about in advance.

As a result, the marketing of this magazine was far too costly. If I sent it to 1,000 farm families, there *might* be 100 of those families—if I'm lucky—that would have kids in my target range for age. So, in effect, 90% of my mailings were *wasted*.

There was another problem I hadn't anticipated: Adult subscribers don't "grow out of" their market. Kids do. Even if I got an avid subscriber to *Country Kids*, as soon as that child turned 13, there'd be *no way* he'd want

to keep receiving a "kids magazine".

While the content was good —and we received many letters from parents saying how much their kids loved our magazine— the marketing was so difficult and costly that we had no choice but to pull the plug after 3 years.

Before I move on to other items, I want to mention one part of the content of *Country Kids* that attracted a lot of interest.

Remember I mentioned my getting a Belgian mare for Christmas one year? Well, one of the reasons I chose "Maggie" was that she'd just become pregnant. I wanted to use her and her "condition" to educate kids reading the magazine.

I was preparing the first issue of *Country Kids*, so we ran pictures of Maggie, telling the young readers all about her. We said we'd named her "*F&RL* Maggie" after *Farm & Ranch Living* magazine. We also wrote about her condition and that we would follow her pregnancy and progress until the birth.

But then we added one of our contests: We told the young subscribers that when the foal was born, *they* would have a chance to name it! And the one who came up with the winning name would get a free trip to Wisconsin to personally meet the colt (male) or filly (female).

> *"We were able to explain why almost all horses are born at night..."*

That *really* drew a response. After the little one arrived—a filly— we printed pictures of her and began the naming contest. The winner was a young boy from Minnesota, who came up with a *great* name: "Maggie's Paige". (Get it? "Magazine page".)

It was a shame this magazine didn't make it, because of the educational aspect it afforded rural children. For example, with all this about Maggie and Paige, we were able to explain to young readers why almost all horses are born at night. That's true.

Experienced horse people give this reasoning: A colt or filly can run at 75% of its mother's speed within a few hours of birth. So, in early days, when horses foaled in the wild and predators were about, a newborn would not have much chance of out-running anything if born during the day. But when born at night, that little one could make some fast tracks by dawn and have a much better chance of survival by the time a predator was looking for breakfast.

This historical fact is believed to be why almost all horses are born at night. It's cool to think it's one of nature's ways of protecting young foals.

Another "semi-failure". Several years after we had launched *Farm & Ranch Living*, the magazine was faring well. But when I studied a circulation chart one day, I discovered that we had fewer than 20,000 subscribers across the entire Southeastern states.

That surprised me. After all, I was well aware of the huge success of *Southern Living* magazine there. (I've often thought part of the success of that magazine is that it makes a *statement* for its subscribers: Displayed on the coffee table, it says to all visitors, "You bet I'm *Southern!*")

So, using the "If you can't beat 'em, join 'em" approach, I decided to turn out a Southern Edition of *Farm & Ranch Living*. I hired a Southern editor, Tom Cooper, and stationed him at a small town in southern Georgia. We changed the cover as well as the 16 outside pages for that edition, then wrapped that section around the body of our regular edition.

And we changed the cover logo on this edition to read, *SOUTHERN Farm & Ranch Living* (see above). Should work, right?

Wrong. I never figured out quite why, but it was a dismal failure. What's more, the *Southern Living* attorneys started getting on our case because they felt our name was infringing on theirs.

That seemed a stretch to me since *SOUTHERN Farm & Ranch Living* seemed decidedly different than *Southern Living*, and the typeface was far different, too. But we weren't gaining enough circulation anyway, so after 2 years, I gave up trying. Some "can't miss" ideas just…miss.

Got burned on cookie idea, too. In 1998 we announced a "Cookie of All Cookies" contest, for which we received *over 34,000 entries* in a little more than a month! The main reason for this incredible response was that we offered the winner of the contest *a percentage of all the sales proceeds* from the cookie. To add to the intrigue, we promised to keep the win-

If you want life to run smoothly, grease it with gratitude.

293

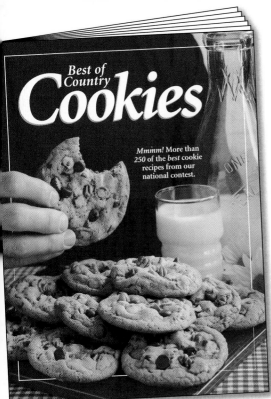

Mmmm! More than 250 of the *best* cookie recipes from our national contest.

AFTER SUBSCRIBERS judged the recipes at our company Visitor Center, book at left became a hit with over 280,000 copies sold to date. It is "full-color throughout" as shown at right.

ning recipe a *secret*. We conducted this contest at our company Visitor Center in downtown Greendale, which is within walking distance of our editorial headquarters.

It was a huge draw for sub-scribers, who enjoyed "judging" this contest. Each day, our food staff would turn out a half dozen or so of the cookie entries. The visi-tors were invited to taste them, indicating their preferences and detailing why on an "Official Judging Form".

The eventual winner was a re-ally *great* cookie from a woman in northern Minnesota. Everyone said it tasted "like a turtle sundae". The cookie didn't have an attention-get-ting name, so we gave it one. We called it the "*Mmm*minnesota Muncher".

Well, the contest and the resulting *Country Cookies* book (280,000 copies sold to date) were a huge success, but there was one problem: Since the win-ning recipe was a *secret*, the *only* place our 16 million subscribers could taste that cookie was at our Visitor Center.

And they complained about that. One subscriber from North Carolina wrote, "I'm 80 years old and I want to taste that winning cookie. How do you expect me to get to Greendale to taste it?"

I came up with part of the solution while vacationing in Florida. I was sitting on John Gardetto's patio in Naples. John and his wife, Judy, had been neighbors of ours for years and are still close friends; we'd watched their small Gardetto Bakery company grow to national prominence with its sale of Gardetto's Snak'Ens, breadsticks and other bread products.

Maybe it was because John was in the bakery business or something, but while I sat there on his patio mulling over this "How can we taste the cookie?" problem, a solution suddenly occurred to me: "Why don't we sell a *mix* and let subscribers bake their own Munchers?"

Well, that idea more than paid for our vacation trip. To date we've sold over 180,000 packages of cookie mix ("Just add butter, water and an egg") by mail and through our Visitor Center. It has also resulted in more than $65,000 in royalties for the contest winner to date.

But even that didn't totally solve the problem. The fact is, some people just don't *bake* anymore. And if they can't buy that cookie over the count-

It's almost impossible to smile on the outside without feeling better on the inside.

er, they're likely never going to taste it.

Frustrated by this, I came up with what I *thought* was an even *better* idea: "Why don't we sell the mix of this now famous cookie to some national chain—like McDonald's or Wendy's or Starbucks?"

This would be good for us—we'd make money off the mix we'd sell to them in bulk—but it could be even more *incredible* for them! We would tell over *50 million people* (16 million subscribers times 3.2 readers per copy) every other month that they could now taste the famous *Mmm*minnesota Muncher at the outlets of one of these chains!

Just think what this could mean to a McDonald's or Wendy's:

1. We would regularly urge 50 million people to head for their door.

2. We would do this at *no cost*! By comparison, can you imagine what it would cost one of these chains for advertising to reach 50 million people every other month?

3. This might well attract a whole new audience for them. Our average subscriber is around 55 years old. A lot of these people likely haven't visited a McDonald's or a Wendy's in years; too much of a noisy kids place.

But now they'd have a *reason to go there*—to try this incredible cookie. And older people *love* cookies. After these folks got inside, they just might find the place more pleasant than they'd thought…and come back again, cookie or no cookie.

I have an Iowa friend who owns 12 McDonald's franchises, so I ran the idea past him. He loved it and gave me the name of the V.P. of marketing at McDonald's headquarters.

So I started my usual letter-plus-gimmick mailings. I included the cookie book, details of the contest, copies of our magazines and other cook-

To get something done, a committee should consist of three people, two of whom are absent.

books. I sent everything *but* the mailbox. He never responded. Not by mail or phone. Nada.

Then I started the same campaign with Wendy's. Then Starbucks. Then Arby's. I never got a response from *any* of them.

I couldn't believe it—and still can't. This seems like something far more beneficial for *them* than for us. Again, it has the potential of driving *50 million people* to their door, every other month, *FREE*.

I don't give up easily. One day while walking through an airport I noticed a Mrs. Fields cookie outlet. *Hey, why not get them to add the Munchers to their line?* Why hadn't I thought of *that* before?

The fit would be even better with Fields than those other firms. They already are a "cookie outfit". We'd urge our readers to try our famous cookie at any Mrs. Fields outlet...and while there these new customers would likely buy some of Fields' regulars as well. A win-win!

I hurriedly started another letter campaign, this time to the president of Mrs. Fields in Salt Lake City. I really got into the mailings this time, inserting not only the cookie book, but a whole "care package" of books, magazines, brochures and even some of our catalog items with each mailing. I just unloaded on him.

This time I sent the mailings back-to-back, day after day. I told him he was going to get a letter and a heavy package like this *every day* until he called me.

I made a brief point with each mailing, that we were offering him the opportunity to reach 50 million potential customers *free* on a regular basis...that this would add "new energy and excitement" to his outlets...that these new customers would buy many of his existing cookies while they were there...and more benefits.

After a half dozen of these, I hit him with this: "All I need is 15 minutes of your time. If you don't feel by then this has potential for you, I'll walk out of your office and never bother you again.

"If you'll grant me those 15 minutes, I'll bake a batch of our famous cookies in the morning and charter a plane to Salt Lake City so you can taste them while they're still fresh. I'll be out of your office and on my way home in less than an hour."

That did it. He called.

I did *exactly* that. I chartered a flight from Milwaukee to Salt Lake the next morning, and with the change in time (2 hours), I was there with a fresh batch of Munchers by mid-morning. He was cordial but guarded. Yet he seemed interested and asked numerous questions.

Keeping my promise not to wear out my welcome, I left after an hour. I told him, "The next call is yours. I won't bother you until I hear from you."

Still, as I left, I felt I *had* him. He'd paid close attention and even asked that I leave my display and presentation materials for him to review. I felt very good about my chances when I whizzed back to Milwaukee, getting back on that charter in time to be at my desk that afternoon.

I never heard from him. I just couldn't believe it. I really thought I had the whole program *sold*. It would have meant a big profit to our company, but again—in my opinion—a far bigger profit to his. I have no idea why he didn't call. I didn't call him. I kept my word.

I just *can't believe* I cannot get this program sold to some big company! I tried IGA Food Stores, too, and managed to get an appointment with their top marketing manager in Chicago.

I explained how IGA could offer our famous cookie through their bakery department...that they could also sell our cookie book and make additional profit from that...that their small, independent grocers were *perfect* for our somewhat rural audience...that it would motivate people who regularly shopped at other stores to try IGA, and they

> *"Offered them a chance to reach 50 million people FREE... they turned me down!"*

then might become regular customers...we'd urge 50 million to their stores regularly, FREE, etc., etc., etc.

Again, there seemed to be real interest, and they'd give it serious thought. But they never called. Never heard a word. More nada.

Is there something about these big companies and this big potential I don't understand? I would think the marketing people at these firms would just *salivate* at the opportunity of having all this free exposure in our magazines, nudging our *50 million* readers to their door.

To date, we're still only offering the baked cookie at our company Visitor Center. I'm not giving up, though. I'm still working on it, and someday soon I hope I come up with a way to give that little old lady in North Carolina a chance to taste our Munchers.

Something else to chew on. When you send out a letter soliciting a subscription to a magazine or to order a new book, the first challenge is to *get the prospect to open the envelope.*

According to direct-mail marketing studies, the "teaser line" on the outside of the envelope—that is, the brief statement that results in a person opening or not opening the envelope—is a *major* factor in your mailing's success. If they don't open the envelope, you don't have a chance at selling something.

There are national seminars in which experts share secrets and *train* direct-mail writers. Early on I attended several of these sessions, where some of the best teaser lines ever written were shared. One was, "Are you the kind of person who closes the bathroom door even when you're home alone? Then what you'll find inside is perfectly suited for *you*..." That was said to be one of the most effective envelope openers ever.

Anyway, I was developing a promotional mailing for *Reminisce*, our highly successful nostalgia magazine, and was trying to come up with something that would make this older audience open that envelope.

Suddenly, I hit on a *great* gimmick: We'd put a stick of Blackjack gum inside each envelope! That had a lot of things going for it—it was a "nos-

Be careful about living in the lap of luxury. Luxury may suddenly stand up.

talgic gum" that our older readers would recall from their childhood…it was now hard to find…and older people never throw away food.

So, if we told them right on the envelope, *"There's something inside to chew on while you consider our offer…"*, and they felt that stick of gum inside, we'd get 99% of those people to read that piece. If the test mailing of this worked—and why wouldn't it—we'd likely end up ordering a *lot* of Blackjack. We mail *millions* of promotional pieces like this per year.

I called the gum company's headquarters and explained what I wanted *fast* in time for this mailing. "Sorry, we only make that gum once a year," was the answer from the unenthusiastic woman on the other end.

"But this could become a big order—we might order *millions* of sticks of Blackjack," I said.

Same slow response: "Sir, we only make that gum once a year."

"Well, you must have a lot of this gum on your shelves somewhere. How about some of that?"

"No, we don't make a lot in advance—we just make it once a year."

"But this could be a *HUGE* order!"

"Sorry, we only make that gum once a year."

"What's the name of your supervisor? Could I talk to him or her?"

"You could, but she's only going to tell you that we o-n-l-y…m-a-k-e…t-h-a-t…g-u-m…o-n-c-e…a…y-e-a-r."

"Can I talk to her?"

"She's not here now."

"Could you have her call me?

"Sure, but it won't do you any good. Give me your name and number."

I gave it. Never got a call. I sometimes wonder how big companies survive when they grow to the point of apathy.

This company not only lost what could have been a large order, but we likely lost a good deal, too. I think that gum-in-the-envelope would have been highly successful.

A couple more that never flew. It occurred to me one day that anyone who buys a 10-pound bag of baking flour is a real *baker*. So why don't we go to Pillsbury or some other flour company and have them insert a small coupon in each of those bags, offering one of our food magazines, *Taste of Home*, for a dollar off?

We'd offer the flour company a dollar or so for every conversion…it would be a nice gesture for them (the magazine's reduced price being "compliments of Pillsbury")…we'd save the cost of a mailing…and we'd reach a "screened" prospect—that is, an enthusiastic baker. By comparison, we have no way of knowing who bakes and who doesn't when we make a normal mailing.

I turned that idea over to our Marketing Department. But they've never been able to sell it. Just never got wings under it.

Another idea I had that never sailed: Why not attend a national residential Realtors convention, set up a booth and urge them to give gift subscriptions of *Taste of Home*?

A key chain is something that allows you to lose all your keys at the same time.

298

A Realtor makes some good money at 6% or so of the home's price and could afford a $9.98 gift for a buyer. And wouldn't that buyer be appreciative if—the first time she came into her new home—there was a copy of our magazine on the kitchen counter with a note, "Here's a *Taste of Home* to welcome you to your new home!"

The note would explain that the agent was giving the owner a year's gift subscription and "If you hear of anyone interested in buying or selling a home, please contact me."

> **"Failure is frustrating, but you have to keep trying..."**

Plus, we'd print, "This is a gift from (REALTOR'S NAME)" on the mailing label of every issue all year long.

Good idea? I think so. Apparently Realtors don't. Our Marketing Department has never been able to sell that program, either.

All these frustrating failures add credence to the saying "You have to have a lot of ideas...because only one out of 10 is any good."

Life is like a taxi—the meter keeps ticking whether you're getting anywhere or not.

.

Ideas are like rabbits.
You get a couple and learn how to handle them,
and pretty soon you have a dozen.
—John Steinbeck

CHAPTER 40

'Why Doesn't Somebody...?'

GOD KEEPS GIVING ME lots of ideas. I don't know why. It's just a gift I've been blessed with. I don't dwell on it or think this makes me superior or more talented than anyone else.

See, I think God gives *everyone* gifts. Surely every person reading this has some specific talent or ability that I lack. I figure God just spreads these gifts around to offer the world some "balance".

So my gift happens to be creativity, and I just accept it for what it's worth, not something that's necessarily special. One time one of our daughters, Joni, asked me, "Dad, aren't you pleased with all the creativity God gave you?"

And I answered, "Not really. Frankly, what others seem to find 'creative' just seems like common sense to me."

For whatever reason, I keep coming up with ideas. Sometimes I'll be aware that something *big* is swirling around inside my head. I won't at the moment know what it is…but I know something's going on and that some new concept is about to be "born". Sure enough, a few days later, I'll come up with something and say to myself, "So *that's* what it was!"

That's just the way it works for me. I've often said, "I have ideas I haven't even thought of yet." And I'm dead serious—I just know I can count on more continually coming my way.

Some of the ideas that come are pretty good, and some are far-fetched. Quite often I come up with ideas I personally can't use…but still feel they have potential for *somebody*. Here are a few samples that come to mind:

Why not a "woman's car"? It must have been a dozen or more years ago when my wife and I were shopping for a new car. I found one in a dealership that I particularly liked and asked Bobbi to get behind the wheel to "see how it feels".

She got in, looked around for only a few seconds, then got out of the car. "I don't like it," she said.

"Why?"

"There's no place to put my purse."

"What?"

"I like my purse right next to me like I've always had it in our old car—in that little niche in the center of the seat."

"Hmmm…let's try this car over here. Sit in this one."

She got in, got out. "I don't like it."

"Why?"

"There's no place to put my purse."

"Let me get this straight—you're *judging a car* by whether there's a place to put your *purse?*"

"Well, that's important to me. Actually, I don't like the seat in either of these, either—it doesn't feel right for my legs."

I thought back on that episode later, and what a "gender thing" car buying has become. Then it occurred to me: Why doesn't some car company design a car *just for women?*

I'd seen figures that indicate women are individually or jointly responsible for close to 50% of car buying decisions.

So why doesn't some auto manufacturer turn out a car that's designed to better fit the torsos of women, has larger vanity mirrors (maybe better lit with part of it magnified), has softer leather, a console with compartments for lipstick and makeup, maybe even comes in pastel colors…and *has a place to put a purse!*

> ## *"You judge a car by whether there's a place for your purse???"*

I started thinking this had potential for our *Country Woman* magazine, one that would result in a lot of national publicity: We'd select 50 women—one from each state—fly them to Detroit and invite designers from the major auto companies there to meet with them, to hear *What women really want in a car.*

I felt women across the country would notice this, appreciate it and just might subscribe to the magazine that made it happen—a car finally designed for *them*. But when I totaled the cost and the time it would involve with our limited staff, I didn't think we could afford to carry it off.

Still seems like it has potential, though, and it's just one of my "Why doesn't somebody…?" ideas.

While I'm talking cars, why doesn't somebody invent a "His & Hers Rearview Mirror"? Every time I get in our car, I have to readjust the mirror from where Bobbi had it set. And then she has to do the same after I've driven.

So why not have two preset adjustments on that mirror, one marked "His" and the other "Hers"? You get in the car, push on the mirror and presto, it's immediately at your setting.

And why doesn't somebody try this? I'm a "car nut". I love cars, so when I travel and rent, I usually request a different manufacturer's car each time just to see how another type drives.

So…why doesn't some car leasing company offer guys like me a chance to drive *six different cars each year*? Here's how it would work: The leasing firm would get a group—say 12 car nuts like me—and each member of this "fraternity" would sign up for a 2-year lease. Then the new cars would be rotated—we'd each get a different car every 2 months.

The cars would be different types and models—likely high-end, pricey ones that all these car enthusiasts would love to drive. This group of 12 would form sort of a "car club"; the leasing agency would set up a quarterly dinner meeting at a nice restaurant or country club to allow the participants to "talk cars" and get the inside scoop on upcoming models.

I'm sure a lot of other car-crazy guys would be willing to pay a little extra for the fun of driving a different car every 2 months…and for the fun of driving their neighbors nuts at seeing six "new cars" in the driveway in just 1 year!

Tee off on this one. Why doesn't someone make biodegradable golf tees? Then there wouldn't be all those busted wooden tees lying around that are both an eyesore and hard on mower blades. Or, make the tees out of hardened fertilizer that would dissolve in water.

And since it's estimated 1.25 billion golf balls are lost every 6 months, why doesn't someone develop some type of glasses or lenses that would make them easier to find?

Ever see a happy jogger? Most of them look like they're in pain. And those on indoor treadmills look bored.

While I greatly admire what these people are doing for health reasons, it bothers me that all of that energy isn't put to some use.

So…why doesn't somebody invent a treadmill or stationary bike that produces electricity? Maybe it could power the TV they're watching while they're working out. Maybe, as an incentive, they even have to jog or pedal at a certain speed just to keep the TV on.

I know *nothing* about electricity, so maybe that's totally impractical. But it just seems a shame that all that energy is going to waste. Why not make it productive? I wish someone would look into this.

Another thought about joggers: Many of them get up early, run several miles outdoors or on a treadmill, then take a shower and drive to work. They pay a premium to park as near to the office as possible, then ride the elevator up to work. Why not, instead, jog less, leave for the office earlier, park at a cheaper lot some distance from the office, enjoy the exercise of that longer walk, then climb the stairs instead of taking the elevator?

I know, I know…a lot of you joggers are thinking by now I'm a little goofy, and you have every right. You likely have good reasons why this doesn't make any sense.

But remember, I was just trying to give you examples of the "Why doesn't somebody…?" ideas that often go through my head…ideas that I can't use…and likely ones that others can't use either.

Give 'em a whiff of this! Almost everyone who feeds birds is driven nuts by squirrels. These ingenious thieves can figure out a way to steal from

Change is inevitable, but growth is an option.

practically any feeder. Over 80 million people in the U.S. feed birds, and they likely spend as much on squirrel *foils* as they spend on birdseed!

So…since you can now buy scents to keep deer and rabbits out of your garden, why doesn't *somebody* come up with a scent that squirrels can't *stand*? Just spray it on the seed. Birds can't smell, so it wouldn't bother them. Somebody could end up smelling like roses with this idea!

Here's a really BIG idea. There are lots of retirement communities in the country, ranging from the Del Webb Sun City developments in Florida, Arizona and California…to the Padre Island places in Texas and a host of other developments across the South. But none of them really cater to the unique interests of *country people*.

Rural folks—especially ex-farmers—likely find most of these places pretty boring. After such an active life, they can't turn off the motor and just *sit*. Even the social activities offered in these retirement villages don't cut the cake for them; they have completely different interests than urban retirees. They'd like someone to talk to about tractors, crops, the price of corn and the weather.

So…why doesn't some developer buy a whole section of land somewhere, with a pretty creek winding through it? For you city folks, a section is a square mile of land containing 640 acres.

For a location, I wouldn't suggest any of the Southern states for this rural retirement village. Farmers have dealt with seasons all their life, and Northern farmers now living in the Sun Belt very likely kind of miss winters. While they no longer want to deal with heavy snow and numbing cold, most of them wouldn't mind seeing a few snowflakes and an occasional light "dusting" during the winter months.

So I think this "Country Place" (not a bad name for it) facility would be best located in southern Missouri, Kansas or Oklahoma. Kentucky or northern Tennessee might be good, too, but they're not as centralized.

I wouldn't locate this village near a large city. I'd locate it in a rural area to make it easy for retired farmers to get off this homestead and "check the crops" in the surrounding area now and then.

Usually there are several farmsteads on a section, so the developer should check which has the best buildings and most attractive farmstead layout, and retain that one. Then get rid of the others to make more room for all the new houses and their good-size lawns…lawns big enough to do some serious grass cutting on a serious garden tractor. And room for a good-size garden plot as well. Sort of a "mini farm".

> *"…And lots of baling wire. Farmers can fix anything with baling wire."*

Now, in the very center of this section you'd have a *large* "meeting facility", where folks could gather to play cards, shoot pool, work on crafts, bowl, swim, dance, watch movies… and chat with people who have similar backgrounds and interests.

The main streets would be diagonal from all four corners; that would provide easy access in all directions. And there'd be a large pond stocked with fish of a different type than those in that winding stream. But the pond would have to have one whopper like "Big Walter" from the movie *On Golden Pond*. Anyone who caught Wally Whopper would know that fish is catch and release; he's only for bragging, not eating.

Now, that farmstead the developer retained would be put to good use. The machine shed would have a dirt floor that had years of oil and grease spilled on it—that smell is like *perfume* to any old farmer.

There would be several old tractors in the shed for the guys to tinker with. When they got them renovated like new, the developer would bring in several more for them to work on. The renovated ones could be sold, with the cash going in the "party fund".

This machine shed would contain the workshop of all workshops, with every feasible kind of new tool on hand, but a lot of the old ones, too. Especially pliers. Lots of pliers. And a lot of baling wire. Farmers can fix almost anything with baling wire. It's their duct tape. There'd be a large coffeemaker in that shed, too, and *real cream* in a small refrigerator.

Over in the old livestock barn, there might be a team of Belgian horses. That would give the guys something to feed, pet, harness and drive. They'd have to clean out the barn regularly, since there will be houses nearby. But only two horses would hardly do much to the air…and it just might be the kind of air a lot of their friends who retired and moved to the Sun Belt are likely missing. They'll also need to polish those harnesses regularly.

For the same reason, it might be a good idea to keep just one cow there, too, that has to be hand-milked twice each day. The guys can take turns. They'd probably put a clipboard on the barn wall to schedule milking and cleaning assignments. And they likely wouldn't mind when their turn landed on Sunday or a holiday; that's the way it used to be for them all year long.

> *"The haymow could be swept out for an old-fashioned square dance…"*

The farmhouse would be a welcome gathering place, too. It would have a large, modern "country kitchen" with lots of large pots and pans, plus plenty of stoves and ovens so the "womenfolk" could gather to can tomatoes, make sauerkraut and freeze peaches. There would be picnic tables under the trees to be used not just for eating, but for cutting and cleaning garden crops…and for sittin' and chattin'.

I think the developer should move an old schoolhouse onto the property as well and fix up the inside just like it was in "the old days". Then when grandchildren came to visit during their spring break, some retired teacher could keep those kids occupied for a few hours and give them a little history at the same time, of how things were when their grandparents were kids.

And while those youngsters are there, the haymow in the barn could be put to good use, with gunnysack swings to ride, piles of straw to tumble

Few things are more exhausting than looking for an easy way to make a living.

in, tunnels through hay bales to crawl through, and a basketball hoop to shoot at. Best of all, the rule would be that kids could shout and make all the noise they want up in this haymow. "*Shhh!*" and "Hold it down!" would not be allowed in the mow. An old barn is great for noise and loud echoes.

Why limit this kind of fun to kids? The adults would nostalgically enjoy many of those same things. And once a year the haymow could be swept out for an old-fashioned square dance up there.

Now, doesn't this sound like a place where country folks would like to retire? A place like this where everyone has a similar background and is interested in talking about the same things?

If you agree, pass this idea along to a developer you know. *Somebody* oughta do it.

Full-time halftime show? Okay, finally, here's an idea that just has *fun* written all over it. It involves halftime shows at college events.

I've often remembered what I enjoyed during the mid-game break long after I've forgotten the game itself. Some of the things college kids come up with are highly creative and entertaining.

I've seen a guy dressed up as a mascot do a complete flip off a trampoline and, as he came out of the turn, slam-dunk a basketball. He made two out of three that way.

At another game, after a group of pom-pom girls finished performing, four hefty guys rushed out in costume and mimicked the routine. They'd obviously practiced a good deal, because their choreography was as good as the pom squad's. Well…almost. But it was funny and memorable.

I saw a college sophomore put on a Frisbee show with his dog that was amazing. And another student donned a clown suit and did a comedy act with his dog that had the crowd roaring.

I watched a family acrobatic team do such an incredible gymnastic routine that it deserved and received a standing ovation. I remember an overweight college kid making 53 free throws in a row…he didn't miss; the buzzer sounded for the second half and he had to quit.

I saw a majorette who could throw a baton over an arena rafter, then do two flips before it looped over and she caught it on the other side. I've seen six guys playing tubas who were as funny as they were musical.

Then there was the "rubber chicken contest". A team member tosses rubber chickens from one free throw line to his partner at the other free throw line, who tries to catch them in a basket. The team that catches the most chickens wins. Anyway, the crowd went wild.

And I once enjoyed a Ping-Pong match at center court in which individual points went for as long as 5 minutes or more. The one guy was a "slammer" who would kill the ball, and the other guy was a "human backboard"; he was sometimes back by the free throw line but just kept returning the balls! I have no idea who won the game that night, but I vividly recall this Ping-Pong match that had the crowd oohing and aahing.

The point is, there is a *lot* of talent on college campuses that often makes the mid-game break more memorable than the game itself.

So…*what if* you put the BEST of all college halftime shows together into one show…and took the show on the road? What an evening of entertainment that would be!

You'd bill it as "The Best of (Half) Times", or "The Full-Time Halftime Show". Who wouldn't come out to watch a whole evening of good, clean *family* fun like this? I know I would…and so would thousands of others when they saw what was on the bill.

You'd schedule these shows during the summer season when these college students aren't in classes. You'd book them at college basketball venues…readily available during summer months, so the event could be held rain or shine. You'd keep the show moving, from one state to another, with the performances just a day or two apart.

And how would you attract the *best* halftime talent from across the country to appear in this show? Well, you'd not only pay these college kids a nice salary for this great summer job…but you'd give these students *10% of the net profit* as a bonus! With that kind of carrot, you'd surely attract the top talent. It would allow you to be really selective.

The evening performance would include everything from music to comedy to acrobatics to "I don't believe I saw that!" stuff. For an hour before the event began, you might warm up the crowd by holding a free throw or three-point shooting contest at each end of the court.

Or…you could have a free throw *demonstration* by someone like that can't-miss guy who made 53 in a row…or perhaps we could get Ted St. Martin, a dairyman from Washington, to put on a free throw shooting clinic for the crowd.

Let me tell you about Ted. We did a story on him in *Country* a number of years back after I spotted an article about him in *Sports Illustrated* (which had previously verified the facts you're about to read).

Ted was milking cows for a living when he started reminiscing about his high school basketball days in Naches, Washington. He wasn't even the star on that team, but the one thing he could do well was shoot free throws.

"Here I was," Ted remembers, "35 years old, a dairy farmer, and I got to thinking while out on the tractor one day what a shame it was that I'd become rusty at the one sport I loved so much as a kid."

> **"Dairyman Ted made 2,036 free throws in a row!"**

So he nailed a hoop to the side of his dairy barn and started shooting. After a while he was able to hit a couple hundred free throws in a row.

Ted didn't think much of that—after all, he'd always been able to hit free throws with consistency. But others did. One evening during a barbecue, he amazed family and friends by firing off *514* free throws without a miss.

Someone checked what the all-time record was and came back with 144. So, soon after, his friends assembled a group of doubters, including the local newspaper's sports editor, for a shooting exhibition. That time 5-foot-7 Ted sunk 200 in a row.

After that, he set new records again and again. Then again and again. His all-time record was *2,036 free throws without a miss!* (The NBA record for consecutive free throws is 97, set by the Minnesota Timberwolves' Micheal Williams in 1993.)

With this kind of uncanny ability, Ted's talent was soon in demand at local events. Then word spread to other areas as well. Appearance fees began getting as high as his shooting average—to the point that he eventually sold the farm and began making his living at basketball free throwing.

Sponsored by Coors Light, he traveled the country, putting on demonstrations and taking on all challengers. He performed at the NCAA Final Four weekend, at NBA games, at various benefits, conventions and grand openings.

Did Ted ever lose to anyone? "Yep," he says, "about once every 250 challengers. And it was never to the local basketball star or some great college athlete. It was usually to some short, middle-aged guy like myself who just got in a groove."

"He can shoot 'em left-handed, too!"

As you'd expect, Ted thinks it's a shame that there are guys in the NBA who "shoot only 50% at the line for the money they get!" (Every time I see Shaq miss another free throw on TV, I wonder what would have happened if he had hooked up with Ted.)

After the Coors commitment ended, Ted and his wife spent years in their

DEADEYE. Ex-dairyman Ted and wife spent years on road teaching free throw technique.

van, traveling coast to coast, making a living by conducting clinics at high schools and colleges, and selling a how-to instructional videotape.

Now, wait'll you hear this: Midway through these years on the road, Ted slipped and fell off a stage during a clinic in Syracuse, New York. He severely injured his right shoulder, so badly that a week later he couldn't even raise a fork to his mouth.

He had no choice but to undergo surgery. Even then, he was told by the surgeon that his shoulder would likely take months to heal…and that it might never get back to normal.

"As I was lying there in the hospital, it occurred to me that I still had the other arm to use," Ted says. "All these years I'd been telling people they could teach themselves accurate free throwing. I'd also learned that some people develop habits that are hard to break, and that they'd been better off if I could have started teaching them from scratch.

"Well, here was my chance to prove it myself. So I went out by the garage and applied all my own rules, this time using my left arm."

In 2 weeks he was able to make 94% of his shots with his new, one-handed, left-handed technique. Eventually his right shoulder healed and he was able to shoot with his right arm again. After that he found he could win most contests either way.

I haven't had contact with Ted since we did that story on him, and I doubt that he could be lured out of retirement to be part of this half-time show circuit.

Besides, this show would be made up solely of college students, and there are likely other specialists out there who don't have what it takes to make the team, but—like Ted—have the knack of swishing the net with amazing consistency when no one has a hand in their face. And that would be a great warm-up for this road show.

Whatever, I think this "Full-Time Halftime Show" has so much potential that I've already registered the name. And if there's anyone out there who would be interested in organizing, producing and investing in it, let me know.

This just seems like such a fun idea that *somebody* ought to do it. The country could use more good, clean family entertainment like this…and certain college kids should have the opportunity to show and share their unique talents. Stay tuned…

A fool and his money...
are soon invited everywhere.

CHAPTER 41

The Town with 'Backward Houses'

IT HAPPENED BY CHANCE, but I've often thought there could be no more appropriate town for the location of our company headquarters than one named "Greendale".

Reader's Digest deservedly covets Pleasantville (New York) as its headquarters town. But for us, with our country-oriented magazines that glorify outdoor beauty, *Greendale* is perfect.

If I were both smarter and a visionary, I might have chosen to publish from this town for its name alone. That way our subscribers would think of what "Greendale" implies every time they contacted us by mail. But it didn't happen that way.

The home where we'd started our business in the basement was in a neighboring suburb, Hales Corners. When Bobbi was in the hospital after the arrival of one of our kids, she shared a room with a woman from Greendale who went on and on about how "pretty, charming and historical" this little village was.

When I picked up Bobbi and the baby, she suggested we drive through the small suburb on the way home. We were immediately enthralled with the village center and quaint little homes surrounding it...so much so that several years later, when a nice home came on the market there (our family had grown and we needed more space), we bought it and became Greendale residents.

Gradually we learned why this village was so historic. It's one of only three "Greenbelt Towns" in the U.S. that was built by the Roosevelt Administration during the Great Depression. Roosevelt recognized at the time there was a great need for new homes and a great need to provide jobs.

Over 100 major cities were first considered...and finally Milwaukee was one of the three chosen. The selection was partly due to the large, attractive tract of rolling farmland on Milwaukee's southern border—it seemed a perfect fit for the designer's plan.

Just imagine that group's challenge back then in 1934, as they walked

May it not matter that we are stars, but that we twinkle.

311

over this land—*3,410 acres*, which had previously been dairy farms—and decided where to put the business center, the schools, the parks, over 500 homes, where to place the streets, etc. But accomplish it they did, creating one of the prettiest villages in all of the Midwest.

They named the town "Greendale". When it was finished, 572 families —each selected basically because they were poor—moved in. They would all be renters, albeit at a reasonable rate, and since the government continued to own the entire town, the government became their landlord.

Some say it looks like New England. There definitely are aspects of New England that appear in Greendale's design, especially the downtown buildings. That's likely because the town planner, Elbert Peets, was from New England.

Peets created a village that is truly unique in many ways. Due to his vision, Greendale is likely the only town in the country with "backward houses". Here's why: Peets reasoned most of these poor people never had a lawn or garden of their own, so he wanted to maximize their backyards and the tenants' view of it.

> *"Gradually, this once-proud village became a ghost town..."*

To accomplish this, he placed each house very close to the curb and turned it backward, with the rear entrance near the street and the large living room window facing a big backyard. Some span 5,000 square feet, providing plenty of space for flower beds and vegetable gardens.

Peets' favorite building in America was the main building at Williamsburg in Virginia, so he made the Village Hall in Greendale a miniature copy of it—right to the rooster on its tower. Positioned at the end of Broad Street, it's Greendale's crowning glory.

In 1948, the government decided to get out of the home rental business. All the houses were sold, with the tenants of each unit getting first chance to buy. In 1952, the government sold the commercial buildings in the village center as well.

Greendale prospered after that, especially after 1958, when Allis-Chalmers built three large research buildings near the downtown area. (As mentioned in Chapter 34, these buildings became our publishing headquarters after we purchased them from A-C in 1980. We're still there.)

The cluster of businesses along Broad Street fared well, too...they did, that is, until 1970. That's when Southridge Shopping Center was developed within walking distance of downtown Greendale. The result was one of the largest malls in the nation—it's still the largest in Wisconsin today.

That was the beginning of doomsday for downtown Greendale. Shoppers soon shifted to the new mall, with its 130 stores. One by one, the shops along both sides of Broad Street began closing.

In retrospect, it was a classic case of absentee ownership. Most of the Greendale business buildings were owned by an Ohio corporation, and for them it was pretty much a "paper investment". Locals contended that not

THINGS LOOKED BAD for the Greendale business district after Wisconsin's largest mall was built nearby and drew shoppers away. One by one the businesses began closing. Eventually, the buildings badly needed paint and repairs, and by the early 1990s, only seven of the 29 businesses along Broad Street remained open.

one representative of the Ohio investment firm had paid a visit to Greendale for more than 12 years.

As businesses continued to shut down, the Ohio investors were unwilling to put any money into maintenance and cosmetic touches; they didn't know how long they could count on tenants to occupy the buildings.

The tenants, likewise, were unwilling to put any of their own money into fix-ups because they didn't know how long they would last. By the early 1990s, only seven of the 29 businesses were still open.

It was sad to see. Gradually, the center of this historic village became a ghost town. Many buildings were badly in need of paint, pieces of the facades were torn away, shingles were missing, roofs leaked, windows were broken, curbs were crumbling and some streetlights flickered.

Many Greendalers bemoaned the appearance of their once-prosperous, attractive Greenbelt Town. But no one had a cure for it.

To the chagrin of many who had grown to love this little village, it now appeared once-proud Greendale was doomed.

Ability is important, but dependability is critical.

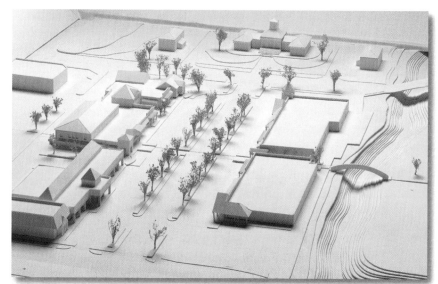

A VISION OF WHAT COULD BE. As the plan (described in the following chapter) began to take shape, the architectural firm wanted to show residents what a renovated Greendale could look like. But they didn't feel that most people could "picture" the end result with a set of blueprints and drawings. So the designer created the three-dimensional scale cardboard model pictured above. It showed the storefronts and new boulevards, new trees, wide strips of grass and abundant flower beds. This model was placed in a storefront along main street. It worked—residents were better able to see and understand what the "new Greendale" would look like.

Life is more accurately measured by the
lives you touch than by the things you acquire.

CHAPTER 42

A Chance to Save a Town

MY WIFE AND I were as saddened as other Greendale residents to watch what was slowly happening to our charming little town. We'd lived here for more than 30 years, our kids had been well-served by the community's schools and many of our 500-plus employees also lived in the Greendale area. Many of them walk to work.

I was mulling over the village's slow demise when the solution came to me while working in my garden one Saturday. It suddenly struck me that I could solve two problems at once!

The first was the one at our corporate offices—too many of our subscribers were "stopping in for a visit" unannounced. The second was the lack of customer traffic at the shops in downtown Greendale.

So…what if we put a *company visitor center* in downtown Greendale and shifted that traffic from our door to that door? That could be the solution to both problems!

Let me pause here for a bit of background: Our average subscriber is 55 years old. That means nearly half of our 16 million subscribers are retired, and retired people love to travel. Since we publish these "friendly" magazines, it seemed whenever these subscribers got close to Greendale, they'd just stop in at our offices for a visit.

This was flattering on one hand and frustrating on the other. They were all nice people, but they kept showing up, and they all wanted a tour.

We didn't have a "tour guide", so some busy editor (they always wanted to meet an editor) would be called to the reception area to meet and walk them slowly through our offices. Understandably, they were in no hurry whatsoever. Just as understandably, we had deadlines to meet.

They wanted to walk through our entire facility, meet as many of our staffers as possible, then sit down and visit. And if they ever got into our test kitchens, they didn't want to leave, period! They'd taste and test for an hour. Or more.

In addition to the time this took, there were other problems. Our offices—

Y'ALL COME SEE US, we told readers after our company Visitor Center (above) in downtown Greendale was completed. Over 200,000 people now visit annually.

with narrow hallways and open cubicles—were never designed with tours in mind. We're set up for publishing. Plus, the loud voices and laughter became a major distraction to creativity.

Finally, we had no choice: *No more tours.* While I agreed with that decision, I felt badly about the disappointment of supportive subscribers who came to our front door, eager to meet editors they'd come to know in print and to see where our magazines and cookbooks were created.

I was concerned about what they thought of us and what they told their friends. I was afraid they went home and told 20 people, "Sure, they put out those friendly magazines, but when you get to their front door, they tell you to go away!"

> *"If they ever got in our test kitchens, they wouldn't leave, period!"*

So, that Saturday in the garden, I suddenly came up with the solution: Why not rent the long-empty liquor store on the corner of Greendale's village center and turn it into a company visitor center?

I envisioned it emulating all the things subscribers would normally see at our company, only better. It would have a working test kitchen, an editor's office, a display of items sent in by readers, a small theater with a video

It isn't the load that breaks you down; it's how you carry it.

316

detailing the company's history, a bargain basement offering closeout items from our catalog and more.

We'd then *urge* our 50 million readers to "Come for a visit"…but not to our offices. Instead, we'd invite them to this new Visitor Center in downtown Greendale.

Perfect. This would steer subscribers away from our door and toward the village, where they were desperately needed.

Oops! Wait a minute… The more I thought about the idea, the more sense it made. But by the end of the weekend, a discouraging concern came to mind.

I began to think about those Ohio investors, who hadn't done one thing for the village in over 12 years. With this new Visitor Center of ours, customer traffic would come back to the downtown area in a big way, and those investors would begin eagerly renting out all those closed business spaces. But…to whom?

I just knew our subscribers would have a certain perception of what Greendale should be. (I proved to be right about that. Last summer a friend of mine was sitting on the bench in front of the Visitor Center, next to an older man wearing a "Michigan" cap. "Whaddaya think of Greendale?" my friend asked. Answered the fellow from Michigan: "It's exactly like I pictured it.")

So, I reasoned, if the current investors continued to own the property, neither our company nor Greendale's residents would have any control over the choice of future tenants. They could rent these empty spaces to adult bookstores, palm readers, tattoo parlors or whatever.

That just wouldn't fit the image of the quaint, historic village we'd been describing to our subscribers for years before things started going downhill.

The only solution: Buy all the business buildings. That would give us total control over the selection of new tenants.

What's more, it would offer us the opportunity to give the village center a cosmetic makeover—with new storefronts, new lampposts, new trees, more green spaces (to put "the green back in Greendale") and more flowers. Lots and lots of flowers. I love flowers.

We did it.

Through our family's investment company, Grandhaven, we bought the village center properties and started an extensive renovation of the downtown area that took nearly 2 years.

The architects took great care to retain the "New England feel" of the existing buildings. We installed an attractive walking bridge across a

Good enough isn't.

317

GREENDALE'S alive and thriving again, with "Eleanor's Fountain" (top left), a large gazebo, hanging baskets from "gaslight" lampposts and an abundance of flowers.

creek to connect the village center to a lovely park…planted numerous trees along Broad Street…installed nostalgic lampposts reminiscent of gaslight days…added multiple flower beds and hanging baskets…and installed a carillon in the tower of the tallest building—its bells mark each quarter hour and toll out patriotic songs several times a day.

A special fountain was also constructed in front of the old post office. It's called "Eleanor's Fountain" in honor of Eleanor Roosevelt's personal visit to the village during its construction in 1936. Large metal plaques surrounding the fountain provide the gist of Greendale's history in chronological order.

Even before the renovation was complete, small business owners from other areas began showing interest, and leases were signed. We had two goals: To choose businesses that benefited residents first and visitors second…and to make sure not to duplicate anything the Southridge mall already offered.

It was a great success.

All 29 business spaces in the village center are now fully occupied, with inquiries coming in from other tenants eager to locate there. An estimated 200,000 people now visit annually. Greendale has been reborn and has become an enjoyable tour destination for many of our subscribers.

Yet, the renovation was a time-consuming, highly costly process. Before we began the project, our son, Scott—who heads up our investment interests—took me aside and said, "Dad, I hope you aren't looking at this as a good investment. This won't pay off in your lifetime or mine."

"I know," I told him. "But some 'investments' are done for different reasons. I agree this will never pay off financially, but it can pay off in many other ways. How many times in life do you get the chance to change a town…and enhance the enjoyment of its 15,000 residents, plus that of thousands of visitors?

"This renovated village can become a legacy to our company, our employees and our Greendale roots." Scott understood, and agreed.

Who takes care of all those flowers? That's a story in itself. More than 37,000 annuals are planted each spring in downtown Greendale in beds, baskets, pots and window boxes. And the care of all these flowers is undertaken in good part by more than 60 Greendale volunteers.

They're called "Greendale's Weed-Out Warriors" and they love their job. The idea of organizing these Warriors came to me after a conversation I had with a resident of a senior apartment facility that's within walking distance of the village center. She mentioned how much she missed her flower garden since she'd sold her home and moved into her apartment.

I gave it some thought, then simply swiped the concept of the "Adopt a Highway" program and initiated an "Adopt a Plot" program in the village. It was an immediate hit. Any resident can "adopt" as large or small a plot along Broad Street as they'd like.

A small sign is placed in each bed, "This Plot Cared for by Ella Smith" or whomever. Our Grandhaven grounds crew takes care of the watering and

If you receive invitations to three really desirable social events, they will all fall on the same evening.

WALKING BRIDGE over Dale Creek now connects village center to nearby park.

"WEED-OUT WARRIORS" take care of all the flower beds along Broad Street.

fertilizing, but these volunteers take care of the weeding and deadheading.

They do a terrific job and enjoy the sense of involvement. We give the volunteers a newly designed shirt each spring that says "Greendale's WEED-OUT WARRIORS" in large letters on the front. On the back of the shirt it says, "We're making Greendale the best blooming town in the country!"

It may be corny, but it works. What's really gratifying is to hear visitors say they're going to start a program just like this in their town when they get back home.

The "Daffo*dale* Capital of the Country". Greendale has also become known for its daffodils. As I mentioned earlier, this all started as a result of an article in our company's *Birds & Blooms* magazine.

It announced plans to make Greendale "The Daffo*dale* Capital of the Country". To get the project under way, our family's investment company, Grandhaven, would donate 2,000 bulbs. Subscribers were told they could consider sending in a few bulbs of their own, so one day they could say they helped make Greendale the "daffo*dale* capital".

The article stated that these bulbs would be used to plant a large daffodil garden in Dale Park. This garden would be designed in the shape of a "sun". The center would be planted in red tulips, and the daffodils planted in 50 long rows to form the "rays" spreading out from the sun.

Why 50 rays? There would be one row for each state—Alabama through Wyoming—and bulbs from each state would be planted in their respective row. (Ultimately there were 51 rows, with an extra one added for bulbs received from Canadian subscribers.)

After the issue with this article went in the mail, we and the Grandhaven

SUBSCRIBERS sent more than *54,000* daffodil bulbs to create this big sun-shaped bed and to help Greendale become well-known as the country's "daffo*dale* capital".

staff waited to see what kind of response it would receive. In 2 weeks, we were surprised. In 3 weeks, we were amazed. And in a month, we were overwhelmed. *More than 54,000 daffodil bulbs* were sent in by subscribers!

Some subscribers had sent two or three, but others sent a dozen or more, with handwritten notes saying how proud they were to have their bulbs be part of making Greendale known for its abundance of daffodils.

They'd all followed our recommended directions, too, cleaning soil off the freshly dug bulbs, inserting them in a plastic bag and then attaching their name to the package.

On one hand, we were delighted; on the other hand, we were now facing a dilemma: Only 7,000 bulbs were needed to plant the "sun bed" we had in mind. What would we do with the *42,000 extra bulbs*, which were now stored in a huge pile in the basement of the hardware store?

After giving it some thought, we came up with a good solution. We announced in the local newspaper that, on a specified Saturday, Greendale residents could pick up as many of the bulbs as they wanted, as long as they showed their driver's license to assure they were locals.

Plus, each recipient had to promise two things:

1. That they would plant the bulbs in their *front* yard so the daffodils could be seen from the street and appreciated by people driving through the village.

2. That they would save the donor's name and address, then send a thank you note and a photo when the flowers were in full bloom.

As a result of this second provision, "daffodil connections" have been

You can't leave anything for posterity if you don't get off your posterior.

CROWNING GLORY of Greendale is its Village Hall at the end of Broad Street, which is a miniature copy of the famous main building at Williamsburg in Virginia.

FLOWERS ABOUND along Broad Street, in baskets and in multiple beds, and are tended by local volunteers. Summers provide visitors many "Kodak moments".

formed across the country. Many donors and recipients started corresponding, and in some cases they developed such a friendship that the two parties have even visited back and forth.

Our springs are now golden. Since daffodils propagate quickly, the number of yellow and gold blooms has annually doubled and redoubled throughout Greendale.

Plus, Grandhaven has contributed and planted several thousand additional bulbs each fall in selected areas, further enhancing the village's image as the Daffo*dale* Capital of the Country.

As for the original daffodil garden in Dale Park, the "rays" of the sun have multiplied and have gradually grown together, yielding a burst of blooms each spring to welcome hundreds of flower-fancying visitors.

The garden isn't left idle after the daffodils die out in mid-May. Red salvia is then planted in the "sun" and gold marigolds are planted to replace the "rays", offering summer-long beauty for the park's frequent visitors.

These flowers, along with the 37,000 annuals planted on Broad Street each spring, provide a kaleidoscope of blooms that quickly becomes the focus of thousands of camera buffs. This colorful setting—along with an extensive Rockwell display at the company Visitor Center—have truly transformed Greendale into a "Norman Rockwell town".

I'm not afraid of failing.
I'm more afraid of not trying.
—*A.B. Wallace*

CHAPTER 43

My Biggest Failure...by Far

SHOULDN'T HAVE DONE IT. Norb Whittle, my financial wizard, advised against it. Bobbi had misgivings about it, too.

By now I should have known to listen to her even more than Norb. As I said earlier, I've learned that women are just plain more intuitive than men. And you can double that with my wife. Bobbi just has a *sense* about things.

Here's the background: It was 1999 and we were right in the midst of the complete renovation of the buildings in downtown Greendale (described in the previous chapter).

There'd been a restaurant on the corner of the village center, and it had been closed for some time. The building had great historical significance—it had been the original village tavern when this charming little town was created in the 1930s. So tearing it down was not an option.

That's when I came up with a *great* idea. Or so I thought.

I envisioned that once we finished the renovation project and started urging subscribers to "Come see us soon"—not only for a visit but to take advantage of the closeouts at our company Visitor Center—the village would see *lots* of traffic. I was right on that point.

Our *Taste of Home* magazine had become hugely successful, and *Quick Cooking* was growing fast. As a result we now had a combined circulation of well over 10 million subscribers to our various magazines, and there was an increasing number of people "stopping by" Greendale.

So...with all those visitors...and no other restaurant in the area...what if we started a restaurant of our own...and called it the "*Taste of Home* Restaurant"? What a great idea!

We'd not only invite our *TOH* subscribers to come visit Greendale, but to dine at *their* restaurant as well. Sitting down and enjoying a fine meal—made with recipes right out of *Taste of Home* magazine—would make their visit all the more memorable. Brilliant, huh?

Norb kept saying no. He'd worked at a private accounting firm before

Children learn three ways—by example, by example, by example.

325

HOMEY *Taste of Home* Restaurant. Great food and service, but starving for profits.

joining me, and had handled the books for various taverns and restaurants. He related horror stories about how hard it is to make money in that business, and how hard it was to track money taken in by managers, bartenders and waitresses. "You know publishing, but you don't know squat about running a restaurant," he said, or something like that.

I countered every one of his objections. For beginners, I said we'd hire good people we could *trust*. It would be a warm, friendly place, and we'd serve down-home food at a price locals and visitors alike would find attractive. There was no other really *good* restaurant of this type on the south side of Milwaukee. "If we build it, they will come."

But of all my comebacks, the best I had was this:

"Norb, can you name *one* other restaurant in the entire United States that can regularly invite *50 million people* to come in to dine? That's how many readers we reach every other month, and we can keep talking about this restaurant to all of those people—*free!*"

I was just getting started. "My goal with this restaurant isn't to make a lot of money. If we just break even, that'll be fine. When all these people start coming to Greendale, we need a place for them to eat. Most of these are country people, and enjoying good food is part of a good trip.

"Greendale's going to become a tour destination. We'll need to make the restaurant large enough to handle tour groups of 400 or more at a time. With that many people and all that free promotion, how could we possibly lose money? What's more, Greendale residents would greatly enjoy this restaurant, too. We really need a fine dining facility in this area."

I still wasn't done. "Hey, you want to dream a little? With the constant exposure of our magazines behind it, who knows, Norb, maybe this concept could be so successful that we could *franchise* it. We could have *Taste of Home* Restaurants all across the country!"

When I get excited about something, I'm a heckuva salesman. So good, in fact, Norb eventually relented, though he was still far from enthusiastic.

I hired one of the best restaurant managers in Milwaukee on a consulting basis, then sat down with an architect-designer and his decorator. They kept asking what kind of "feeling" or ambience I envisioned for this restaurant, and I kept answering, "I want it to be down-home and comfortable—sort of like a visit to Grandma's house."

With that, we set off, and with all my optimism, we nearly doubled the size of the original tavern-restaurant. We installed a huge state-of-the-art kitchen and a series of separate dining rooms, each with its own name—there was the Family Room (casual), the Dining Room (upscale), and three rooms named after our magazines—the *Country* Room, the *Reminisce* Room and the *Birds & Blooms* Room—each with appropriate decor.

To accommodate the freezers, storage and office areas, we dug a complete basement below it. And that's when we dug ourselves into our first pile of trouble!

About halfway through the digging, a peculiar odor suddenly filled the air…then drifted down main street. Potent stuff. The Wisconsin Department of Natural Resources was called, and sure enough, we'd run into serious contamination.

Turned out that years earlier, a dry cleaning establishment had operated next door, and with pollution not much of a concern back then, they'd just run those strong chemicals out of a pipe and onto the ground. That stuff had soaked down as deep as 25 feet and reached way out below the street! The DNR shut down the project completely and allowed no work to continue until it was *all* cleaned up to their satisfaction.

> "Whatever happened to 'Going to Grandma's house'?"

That cleanup took *months* and delayed the site's completion by nearly a full year. Some of the soil was so badly polluted it had to be trucked to the only fill that would accept it—in *Canada*. This cleanup was incredibly costly—so much so that it eventually matched the entire construction costs of the building itself.

Finally the restaurant was finished and we opened in 2000. The result—both inside and outside—was beautiful, but *way* over budget. I'd been too busy with many other projects to provide close supervision, and the costs had simply run amok. *Way* amok.

By the time a man realizes his father was right, he has a son who thinks he's wrong.

People spend money differently when it isn't their own. Something had happened to my "Going to Grandma's house" concept; if she'd lived at the Ritz Carlton, the decor would have been spot on!

The curtains were custom-made, the carpet was spongy, the dishware was fine china, the wine glasses were hand-blown, the walls featured murals, clouds were painted on ceilings by a noted area artist. You get the picture. My "down-home" had been taken upscale. Make that UPscale.

Costs and overhead didn't drop off after we opened, either. The manager hired those *quality people* I'd suggested, he paid them well and he served the *best* food made from the *best* ingredients. The seafood was flown in fresh from Boston twice a week, the steaks were bought from the same purveyor as Ruth's Chris Steak House, and there were things on the menu I found hard to pronounce.

My involvement was pretty much limited to eating there, at least once a week. My wife and I loved it. Fine food, super service, warm ambience. The place had such a presence that you felt compelled to dress up when you went there. But the combination of these very things became the heart of the problem:

We could never charge enough to cover the costs. If we raised the prices to the break-even point, the customer count dropped drastically. If we lowered the prices to a level that lured them in, we lost money on every seating. Most days we lost $3 to $5 a serving. I'm serious.

If I told you—and I won't—what we lost *per month* in this restaurant, you would think I meant *per year* and that I was exaggerating. Our books not only bled, they hemorrhaged.

I lost more on this restaurant than any magazine launch or any other business venture I've ever been a part of. It was a costly lesson in "stick to what you know" and "limit yourself to what you can personally oversee".

The experience has given me a whole new respect for *anyone* who runs a restaurant. It's *hard work* with *long hours*, most often 7 days a week. And the single most important ingredient to succeeding is *the owner better be there.* I can think of no other business as challenging for an absentee owner.

We closed the doors of this beautiful place in December of 2002, then rented the facility to Heinemann's, a small chain operation with a good reputation that has six other locations in the area. They're doing well, serving health-conscious, down-home food at prices that residents and visitors can afford.

Yet, subscribers who return to Greendale for second visits—as well as many village residents—often mention how much they miss the *Taste of Home* Restaurant, with its fine food, great service and warm ambience. I miss it greatly, too…even though it gave me my first taste of serious business failure outside of the publishing field.

Shudda listened.

If you planted the grapes,
you deserve to taste the wine.

CHAPTER 44

Ideas Grown in My Garden

The trouble with being a good sport is you have to lose in order to prove it.

I'M A GARDENING NUT. It likely stems from my farm background and the urge to grow things. I have a huge garden plot near the house that Bobbi fondly refers to as "Roy's farm".

I spend a lot of time there, especially on weekends, growing a wide variety of vegetables. The garden's appealing to the eye through a trick I learned while conducting one of our tours to Switzerland—I plant flowers every fourth row.

Mostly, I grow tomatoes. Do I grow tomatoes! I had 48 plants last year, fewer than the year before, of various varieties. At harvesttime, I bring buckets of tomatoes to the office and feed a large number of friends. I could probably feed the National Guard, too—I just love to grow tomatoes.

But I enjoy gardening for more than just the green thumb aspect. A garden is a great place to *think*. There are no telephones, no radios, no cell phones (phew!), no conversation. There's just the birds, the breeze…and your thoughts.

A lot more than vegetables have come out of my garden. It's produced concepts for new magazines, new books, wild ideas aimed at getting readers excited and even a few inventions.

So far I have three patents, and am now working on the fourth. Three of these inventions took root while I was digging in that garden.

The first and by far most successful product is the Tomato Booster. We've now sold over *3 million* of those Boosters, all by direct mail.

The seed for that idea was planted as a result of a couple of contests held at the company. We'd done a story on a fellow from Indiana who that year had grown the country's largest pumpkin—over 300 pounds! After we'd published it, I wrote and asked if he'd share a few seeds from that whopper so we could have a pumpkin-growing contest in part of the flower bed just north of our offices.

He sent me only six seeds, but they were *HUGE*. Each was as big as a quarter or larger—after all, they'd come from a 300-pound pumpkin. I announced this growing contest we were going to have just outside our offices and gave two to the Editorial Department, two to the Art Department, and two to the Catalog Department.

I said the prize for the winning department would be…let's see…a free pumpkin pie from Baker's Square for everyone in the department! Now, if the catalog group would win, that would cost us over 150 pies. But, hey, the cost would be worth the excitement for that big group. You gotta keep fun in the ranks.

After the contest began, it wasn't long before it was obvious the artists were taking this thing seriously. They checked the article about the winner and applied all his tips—they pinched off all the runners but the healthiest one, then isolated just one pumpkin and eliminated the others. They fertilized the dickens out of it and near the end even added milk to the water, because that's what the winner had done.

This sucker got so big by late season that they got tired of lifting it on a scale periodically to check its weight. So they rigged up a "chicken scale", as we ex-farm kids would call it; they put some canvas straps around the pumpkin and *suspended* it from a large scale with big numbers. That way, since it was right along our access road, everyone could check the weight of the pumpkin as they drove by each day.

Predictably, the artists won, pumpkins down. It weighed over 140 pounds. And cost me 16 pumpkin pies.

One fun contest deserves another. The following spring we announced a tomato-growing contest on a larger portion of that plot. We put about 40 plants out there and announced the rules: "This tomato contest is solely for individuals. Once you choose a plant and put your name by it, *nobody* is going to help you with it. You have to water, fertilize and prune it on your own."

Prize for the individual winner: *Hmmm*…let's see…a family-size pizza every month for a year.

This time I got seriously involved. After all, tomatoes are my thing—no one was going to beat me in this contest! So I was diligent in caring for it every weekend.

One Saturday while watering *my* plant, I noticed that, because the plot was sloped, the water kept running away from the base. Looking for a cure, I walked behind our warehouse where all the leftover packaging is discarded in a large Dumpster.

> *"A garden is a great place to think…"*

There I found some sort of large plastic dish and hauled it back to my plant. I used a shears to cut a hole in the center, just big enough to slip over the plant if I folded up the branches. This time when I watered, the water didn't run away—all of it went directly to the plant's roots.

Hey, I'm onto something here! That's a problem even with tomatoes on level ground—once the soil gets firm, the water tends to run away from the plant instead of soaking down to its roots.

OVER 3 MILLION of these "Tomato Boosters" have been purchased—all by mail—since this product was introduced. Illustration shows how this unit allows water and fertilizer to seep directly to plant's roots. It's *guaranteed* to increase yields.

I thought about it more that afternoon as I worked in my own garden. Later I doodled a couple drawings, and by the next weekend I met with an old neighbor, Art Beutler, who I knew had at least two inventions of his own. He agreed the idea had potential, and I asked him to make a mold for a prototype.

After that, I spent part of my Saturday afternoons with him in his basement shop. I told him I wanted this apparatus to be a round dish with an elevated hole in the center...I wanted it made of black plastic to absorb heat...big enough to hold a gallon of water...high enough to hold the branches of the tomato off the ground...and slick enough that inchworms couldn't climb it. Then I wanted three small holes the thickness of matchsticks at the bottom, so the water would *seep* directly to the roots.

One Saturday after we'd gotten the mold that far, I told Art I had another idea: "Let's make a small cup at the base of each of those holes."

"Why?" Art asked.

"We'll call them 'fertilizer cups'. We'll advise growers to put fertilizer in those little indentations—that way the nutrients will leach right down to the roots every time the plant is watered."

On my way home from Art's house that day, something else occurred to me: "Why not sell the *fertilizer*, too? We could offer it in small packets that will carry each plant through a season."

While Art finished the prototype, I sought out fertilizer suppliers. I eventually found a good product especially suited for tomatoes, and I named it "Maxi-Mix". (I compare it with Miracle-Gro in my garden each year and it does as well or even better.)

By February we had samples of the finished product, which I named and registered as the "Tomato Booster". Then we offered it in our magazines, right at the time nursery companies were sending out their seed catalogs

The best way to get your tomatoes to ripen is to go on vacation.

HOTHOUSE protects against late frost, warms plant and aids growth.

and gardeners were itching for the growing season ahead.

The response was amazing—we filled orders for over a *half million* of those Boosters that first spring!

Our "baker's dozen" offer of 13 for the price of 12 did especially well. What's more, *54%* of the people who ordered the Boosters also ordered the Maxi-Mix fertilizer packets, nearly doubling our profit. Suddenly, we were in the tomato business.

The "Hothouse" came next. That spring, we headed to western Iowa for our annual Easter vacation trip to visit relatives. On the way, I noted dozens of large plastic milk jugs in people's gardens, protecting young plants from frost.

I pondered how difficult it must be to use a heavy shears and cut up that many of those thick, plastic jugs. There has to be a better way to protect plants from frost. Hey…why don't we make some sort of "hothouse"?

When I got home, back to Art's house I went. Within days, Art came up with a concept that would make the product easy to ship, which is always a plus in the catalog business.

Basically, the product is a tiny tent (see photo above). It has four heavy wires that curve together at the top, where they're inserted into a plastic spool. This forms the frame for a clear plastic bag, which has perforations in it to allow for aeration. You stretch this bag over the frame in tent-like fashion.

We turned out some samples and tested this new hothouse extensively in cool temperatures. It worked wonderfully.

The following year, along with the Tomato Booster and Maxi-Mix fertilizer, we offered our exclusive Tomato Hothouse with the luring headline, "Plant 5 Weeks Ahead of Your Neighbors!"

Almost anyone who grows tomatoes wants to have the *first* tomato in his neighborhood, so this Hothouse proved to be another winning product. We nearly doubled the sales of both the Booster and fertilizer the second year, and sold more than 300,000 Hothouses. (The new headline that boosted Booster sales was, "Honey, Wait'll You See This One!")

To date, the total combined sales since 1996 of the Tomato Booster, Max-Mix packets and Hothouses is $7,220,808. And because we keep guaranteeing results with our standard "Double Your Tomatoes or Double Your Refund" offer, the orders keeps coming. These products simply *work*.

Oh, and I won that tomato contest, too.

Unexpected competition. I've learned a little about patents through experience with these products, and one thing that's impressed me is that a patent *pending* seems to offer more protection than a patent, period.

Why? Because when it's pending, potential competitors don't know exactly what the patent is and how close they can come to a product without infringing on it. But as soon as the patent is affirmed, they can study it and find ways to come up with something very close to the concept…but not so similar they can be sued.

Our Tomato Booster is a prime example. While the patent was pending, we had no competition. But shortly after it was finalized, somebody in New York began marketing a product *so similar* that we immediately knew he'd just adapted ours.

For example, our Booster is round, he made his square. Ours has three holes at the bottom, his has four. Ours has a 3-inch hole for the plant, his has 4 inches. Then the dummy made it obvious where he'd gotten the idea— he gave it the *same name*, the Tomato Booster!

Because we had that name registered, we were able to stop his use of that, though it took a full year and costly attorney fees to do so. But we can't stop him from making and marketing the product—the differences are *just enough* to make it legal.

He's been selling *thousands* of them through garden supply stores throughout the country for several years now. Worse, he obviously gave more thought to "planned obsolescence" than we did, which is a key to repeat sales. His are so flimsy that you have to discard 'em and buy new ones each year. By comparison, I'm using some of my sturdy ones for the fourth year. As it's said, experience is expensive.

Bird in hand—in only 14 minutes. The third patented item came as a result of a series we did in *Birds & Blooms* about people who had managed to train wild birds to eat from their hands.

I've been a bird enthusiast for many years—"Peanut" (Kristin), one of our granddaughters, once counted 27 birdhouses and bird feeders around our wooded home site. So after editing that series, I told Bobbi, "*Someday* I'm going to get a bird to eat out of my hand."

But I didn't think there was much chance of that in view of the *time* it took for these people to accomplish this. The normal training period takes *30 days*.

IT'S THRILLING to have a bird eat from your hand…and it doesn't have to take you a month.

"BILL BIRD-IN-HAND" is the dummy on the left; I'm the one on the right with a house finch eating from my hand. We started with "Bill" in standing position, but switched to sitting position to make it easier for the "trainer" to stay *statue still* for long periods. I have now had a wide variety of birds eat from my hand—it's always exciting!

Here's how they do it: You note the time of the usual morning feeding frenzy of birds near your home, and then stand—still as a statue—about 30 feet away from the feeder for a *half hour* or more. Next day, same time, you move a step closer and again pretend you're a statue for another half hour.

This act is repeated, one step closer each day, for nearly a month, until you're finally right next to the feeder. If the birds continue to feed while you're there, the next day you close off the feeder and put a few seeds on a plate, holding it right next to the feeder tray.

If the birds become comfortable with that after a few days, you remove the plate, put the seed directly in your hand, and soon you have a chickadee, nuthatch or whatever eating right from your hand.

Great idea. Great experience. But who the dickens has the time to spend a *half hour every day for a month* to make that happen? Not me. I hope my life never slows down enough to allow that kind of effort.

Yet, I envied the experience. I decided that during my next session in the garden, I'd concentrate on coming up with a shortcut version of that training period.

I did. And I've now had the pleasure of having finches, nuthatches, chickadees and even a male cardinal eating from my hand! And the total "training" on my part took about 20 minutes.

While gardening, I concluded the key was to get somebody else to do the training for me. So what if I used a *mannequin* to do it? What if I made a life-size mannequin and had *him* stand out like a dummy for a month, moving him closer to the feeder each day?

I went to a custom display company in town and told them I wanted this guy to be made of coated cardboard or plastic (for sturdiness and to withstand the weather)…I wanted him about 5-foot-10 (my height)…he needed to fold at the waist (to fit a smaller shipping box)…and he had to have an arm that could be attached at the shoulder…with a hand at the end featuring a depressed area for the seed.

We also needed a metal pole to go through loops along his back side to straighten him up, then be pounded into the ground to support him.

The end product looked great, and I immediately named him "Bill Bird-in-Hand" (now trademarked). I took him into my backyard, placed him about 30 feet from our main feeder, *then put one of my caps and shirts on him*. That would be the key, I felt, to making him look like me when I was ready to change places with him.

I didn't spend 30 days training. It became obvious the birds were quickly becoming comfortable with "Bill". After all, he wasn't out there playing statue just a half hour each day. He was there 24 hours a day.

So I moved him about 5 feet closer each morning before I left for work. By the middle of the second week, I already had him right next to the feeder, and the birds kept coming and going. Saturday morning, I

> *"He landed on my cap, then flitted to my hand!"*

closed off the feeder and put some seed in Bill's hand. When I came home at noon, the seed was gone. I reloaded twice more that day.

Sunday morning, I fed Bill and the birds one more time. Then mid-morning I made the switch—I removed Bill, put on a matching shirt and cap and stood in his place with seed in my hand. And waited. And waited.

Ten minutes is longer than you think when you're standing *very still*. But a few minutes later, just as I was getting discouraged, I heard a couple of chickadees doing their "chick-a-dee, dee, dee" behind me. Suddenly one landed on top of my cap!

He hopped to the bill, and I could see his little tail flitting over the end of it. This was *exciting*. Then he hopped on my arm, bounced there a bit and flitted to my hand. It all happened in just 14 minutes.

What an exhilarating experience!

I could feel that little fellow's feet and how light he was. He poked through the seeds, picked one he liked and took off. I kept my statue pose, and that little guy came back four times.

When he finally had enough, I bolted into the house and yelled, "Bobbi, bring the camera—I need photo evidence!" The birds came back, she shot

335

several pictures, and I knew we had a new product that would delight bird lovers across the country. Forget about any profit—just for them to have this same exhilarating experience would be satisfaction enough.

I needed more credibility. Not only for others, but for myself. Maybe my birds were just tamer than others.

So I had the manufacturer make 20 more of the same unit, and we sent them to *Birds & Blooms* field editors in 20 different parts of the country. We told them exactly how to use "Bill" and asked them to share their experiences.

The reports were supportive and enthusiastic. One by one, they'd had the same success as I did, some after only 1 week and then in just minutes after they made the switch. The reports were lengthy, too, as they thrillingly related things such as, "This goldfinch sat on my hand, dug between my fingers for the seed and looked right at me!"

The experiences of these field editors were so interesting and exciting, I felt they just had to be shared. Yet there just wasn't enough space in our magazine to do that adequately as we got ready to market Bill. So I decided to do a small book that included the best of their comments, plus recommendations and some tips that they and I had learned. I named this book *Bill's for the Birds.*

I was about three-quarters finished with the writing when I got a letter from an activities director at a senior center in Kansas who had seen one of our field editors' trial versions of Bill. "This is a great idea," she wrote, "but could you get it to work in a *sitting* position so our residents who can't stand that long or are in wheelchairs can try it?"

Great idea! So I stopped the book, got another Bill and scored the model at the knees so he could sit. I picked another location where I'd have a whole new set of birds, plopped him in a lawn chair, then moved the chair closer to the feeder each day.

By the following Sunday, the birds seemed ready, so I pulled Bill out of the chair, put on my matching shirt and cap and *bingo*, I had finches in my hand in about 20 minutes. Finches, by the way, are spookier and much harder to draw near than chickadees or nuthatches.

Again, I ran to the house and had Bobbi bring the camera. In no time at all, she shot a roll of film with finches on my hand (that's one of her photos on page 334).

When I suggested we switch places, she said she didn't think it would work because she was wearing a skirt. I contended birds aren't into legs, that if the shirt and cap were the same, it should work.

We traded places, and I hardly got the camera focused before she had a finch on her hand. She was pretty excited!

Since she didn't look as cute in my cap, I said, "Let's try it without the cap." The birds wouldn't come near her. They immediately seemed to know the difference.

I've since placed Bill in my backyard. I usually don't put him out there until early fall, when birds are more dependent on feeders. But he's worked wonderfully—I've gone out during halftime of a Packers game and had a chickadee on my hand before Brett Favre threw his next pass. And once I had a male cardinal land on my hand—not for long once he saw my eyes move, but long enough to feel his weight and see that beautiful bird closer than ever before.

A side benefit to having Bill in your backyard is that birds seem to get accustomed to a "human presence". I notice birds come closer to me now when I'm working there, and they often sit right on or next to my feeders when I'm refilling them.

Some Bill Bird-in-Hand users report their birds actually fly right to them—a New England customer says he now carries seed in his pocket to feed chickadees that regularly come begging!

Wrapping up, we've now sold over 10,000 Bill Bird-in-Hands. But the sales aren't half as satisfying as hearing people across the country extoll how exciting it is to have a wild bird eat out of their hand.

Rain yielded next idea. I'm working on my fourth patent now, and I'm getting close. Bobbi and I were headed out of a restaurant last summer, only to find it was pouring outside.

She didn't want to go to the car, for the same reason any other woman would have given: Her hair.

"Where's your umbrella, hon?"

"It's in the car."

"What about that little fold-up one, don't you keep one of those in your purse?"

"No way. Those things are as big as an ear of sweet corn. You can't get one of those in today's small purses."

Hmmmm...

That's what I'm now working on, "The World's Smallest Umbrella". The prototype is being developed, and it's beginning to look promising.

My guidelines to the supplier were: It needs to be no more than 6 inches long (about the size of a magic marker or one of those new, tiny eyeglass cases). The "tent" portion needs to fold out to twice its size, 12 inches (just large enough to cover a woman's hair). Its handle also needs to fold out to twice its length, 12 inches (easier to hold).

"This idea could be my best—or worst—yet!"

And, because this is a product strictly for women, it needs to have such a colorful, whimsical, eye-catching design that it's a fashion statement. If we get it right, every woman who sees it will want one.

Lastly, it has to be so cost-efficient to produce that we can offer a half

Some people spend their life stewing, others doing.

Bill's for the Birds

The complete story of "Bill Bird-in Hand"... and how he can have birds eating from your hand... in just 30 minutes!

Compiled by the Editors of *Birds & Blooms* magazine

dozen of them for $5. That way women can keep one in each purse.

This tiny umbrella will be inserted into an attractive sleeve, for which I already have the fitting slogan: "Protect Your Hair from Here to There!"

When it's ready, I plan to hand out a thousand of them on a rainy day in Seattle as a marketing ploy. Then I'll take it to a national restaurant convention and suggest it as a handout imprinted with "Moe's Steak House" or whatever. It should be even more perfect for hairstylists to consider as handouts to their customers.

And how about giving these away for "Umbrella Night" at the ballpark? Especially at some baseball venues that in recent years have begun promoting "Wednesdays Are for Women" outings.

This World's Smallest Umbrella idea could be terrific or terrible. Not knowing is what makes it exciting. It could end up being my biggest bomb…or prove so popular it'll put my three other patents in its shade.

*Once I became rich, I was willing to pay my share.
But all of a sudden a whole lot of people
expected me to pay their share, too.*
—Sam Walton

CHAPTER 45

Musings, Memories and More

HOW MANY JOBS would lead you to become close friends with a movie star like Ernest Borgnine? That's just one of the many highlights that have come my way over the years, all due to being in "the magazine business".

This "job" has allowed me to travel in all 50 states—and that includes the *rural areas* of those states, gathering stories, taking pictures and running country-oriented tours. Along the way, I've had the privilege of meeting thousands of really good, down-home, honest people.

While I've enjoyed getting to know those people just as much as celebrities I've met along the way, there are a few of the latter who stand out, especially Willard Scott and Ernie Borgnine.

We contracted with *The Today Show's* Willard Scott to narrate a video of our cross-country hitch that trekked from Maine to California. I spent a full day with Willard getting the narration right (he'd slap his forehead every time he blew a word and had to do it over), and we had so many laughs and hit it off so well, we stayed in touch after that.

But let me tell you how I met Ernie. As you know by now, we're fond of "hiding" things in our magazines. Well, I didn't even know Ernie Borgnine was a subscriber to *Country* until I got a letter from him one day. You could tell by the mistakes and typos that he'd typed it himself. I still have it in my files.

It said: "Hard as I've tried, I cannot find that danged 'needle in a haystack' in this issue. But I want one of those pies you're offering as a prize—the one baked by that Amish farm woman in Ohio.

"So just send me one of those pies and bill me, okay?" Then below his carefully signed name he added a P.S. "Yes, it's really me."

I figured a guy like him had a good sense of humor, so I wrote back, "Ernie, I'm sorry, there are some things in life that you can't buy. You first have to find the needle, and then you'll be in the drawing for one of the 50 pies."

ERNIE BORGNINE got his wish to be a clown at the annual Great Circus Parade in Milwaukee. Here he takes a deserved rest with Bobbi, his wife, Tova, and me.

I would have probably given in and sent him a pie anyway, but I just wanted to see what his response would be. A week later, he wrote, "Okay, I found the danged needle. It's on page 57. Now send me one of those pies!"

I replied, "Well, Ernie, you're only halfway there. As our contest clearly states, if you find the needle and identify the correct page (you did), then you get in a drawing with about 100,000 other subscribers, and if yours is one of the 50 names drawn, you get the pie."

I figured I'd led him on long enough, so I added a postscript: "Oh, all right, for all you do for Milwaukee's Great Circus Parade each year, I'm going to have Maudie Raber, the Amish farm wife, send you one of those pecan pies. Enjoy!"

The latter needs a little explaining. Milwaukee has hosted the nation's largest circus parade for years. One evening in the early 1990s, Ernie was a guest on *The Tonight Show* and Johnny Carson asked him, "With all the years you've been acting, is there any role you would have liked to have played but didn't?"

Ernie immediately answered, "I always wanted to be a clown, but that role was never offered to me."

Ben Barkin, the founder and annual organizer of the Milwaukee parade, was watching that show. He picked up the phone and eventually connected with Ernie. Ben said, "You want to be a clown? We need a 'famous clown' for our circus parade here. If you'd like to be involved, I'll send you a plane ticket."

From that year on, Ernie Borgnine donned a clown costume and walked in the Milwaukee circus parade. The crowds love Ernie, and he loves them.

He'd performed at the parade several years before we had that "needle-pie" letter exchange. I had Maudie send him one of the pies, and when Ben Barkin heard about it, he introduced me to Ernie at the next parade: "Roy's the editor of *Country* magazine," he said. "He's your 'pie guy'."

Ernie roared with laughter, shook my hand and that was the start of a long relationship. We've had him to our house for dinner during the parades to give him a little relief from the crowds; he invited us to join him at an Angels game when we were in Los Angeles, and best of all, his wife, Tova, invited Bobbi and me to Ernie's 80th birthday party at the Beverly Wilshire Hotel.

What an evening that was! It was a surprise party for Ernie, and it turned out to be a 3-hour "roast". The "roasters" included some of the biggest names in show business—Milton Berle, Red Buttons, Harvey Korman, Stefanie Powers, Anthony Quinn, Steve Allen, Jayne Meadows, Gene Autry, Karl Malden, Les Brown and many more.

Tim Conway and Don Rickles sat at our table, and we had a chance to talk personally with them and several of the others. I still remember the typically caustic opening remark of Rickles when he grabbed the mike: "Ernie, I gotta be honest with you…before I got your invitation, I thought you were dead!"

It was an incredibly memorable evening, but what particularly impressed me was how *nice* these people were to us, pure "nobodies" in this crowd, and how much they obviously liked and respected Ernie. I came away thinking that these talented people are just as "close" to each other as I am to my best friends.

Wait—the Ernie story does not quite end there. The following fall, I was escorting one of our "Amish Tours" through Ohio, and our tour

LOVES KIDS. Ernie poses with Bobbi and our grandchildren Ryan and Kristin before parade.

group made a planned stop at Maudie Raber's farm for lunch. While the tour members were eating, Maudie beckoned me into the kitchen. She opened up a drawer, pulled out an 8x10 picture and said, "Who is this guy?"

It was a picture of Ernie, which he'd boldly signed. What Ernie didn't realize is that Maudie, being Amish, didn't have a TV nor a radio and had never been to a movie. She had *no idea* who some guy named Ernest Borgnine was!

Ernie hasn't heard the end of that, either. Tova's told me that whenever Ernie "gets a little full of himself" (which isn't too likely), she says, "Remember, Ernie, you may be famous—but nobody knows you in Holmes County, Ohio!"

My most embarrassing moment involved another celebrity. Shortly after I'd moved out of my basement to a small office in downtown Milwaukee, I landed an assignment from the A.O. Smith Harvestore company to write the script for a promotional film lauding their "blue silos".

I'd mentioned this to a friend, Bob Meyers, adding that I had written to Chet Huntley's agent to see if Huntley would narrate it and what the fee would be. Huntley at the time was the lead half of NBC's nightly *Huntley-Brinkley Report*, and I'd learned he did some freelance narration.

"Oh, no—I'd said that to Chet Huntley!"

Now, my friend Bob was a jokester. When he called my office, he'd come up with a new opener each time. He'd use a deep voice and tell our receptionist things like, "This is the Secretary of Agriculture…" She'd laugh and forward the call.

Well, one day she buzzed me and said, laughing, "Chet Huntley's on the phone." I just *knew* it was Bob, since I recalled telling him about contacting Huntley's agent.

So I picked up the phone and said glibly, "Hi, Chet baby!"

It was Chet Huntley!

As soon as I heard his voice, I knew my blunder and sputtered an apology, but he acted as though he hadn't noticed and got right down to business. He took the job. His fee? $400. Can you imagine getting a national anchor like Peter Jennings or Tom Brokaw to narrate a 20-minute film today for *$400*?

While meeting a few celebrities such as these certainly provided some of life's highlights, I don't value them any more than getting to know some of the more "common folks" along the way. Such as J.B. Hennings in Louisiana, who proudly gave me a tour of his wooded land in his pickup, then drove me to a little shack along the river, where he cooked up the best fish fry I've ever eaten. Others come to mind:

…The farmer in Oregon who showed me how he grows hops for the beer companies, then sliced up a big watermelon that we enjoyed on his porch, spitting the seeds on the lawn while looking out at Mount Hood.

…The seasoned fisherman along the coast of Maine who showed me how

If you don't learn from mistakes, there's no sense making them.

he catches lobsters in those wooden box traps 25 miles out in the Atlantic. Man, the big ones he caught were scary-looking things!

…The cowboy in Cheyenne, Wyoming who would climb on any horse you showed him, but absolutely refused to get on any airplane: "You do your thing, I do mine."

…The "singing dairyman" (Paul Miller) of Pennsylvania, who with his family came up with a unique way of thanking his neighbors for hurriedly rebuilding his barn just before winter set in—they went farm to farm and sang Christmas carols.

…The tobacco grower in North Carolina who saw me starting to dance and swat when fire ants climbed up my pants, and with a slow smile he couldn't hide while watching this Yankee's reaction, said, "Yep, they'll kinda nip at 'cha."

…The vegetable grower near Fairbanks, Alaska who showed me strawberries so large they wouldn't fit into the mouth of a pint jar—*really*—due to long summer days there. "On June 21," he said, "we have an all-night softball game here—we can see the ball clearly without lights."

…The Texas foreman who drove me to the bunkhouse at the center of King Ranch—and drove and *drove*. Hey, that ranch is over 120 miles long and 30 miles wide! It includes 825,000 acres, covers 1,300 square miles and is larger than the entire state of Rhode Island.

…The Florida orange grower who taught me why oranges eaten there are so much sweeter than those we get up north: "The juice that makes 'em sweet comes from the trees in the last 10 days, but we have to harvest them before that if they're going to be shipped a distance."

…The Minnesota farmer who plays recordings of music-like sounds to his crops to increase yields—and showed me plenty of evidence that it works with walnuts and tomatoes nearly *twice* the size of those in the "music-free" area a hundred yards away.

…And finally, Dave "Booga Bottom" Harris of Greenville, Mississippi, a seasoned crop duster who *insisted* I take a ride with him at the end of the day. *Whoooie*, I never should have caved in to that!

I'd hardly strapped into the backseat of the open cockpit when Dave—who preferred to be called "Booga Bottom" and even had it painted on the side of his plane—taxied wildly right toward a row of trees, then pulled up just in time to top them.

"I kissed the ground… he thought I was kidding!"

He was obviously showing off for his friends below, so he zoomed straight up, way up, then cut the engine and we did sort of a free fall straight toward the ground…and seemed to wait forever before he roared back up again.

He leveled off, then shouted back to me, "You all right back there?" I made the mistake of nodding "yes", so he immediately turned the plane upside down and we flew that way awhile.

Next he swooped so low to the ground that he made his buddies hit the deck, then headed toward the end of the field and flew *between* the fence and the telephone wires! I learned later there was only a 20-foot clearance, and was shown marks on the wings where he'd hit wires before.

When we finally landed on that bumpy pasture, I fully satisfied him by climbing out of the plane, wobbling a few steps, then laying on my belly and kissing the ground. I think he thought I was kidding. Every plane flight I've had since seems *smooth,* no matter what the weather.

He invited me to his huge plantation home for dinner that evening. After handing me some sort of mint julep, he took me on a tour of this incredible mansion—each of its 10 bedrooms had a separate fireplace. I couldn't help but note the contrast between a guy who flew so wildly and lived so elegantly.

I could list a hundred more country characters like "Booga Bottom" and the others I've gotten to know over the years, but this brief sampling should show why I found them as memorable as the celebrities. Someday I might find time to do a book just on them, titled *Country Characters.*

But for now, I'm going to switch gears, check my pre-book notes and share some of the other things that have made my life interesting. No need for separate chapters here…just more musings and memories as they come to mind:

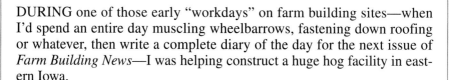

DURING one of those early "workdays" on farm building sites—when I'd spend an entire day muscling wheelbarrows, fastening down roofing or whatever, then write a complete diary of the day for the next issue of *Farm Building News*—I was helping construct a huge hog facility in eastern Iowa.

About mid-afternoon, Gary, the owner of the company said, "You mentioned during lunch that you like golf. You have your sticks in the car?"

By coincidence, my clubs were still in the trunk from having played the previous weekend.

With that affirmed, he said, "Why don't you join me for 9 holes after work before you head back? It's men's night at our country club."

This being a tiny town of only 300 or so, I responded, "You have a *country club?*"

Gary got a little indignant. "Sure do! We even have watered greens. It's a really nice course."

That piqued my curiosity. I wondered how nice this little course could be, and what "men's night" would be like in a small town like this. So I agreed to join him.

Right after 5 o'clock, we headed to his home in town, where he directed me to a bedroom to change clothes. While I was changing, he yelled, "You want steak or pork chops for dinner?"

I assumed he must be calling the club to order ahead of time, so I said, "Whatever you're having is fine."

When I came out, he slapped a package of cold meat in my hand. "We're having steak," he said. "Let's go."

I started for the front door until he waved, "No, this way," and headed for the back door. Surprise—behind the house was his own golf cart, albeit an old, used one with a gas motor that definitely needed a muffler.

As we growled down the gravel street, similar old carts appeared from behind other houses, driven by his buddies, who smiled and waved as they fell in line. We headed toward the edge of town, dust whipping up behind from the "convoy".

I was eager to see the clubhouse at this rural country club. Suddenly, as we came to the edge of town and made a turn, there it was—a large old mobile home propped up on concrete blocks! Smoke was rising in a cloud at one end from at least a half dozen charcoal grills, each hovered over by rugged, suntanned men.

"Here," said my host, "everyone cooks their own. Find a grill and I'll grab you a beer." He returned after thrashing around in an ice-filled cooler and handed me a cold Miller.

There were so many men, so much smoke and such loud conversation, it was a scene fit for a movie. I studied the group and noticed how many of the guys in shorts had *brown* arms and *white* legs. And the ones who weren't wearing caps had brown faces and white foreheads. I also noted one big guy was cooking a little pork chop while a short, slight fellow was flipping a huge porterhouse.

When my steak was done, Gary said, "Follow me" and we headed inside the "clubhouse". There, along one wall, was a long table tended by several women. As you walked along, they smiled and plopped a baked potato, barbecue beans, salad, Jell-O and a warm homemade roll on your plate. Then you headed back outside and found any place left on a few benches, some stumps or right on the grass.

I'd put in a hard day, and the food was *great*. So was the camaraderie— these guys were close friends. I couldn't contribute much to the conversation—it was all about the height of the corn, the price of hogs, last week's rain, etc. These were the things that were important and of interest to them.

> **"With this kind of golf, I should have worn a helmet!"**

Finally, it was time to *play golf*. It was a shotgun start, so the sputtering carts scattered all over the course. Some guys just used pull carts, and others hoisted tiny bags of sundry clubs over their shoulders.

They didn't use a siren as the shotgun starting signal as done at most courses. When everybody appeared to be at their designated tees, some guy back at the "clubhouse" gave a long blast on a car horn followed by two toots.

"Let 'er go," said Gary, and we all teed off. The course was…well, a pasture. It had no trees separating the fairways, and balls were soon flying all over. After a couple of holes, I decided a *helmet* would have been far more appropriate than a golf cap!

Cheerfulness is the window cleaner of life.

Most of these guys were hackers, but it didn't dim their fun in the least. Neither did golf hinder their conversation—which continued on about corn, beans, cattle, hogs and rain right through anyone's backswing. And a few frisky jokes were mixed in there, too.

As we putted on No. 5, I commented to Gary how good the green was and asked about that watering system he'd mentioned. He quickly demonstrated by picking up a curled hose with one of those back-and-forth spray units on the end and plopping it in the middle of the green. "Nothing to it," he said. "See? Watered greens."

We finished swinging (and ducking) just before dark, then everybody gathered around the mobile home-clubhouse again for a few more beers. As those men laughed and talked—I don't recall anyone discussing their scores—I concluded that these guys were just as close and had just as much fun as my buddies and I do at our "swanky" country club on the edge of Milwaukee.

I stuck around an extra hour before hitting the road, soaking up the atmosphere and committing it to memory. So much so that I was able to relate that whole "men's night at the local country club" again now nearly 30 years later.

❖❖❖

MY WIFE AND I have conducted more than 40 of our company group tours over the years, many of them in the States and many to the far reaches of the world. My favorite "tour story" happened on a trip to Switzerland a number of years ago.

We normally set up the lodging in small Swiss towns rather than Zurich or Bern, because our country-oriented tour members are more comfortable in that atmosphere.

On this particular trip, we'd left Chicago's O'Hare at about 10 p.m. with 90 people (the limit for two motorcoaches). We flew through the night and arrived in Switzerland shortly after dawn. Then we boarded the coaches for a long drive, stopped along the way for lunch and finally arrived at our hotel in the tiny town of Unterwasser.

We told the tour group to take a good nap that afternoon; after all, they likely hadn't slept well on the plane, there was a drastic time change (7 hours) and we were going to have a busy week beginning at 7:30 the next morning.

Well, there were a couple of Midwestern farmers in our group. You try to tell two active farmers to take a *nap* in mid-afternoon. Not much chance of that happening! So, unbeknownst to me, these two farmers strolled outside the hotel that afternoon.

In Switzerland, they don't waste any productive land. The average farm there is only 23 acres, so grazing land is highly valued—cows graze right up to the sides of rural hotels like the one we were staying in, and you can hear their bells clanging all night long. I've never found it a bother; it adds to the atmosphere.

Anyway, our two farmer tour members wandered a bit and began watch-

Many ambitions are nipped in the budget.

ing a Swiss farmer who was raking hay—*by hand* with a huge rake. They walked toward him and tried to converse, but they couldn't communicate a lick—they spoke only English, he spoke only German.

Finally one of our guys reached out, grabbed the rake from the Swiss fellow and started raking. The Swiss farmer immediately turned and started walking back to his nearby farmstead. Our guys wondered if they'd insulted him.

Not the case. The Swiss farmer came back with *two more rakes.* And now all three were merrily raking, smiling and trying to talk but still not making any sense to each other.

After nearly an hour, the Swiss farmer stopped, pointed back at his farm, then made milking motions with his hands. "Oh, you're going to *milk*," said the U.S. guys. "We haven't milked cows by hand in years. We'll help you!"

With that, they followed him and each milked two cows in his large barnhouse before heading back to the hotel. They told our whole group about their experience at dinner that evening.

From that day on, those two farmers caused a lighthearted fuss every afternoon as it neared 5 o'clock. "Hurry, Roy," they'd tell me, "we gotta get these buses back in time to help 'Fritz' with chores!" And as soon as we'd get back, they'd hustle over to help Fritz, the name they'd given him, with his milking.

Now, here's the good part: The last night of our stay, that Swiss farmer somehow managed to invite these two farmers and their wives over for supper at his house. And they went. I'd loved to have been a fly on the wall in that home that evening, with the parties understanding little or nothing of what was said!

No matter, they must have communicated somehow, because the next morning at 7 a.m. when we were loading to head to the airport, that Swiss farmer and his wife were there by the coach, and all six of them hugged a tearful good-bye, knowing they'd likely never see one another again.

> *"Hurry, we have to help Fritz with chores!"*

After running tours to a number of distant lands, I've often thought that *travel* is perhaps one of the best deterrents to war.

Why? Simply this: Because the more you travel, the more you learn that people are pretty much alike everywhere. They have close families, they love their children, they work for a living, and they share many of the same concerns and characteristics we do. Why would we ever want to harm anyone who's a lot like us?

The epitome of that conclusion, for me, is my strong, vivid memory of that emotional hugging scene between a rugged Swiss farmer and two big American farmers. All three didn't look like they were much accustomed to hugging, yet they obviously felt so strongly about the bond they'd formed that they were compelled to communicate physically the feelings they couldn't communicate verbally.

The best safety device in a car is a rearview mirror with a police officer in it.

347

IT WAS DURING THIS VERY TRIP that we began a travel technique that we've made a standard practice ever since. We have tour members "rotate seats" on the motorcoach every day of the tour, moving two seats ahead on the left side each morning, two seats back on the right side.

Sounds pretty "juvenile", doesn't it? Not when you learn why. The third morning of this tour, it was raining cats and dogs. A half hour before the 8 o'clock coach was to pick us up, I grabbed an umbrella and headed to the pickup point, just to be sure everything was set before bringing the group out in the inclement weather. The coach wasn't there as yet, but to my surprise, a dozen of our people were—huddled in the wind and rain, getting soaked.

> ### "What time does the 8 o'clock bus leave?"

"Why are you here so early?" I asked. "The coach isn't due for nearly a half hour."

"We want to get a good seat near the front today," they chimed. "We've had to sit way in the back the last 2 days."

Right there, right then, I decided we weren't going to let that happen again—having people get soaked to get good seats. I announced our "rotation schedule" that day on the coach, and we've stuck with it ever since.

Why do we have them move *two* seats rather than one? We find it mixes the conversation better; it puts them with a different set of people than those they visited with yesterday.

One last travel comment. If you run enough tours, here's the one question you hear so often that it raises the hair on your neck: "What time does the 8 o'clock bus leave?"

In matters of style, swim with the current;
in matters of principle, stand like a rock.

CHAPTER 46

More Musings, Memories and Tidbits

I'M STARTING a new chapter here because the last one was getting long. Yep, that's my honest reason.

See, my wife's a voracious reader—it's not uncommon for her to read two or three books a week. She tells me she prefers short chapters: "It breaks up the book a bit," she says. "If you have something you need to do, the end of a chapter is a good place to break away and then come back later."

Maybe it's like TV, where commercials often afford a convenient bathroom break. Since there are no commercials in this book, I thought I'd just start a new chapter here, allowing you a short break if you need it, then get on with more Musings and Tidbits. Starting right here:

——————— ❖❖❖ ———————

I'VE ENJOYED BEING A JOURNALIST. Not just because I've always liked to write, but because this job has given me a license to look into other people's lives. In any other situation, if you asked people such personal questions, they'd rightly say, "None of your business!" and maybe even punch you in the nose.

But when you identify yourself as a reporter or an editor, the same people readily bare their souls. I've often been amazed at things total strangers have freely volunteered as I scribbled notes. People have told me things I just *knew* I'd better not print.

It's been a joy to hear everyone's "story". I've always had a fascination with other people's lives, especially how they got involved in whatever business they're in. Even now, when we meet people socially, one of my early questions is, "How did you get into your line of work?"

——————— ❖❖❖ ———————

I GREW UP FASCINATED WITH HOBOES. The farmhouse in which I was born was only 200 yards from a railroad, and I often sat on the bridge over those tracks and waved at the conductors. Obligingly, they'd smile and sometimes even hoot their loud whistle at me.

But the scary part of living that close to the tracks back then was the

These days, it seems a pedestrian is a person en route to or from a parking lot.

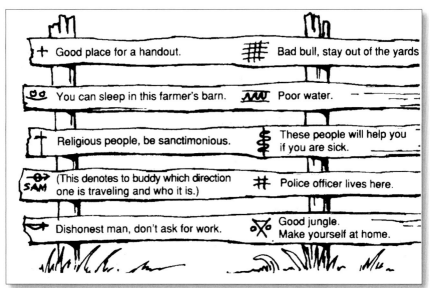

Good place for a handout.

Bad bull, stay out of the yards

You can sleep in this farmer's barn.

Poor water.

Religious people, be sanctimonious.

These people will help you if you are sick.

(This denotes to buddy which direction one is traveling and who it is.)

Police officer lives here.

Dishonest man, don't ask for work.

Good jungle. Make yourself at home.

FINALLY, after all those years, I'd broken the "hobo code". The symbols above are just as "Steamboat Charlie" drew them for me. And the definitions are what other hoboes understood from each of these symbols scratched on bridges or posts.

hoboes. Every couple of weeks during the summer months, one would show up, tap at our screen door and ask for food. They were usually bearded men, and since no one else I knew had a beard, they appeared all the more scary to me.

While she never openly admitted it, it was obvious my mother was a little frightened by them, too. After all, Dad and my older brothers were usually out on the north forty or somewhere, and it was just her and me—a little squirt then—in an unlocked farm home.

She never turned down a request for food. She'd cut thick slices of her homemade bread, cover it with butter and homemade jelly and hand it to them with a cup of coffee. I'd watch them through the screen as they ate on our front step. Most were very polite and thanked her before leaving.

But one morning when there was a tap at that screen door, and a huge, bearded hobo stood there, Mom panicked a bit. She was out of bread. She looked about, not knowing what to do, until she spotted a stack of pancakes that were left over from breakfast. So she spread jelly on a few of them, folded them over and handed them to the hobo.

> **"My mother was always frightened by those hoboes..."**

That guy must have thanked my mother a dozen times, bowing each time as he did. He'd apparently gotten so tired of all those homemade bread sandwiches wherever he stopped that those jellied pancakes were a real change-of-pace treat!

But the more she fed them, the more hoboes came. My dad had heard

350

that hoboes use some type of codes and leave them as markers for those who follow, indicating where they can get free food or whatever. My brothers and I studied the wood pilings of the bridge, but other than some scratches, we could never detect anything.

About 40 years later, I learned those "scratches" meant more than we thought. I was on the phone with Dave Adams, a draft horse friend from Britt, Iowa; I'd met him when I was involved with Dick Sparrow's 40-horse hitch. Dave told me that Britt was hosting its annual Hobo Convention…that in fact, he had a hobo named Steamboat Charlie in his house at that very minute.

"Can I talk to him?" I asked, and Dave put Steamboat on the phone. After a very interesting conversation, I asked him whether it was true that hoboes left markings for their counterparts.

"Absolutely," he replied. "We did it to help each other out and survive."

So I asked him if he would be willing to share those code markings with me if I sent him a $100 check in advance. I thought it would make an interesting story for *Country* readers.

He readily agreed to do so, and he sounded trustworthy, so I sent the check. Two weeks later, I got his handwritten response with 10 simple markings and the meaning of each. I was right, our readers really enjoyed that piece. At left is a reprint of those codes from Steamboat Charlie.

So now you're set—if you're ever walking near a railroad, see some scratches on a post and are hungry, you'll know where you can get some free homemade bread sandwiches. Or jellied pancakes.

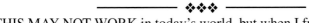

THIS MAY NOT WORK in today's world, but when I frequently flew out of O'Hare Airport, I came up with a good way to find a parking space. Before I tried this technique, I'd drive and drive in that huge lot, sometimes looking for a spot so long, I'd nearly miss my plane.

But not after I got this system down: I'd just drive right up to the area where returning passengers were coming out of the terminal and ask, "Would you like a ride to your car so I can have your space?"

Back then, people more readily trusted each other, so they'd hop in, and I'd have my car parked in no time.

———— ❖❖❖ ————

THAT PARKING ITEM reminds me of when I was exiting a parking lot in Denver last fall. It was the lot where our son, Scott, parks every day.

(By the way, when he was 9 years old, he told me one day that Colorado was his favorite state. "How can that be?" I asked. "You've never been there." And the little shaver answered, "'Cause it's the only state with 'color' in its name." It proved prophetic—he went to the University of Denver and has shown no inclination of ever leaving Colorado.)

Anyway, I pulled up to the lot's little glassed-in booth to pay the bill. The middle-aged woman inside seemed a little bored with her job, so I tried cheering her up with a few comments. Then I asked, "By the way, would you happen to know a Scott Reiman who parks here?"

With that, her face brightened and in halting English she said, "Sc-ought W-reiman? Yes, I know him. He nice young man. On cold winter days, he sometimes brings me cup of hot coffee on his way to work."

"In that case," I said, "I'm proud to say he's my son."

Sometimes little things you learn about your kids make your heart swell.

❖❖❖

NOW ONE ABOUT DAUGHTER JULI. Juli was a sophomore at my alma mater, Iowa State University, when she invited me out for "Dad's Day" at her sorority. She kept telling me about "a picture" that I just *had* to see over in the Agronomy Building.

Honestly, I wasn't too enthused about walking that far on this cold, blustery February day, but she persisted, and finally—more out of love for the daughter than to see this picture—I bundled up and joined her for the long trek to that part of the campus. There, we climbed the stairs to the third floor, where she'd noticed this postcard-size picture pasted on the office door of an agronomy professor.

It *was* a *great* picture! I immediately got excited about it, and Juli said more than once, "I just *knew* you'd like that picture, Dad!"

It was a photo of two little boys—obviously twins—dressed in bib overalls with exquisite expressions on their faces. It was what I call "a captured moment". A professional photographer might have ruined it— he likely would have moved the kids off the gravel onto some grass, got overly concerned about the posts above their heads and used a flash for fill-in lighting.

Instead, you had this "natural" picture. You just knew that it was likely shot by one of their parents as the two little boys were chatting about something.

Since it was a Saturday and the professor's office was closed, I noted his name on the door and called his assistant the following Monday. She got the photo off the door, checked the back of it and gave me the family's name and address.

I eventually got through by phone to the twins' mother, who told me she shot this picture on the first day they'd worn those bib overalls. She entered the photo in a contest at the county fair, but it didn't win anything. Yet, an hour later, she'd come back to the display and several people wanted to buy copies of it.

> *"A professional photographer might have ruined that photo…"*

By the time I reached her, she'd sold a number of them, one of which somehow found its way to this professor's door in Ames, Iowa. We were just getting ready to launch *Country Kids* magazine, and I told her I thought this was the *perfect* picture for the cover of that Premiere Issue. I said I'd consider it if she sent a copy of the photo.

After I received it, I was all the more impressed with it in a larger format…but then soon became frustrated. The focus and color of the photo

FAMOUS PHOTO. We've filled orders for over 3 million copies of this picture that my daughter Juli spotted on a college professor's door and called to my attention.

were terrific, but it was solely a *horizontal* picture. It wouldn't fit the *vertical* format of our magazine. We tried several ways, but it just wouldn't work on the cover.

Dale Miller's office was next to mine and I asked if he had any ideas. I just knew this picture was special and that our readers would love it…but if we couldn't use it on our cover, how could we do it justice inside?

Suddenly Dale said, "What if we made a really large version of it and turned it into a poster?" That idea turned out to be golden.

We'd never offered any type of poster before, but this just seemed like the kind of picture that our country audience would want to frame, tape to their refrigerator, pin to the bulletin board or whatever. It was worth trying.

So…I wrote to the twins' mother and told her the photo didn't work for our cover, but described our poster plans. I enclosed a $500.00 check and a release for her to sign, but told her she should think about this option first:

"You can take the $500.00, or we'll give you a quarter for each poster we sell. We've never sold a poster before—so I don't know whether we'll sell a hundred, a thousand or 10,000. It's your choice. Let me know."

A week later she called, said she'd given it some thought and had decided on "the sure thing" by taking the $500.00. She said she'd already cashed the check and bought a washing machine she'd been needing, and that the clearance form was on its way back to us.

If you can laugh at it, then you can live with it.

We decided the photo needed a caption. I studied it a bit, tried to imagine what these two little fellows might be saying, then penned, *"You been farming long?"*

We labeled it our "Little Farmers" poster and tested it with an offer in our magazines. But since we hadn't tried selling anything like this before (and had been *burned* on some other things we *thought* would sell well), we only printed 2,000 copies of the poster.

They sold quickly. So we printed another 2,000. Then we printed 5,000. Zip, out the door they went. So next time we printed 20,000 copies ...then 50,000...and then more and more and more!

The demand for this poster was absolutely incredible. Many who ordered hadn't even become aware of it through our magazines—they'd spotted it at someone else's house or office and just *had* to have a copy of their own.

I know you're already feeling sorry for the twins' mother and thinking how many washing machines she could have bought if she'd taken the "quarter per poster" instead of the $500.00, but bear with me—you'll see she eventually fared just fine.

With this kind of demand, we decided this photo had such appeal that we shouldn't limit it to just a poster. We could likely sell this picture printed on T-shirts, towels, bibs, cups, you name it.

So, I sent another letter to the twins' mother and advised her to contact a good local attorney; that way she'd know we were being completely fair to her. I explained that while the agreement we'd made earlier exempted any royalty on the poster, we would now give her *6% of all sales* of any ancillary items made from the photo, and this would be *net* for her—she wouldn't have to pay any of the marketing, mailing or promotional costs used in selling it.

In the months and years that followed, I became good friends by phone with her attorney—Brett Aldridge—who handled all the legal matters and was elated with the sizable royalty checks we kept sending his client.

> **"Actual count is now 3,137,101 copies of 'Little Farmers' poster!"**

We marketed this photo in every conceivable form, but one of the best proved to be a set of small figurines made of these two little fellows. There apparently are *lots* of figurine collectors across the country. We sold *thousands* of them.

One day while visiting Bobbi's mother in Kansas, I noticed her collection of salt and pepper shakers. I wasn't aware before that people collected such things. But as I looked at her collection, it suddenly occurred to me that if we just "poked some holes" in the top of these Little Farmer figurines...why, sure!

There apparently are *lots* of salt and pepper shaker collectors throughout the country as well; the supplier could hardly keep up with the demand for Little Farmer shakers.

The poster sales continued well for years. My wife and I eventually spotted that poster everywhere as we ran tours, not only all across the lower 48 but even in Fairbanks, Alaska and in Zurich, Switzerland!

We have a *large* (4 feet by 5 feet) display of this poster at our company Visitor Center in downtown Greendale, and on a small blackboard beside it we keep a running count of the total "Little Farmers" posters sold. As this is written, that total is *3,137,101.*

Now, how well has their mother done in her percentage of sales? To date, she's received *well over $200,000.* Which should not only cover a lot of washing machines, but the tuition of those two little boys as well, who are now in college.

The poster also more than covered the tuition of our daughter Juli, who I've thanked many times for insisting that I take that long walk across the campus that cold February day.

———————— ❖❖❖ ————————

SPEAKING OF PHOTOS, here's another potential cover shot that—like the "bull picture" I described earlier—never developed. Early on while I was still freelancing, I spotted a farm near Dixon, Illinois that had cover written all over it.

It was on a hill, the barns were newly painted red with white trim, the house was attractive, and a beautiful stand of tasseled green corn covered the slope leading up to the farmstead. It was late in the afternoon, the sun was turning orange, and white clouds in a vivid blue sky formed the background.

I had borrowed an expensive Hasselblad camera (worth about $1,500) from Tom Ferderbar, a photographer friend, to shoot some other potential covers on this trip, and this one I'd just come upon had the potential of another cover before I headed home.

So I pulled in, checked with the farmer whether it was okay to shoot some pictures, then asked if he had a stepladder I could borrow. My idea was to stand high on that ladder so I'd have the tops of that tasseled corn as a foreground for those red barns on this beautiful farmstead.

He produced a tall one, about a 15-footer, and it got heavy in a hurry as I lugged it about 50 yards through that thick corn. It was now about 5:30 p.m., and the light was getting perfect for the shot I had in mind.

> *"That's when I <u>really</u> started sweating!"*

But it was July, it was *hot* and very close in that field. And dragging that big ladder between the tall, tight rows—then repeatedly climbing up and down with the heavy camera to see if the view was right—got pretty tiring. So I finally just put the camera next to a cornstalk, kept moving and climbing the ladder, moving and climbing, each time framing the potential photo with my hands.

I probably did that for another 20 minutes or more before I finally found the position that I felt was *just right.* Now all I had to do was get the camera and…

Being kind is more important than being right.

355

That's when I *really* started sweating. I couldn't find it. I'd moved that stepladder so often, and with one cornstalk looking exactly like 10,000 others, I didn't have a clue where it was! I started circling, then going back and forth, retracing my steps…with no success. At one point I even had trouble finding the ladder!

The panic began. This was a *$1,500 camera.* I didn't have $1,500. Worse, it belonged to a friend. I didn't know what to do…until I remembered something Dad had taught us when we were kids on that Iowa farm.

Kids used to get lost in cornfields and get totally exhausted trying to find their way out. Since we used to play hide-and-seek in our corn with the neighbor kids, Dad had told us, "If you ever get lost, don't run in circles. Just follow a row and stay with it until you get to the end of the field. Then you'll know where you are."

I had used that exact method once when I was about 10. I got totally disoriented, but remembered to go in a straight line. I came out on the wrong end of the field, but when I saw the Eischeids' farm, I knew where I was, walked the other direction and found my way back to the house.

So I decided I'd use this same method again 30 years later to find that camera. I went two rows at a time, back and forth, back and forth, about 30 yards in each direction. I did this for most of a half hour, and just about the time I was going to give up and start over, I found the camera! I could not believe how far away from the ladder it was. What a relief.

But guess what—by now the sun was too low to make it worth even attempting a photo. After all that, I had no choice but to just lug that heavy stepladder back to the farmer.

"Get any good pictures?" he asked. I felt so dumb, I mumbled something like, "Well, not as good as I'd liked," then climbed in the car and took off.

I was so disgusted and sweaty, I could have used a shower before driving the hundred miles home…but, thanks to Dad, at least I had that expensive camera going back with me.

PEOPLE SOMETIMES ASK why none of our six kids joined me in the business. My usual response is, "Well, I never discouraged it, and I never encouraged it—we just let things take their course. I've seen that work terrific, and I've seen that work terrible. If it doesn't work out, how do you fire your own kid?"

Our children worked at the company during high school and summer vacations—handling everything from typing and filing to hauling the mail to the post office and mowing the lawn. But I was publishing magazines for *farm* people back then and raising *city* kids, so their interests took them elsewhere.

Yet our son, Scott, ended up working closely with the company by supervising many of its earlier investments, and he now manages the bulk of our family investments and foundation funds. He works hard, is 100% honest and approaches business with the right perspective.

I've sat in meetings with him and heard him say, "We only do business

Life is a journey, not a guided tour.

Horse sense dwells in a stable mind.

IT'S A REAL THRILL to hold the lines and drive 40 horses at once. I've had the privilege of driving this huge team of Belgians twice for short distances—not in a city parade, but in a safe rural setting like this. Still, it's like holding back a *train*.

with good people, and we only invest in things that we feel good about. When we're finished, we want both your firm and ours to say, 'That was a good deal for us.' That way we'll both sleep well."

❖❖❖

PEOPLE ALSO ASK from time to time about the "wheat symbol" that appears on our logo, our stationery and other items representing our company (you've likely also noted it above the chapter headings in this book).

Just after I'd moved from our basement to a rented office in downtown Milwaukee, I felt we needed a business card and a letterhead to make us

357

"official". The designer asked if I'd like anything symbolic worked into it. I told I'd think about it and let him know.

The next day when we met, I'd decided I wanted to work wheat into our logo in some way for three reasons: (1) Wheat would appropriately give it an agricultural touch, since we were then specializing in farm topics. (2) Wheat is one of the few crops grown across the country rather than in one area. In fact, wheat is the single most prominent food crop in the world. (3) I liked its Biblical significance. It implies we're ready to sit down and "break bread" with our readers.

So that's why the wheat symbol has been connected with our company for more than 30 years. In fact, when our new home was built, we had an artist create a version of it that's displayed high over the entrance.

❖❖❖

I MENTIONED earlier that I've driven the 40-horse hitch—twice. This is a bigger feat than you might think.

Just holding that many lines in your hands to direct that many horses is a feat in itself. (This hitch stretches out 40 yards in front of the driver. When it makes a turn on a city street, the first 16 horses actually disappear from the driver's view for a few seconds!)

Well, I've not only driven 40 Belgians, I've also ridden a 4-foot chicken multiple times. And never been thrown. So far. Because you may have trouble believing that, I'm enclosing photo evidence (at right).

Yep, that's me in the black cowboy hat on a big white leghorn that looks like it's been on steroids. I originally bought that monster chicken to show off for our grandchildren at one of our family gatherings.

They all flocked to the window when Bobbi said, "Come here, kids—Grandpa's got a new pet!" Their squeals of delight were enough to justify the price of this crazy chicken I found being offered by a mascot company at a convention in Las Vegas.

In case you haven't figured it out, those are fake legs swinging over the top. I'm actually inside that chicken up to my waist, with my feet covered by those huge chicken feet and spurs.

I rode it in the Greendale Fourth of July parade several times and have since given it to one of our sons-in-law so he can now ride it in his local parade. But that doesn't mean I'm finished fooling my grandkids—this year they squealed at my new clown outfit. (It's worn upside down. Its legs waggle above my head, which makes it look like I'm walking on my hands.)

I spotted another fun outfit for the future…but my grandkids might read this book.

❖❖❖

GOING FROM A 4-FOOT CHICKEN TO DOGS is a rather quantum leap, but I think this is worth sharing. When I grew up in Iowa, I was fascinated with some of the things our farm dogs did. They weren't just pets, they were "hired hands".

For example, during harvest season when we were going in and out of our livestock yard, hauling loads of hay or corn, we never bothered to close the gate to keep the hogs and cattle in—we would just station "Brownie" there, and he'd guard that gate all day long, saving us a lot of time.

Otherwise we'd have had to stop the tractor each time, get off, open the gate, pull through, go back to close the gate, over and over.

Brownie seemed to know that was his job, and he reveled in it. No steer or hog dared come near that gate during his watch. And he seemed to "smile" knowingly at us each time we came with another load.

That dog impressed us even more when we moved from a farm 2 miles north of Halbur to another rented farm about 2 miles south of Halbur. For several weeks after that move,

RIDING A 4-FOOT CHICKEN is a lot easier than driving a 40-horse hitch, but memorable just the same. Fortunately, I have him pretty much under control here.

he'd be lying wet and tired by the porch each morning, as though he'd done a lot of running during the night.

We found out why. The fellow who now lived on our old farm met Dad in town one day and said, "Ed, I don't see you much, but I see your dog a lot. He's digging up his old bones and hauling them home."

Now, Brownie had ridden to our new place in the cab of the truck—how could he have possibly known his way to that farm and back, over 4 miles away?

Remembering this, I started a series called "Dog Tales" in *Country*, asking readers to relate feats of their own dogs. We received a stream of amazing stories, the best of which was this:

A college boy from Tennessee spent his summer working on a farm in Ohio. He took along his dog, a German shepherd, and when the summer

> *"Imagine, that dog found its way from Ohio back to Tennessee!"*

ended, he decided the Ohio farm would be a better home for the dog than staying with his mother in a small town in Tennessee.

Late that fall, his mother was sweeping the front porch when a dirty mongrel approached her. She was about to shoo him away with the broom, then hesitated as something about the dog looked familiar—it was her son's dog!

Somehow that dog had made its way from Ohio all the way back home to Tennessee! Think about it—some humans would have difficulty doing that with a map.

We heard some beauts from readers when doing that series, all verified by friends and neighbors, but this one about a dog that found its way home—from Ohio through Indiana and Kentucky back to Tennessee, roughly 500 miles—was the dog tale of all dog tales.

—————— ❖❖❖ ——————

LET ME WANDER from dogs back to business for a bit. It's highly rewarding to do the right thing, even if it sometimes cuts into your profits. An example is our "Charity Letter".

I composed that letter in the mid-1980s, and our circulation staff still uses it when they receive a heart-wrenching letter from a subscriber. Here's its background:

Our magazines were still pretty much farm-oriented then, and the bulk of our subscribers were farmers and ranchers. In 1985, the ag economy hit rock bottom; farmers were going bankrupt by the hundreds. And many who weren't yet bankrupt were having difficulty hanging on.

During that period, we'd get letters from farm wives that cut right into your heart. So many had the same theme, I remember them almost verbatim. Here's one I saved from that terrible time:

"I'm not renewing my subscription to *Farm Wife News*, but I want you to know why. See, we're in great financial trouble out here. My husband doesn't openly share with me how bad things are, but I can tell by his expression and even the way he walks. I can also tell by the way he tosses in his sleep at night.

"I don't know what to do to help. I can't buy less food or cut back on necessities, yet I want to contribute in some way. So I decided today not to renew my subscription, despite the fact it's absolutely my *favorite* magazine.

"It may only be $9.98, but I want to show my husband in even such a small way that I'm trying to help our situation. I hope you understand, and thank you for so much enjoyable reading."

That letter wasn't an exception, it was typical. We received so many that our editorial staff was getting dispirited; we were all getting a little down when our job was to keep our readers up.

Finally, I went back to the circulation area where these cancellations were coming in and told them, "Look, I don't want you to forward any more of these depressing letters to me and the staff. It's affecting our attitude and the job we're doing.

Don't be called out on strikes. Go down swinging.

"From now on, when you get one of these heart-tugging cancellations, just send out this letter to them. You don't have to check with me or anyone else first; you decide on your own when the situation warrants it, okay?"

That letter became known as "The Charity Letter". It's short and to the point. Here it is:

"We're sorry to hear of your situation. In view of it, we're not accepting your cancellation.

"Because you supported us when we needed you, we're supporting you now that you need our magazine to keep something positive in your life.

"Therefore, we're extending your subscription for one year, free of charge, and hope that things improve to the point that you'll be able to do so on your own in the future.

"Again, we thank you and others for making our ad-free magazines a success. Good luck, and God bless you."

That Charity Letter is still in use today. Most often now it's sent to *Reminisce* subscribers who say that their retirement funds are depleted, or that their spouse passed away and "while we always loved the magazine, it's too costly for just one of us".

We don't give away thousands of free extensions through that letter, but we regularly give out dozens…and feel good about every one of them.

———— ❖❖❖ ————

AFTER THAT SERIOUS NOTE, I'd best turn to a bit of levity. I've already mentioned the *fun* we've had in our offices over the years. Sometimes it's gotten close to going overboard.

An example is the first time a *Wall Street Journal* reporter came to interview me late one autumn. Even that staid financial publication thought our ad-free approach was worth investigating.

The morning interview with the sharp female reporter went well, and as we headed out the front door for lunch, one of our photographers was taking pictures of the best-dressed employees in our annual Halloween costume contest.

I wasn't in costume, but they yelled for me to come pose with them anyway. Turned out it was a setup. Just as I joined the group and smiled at the camera, one of our jokesters, Dale Miller, struck from behind and hit me full in the face with a cream pie!

I'd never had that happen before. I couldn't see a thing; whipped cream had hit me in open eyes and it was all over my face and hair. While I found it laughable, I was headed out to *lunch* with a reporter from *The Wall Street Journal*! How's this going to fly with her?

Turned out okay. She said after I'd cleaned up that any company whose employees would risk "pie-ing" the CEO must have a pretty good relationship with top management. Guess that's true. But I still owe Dale for that one.

———— ❖❖❖ ————

PRACTICAL JOKES have always been rampant at our place, and I'll admit to being a part of them myself. One of my favorite days of the year is

People who buy used cars know how hard it is to drive a bargain.

April Fools' Day.

I've always made sure to get to work particularly early on that day, because I had a lot to do. First, when we still had the old-time phones, I'd tape down the "button" below the receiver, then gave our receptionist a list of whose phones I'd "doctored". As they neared their offices, she'd dial their numbers. They'd pick up the phone, but because the buttons were taped down, it kept ringing. They'd usually answer "Hello" three times or so before they realized what was wrong, but by then she'd hung up on them.

And when we had electric typewriters, I'd bring a bag of jelly beans to the office and drop a few in the cradle of keys. The staffer would turn on the unit and start typing, and the gals would sometimes *scream* as the keys flung those beans against the window and the wall!

> ## "Here's a prank some of you may want to try..."

Now here's an April Fools' prank some of you guys may want to try yourself: You wear a *dark* suit to the office, see, then put a spool of *white* thread in your lapel pocket. From the back side of your lapel, you run some of that thread through the eyelet, and leave about an inch or two of it dangling or flattened against your suit.

Women can't *stand* seeing something like that. You chat with them a bit, and it's a certainty in a minute they're going to say, "You have something on your suit there."

Now you say, "Where?" and look to the *right*, the wrong side. As they keep pointing and saying "There", you act like you still don't know where it is and keep saying, "Just pick it off. Just pick it off."

And surely she will. But as soon as she gets hold of that thread, you start backing away real fast. That spool will quickly unravel, and she'll soon have wide eyes and several feet of thread in her hand! She'll think your shorts are unraveling!

Then, after the excitement is over, you just break off the thread, paste another inch or so against your lapel and go off looking for another victim. It's a "can't miss".

❖❖❖

ON A LARGER SCALE, perhaps the best practical joke played at our firm was when we were adding eight new offices on the other side of an existing wall. We and the construction crew decided to hold off on making the opening for the connecting door until finished, to curb the noise and the dust.

One day the foreman walked in and said they were ready to knock out the hole for the door. So they moved all the furniture out of Bill Freiberg's office (we later called that "Freiberg Hall"), where the connection would be.

Just after a workman began pounding on the other side of the wall, one of our editors hurried into my office and said, "I have a great idea, but I need help!" His idea was to move all that furniture back *into* that office, but

Strength is born from adversity; you may lose the inning but win the game.

totally reposition it, then put a different editor in the chair so the "pounder" would think he'd made the hole in the wrong place!

That sounded worthwhile, so a whole group of us worked like crazy, moving back the desk, files and other equipment. The pounding continued as we raced to finish before he broke through the plaster.

Our timing was like it always is in the movies. We'd just finished, put our biggest guy, Dave, at the desk, with him now facing in the opposite direction. Then the rest of us crowded at the office's little outer curtained window, each getting about one eye to peek in and catch the reaction.

Finally, *BOOM!* A huge chunk of plaster flew into the office, and Dave leaped out of the chair, yelling loudly, "What are you *doing?* You have the *WRONG OFFICE!*"

The crewman on the other side was in shock. He stood there with his sledgehammer in one hand and his other hand on his forehead, as Dave continued to carry on and get even more upset: "*Look* at this *mess* you've made! You're one office too far to the left! What were you *thinking?*", knowing full well we were all watching his performance from the window.

For fear the poor guy was going to have a heart attack or something, Dave finally stopped, put his hand through the hole to shake that of the crewman and said, "Calm down. It's a joke. We were just having a little fun."

> ***"You guys almost gave me a heart attack!"***

Then we moved all that furniture out again, but we felt it was fully worth the effort. More than a year later, we met that same construction crewman in the street and he recognized us.

"You guys almost gave me a heart attack that day!" he shouted. And we had a good laugh all over again. Fun things like that are well worth giving up a little productive time.

--- ❖❖❖ ---

WHILE WE LIKED TO TRICK people for fun, I learned one day that our longtime janitor, Norman Young, did it for good reason.

We were about a week away from moving our offices in downtown Milwaukee to our current site in Greendale. The needed changes were about finished, and I was spending a Saturday morning there, arranging some things in what would be my new office.

Norman was busy all morning. I could hear him out there as he worked in various areas of the large open space in the center, where about 20 office cubicles would eventually stretch to the other end of the building.

Taking a break, I found he was installing multiple thermostats to the pillar supports here and there. I got curious and asked, "Norm, you sure we're going to need *that* many thermostats out here?"

With a totally serious, business-like face, Norman said, "Oh, there's only a few of these that will actually be hooked up. The rest are just to fiddle with."

"*What?*"

Unshared joy is an unlighted candle.

"Look," Norman responded, "I've been at this business a long time. People keep getting hot and cold. If you give them a thermostat they can adjust now and then, they think they've changed the temperature and they'll be just fine. It's mostly mental. I'll show you which ones actually work when I finish here."

You know what? He was right. I kept this secret to myself and was inwardly amused when I often saw employees fiddling with those fake thermostats, then appearing completely satisfied a few minutes later.

Several years later, I learned that Norman wasn't the only one using this trickery. A friend was giving me a tour of a seven-story building when his maintenance man joined us. Somehow the conversation got around to room temperatures and I shared my Norman story.

My friend laughed. The maintenance guy didn't.

"Basically, we do the same thing here," he said. "The *only* place that the temperature can be adjusted on any of these floors is in the control room on the first floor.

"But when people call down and tell us it's too hot or cold, they're never convinced that anything has been done about it until they *see* one of our maintenance people come to their floor. So we send a guy up, he goes into a storage room for a few minutes to pretend he's adjusting something. Then they're satisfied. But there's nothing mechanical in that storage room. All the adjustments are made from below."

Made me wonder how many "placebo thermostats" there are in other office buildings across the country.

Some people are always hot, some people are always cold, and they always work in the same building.

Marriages are not made in Heaven.
They come in a kit and you put them together.

CHAPTER 47

A Chapter Full of 'Leftovers'

OKAY, I'M ALMOST FINISHED. I made one last check of my notes for this book and ran across a few short items that I think will be of interest before I say, "Stick a fork in it, it's done."

Besides, someone may think this book is worth the price when they're told, "Hey, it has 48 chapters…that's a big book. There's a *lot* in it!"

Actually I have much more I could include, but I'm sticking with the aforementioned policy that has served us well for years: When in doubt, leave it out. But here are a few leftovers that may have merit.

 ❖❖❖

THE FIRST EMPLOYEE I hired after moving from my basement to a small office in downtown Milwaukee was Gaylin Morgan. I only had one desk when he arrived; the second one hadn't arrived yet. So for the first few weeks, we faced each other at one desk. I was the boss, so I got the side with the leg inset. He claimed he had bad knees from that time on.

Gaylin—who goes by Morgan rather than his first name—was single when I hired him, but he didn't stay single very long. The business grew to the point where we needed a secretary/receptionist/typist/phone answerer.

Morgan said he knew a young woman named Carol who might fill the bill. I set up an interview and hired her. A couple of years later, Morgan married her.

He and Carol recently celebrated their 37th anniversary. He may have bad knees, but he obviously has a good eye for receptionists.

As the business grew, Morgan headed up our public relations accounts. Eventually, he and another employee, Gary Myers, split off and formed their own PR company, Morgan-Myers. I didn't have a problem with that—I was more into magazines than PR clients anyway, and after all, I also once left a company to go on my own.

We didn't have a lot of contact over the years until "The Typewriter Incident" occurred. I'm sure there were days during that experience that Morgan wished I hadn't gotten back in touch.

TYPEWRITER LOST 21 YEARS...REAPPEARS. First employee Gaylin Morgan, left, put in nearly 4 years of "detective work" before locating my beloved old Royal.

It's strange how things that didn't mean much to you when you were younger suddenly take on more meaning as you get older.

That's certainly true of the old gray Royal typewriter my wife and I used almost daily as we were getting started. When I was still freelancing, I'd pound out each story on that old Royal, then Bobbi would use it to retype each one, cleaning up the typos and making the manuscripts look more professional.

As mentioned earlier, funds were tight in those early days, so I never purchased a typing stand. The Royal was set up on a TV tray. We both recall bracing our knees against the tray legs to keep it from rocking. We also remember the folded rug that kept our feet off that cold basement floor.

That typewriter and I had some highs and lows. I typed the first magazine that failed on that Royal, and I also typed the entire first issue of *Farm Building News*, my first success, on that machine.

After I left the basement for a *real* office and more magazines came along, the old Royal eventually got moved to a back office. When Morgan left to go on his own, I helped him get started by giving him a desk, chair, camera, filing cabinet...and the old gray Royal.

I'm embarrassed to admit that now. But back then, that typewriter was just gathering dust and getting in the way.

I didn't miss it and didn't even think about that machine...until we began building a new home in the mid-'90s. Since I was finally going to have a study in the house, it occurred to me that old typewriter and a few other things from the early days would add a nostalgic touch.

So I dropped Morgan a note and asked if he still had the old Royal. I was unaware till much later—he didn't want to tell me—but that note set him off on a search that lasted nearly 4 years.

I'd call or write him now and then regarding it, and each time the response was hopeful, but vague. After the hunt was over, he 'fessed up to the truth.

"I used the Royal myself until 1979, but then it went to the warehouse," he explained. "As we junked several generations of equipment over the years, someone would ask if the old Royal could be tossed, and I always issued an emphatic 'NO!'

"But when you finally asked about it and I checked, it was nowhere to be found. I tracked down all former employees...nothing. I knew how important that old typewriter was to you, and I began sweating."

The trail went on and on...through an employee who had taken it home...and later given it to now his *ex*-mother-in-law, who'd sold it at a garage sale.

Morgan didn't give up. He composed a want ad for the area paper: "Wanted: Gray Royal typewriter sold in spring 1991 at local rummage sale. Sentimental value. Reward."

Shortly after, he received a phone call from an antique dealer who said she was sure she had the typewriter.

"I hurried to that shop and, as I walked in the door, there it was—*your old Royal* sitting on the floor! My heart skipped a beat when I saw it."

Mine did, too—I hadn't seen that lovable old machine in *21 years*. I drove to his home to pick it up, and we even posed for a picture with it. I placed it in my study as planned, then a few years later moved it along with some other nostalgic things to our company Visitor Center.

It's still there for visitors to see, appropriately propped on a TV tray. Every so often I walk past and stop to rip off a few words. It's as fluid now as it was in the '60s. That old Royal and I went through a lot of words together.

❖❖❖

I SCORED A SLAM-DUNK SCOOP ON WILT CHAMBERLAIN. When I was a student reporter for the *Iowa State Daily*, Wilt Chamberlain was then playing for the University of Kansas. The sports editor and I went to interview Wilt in mid-afternoon prior to a game with our Cyclones.

Athletes weren't treated so grandly back then—visiting teams were lodged in small rooms in our college's Memorial Union. Each room was equipped with single beds that were really more like bunks.

I'll never forget when I saw Wilt for the first time—he was the first person I'd ever seen over 7 feet tall! That would be enough in itself, but Wilt was stretched out on one of the bunks. He was so tall that while his head was on the pillow, his knees were bent at the bed's bottom rail and his feet were flat on the floor!

The sports editor did most of the interviewing while I stayed in the background. I noticed all the while he talked, Wilt kept fiddling with two or three rubber bands that were wound around each of his wrists.

As we started to leave after the interview, my curiosity was piqued, so I stepped back to ask Wilt about the rubber bands. He smiled and said no one had ever asked him about them before, then explained:

"When I was young, I was a 'bleeder' (hemophiliac), and if I ever got hit on the shins while playing, I had a real problem. So I started wearing long stockings and used rubber bands to hold them up. Still do.

"Sometimes the bands break during a game, so I started wearing 'spares' on my wrists. It's become a habit, and now I wear them all the time."

I found that fascinating. When we got back to the journalism newsroom, the sports editor wrote up the interview, but I typed out what I'd learned about Wilt Chamberlain's long stockings and his rubber wristbands.

I sent it to the sports editor of the *Des Moines Register*. He must have found it intriguing, too, because it appeared in a bold box in the next day's edition.

After that, every time I saw Wilt play, in college games, with the Harlem Globetrotters and in the pros, I'd see him wearing those long stockings and recall my rubber bands scoop.

—————— ❖❖❖ ——————

MY INNATE CURIOSITY, such as that described above, has on one hand yielded some fascinating revelations that others never wondered about, and on the other hand sometimes drives my wife nuts.

I tend to persist at asking for detail about little things that seem unimportant to her and likely most others. When I hear one of our kids or grandkids has said this or that, I want to know *when* they said that or *where they were* when they said it. I just want to totally "picture" the moment.

My golf friends look at me a little sideways sometimes, too, due to my questions. Like the time I was playing a course in Arizona. While we were putting, a mockingbird was singing its heart out from a tree next to the green. It went from this warble to that for a full 5 minutes, seemingly never repeating the same sound.

As we walked toward the next tee, I wondered aloud, "How does a mockingbird know what he's going to sing next? I mean, every other bird just opens its mouth and the same sound comes out, over and over. But a mockingbird has a whole repertoire to choose from. How does he decide which song he's going to sing next?"

Response from the other golfers? "Hit the ball, Roy."

But the question still lingered after I returned to the office. So I went to my usual source for the answer: Our readers. I've learned over the years that when more than a million people read your magazine, you can ask just about any question that comes to mind and at least *one* of them will have the answer.

So I mentioned this incident in the "Country Comments" column I wrote for each issue of *Country*. Predictably, I got the answer...and more:

• Researchers have found there appears to be no limit to the number of

Give some people an inch and they'll take the whole bed.

368

songs a mockingbird can pick up. An extensive study showed that most are able to master at least *180 songs* in a single month, and during mating season, they may master more than 400! (While that satisfied my curiosity on that count, now I wondered who *funded* a study like this.)

● A mockingbird can imitate more than just birdcalls. It's been known to mimic squirrels, frogs, crickets, sirens, bells, squeaky doors, home alarms and even alarm clocks so perfectly it awakens people every morning.

● One reader said a mockingbird in his neighborhood learned to imitate his cell phone so closely that he mistakenly answered it again and again.

● But here's my favorite: A reader said a mockingbird learned to mimic the bark of their small dog to the point where they couldn't tell which one was "barking". Every time a car drove into their yard, both the dog and the bird would bark.

Now, here's where it gets really interesting: The dog died. After that, every time someone drove in, the reader said, "We'd rush to the windows to watch people get out of their car, then start staring up when they heard 'barking' coming from the top of a 50-foot tree!"

That's a picture, isn't it? She vowed numerous neighbors would vouch for their "barking mockingbird".

————————— ❖❖❖ —————————

SINCE I'M DEALING WITH BIRDS here, did you know that most birds can't smell or taste? That's what I learned from bird experts while editing *Birds & Blooms*.

If I'd learned that earlier in life, I could have saved a few young birds. I'd been told that if a baby falls out of a nest, there's no use putting it back because once the mother picks up a human scent on the little one, she won't care for it.

Wrong. Mama bird can't smell that well, if at all. A few large birds—such as vultures and parrots—have olfactory glands developed well enough to have a sense of smell, but not the songbirds in your backyard.

Same is true for taste. While humans have 9,000 taste buds, songbirds have fewer than 50. That's why some people put cayenne pepper in birdseed to discourage squirrels. (I'd never do that; squirrels drive me crazy at my bird feeders, too, but I couldn't bring myself to "hot tamale" them.) While squirrels will avoid such seed, birds will eat it without hesitation; they don't detect the strong scent or taste of the pepper.

This means birds you feed around your home locate their food primarily by sight or touch. On the other hand, contrary to some beliefs, birds are not color blind. They see the same colors we do, which explains why hummingbirds are attracted to red flowers, for example.

One more fine feathered item, then I'm off the bird bit: When one of our daughters, Terrin, was 9 years old, she and I were observing some birds near our patio. I asked her if she had any idea why male songbirds are more brightly colored than females. She thought a second and said, "Maybe it's because the female does most of the nesting, so she has to be camouflaged."

I was impressed not only with her logic, but that she knew the meaning

No cowboy was ever faster on the draw than a grandmother pulling pictures out of her purse.

of that word. So I followed with, "Then why is it that any cat of more than two colors is always female?" (Which, by the way, is true.)

She surprised me again. "Maybe it's because the male has to do the hunting while the female takes care of the little ones, so he has to be camouflaged."

Her mother didn't raise any dumb little girls.

❖❖❖

HERE'S ANOTHER QUESTION readers have answered for me: "Why did they cover covered bridges?"

We were choosing a cover photo for one of our magazines one day, and I was studying this beautiful picture of a covered bridge. That's when the question occurred to me. Sure, those bridges are pretty, but early bridge builders wouldn't have gone through all that work just for the cosmetic effect. So why did they cover them?

Questions about offbeat subjects like this tend to linger with me, so I decided to ask readers about it in my next column. Predictably, I got *lots* of answers.

Some folks speculated those wonderful old bridges were built with roofs and sides to provide shelter to travelers during storms. In fact, several readers shared memories of parking their horses and buggies on covered bridges during a surprise thunderstorm.

While that may be okay to do in a pinch, it's not likely that's the primary reason such bridges were covered. After all, being suspended over a rain-swollen stream with the wind whipping waters into a frenzy—that

EVER WONDER why early bridges were covered like this? I did, and learned why.

would be one of the last places you'd want to wait out a storm!

Others felt the reason bridges were covered was to make them look more like barns so horses would feel comfortable entering the bridge, since many are known to get skittish about crossing over water. But subscriber Patricia Dupree of Manchester Center, Vermont didn't buy that theory. She recalled having to blindfold her mare to get across the famous Chiselville Covered Bridge near her home.

Still others contended bridges were covered to keep the snow and ice off the bridge floor so it wouldn't get slick in the winter. Again, other readers pooh-poohed that theory, since they remembered how they had to haul snow onto covered bridges in winter so they could cross over on their sleighs and bobsleds.

Finally, readers—and a few experts—provided the *real* reason why covered bridges were covered: It was to protect their huge bottom trusses and timbers from the weather.

Those massive beams were difficult to come by and were often hauled miles to the site. So it was a lot cheaper to occasionally replace roof shingles and rotting side boards when needed than to replace those rugged trusses. A testament to the effectiveness of this technique is the approximately 870 authentic covered bridges still standing today in the U.S.

So there, if the conversation hits a lull at your next cocktail party and you want to stir it up a bit, why not impress everyone with your vast knowledge of trivia by suddenly spouting out, "Why did they cover covered bridges?"

If you're the only one who knows the answer, you owe me a drink.

——————— ❖❖❖ ———————

MY SON, SCOTT, during a conversation sometime back, said to me, "Dad, you really love business, don't you?"

And I responded, "Well, when you're too old to play football, business is the only sport in town. In a way it's just another *game*. It's like I'm going to line up across from you, and I'm going to play fairly, morally and ethically. But when that ball's snapped, I'm going to knock you on your butt! Then I'm going to get up and see if I can do it again. That's business to me."

I've always felt that way—selling something is sort of a match of wits. It's another "game". Money or profit has little to do with it. If I sell something, I "won" that down or that inning or that hole. Then we'll tee it up and see if I can win again.

I think a lot of people approach it that way. Looking forward to the game of business is what makes it fun to come to work each day. In fact, the challenge, enjoyment and excitement of that are probably some of the reasons I've never found time to get sick in all these years.

I missed a half day once when all of our kids got the flu and it finally caught up with me for an afternoon—but even then I worked on a typewriter at home. Other than that, I've never had a "sick day".

Sure, I've had days when I didn't feel great, but I was there. My Iowa

The mind is wonderful—it works from birth until the moment you stand up to speak in public.

farm father once said, "If you go on with your work, you'll get your mind off being sick. You won't feel good sitting or laying around the house, either—so you might just as well get on with what needs to be done."

Years later I heard that philosophy expressed this way: "An idle mind doesn't heal a body."

I thank God for that kind of health. Again, I believe that totally enjoying what I've been doing for the past 30 years has had a great deal to do with it. I just never found *time* to get sick.

I was too busy having fun. I've found it extremely exhilarating to launch magazines that can survive and thrive without advertising…to have millions of people show they're willing to pay a premium price for them…enough so that we don't *need* to sell ads to supplement the costs.

What could be a nicer compliment than that? And we've now gotten that kind of compliment from over 16 million subscribers.

As I said earlier, I've gotten to work early each day not because I've had so much to do, but because I can't wait to do it. What a "job".

❖❖❖

MENTIONING MY DAD brings to mind a column I did about him. On the back of the first edition of *Farm & Ranch Living*, I wrote a personal column. That was in 1978. I've written a personal column for that back page of every issue since.

I just now did the math—that's *156* (puff, puff) columns over the past 26 years. Since many of these columns were about my family, my observations and opinions, the readers got to know me pretty well. It's probably the reason most of my mail from readers is addressed "Dear Roy". I like it that way.

Anyway, one particular column about my dad drew a significant response. I'd related in an earlier piece that our family had never been demonstrative when I grew up. I knew my parents loved me, but they never said so, and our family seldom hugged. Mom would on special occasions, but never Dad.

So, I told readers, I was heading back to Iowa to celebrate my parents' 68th wedding anniversary the following week, and I was going to correct that situation by hugging my dad.

Well, I did it. I just didn't realize at the moment that first hug would also be the last.

Dad died suddenly before I could get the next column written. When I reported that to readers, and wrote admiringly of the kind of man he was, I received letters, notes and even sympathy cards.

It was appropriate, because my dad was, after all, quite a guy. He was an Iowan through and through—he worked hard, never attained wealth, yet took a great deal of pride in what he had and wanted charity from no one.

Evidence of the latter is my experience when Bobbi and I visited Mom and Dad one spring. He'd retired from farming by then, and they were living in a small house in my hometown, Auburn, Iowa. The house had only one bathroom, on the second floor.

During our visit I said, "Dad, Bobbi and I have talked it over, and we'd like to add a bathroom to the first floor."

He looked at me with surprise and said, "Why would you want to do that?"

"Well, because every time Mom has to go to the bathroom, she has to climb those stairs."

"She's not complaining about that. That's good exercise for her. We don't need another bathroom."

"Well, it would be a nice convenience. In fact, we'd like to add a small laundry room next to the bathroom."

"Why you want to do that?"

"Because Mom has to do all of her laundry out in the garage, and in the winter it's cold out there."

"She's not complaining about that, either. She puts on a jacket and gets along just fine."

"But, Dad…"

"Look, I'm not taking any charity from any of my boys. (That's how he always referred to the five of us.) I don't want to talk about it anymore, okay?"

So I didn't…until our next trip home about 3 months later. I'd had time to give it some thought, and this time I was ready for him.

"Dad, I want to talk about that new bathroom and laundry room again…"

> *"Don't tell me you're going to ruin this visit, too!"*

"Don't tell me you're going to ruin this visit, too," he said stubbornly. "I told you I'm not taking any charity from any of my boys!"

"I know you said that, but I've been thinking about it. Dad, for one person to feel good about giving something, the other has to be willing to accept it. We can afford to do this, we want to do it and you're denying us the opportunity to feel good about doing it."

Dad thought a minute and said, "Okay, you can give it to Mom. On one condition."

"What's that?"

"I want to see the bill from the contractor when it's finished."

"Why would you want to see that?"

"Because I'm putting it in my will…I told you, I'm not taking any charity from my boys!"

That proud old man had outfoxed me again, giving me my way but also having it his way. When he died, though, I was relieved to see it wasn't in his will.

Somewhere along the way, Dad understood. As I said earlier, he never went beyond a grade school education, but he had a Master's Degree in common sense.

— ❖❖❖ —

Humor is hazardous to your stress.

IT WAS MOM who got me interested in gardening. Being the youngest of five boys, I was the one left behind to help Mom tend our huge vegetable garden while my older brothers worked beside Dad with the crops and livestock.

At first I wasn't happy about this; I wanted to do the "important" tasks like my brothers. But eventually I grew to like it. Mom and I talked about a lot of things while we hoed and harvested. But no matter how busy we were, she always took time to stop and admire a butterfly. She loved butterflies.

That's why I decided to fund construction of the Christina Reiman Butterfly Wing on the campus of Iowa State. It's part of the Reiman Gardens complex at the entrance to the university.

Our entire family was on hand in August 2003 when we dedicated this just-completed glass structure (designed in the shape of an artistic butterfly). With more than a thousand live ones flitting about, visitors have a lot of butterflies to admire. Mom passed away at age 92—I wish she'd been able to see *her* butterfly wing. Then again, maybe she has.

The surrounding 14-acre complex—with its rose plots, flower beds, lily pond, plantings, shrub displays and lawn demos—has become a Midwest travel destination. Even during dreary winter months, lavish orchid shows and aromatic floral displays inside the site's large conservatory provide Iowans with "something green and growing".

Funding these beautiful gardens provided me with an opportunity to give something back to Iowa State for all it gave me. Best of all, dedicating this facility in my parents' memory presented a fitting way to honor them. To a great degree, what they were, I am.

—————— ❖❖❖ ——————

NOW AND THEN I'd hit on subjects in personal columns that would spark an extraordinary response. But no column I ever wrote brought in more letters than the one I wrote when my wife and I drove daughter Cindi off to college.

Here is that column, from nearly 20 years ago, which was headlined, "Oh, For One More Walk…":

MY HEART'S hurting today. See, I took Cindi to college yesterday. My wife and I loaded (and I mean *loaded*) all of daughter No. 3's things into the van and drove all the way to Bloomington, Indiana, where Cindi's enrolling as a freshman at the University of Indiana.

The time to say good-bye came all too quickly. I have a different soft spot for each of my five daughters, and I got so emotional when I hugged Cindi that I got embarrassed as other parents walked by.

I quickly hopped behind the wheel of the van, waved and drove off. But I'll never forget looking back at that girl standing so alone in front of that big dormitory, holding back tears of her own and waving good-bye not only to her parents, but to a past chapter of her life and ours.

I couldn't talk for the first 20 miles. It was all I could do to keep from turning around to go back and get her. There were so many things that I still wanted to tell her…

More than anything, I just felt I wasn't "finished" with her. It was as though I was molding something, and someone took it out of my hands before I was done with it.

Finally, when my voice came back, I told my wife how I felt. And she rightly pointed out that you never really "finish" a child.

"That's up to Cindi to do," she said. "We just sort of put the clay together, and now it's up to her to shape the final mold."

Yes, I'm sure that's true. But I couldn't help but think how much I wish I could have taken just *one* more walk through the woods with Cindi, and have just *one* more father/daughter chat before she moved out of our home.

If you have a son or daughter, be sure *you* take time or *make* time to do things like that…while there still *is* time. A child's life goes so fast…

—*Roy Reiman, Editor/Publisher*

That column drew well over a hundred letters of the "I know…I know" variety. Apparently everyone who's ever dropped off a kid on campus for their freshman year—and knows that life will never be the same on either end after that day—can relate to that experience. Some writers expressed even more emotion than I did.

It made me emotional again as I retyped it just now. And I think these three recollections—about my dad, mom and one of our daughters— might be an appropriate place for me to wind up the body of this book.

…But not before I needle you a bit.

Those who speak well of people need never whisper.

Don't cry because it's over;
smile because it happened.

CHAPTER 48

Okay, Now I'm Gonna Needle You...

SEVERAL TIMES in this book, I detailed our fondness for *hiding* something in our magazines. That includes "Hattie's Hatpin" in *Reminisce*, "Ted's Toothpick" in *Taste of Home*, an elusive acorn in *Birds & Blooms* and so on.

Any reader who finds one of those items in those magazines can send us a note, and if they correctly identify the page where the object's hidden, they could be one of 50 winners of a country-oriented prize.

Easily, though, the most popular hidden item is the one we started with: "A Needle in a Haystack", which we hide in each issue of *Country*. We've often received "I found it!" notes from more than *125,000* readers after an issue.

Sometimes it's partly the unique prize that interests them. We try to come up with something that most people can't buy. In most cases, that's something homemade or handcrafted by one of our rural subscribers.

Of these, nothing has ever proven more appealing than "a pecan pie from Maudie Raber". Maybe it's because Maudie is such a great cook...and maybe it's because people enjoy picturing all that goes into getting one of those pies delivered overnight to their house.

See, Maudie's an Amish farm woman who lives near Millersburg, Ohio. She has no electricity in her home, so she bakes these incredible pies in her small kitchen stove, then hauls them to town in her buggy with "Molly" trotting up front.

There, the speed of the transport picks up a bit, from buggy to jet airplane. The pies are shipped via FedEx overnight to each recipient. We call it our "pie in the sky" approach to delivering "a fresh slice of the country".

Since we were the first to hide anything in our magazines, I'm now going to be the first to do it in a book. And since the "needle in a haystack" has been the favorite hidden item, I'm having Judy Larson, the Art Director, hide a needle *somewhere* in this book.

Hardening of the heart is worse than hardening of the arteries.

377

It's a drawing of a needle, very small, and it could be hidden anywhere. It may be along a margin, in a photo or illustration, or in a headline (nope, we didn't use it as an exclamation point!). It could be just about anywhere, which is why it's like looking for a needle in a haystack. But it *is there*, hiding on some page somewhere in this book.

If you find it, send a note to: Book Needle, Reiman Publications, 5925 Country Lane, Greendale WI 53129.

If you identified the right page, we'll include you in a drawing for…yes, we're asking Maudie to crank up that stove again. If yours is *one of the 50 names drawn*, you'll receive one of her 50 mouth-watering pecan pies by next-day delivery.

Normally our deadline for these drawings is about a month after our magazine is mailed. But since this contest is in a *book*, which is coming off the press this summer (in 2005) and will likely be purchased throughout the summer and into the fall, we're moving the deadline for these entries all the way back to *November 15, 2005*.

This will also allow Maudie to ship those pies after the weather cools a bit in most parts of the country. (For those of you who just came across this book and are reading this after that deadline date—sorry.)

Wait…now I'm going to needle you…with _real needles_. Yes, to add even more fun, I'm starting a "national treasure hunt". I've asked our field editors (we have over 1,000 of them) to help me hide some *real needles* throughout the U.S. and Canada!

In fact, they've already done it. They've hidden *one wooden needle* in each of the 50 states and in each Canadian province.

That's right, one of those wooden needles is hidden in *your* state or province right now. If you find it, it's worth *$500.00!* Of that, $250.00 will be yours, with the other $250.00 donated to a local school or library of the winner's choice. (Many libraries are in financial trouble now, and we want to encourage reading for all ages.)

Wait…there's still more: *ONE* of those 50 needles—yes, just one, is *WORTH $5,000.00!*

Again, half of that prize money—*$2,500.00*—will go to a local school or library. Since I'm planning to put *all* the proceeds I receive from this book into our family foundation, which contributes to various causes, the half I'm giving to each winner's school or library will be an appropriate gift.

I studied our list of field editors across the U.S. and Canada carefully before selecting several in each state and province. I then wrote and asked if they would be interested in helping me with this one-of-a-kind treasure hunt by hiding one of the wooden needles. I also asked whether they could keep its location a *solid secret*.

I then screened the responses and chose the field editors I wanted to hide a wooden needle (exactly like the one I'm holding in the photo at right). The needle is 12 inches long and about 1/2 inch in diameter.

To protect each needle, we wrapped it in clear, biodegradable shrink wrap so it can be easily seen through the plastic. In addition to the needle, there's

IT'S TRUE! There's a *real* needle, a wooden one just like the one I'm holding here, hidden in your state or province. This national treasure hunt can result in some handsome cash prizes!

a note inside stating, "Hay, You Found It!", plus instructions on whom to call to report the finding and thereby collect the prize.

Now, unless you're from Rhode Island, there's an awful lot of territory in your area where one wooden needle could be hidden.

So, here's how you can get your first "clue" on the *proximity* of the needle that's hidden in your state or province:

Just send a self-addressed stamped envelope to the address on the next page. You needn't put any note inside (unless you can't resist saying something like, "I like being needled...send me your first clue"). When we receive your envelope mailed to that specific address, we'll know what you want.

We'll then send you a small map showing you the *20-square-mile area* in which the needle is hidden in *your* state or province.

A month later, you can send a second self-addressed stamped envelope. If the needle hasn't been found by that point, we'll then send you a *second* clue and map, now narrowing down the search area to *5 square miles*. We'll inform an area newspaper as soon as it's found. (Note: This contest ends December 31, 2005.)

I can tell you this much right now:

1. Each wooden needle is hidden in a *public park*. Why not take along a garbage bag while you're searching and clean up a little litter?

2. Each needle has a confidential code number on it, so we know it's ours and not a duplicate.

3. *Don't bother to ask* any of our field editors where the needle is hidden. We've instructed *all* of them to respond: "Sorry, I can't discuss it" to any questions. And we've had the editor who actually hid the needle vow to the secrecy of the needle's whereabouts.

4. *Don't call us.* No phone calls will be accepted at Reiman Publications about this program.

5. No Reiman Publications employee or relative of an employee—nor any relative of any of our field editors—is eligible to win.

6. As the needles are found, the names of the winners will be printed in

Sometimes you must stand alone to be sure you still can.

379

Again, the finder will win half of the designated prize and will get to choose the library or school that receives the other half. With this type of added benefit, I'm hoping schoolchildren may want to get involved in the search…and in cleaning up area parks as well.

So, *the search is on.* To get your first clue immediately and then a second clue (available only to those who requested the first clue) 4 weeks later, write to: "Hay, Clue Me!", Reiman Publications, 5925 Country Lane, Greendale WI 53129.

That's it. That's my story. I feel I've had a fascinating life. I'll let you decide whether it was worth a book.

Now I need to turn to other things—visiting my kids, working with charitable causes and spending more time in the garden. I still have lots to do and lots of dreams still unfulfilled.

After all, I have ideas I haven't thought of yet.

Do the headwork before the handwork.

If you find a dream inside your heart,
don't ever let it go…
for dreams can be the tiny seeds
from which tomorrows grow.

Launches Over the Years...
from Farm...
to Country...
to General

1970s
Farm Wife News (1970)
Country Store catalog division (1971)
World Wide Country Tours (1975)
Farm & Ranch Living (1978)

1960s
The Pepperette (1963) failed
Freelancing, custom publishing (1963-67)
Farm Building News (1967)

2000s

Light & Tasty (2001)
Backyard Living (2004)
Cooking for 2 (2005)

1990s

Country EXTRA (1990)
Book publishing becomes major business (1991)
Reminisce (1991)
Reminisce EXTRA (1993)
Taste of Home (1993)
Birds & Blooms (1995)
Purchase of Homemaker Schools (1995)
Cookbook sales top 2 million (1997)
Quick Cooking (1998)
Country Discoveries (1999)

1980s

Crafting Traditions (1982)
Farm Wife News becomes *Country Woman* (1987)
Country (1987)
Country Kids (1988) **failed**